TRUST AND RECIPROCITY

TRUST AND RECIPROCITY

INTERDISCIPLINARY LESSONS FROM EXPERIMENTAL RESEARCH

ELINOR OSTROM AND JAMES WALKER

EDITORS

VOLUME VI IN THE RUSSELL SAGE FOUNDATION SERIES ON TRUST

Russell Sage Foundation • New York

The Russell Sage Foundation

The Russell Sage Foundation, one of the oldest of America's general purpose foundations, was established in 1907 by Mrs. Margaret Olivia Sage for "the improvement of social and living conditions in the United States." The Foundation seeks to fulfill this mandate by fostering the development and dissemination of knowledge about the country's political, social, and economic problems. While the Foundation endeavors to assure the accuracy and objectivity of each book it publishes, the conclusions and interpretations in Russell Sage Foundation publications are those of the authors and not of the Foundation, its Trustees, or its staff. Publication by Russell Sage, therefore, does not imply Foundation endorsement.

Library of Congress Cataloging-in-Publication Data

Trust and reciprocity : interdisciplinary lessons from experimental research / Elinor Ostrom and James Walker, editors.
    p. cm.
    Includes bibliographical references and index.
    ISBN 0-87154-647-7
    1. Social interaction. 2. Trust. 3. Cooperativeness. 4. Social exchange. I. Ostrom, Elinor. II. Walker, James, 1950–
HM1111 .T78 2002
302—dc21   2002026991

The paper used in this publication meets the minimum requirements of American National Standard for Information Sciences—Permanence of Paper for Printed Library Materials. ANSI Z39.48-1992.

Text design by Suzanne Nichols

RUSSELL SAGE FOUNDATION
112 East 64th Street, New York, New York 10021
10 9 8 7 6 5 4 3 2 1

The Russell Sage Foundation Series on Trust

T he Russell Sage Foundation Series on Trust examines the conceptual structure and the empirical basis of claims concerning the role of trust and trustworthiness in establishing and maintaining cooperative behavior in a wide variety of social, economic, and political contexts. The focus is on concepts, methods, and findings that will enrich social science and inform public policy.

The books in the series raise questions about how trust can be distinguished from other means of promoting cooperation and explore those analytic and empirical issues that advance our comprehension of the roles and limits of trust in social, political, and economic life. Because trust is at the core of understandings of social order from varied disciplinary perspectives, the series offers the best work of scholars from diverse backgrounds and, through the edited volumes, encourages engagement across disciplines and orientations. The goal of the series is to improve the current state of trust research by providing a clear theoretical account of the causal role of trust within given institutional, organizational, and interpersonal situations, developing sound measures of trust to test theoretical claims within relevant settings, and establishing some common ground among concerned scholars and policymakers.

Karen S. Cook
Russell Hardin
Margaret Levi

SERIES EDITORS

v

Previous Volumes in the Series

Contents

Contributors

Elinor Ostrom is the Arthur F. Bentley Professor of Political Science and codirector of the Workshop in Political Theory and Policy Analysis and the Center for the Study of Institutions, Population, and Environmental Change at Indiana University, Bloomington.

James Walker is professor of economics and a member of the research faculty of the Workshop in Political Theory and Policy Analysis at Indiana University, Bloomington.

T. K. Ahn is a research associate at the Workshop in Political Theory and Policy Analysis at Indiana University, Bloomington.

Karen S. Cook is the Ray Lyman Wilbur Professor of Sociology and Cognizant Dean of the Social Sciences at Stanford University.

Robin M. Cooper is a doctoral candidate in the Department of Sociology at Stanford University and is a research associate at the Laboratory for Social Research.

Frans B. M. de Waal is the C.H. Candler Professor of Primate Behavior in the Department of Psychology and director of the Living Links Center for the Study of Human and Ape Evolution at the Yerkes Primate Center, both at Emory University, Atlanta, Georgia.

Catherine C. Eckel is professor of economics at Virginia Polytechnic Institute and State University, where she also directs the Laboratory for the Study of Human Thought and Action (LSHTA).

James Hanley is a visiting instructor at Adrian College, Adrian, Michigan.

William T. Harbaugh is associate professor of economics at the University of Oregon, Eugene.

Russell Hardin is professor of politics at New York University and professor of political science at Stanford University.

Kate Krause is associate professor of economics at the University of New Mexico.

Robert Kurzban is assistant professor of psychology at the University of Pennsylvania.

Margaret Levi is professor of political science and the Jere L. Bacharach Professor of International Studies at the University of Washington, Seattle.

Steven G. Liday Jr. is a former undergraduate student at the University of Oregon, Eugene.

Kevin A. McCabe is professor of economics and law at George Mason University.

Tomonori Morikawa is associate professor of political science at the Center for International Education at Waseda University, Tokyo, Japan.

John Orbell is the Distinguished Professor of Political Science and Cognitive Science at the University of Oregon.

David Schmidt was assistant professor in the Department of Economics at Indiana University and a member of the research faculty of the Workshop in Political Theory and Policy Analysis at the time of this writing. He is currently an economist at the Federal Trade Commission.

Vernon L. Smith is professor of economics and law at George Mason University, a research scholar in the Interdisciplinary Center for Economic Science, and a fellow of the Mercatus Center, all in Arlington, Virginia.

Lise Vesterlund is assistant professor of economics at the University of Pittsburgh.

Rick K. Wilson is professor of political science and director of the Behavioral Research Laboratory at Rice University, Houston, Texas.

Toshio Yamagishi is professor of social psychology at Hokkaido University, Japan.

Preface

This book is the result of a series of meetings on trust held at the Russell Sage Foundation. All of these meetings, in turn, have been a part of a much broader project on trust organized by Karen Cook of Stanford University, Russell Hardin of New York University, and Margaret Levi of the University of Washington. The first meeting, a Roundtable on Trust As a Political Variable, was organized by Margaret Levi and held on February 25 and 26, 1995. Participants included Valerie Braithwaite, Robert Frank, Margaret Levi, and Toshio Yamagishi. It was at this exciting meeting that Elinor Ostrom was first introduced to the Russell Sage project on trust. Immediately after this conference, Yamagishi, Levi, and Braithwaite joined Ostrom and James Walker at Indiana University to discuss some of the experiments that could be run to examine the role of culture in the creation and maintenance of trust. That small meeting resulted in an exciting research program with parallel experiments being conducted in Japan and the United States (see Nahoko Hayashi, Elinor Ostrom, James Walker, and Toshio Yamagishi, "Reciprocity, Trust, and the Sense of Control: A Cross-societal Study," *Rationality and Society* 11(1): 27–46. As an outgrowth of that effort, Nahoko Hayashi spent the spring semester of 1997 at Indiana University, allowing for considerable discussion there of the cultural foundations of trust. The pursuit of these activities was greatly helped by the support provided us by Peter Evans as part of a project on "Social Capital" administered by the American Academy of Arts and Sciences.

Although skeptical of the use of experimental methods to study trust, as is evident in chapter 14 in this book, Margaret Levi invited Ostrom and Walker to organize a conference focusing on experimental methods for the study of trust. One must deeply respect a scholar who is willing to invest precious resources in exploration of a new research method for addressing a topic of considerable importance. Not only does Levi conduct her own research with extensive care and insight, but she is also willing to explore new and different ways of examining questions.

Margaret Levi, Russell Hardin, and Karen Cook then invited us to organize a conference on trust to meet at the Russell Sage Foundation from November 14 to 16, 1997. The participants in that conference were Karen Cook (Department of Sociology, Duke University), Russell Hardin (Department of Politics, New York University), Margaret Levi (Director of the Center for Labor Studies, University of Washington), Kevin McCabe (Economics Science Laboratory, University of Arizona), John Orbell (Department of Political Science, University of Oregon), Elinor Ostrom (Workshop in Political Theory and Policy Analysis, Indiana University), David Schmidt (Department of Economics, Indiana University), Vernon Smith (Economics Science Laboratory, University of Arizona), James Walker (Department of Economics, Indiana University), Rick Wilson (Program Director, Political Science, National Science Foundation), and Toshio Yamagishi (Faculty of Letters, Hokkaido University). Most of the participants at this one-and-a-half-day meeting focused on an in-depth discussion of the theoretical work that Hardin, Cook, and Levi were engaged in and the experimental traditions of Yamagishi, Smith, McCabe, Ostrom, Schmidt, and Walker. This meeting also gave us an opportunity to begin to explore the possible evolutionary foundations of trust with a key paper presented by John Orbell. The working title of that conference was Behavioral Evidence on Trust.

From that working group, a plan emerged for a series of papers that would be presented at a larger conference to be held at Russell Sage and would eventually be incorporated into a book. Most of the chapters in the current volume were initially planned at that mid-November 1997 meeting. At that same meeting, Russell Hardin raised some serious questions about survey evidence in measuring trust. Hardin's concern with the overreliance on a few general questions led to the examination of that question at Indiana—an issue that is discussed here in chapter 12.

During the next year, many of the chapters were put into initial draft and a second conference on experimental work relating to the study of trust was held at the Russell Sage Foundation on February 19 and 20, 1999. The participants at this meeting were Karen Cook (Center for Applied Social and Behavioral Sciences, Stanford University), Catherine Eckel (Department of Economics, Virginia Polytechnic Institute and State University), Russell Hardin (Department of Political Science, Stanford University), Margaret Levi (Department of Political Science, University of Washington), Kevin McCabe, John Orbell, Elinor Ostrom, Carl Rhodes (Department of Government, Franklin and Marshall College), Bo Rothstein (Russell Sage Foundation), David

Schmidt, Vernon Smith, James Walker, Rick Wilson (Department of Political Science, Rice University), and Toshio Yamagishi. The work of Smith, McCabe, and Orbell drew sufficiently on recent work in evolutionary psychology that participants urged us to include two papers in the volume that were not presented at the conference. One is a classic paper by Frans de Waal. Colleagues thought the paper would help to illustrate that some of the patterns we were looking at in humans could also be studied in animals. We also asked Robert Kurzban to write a paper for our volume that would summarize some of the recent work in evolutionary psychology. When the volume was finally brought together and sent out for review by external readers, one of the reviewers asked whether there had been any foundational work on the development of trust in children. That led us to ask William T. Harbaugh and his colleagues to contribute a chapter to fill in this essential missing link.

Obviously, without the substantial support of the Russell Sage Foundation this volume would not exist. It is also important to say at this point that the intellectual leadership of Karen Cook, Russell Hardin, and Margaret Levi has been essential throughout the entire process. Bringing together work from economics, sociology, psychology, biology, philosophy, and political science in one volume is a challenge. We deeply appreciate the enthusiasm and hard work of our colleagues in writing and rewriting their papers to create a coherent set of chapters in this book. Finally, we owe a special debt of gratitude to the staff at Indiana University's Workshop in Political Theory and Policy Analysis for their help in bringing this manuscript to completion. In particular, we would like to thank Patty Zielinski, Sarah Kantner, and Johanna Hanley for their expert production and editorial assistance.

PART I

INTRODUCTION:
SOCIAL DILEMMAS AND TRUST

Chapter 1

Introduction

ELINOR OSTROM AND JAMES WALKER

I MAGINE the following decision situation involving two individuals. Individual 1 is endowed with $10.00. She can keep the entire sum or send some part of the $10 to individual 2, an anonymous counterpart. Individual 1 knows that any money sent to individual 2 will later be tripled in value. Furthermore, individual 2 knows that he will have the option of sending back to individual 1 some part of the tripled sum of money, a sum determined by individual 2.

Imagine that this game is to be played only once and that both individuals know that all decisions will remain completely anonymous. How might individual 1 go about making a decision in this situation? Based on motivations rooted only in pecuniary payoffs from the game, the noncooperative game-theoretic equilibrium is for individual 1 to send no money to individual 2. Individual 1 would reason, by *backward induction,* that individual 2 would have no incentive to send any money back. Thus, individual 1 would send no money to individual 2. On the other hand, there would be obvious gains to both players if individual 1 were to trust individual 2 to return an amount at least as great as the sum she sends him. The joint gains would be as much as three times the original endowment to individual 1.

What types of decisions will individuals make when they actually encounter this one-way game of trust? (see chapter 3, this volume). Joyce Berg, John Dickhaut, and Kevin McCabe (1995) conducted just such a study. Using a *one-shot* decision setting with double-blind experimental procedures to ensure complete anonymity, these researchers find that thirty of thirty-two subjects in the role of individual 1 sent money to their counterparts (in the role of individual 2)

($5.36, on average). Of the thirty subjects in the role of individual 2 who received funds, eighteen returned more than $1.00 ($4.66, on average), and eleven sent more than the original amount allocated by their partners. Interestingly, on average, those who sent at least $5.00 received an average return in excess of the amount they sent; those who sent less than $5.00 received a negative net-average return. In other words, those individuals in the first position who trusted their counterparts more were more likely than those who were less trusting to leave the game with more wealth than they had entered with.

In a follow-up study, Nancy Buchan, Rachel Croson, and Eric Johnson (1999) implement the experimental decision setting of Berg, Dickhaut, and McCabe (1995) in a cross-national design. They investigate the same game with 188 subjects from China, Japan, Korea, and the United States. They find no pure country effects in terms of the amount sent by subjects in the role of individual 1 (on average, 67 percent of the endowment) or in the amount returned (on average, 31 percent of the amount received). The researchers examine several other potential explanatory variables, in addition to country effects, including culture (based on survey data in which questions relate to an individual's attitude toward group versus individual outcomes), *social distance* (manipulated experimentally), and *communication* (manipulated experimentally). Culture, in the form of subjects' showing a greater orientation toward group outcomes, significantly and positively affects the amounts sent and returned.[1] The opportunity to communicate information about one's self and learn something about the other person with whom a subject is paired also had a positive effect on the amounts sent. Buchan, Croson, and Johnson find that "trusters prosper." "Subjects who sent above-average amounts to their partners took home greater wealth than did subjects who sent only average amounts or less" (Buchan, Croson, and Johnson 1999, 22).

In a third study, John Dickhaut and colleagues (1997) examine the impact of allowing individual 2 to build a reputation by adding a publicly announced second round to the basic structure of the first (Berg, Dickhaut, and McCabe) experiment, in which the individual continued to play with the same counterpart. According to standard *noncooperative game theory*, the existence of this second round should make no difference in the behavior of individuals in the first round. Dickhaut and colleagues wanted to ascertain whether individuals in the position of individual 2 would act even more trustworthy than those who had participated in the first study to assure those in the position of individual 1 that they could be trusted. In the first round, all twenty-three subjects in the role of individual 1 sent some money to their counterparts, and ten of the twenty-three sent the maximum sum ($10.00). Those in the position of individual 2 showed higher levels of reciprocity in the first round than had been exhibited in the Berg, Dickhaut, and McCabe study. Twenty of them returned more than the original sum received, leading to a positive-sum outcome for all involved.

The second round followed a different pattern. Nineteen out of twenty of the individual 1s who had received positive returns in the first round made positive investments again in the second, and all three of the individual 1s who had received a negative return in the first round sent zero to their counterparts in the second round. The most significant difference in outcome was that only seven of the nineteen individual 1s received a positive net return in the second round. The reciprocity that had been exhibited in the first round was substantially reduced in the second and final round.

These three studies illustrate the intricate relation between trust and expectations of reciprocity.[2] In these experiments, a substantial proportion of individuals trusted that the person with whom they were paired—a stranger—would reciprocate trust by returning at least as much money as he or she had been sent by the first player. In all of these games, the predicted subgame-perfect equilibrium, assuming that utility is adequately captured by monetary payoffs, is for individual 2 to return zero. Because individual 2 is predicted not to reciprocate, the prediction is also that individual 1 will not invest anything, owing to the risk of losing everything that is sent. In all three studies, trust and trustworthy behavior exceeded predicted levels.

On the other hand, the degree of trust and trustworthiness varies substantially.[3] A variety of contextual factors associated with the structure of these experiments helps to explain the variance. Individual preferences toward payoffs, prior experience with this game structure, players' capacity to learn more about the personal characteristics of each other, and ability of players to build reputations all appear to affect the decisions of players in both positions. A second major finding is that the rates of trusting, reciprocity, and trustworthy behavior exhibit high variance across experimental conditions. Thus trusting and trustworthy behavior are not unchanging, universal attributes of all individuals but are rather the result of multiple contextual and individual attributes. Understanding trust and the conditions that are conducive to trust is a challenging task.

These three studies illustrate how experimental methods can help social scientists learn more about trusting and trustworthy behavior and contribute to the testing of diverse theories about the origin, sustenance, and outcomes of trust and trustworthiness. Furthermore, the structure of these experiments has a parallel structure to situations that Robert Trivers (1971) has posited as key for the expression of *reciprocal altruism.* For an act to be an instance of reciprocal altruism, the following ingredients must be present:

- An action of the first actor is beneficial to the recipient but costly to the first actor.
- There is a time lag between giving and receiving.
- The actor who gives has an expectation of receiving an equal or larger benefit in the future.

In all three studies, the experimenter controls the pecuniary incentives associated with alternative decisions, the level and form of information subjects have about other subjects, and the extent to which reputations for trustworthiness can be built or destroyed. These studies are illustrative of the types of experimental environments, analyses, and outcomes that are reported in this volume. The studies reported here focus on multiple alternative decision settings that have been created to examine particular questions related to how pecuniary and nonpecuniary incentives and other structural variables affect trusting behavior, as well as trustworthiness.

Why is trust so important? These three studies also begin to provide a hint about the importance of trust in every society. In all of the gaming situations just described, an individual is faced with an "investment" decision that holds out the possibility of a substantial return if a counterpart proves trustworthy and returns more than the first individual invests in the relationship. Each individual 1, however, also faces the risk that his or her counterpart will take the money and run. A core aspect of most definitions of trust is the "intention to accept vulnerability based upon positive expectations of the intentions of the behavior of another" (Rousseau et al. 1998, 395).

Situations that have this core structure abound in all societies and at all times in history. Kenneth Arrow (1974) stresses the ubiquity of trust in almost every economic transaction. An empirical study of trust using a variety of cross-national indicators finds that trust is positively associated with homogeneity with respect to ethnicity and social and economic relationships and in situations in which diverse legal and social mechanisms for counteracting opportunism are well developed (Zak and Knack 1998). Furthermore, Arrow finds that higher rates of investment and growth are positively associated with higher levels of trust. The basic relationship between management and employees is one of mutual trust (see chapter 3, this volume) in which each player has to trust that contributions beyond the minimal will be forthcoming from the other (Fehr, Gächter, and Kirchsteiger 1996).

Elias Khalil argues that market-based societies, which are frequently characterized as encouraging self-interested, untrusting behavior, have a greater need for trust than kin-based or other forms of economic organization. "First, as economic exchange becomes less intermingled with kinship and more based on formal contractual relationships, the monitoring conducted by the kin members and the threat of ostracism almost vanish. Second, the modern judicial system, which replaces the threat system of ostracism and shunning, cannot practically monitor the extensive growth of contractual agreements—even the explicit ones" (Khalil 1994, 340). Simply thinking about the problem of buying a used car should remind every reader of the risks involved in the large number of diverse contractual arrangements that characterize life in a market economy (Buskens and Weesie 2000). Furthermore, our humanoid and primate ancestors faced many situations in which, to obtain long-term joint benefits, they had to decide to make themselves vulnerable based on positive expectations of the intentions of others (de Waal 1996; Boehm 1999). Part of the evolutionary heritage of the modern human is the capacity to recognize human faces and engage in a rough form of mental accounting so as to trust some individuals more than others in particular types of situations.

This book examines the foundations for trust and trustworthy behavior. The central theme that links all discussion relates to the gains from association that are achieved when individuals are able to develop trust and reciprocity. Whether they come in the form of market exchange or personal relationships, the gains from association depend on the willingness of individuals to take risks by placing their trust in others. Whether that trusting behavior is mutually beneficial and lasting depends on the trustworthiness of those in whom trust has been placed.

Concepts of Trust and Reciprocity

Chapter 2, by Elinor Ostrom, considers the abundant evidence of cooperation and reciprocity, focusing on the issue of how traditional noncooperative game theory might be enriched to become a behavioral-based theory. The author reviews the theoretical predictions of currently accepted *rational-choice theory* as it relates to *social dilemmas* and summarizes challenges to the reliance on a complete model of rationality. She focuses on how individuals achieve results that are "better than rational" by building conditions under which reciprocity, reputation, and trust help to overcome short-run, self-interested temptations. This parallels the arguments made in the experimental chapters in part IV of this volume—in particular, the arguments made in chapter 10. Ostrom develops an initial framework for examining how contextual variables tend to affect reciprocity, reputation, and trust. She embeds this core in settings involving both small face-to-face groups and larger groups.

Russell Hardin concludes part I with his chapter, "Gaming Trust," by specifying the basic elements of a trust relationship between a truster and a trustee. First, the truster faces a situation in which he or she will be better off if the relationship is initiated and the trustee reciprocates. Second, the trustee may face some incentives to be trustworthy with regard to the specific relationship, such as internal norms or the prospect of extended relationships. Third, this incentive to be trustworthy can be overruled by a variety of other considerations, such as short-term gains from not being trustworthy. Hardin points to the cognitive structure of trust—the belief an individual has in the likely behavior of the other.

Hardin argues that to account for trust, one must first account for trustworthiness. Trustworthiness can be seen as primarily based either on incentives or on the normative attributes of the decision maker. Trustworthiness is incentive based if the trustee has reason to encapsulate the interests of the truster into his or her own preferences; an example is a situation in which the trustee values the continuance of the relationship. Trustworthiness is normatively based if the trustee feels morally obligated to fulfill the trust.

Building on the conceptual nature of associations dependent on trust, Hardin distinguishes between three models of trust that have been used in the literature: mutual trust, one-way trust, and thick relationships. Mutual trust is seen as an interaction that is part of a long sequence of association between the same parties, a relationship in which both parties play a role as truster and trustee. In one-way trust, the truster must trust the trustee in order to gain from their interaction. If the truster does not trust, the association ends, and potential gains are not realized. Once the truster demonstrates an act of trust, the trustee then is faced with a unilateral decision regarding how to respond to the trust. This game is one-way trust because only the truster faces the risk of trusting the trustee. The thick-relationship theory focuses on the idea that real relationships are experienced in complex settings based on diverse layers of interactions and that actions at one level may, in fact, depend on the action's ramifications at other levels. Actual motivations for trusting or being trustworthy are better understood when reputations in repeated relationships and third-party relationships are taken into account.

Biological Foundations of
Trust and Reciprocity

A common theme found among many of the chapters in this volume is an evolutionary approach to understanding the bases for trust and trustworthiness in modern-day associations. The two chapters of part II lay the foundation for understanding this approach.

In chapter 4, Robert Kurzban presents a well-structured argument for the coevolution of cooperation and reciprocity. Biologists have struggled with the notion of altruism and cooperation, as the two behaviors appear to go against the principles of natural selection. If altruism is defined as helping another organism at a cost to oneself, then it seems logical that natural selection would eventually eliminate this behavior. The evidence of altruism as a stable evolutionary behavior is explained as a result of reciprocal behavior.

To explain the existence of altruism on the basis of reciprocity, Kurzban defines natural selection in terms of design or adaptations rather than behavior. Specifically, an organism can be thought of as being made up of subsystems, each designed to solve a particular problem and contribute to reproductive success. In this view, natural selection is a process that, over time, selects the best designs in solving a problem.[4]

Kurzban discusses two ways in which natural selection can lead to altruistic behavior: kin selection and reciprocal altruism. Kin selection theory (first articulated by William Hamilton [1964]) is the capacity of a gene to increase its rate of replication by facilitating the replication of exact copies of itself, even in different organisms. According to the kin selection theory, a gene would cause behavior in organisms that would benefit another (even at a cost to itself) if there is a high enough probability that the other organism contained that gene. Reciprocal altruism (first articulated by Robert Trivers [1971]) is used to explain altruistic behavior by unrelated organisms. The theory relies on one organism conferring a benefit on another, contingent on the second organism's having conferred a benefit on the first.

Certain conditions are necessary for both forms of altruism to occur. First, both rely on the contingent delivery of benefits. In kin selection, the contingency involves a cue to relatedness. In reciprocal altruism, the contingency is a particular history of interaction and conditions for the forms of such interactions. Second, the environment must be one in which there are benefits to be conferred. Third, organisms must have repeated interactions with one another. Fourth, organisms must have sufficient information-processing abilities to be able to distinguish among individuals and remember which ones have or have not delivered benefits in the past. Finally, organisms must have sufficient information-processing sophistication and behavioral flexibility to interact with other organisms contingent on the history of interaction. Kurzban's discussion of the evolution of cooperation and reciprocity in human and nonhuman species focuses on how these conditions may have impacted the selection of specific kinds of behavior.

Kurzban's chapter is complemented by the detailed analysis found in chapter 5, by Frans de Waal, which stresses the deep evolutionary roots of trust and reciprocity. De Waal presents well-documented evidence to support the thesis that the exchange of social services among chimpanzees rests on cognitive abilities that allow current behavior to be contingent upon a history of interaction. Two types of behavior are formally supported: grooming increases the probability that the recipient will share with its donor at a later time, and sharing decreases the probability that the donor of the service will groom its recipient at a later time. In summary, evidence is presented for an exchange mechanism in which donations and receipts of services are stored in memory and exert partner-specific effects on subsequent behavior of donors and recipients.

Testing a model of reciprocal altruism, in which kin relationships are not a necessary condition, is a crucial step in establishing the evolutionary roots of observed reciprocity and trust. Although it is not possible to develop a quantitative test based on a large number of observations of very costly acts, de Waal does develop an ingenious experimental design for observing whether individual chimpanzees who had given something of value to other chimpanzees were more likely to receive something in return. De Waal concludes that we have evidence "for the entire set of features expected if reciprocity is cognition-based: partner specificity, selective protest, retaliation, turn taking, and the effect of one service on another."

The chapters in part III build on the biological foundations of trust. In particular, two modeling chapters are presented that summarize key arguments related to the linkages between trust, intention detection, and cooperation in complex societies.

The Links Between Evolution, Cognition, and Behavior

Kevin McCabe's chapter 6 can be viewed as a modeling "bridge" to the preceding chapters by Kurzban and de Waal. McCabe develops a theory of exchange based on the idea that one can conceptualize decision makers as using "mental modules" in their behavioral decisions in social exchange. In this theory of exchange, the expectation of reciprocal behavior is fundamental to the implementation of exchange through trust and conciliation.

As McCabe notes, however, "Trust and conciliation are relatively easy to explain once reciprocity is established, but how does one explain reciprocity?" He explores three areas important to addressing this question. First, he examines evidence of the adaptation of the human mind to allow for complex commitments that are required for reciprocal actions. Second, he argues that commitment and reciprocal actions are dependent on adaptations that allow for delay of gratification: "cool" mental mechanisms may have evolved that overcome "hot" mental mechanisms that call for immediate gratification. The final area focuses on the notion of a cognitive accounting system utilized to implement delay of gratification and resulting in reciprocal decision making. A "goodwill" accounting system tracks trading partners and forms the foundation for decisions regarding whether to trust, based on expectations regarding reciprocity. Such an accounting system is seen to be dependent upon a form of "mind reading" whereby decision makers contemplate the possible behavior of those with whom they may interact.[5] McCabe ends his chapter with a summary of a thought-provoking set of brain-imaging experiments that supply evidence of how the human brain may encode goodwill accounting. These experiments suggest that the frontal lobe regions of the brain are activated in situations in which subjects are attempting to cooperate with other human subjects, in a manner that does not occur when these subjects are playing against computer-simulated decision makers.

In chapter 7, James Hanley, John Orbell, and Tomonori Morikawa develop an evolutionary framework and computer simulations to examine more closely the role of evolutionary processes in altering dispositions toward trust and cooperative behavior. In particular, they examine a simulated world in which decision makers play both cooperative and conflictual games and players control information related to the accuracy of intentions. A key presumption in this analysis is that "if cognitive evolution has made it easy—or at least cost-effective—to detect cheaters, then cooperators will be able to avoid exploitation, and cooperation is likely to flourish." In the simulation study, cooperative games are modeled as *prisoner's dilemma games*, and conflictual games take the form of *hawk-dove games*. In the latter, decision makers must decide either to fight or not to fight. In the games investigated, if both fight, the winner captures the resource and the loser incurs a cost. If both do not fight, they both receive a reservation payoff that equals the value incurred by not playing.

The simulations suggest several key findings that researchers interested in complex systems and evolutionary processes should find interesting. Cooperation does not prosper in simulated worlds void of opportunities for fighting. The results suggest that in such worlds, over time, increases in mutual defection and corresponding decreases in mutual cooperation occur. Over time, the population of agents becomes relatively more adept at issuing persuasive lies than at penetrating the lies of others. The inclusion of the hawk-dove option yields a different dynamic. Over time, there is an increase in mutual cooperation and a decrease in mutual defection. Why? With the hawk-dove option, decision makers who believe they face protagonists who are not sufficiently cooperative have a choice beyond opting out of the prisoner's dilemma game. Furthermore, such agents are disproportionately inclined toward cooperation.

Each of the modeling chapters points to the complex relationship between agents' dispositions toward trust and cooperation and their resulting behavior. In part IV, the authors examine such behavior in laboratory-created decision environments, in which subjects face salient rewards for their decisions and those of their counterparts.

Experimental Evidence

Part IV of this volume contains several chapters that review previous experimental work and recent research by the authors. The overriding theme linking much of this work is stated clearly by McCabe and Vernon Smith: "We summarize and report data from a research program motivated by concepts of reciprocity and intentionality detection that we propose as supplements to the standard game-theoretic principles. The question is not whether game-theoretic principles find application in the data—they do—but rather whether they suffice as the only principles that govern behavior."

In chapter 8, Karen Cook and Robin Cooper provide a review of experimental studies in sociology, social psychology, and economics that focus on issues of trust. They begin by confronting the issue of attitudinal versus behavioral measures of trust and the difficult task of disentangling acts of cooperation from trust. They stress that sequential games that allow one player to move before the other, and games that allow players to exit, provide clear evidence regarding "trust" as contrasted to simple cooperation.

They then turn to a review of selected studies focusing on subjects' inherent motivations, the incentive structure and strategic nature of the game facing experimental subjects, and the social context in which decisions are made. In conclusion, Cook and Cooper argue for the need for a more complete theory of the basis of trust, as well as a more complete and unified experimental approach, that examines trust more extensively in terms of the social context in which decision makers find themselves.

Parallel to the evolutionary approach discussed by Kurzban, in chapter 9 Catherine Eckel and Rick Wilson conjecture that humans are conditional cooperators and that the decision to cooperate is based on initial expectations about the likely behavior of others with whom an association is contemplated. They explore the idea that "humans share a capacity to read one another's intentions through a set of cues such as facial expressions, body language, and tone of voice." They report results from two experiments designed to examine how facial expressions may affect an individual's perception of the trustworthiness of a total stranger and the resulting behavior of this individual. Similar to arguments made by Kurzban and McCabe, Eckel and Wilson develop the notion of a "theory of mind"—the ability to read directly another's intentions. In their principal study, subjects in a one-shot trust game view the faces of their presumed counterparts. They move first, in what is in essence a decision to trust or not to trust their counterparts. The main result is that, at the margin, subjects draw inferences from the images they observe and act accordingly. Subjects choose the trusting move 62 percent of the time. The rate is significantly increased if subjects have been paired with counterparts who display smiling images. Trusting behavior is also increased in cases in which subjects have rated their counterparts high on a trustworthiness index, based purely on the inferences they have drawn from their counterparts' photographic images.

In their chapter 10, Kevin McCabe and Vernon Smith offer evidence from a series of one-shot and repeated games in which players are randomly matched or matched repeatedly with counterparts. Reciprocity is based on triadic knowledge—information gained through the shared-attention mechanism. Shared attention, as a mental module, operates on two kinds of information: *focal points,* such as symmetry and *Pareto dominance* of payoffs that are likely to be observed by the other player, and move information, which communicates intentions through both foregone opportunities and assessment of the payoffs that remain as admissible future opportunities.[6]

McCabe and Smith test reciprocity theory by performing experiments based on three variations of an *extensive-form* bargaining-tree structure in which players alternate moves. Each variation has a *subgame-perfect Nash equilibrium* and a symmetric cooperative outcome. Following player 1's decision either to take a sure payoff or to continue the game, player 2 makes the choice as to whether to head toward the subgame-perfect Nash equilibrium or to put the decision back into the hands of player 1. At this point, player 1 can choose the cooperation outcome. In games 0 and 1, player 1 can deviate from the cooperative equilibrium, attempting to raise his or her payoffs and reduce player 2's payoffs. However, player 2 can punish this action at a cost to his or her own payoff. In game 2, however, player 1 can deviate from the cooperative equilibrium with no threat of punishment from player 2 (note that game 0 differs from game 1 in that the cooperative payoffs are equal to subgame-perfect Nash equilibrium payoffs in game 0, whereas in game 1 subgame-perfect Nash equilibrium payoffs are less than cooperative payoffs).

In summary, McCabe and Smith find support for several key findings: first, analysis identifies factors affecting choice other than those predicted by noncooperative game theory; second, no meaningful support is observed for the hypothesis that subjects attach a personal and positive utility to the payoff of their counterpart; third, reciprocity does not require a positive probability of repeat interaction with the same person; fourth, reciprocity increases with the probability of repeat interaction with the same person; fifth, players use the payoffs of counterparts in their strategic analysis. Concerning the last finding, players use the payoffs of their counterparts not to identify the subgame-perfect Nash equilibrium, however, but to identify and try to achieve the cooperative outcome through reciprocity. The possibility that cooperative play results from the threat of punishment by player 2 for player 1's deviations from the cooperative outcome cannot be ruled out. When the threat of punishment is removed, the cooperative outcome diminishes, and the defection rate increases. However, individuals in the position of player 2 rely largely on trust in attempting to achieve the cooperative outcome, with no decline in play toward the cooperative outcome.

William Harbaugh, Kate Krause, Steven Liday, and Lise Vesterlund, in chapter 11, examine how children in third, sixth, ninth, and twelfth grades play the game of trust as designed by Berg, Dickhaut, and McCabe (1995). They do find trusting behavior among children. Even eight-year-olds pass at least one token to the trustees in this game and thus do not behave consistently with the game-theoretic prediction. On the other hand, they find the children and teenagers in their study to be somewhat less trusting than the adults in the Berg, Dickhaut, and McCabe study and the extensive replications of this study with adult subjects. Consistent with a similar finding by T. K. Ahn, Elinor Ostrom, David Schmidt, and James Walker, in the following chapter, Harbaugh and colleagues find a negative relation between the passing of funds from a truster to a trustee and the response made by subjects to a general question used extensively to measure trust on national sample surveys. Trust appears to be a complex concept strongly affected by context. General survey responses may not be a valid measure of the level of trusting behavior found in particular situations.

In chapter 12, Ahn, Ostrom, Schmidt, and Walker turn the focus to play in one-shot and repeated play prisoner's dilemma games. The authors concentrate on four attributes of strategic games as components in understanding cooperation, trust, and reciprocity: pecuniary benefits, player types, information about player types, and the linkages between players that occur in repeated game situations. Results from several experimental decision settings are presented. Cooperation is shown to be significantly related to previous gains from cooperation. The level of cooperation and trust is also shown to be minimal in situations in which reputations for trust cannot be established. In settings in which players have the opportunity to build associations with others of their type, gains from association are larger, less dependent on game parameters, and more dependent on the exact nature of repeated play.

Toshio Yamagishi, in chapter 13, confronts the common characterization of American society as relatively less trusting and Japanese society as relatively more so. Consistent with the findings reported by Buchan, Croson, and Johnson (1999) discussed earlier, Yamagishi challenges the presumption that national identities are reflective of the degree of general trust in a society. Yamagishi provides clear evidence that what has been labeled in Japan as "trust" might be better conceptualized as assurance of mutual cooperation in commitment relations. He argues that trustworthy behavior is assured in Japanese society by the nature of the incentives surrounding exchange partners. "This assurance of mutual cooperation in Japan, however, does not imply that the Japanese are generally trustful." Reporting on a series of experiments conducted by himself and his colleagues, Yamagishi shows that in the context of games requiring trust, but in the absence of mutual commitment relations, Japanese and American subjects behave in fundamentally similar manners. Yamagishi develops an institutional view of culture that is useful in understanding what seems to be contradictory evidence between survey instruments and experimental behavior. Building on the idea of the link between social uncertainty and cooperation, Yamagishi shows that one can predict alternative institutional arrangements in associations dependent on the extent of a lack of common information present in particular settings.

Conclusion

Our conclusions are similar to those expressed by Margaret Levi in chapter 14 of this volume. Whereas she started out a skeptic of the usefulness of experiments, we started out, and continue to be, strong enthusiasts of the experimental method. We are glad that the experience of participating in the two workshops held at the Russell Sage Foundation and a careful reading of the final set of papers has transformed her views. Although the experimental method is certainly not the only way to study trust and trustworthiness, we are confident that a great deal has been learned by utilizing the experimental method to test an evolving set of theories relevant to the study of productive social and economic relations.

Another development that has grown out of experimental studies of trust and reciprocity is a better connection to the biological foundations of human behavior. The determinism of some forms of social Darwinism so alienated many social scientists that the important presumption that human development has been shaped by evolution has repeatedly been rejected. Many of the chapters in this volume presume that humans are also evolved creatures. As such, they have the capacity to learn cultural norms and institutional rules that affect the incentives they face and their resulting interactions. These are the factors that strongly affect how trust can develop in ongoing situations.

Although the original intent of this volume was to study trust using the experimental method, we are pleased that the effort broadened to include a wider discussion of conceptual and modeling issues that must be faced in studying trust. It is, of course, a truism of the social sciences that more research is needed. In this case, more research is indeed needed to sort out exactly which combinations of contextual variables are most conducive to high levels of trust and trustworthiness. In addition to the normative foundations of trustworthy behavior, knowledge of the "other," repeated interactions, and the strong possibility of future interactions are strong predictors of both trustworthy and trusting relationships. How these can be enhanced by various structural conditions will provide a rich set of questions for future work.

Notes

1. Joseph Henrich and colleagues (2001) briefly report on an experimental study conducted in fifteen small-scale cultural groups from multiple continents. Each group was asked to play *ultimatum, public-good,* and *dictator games.* The variance in the level of the amount of funds offered by the first player in ultimatum games is substantial and varies in a systematic way with the general cultural orientation of the groups.

2. Still further experiments with the basic trust game have been reported by Friedel Bolle (1998), René Fahr and Bernd Irlenbusch (2000), and Ernst

Fehr, Simon Gächter, and George Kirchsteiger (1996). Jörg Rieskamp and Gerd Gigerenzer (2001) report on an interesting effort to program the heuristics that individuals tend to use when faced with situations involving the structure of the basic trust game. Thomas Gautschi (2000) provides yet a further test of the findings in the trust game, with consistent results.

3. A modification of the trust game was run by Werner Güth, Peter Ockenfels, and Markus Wendel (1997). In this experiment, they had the players experience the game once and then bid for the roles of player 1 and player 2. Very low levels of trust were extended when the game was played by those who had bid for these positions (and low levels of reciprocity were extended by those who were trusted). Thus, as Karen Cook and Robin Cooper stress in chapter 8 of this volume, context makes a substantial difference in how trust is developed.

4. The position that natural selection picks out optimal designs is vigorously debated in contemporary evolutionary biology literature.

5. The experiments by Kathleen Valley, Joseph Moag, and Max Bazerman (1998) on the effect of face-to-face communication in two-person bargaining games are particularly relevant to the question of goodwill accounting.

6. Given the number of disciplines represented in this volume, some technical terms used will be unfamiliar to some readers. We hope the glossary helps all readers understand the terms used in this book.

References

Arrow, Kenneth. 1974. *The Limits of Organization*. New York: Norton Press.
Berg, Joyce, John Dickhaut, and Kevin McCabe. 1995. "Trust, Reciprocity, and Social History." *Games and Economic Behavior* 10(1): 122–42.
Boehm, Christopher. 1999. *Hierarchy in the Forest: The Evolution of Egalitarian Behavior*. Cambridge, Mass.: Harvard University Press.
Bolle, Friedel. 1998. "Reward Trust: An Experimental Study." *Theory and Decision* 45(1): 83–98.
Buchan, Nancy R., Rachel T. A. Croson, and Eric J. Johnson. 1999. "Getting to Know You: An International Experiment of the Influence of Culture, Communication, and Social Distance on Trust and Reciprocation." Working paper. Madison, Wisc.: University of Wisconsin, Department of Marketing.
Buskens, Vincent, and Jeroen Weesie. 2000. "An Experiment on the Effects of Embeddedness in Trust Situations: Buying a Used Car." *Rationality and Society* 12(2): 227–53.
de Waal, Frans. 1996. *Good Natured: The Origins of Right and Wrong in Humans and Other Animals*. Cambridge, Mass.: Harvard University Press.
Dickhaut, John, John Hubbard, Kevin McCabe, and Vernon Smith. 1997. "Trust, Reciprocity, and Interpersonal History: Fool Me Once, Shame on You, Fool Me Twice, Shame on Me." Working paper. Tucson, Ariz.: University of Arizona, Economic Science Laboratory.

Fahr, René, and Bernd Irlenbusch. 2000. "Fairness As a Constraint on Trust in Reciprocity: Earned Property Rights in a Reciprocal Exchange Experiment." *Economic Letters* 66(3): 275–82.

Fehr, Ernst, Simon Gächter, and George Kirchsteiger. 1996. "Reciprocal Fairness and Noncompensating Wage Differentials." *Journal of Institutional and Theoretical Economics* 152(4): 608–40.

Gautschi, Thomas. 2000. "History Effects in Social Dilemma Situations." *Rationality and Society* 12(2): 131–62.

Güth, Werner, Peter Ockenfels, and Markus Wendel. 1997. "Cooperation Based on Trust: An Experimental Investigation." *Journal of Economic Psychology* 18(1): 15–43.

Hamilton, William D. 1964. "The Genetic Evolution of Social Behavior." *Journal of Theoretical Biology* 7(1): 1–52.

Henrich, Joseph, Robert Boyd, Samuel Bowles, Colin Camerer, Ernst Fehr, Herbert Gintis, and Richard McElreath. 2001. "Cooperation, Reciprocity, and Punishment in Fifteen Small-Scale Societies." *American Economic Review* 91(May): 73–78.

Khalil, Elias L. 1994. "Trust." In *The Elgar Companion to Institutional and Evolutionary Economics*, edited by Geoffrey M. Hodgson, Warren J. Samuels, and Marc R. Tool. Hants, England: Edward Elgar.

Rieskamp, Jörg, and Gerd Gigerenzer. 2001. "Simple Heuristics for Social Interactions: The Role of Trust, Reciprocity, and Fairness." Working paper. Berlin: Max Planck Institute for Human Development.

Rousseau, Denise M., Sim B. Sitkin, Ronald S. Burt, and Colin Camerer. 1998. "Not So Different After All: A Cross-Discipline View of Trust." *Academy of Management Review* 23(3): 393–404.

Trivers, Robert. 1971. "The Evolution of Reciprocal Altruism." *Quarterly Review of Biology* 46(4): 35–57.

Valley, Kathleen, Joseph Moag, and Max H. Bazerman. 1998. "A Matter of Trust: Effects of Communication on the Efficiency and Distribution of Outcomes." *Journal of Economic Behavior and Organization* 34(2): 211–38.

Zak, Paul J., and Stephen Knack. 1998. "Trust and Growth." Working paper. Claremont, Calif.: Claremont Graduate University, Department of Economics.

Chapter 2

Toward a Behavioral Theory Linking Trust, Reciprocity, and Reputation

ELINOR OSTROM

A CENTRAL question has overshadowed the thinking of social scientists at least since the work of Thomas Hobbes (1960 [1651]): How do communities of individuals sustain agreements that counteract individual temptations to select short-term, hedonistic actions when all parties would be better off if each party selected actions leading to higher group and individual returns? In other words, how do groups of individuals gain trust? Hobbes's answer is that communities have to rely on an authority external to themselves to impose and enforce commands that extricate them from the traps of their own making. Hobbes considers it impossible for individuals to escape from what we now call *social dilemmas* and argues that a strong, centralized, and external authority is therefore necessary. Thus, for Hobbes, trust is created by the presence of strong external actors.

The modern garb for the Hobbesian question is the puzzle of how individuals themselves cope with social dilemmas. The answer given by *noncooperative game theory* for *one-shot* and finitely repeated social dilemmas has effectively been the same as that of Hobbes: Agreements, if they are to be followed, must be enforced by external authorities.

The term "social dilemma" refers to a great number of situations in which individuals make choices in interdependent circumstances. If each individual in a one-shot or finitely repeated social dilemma selects strategies based on the currently accepted, *rational-choice* model of the individual, all individuals will realize a payoff at an equilibrium outcome of less value than one or more of the available alternatives (Dawes 1975, 1980; Hardin 1971). Because the less valued payoff is at an equilibrium, no one is independently motivated to change his or her choice, given the choices of other participants. These situations are considered to be dilemmas because at least one outcome exists that would yield higher returns for all participants. To get to this outcome, however, individuals have to trust one another. Rational participants making independent choices are not predicted to realize this *Pareto-optimal* outcome. A conflict is thereby posed between acting from individual rationality and gaining sufficient trust to achieve the optimal outcomes for a group. The problem of *collective action* raised by social dilemmas is finding a way to avoid *Pareto-inferior* equilibria and to move closer to the optimum. Those who find ways to coordinate strategies in some fashion receive a "cooperator's dividend" equal to the difference between the worst outcome and the outcome achieved.

Social dilemmas abound in human affairs. They have been studied by biologists, economists, evolutionary psychologists, game theorists, historians, legal scholars, mathematicians, philosophers, political scientists, sociologists, and social psychologists. The problem of providing essential *public goods,* including national defense, clean air, and safe streets, is one example. Another is the conflict that arises when appropriators using an open-access *common-pool resource,* such as the ocean fisheries, could jointly harvest at a rate that would maximize economic returns to the group (or the sustainability of the resource), but the incentives facing each appropriator threaten the destruction of the resource. Members of a potential cartel also face a social dilemma, but one that, if solved, generates externalities for others. The most famous form of social dilemma is the *prisoner's dilemma.* The prisoner's dilemma is an imaginary construct in which two partners in crime, separated from each other in prison, are individually motivated to defect (that is, to tell the prosecutor about the other prisoner's involvement in a crime). The partner who defects will improve his or her outcome, earning release or a diminished sentence. If both partners defect, both will face the maximum punishment for the crime. On the other hand, if both partners remain silent (that is, if they cooperate with one another), the penalty for both will be less (Luce and Raiffa 1957).

Social dilemmas are called by many names, including generalized social exchange (Emerson 1972a, 1972b; Ekeh 1974; Yamagishi and Cook 1993), shirking (Alchian and Demsetz 1972), the free-rider problem (Edney 1979; Grossman and Hart 1980), social traps (Platt 1973), *moral hazard* (Holmstrom 1982), the credible-commitment dilemma

(Williams, Collins, and Lichbach 1997), the public-goods or collective-goods problem (Samuelson 1954; Olson 1965), and the *tragedy of the commons* (Hardin 1968). Among the types of individuals who are posited to face these kinds of situations are politicians (Geddes 1994), international negotiators (Snidal 1985; Sandler 1992), members of Congress (Shepsle and Weingast 1984), managers (Miller 1992), workers (Leibenstein 1976), long-distance traders (Greif, Milgrom, and Weingast 1994), ministers (Bullock and Baden 1977), labor union organizers (Messick 1973), revolutionaries (Lichbach 1995), homeowners (Boudreaux and Holcombe 1989), and even cheerleaders (Hardy and Latané 1988)—and, of course, all of us.

All major economic, political, and social projects requiring individuals to associate in allocation activities contain the seeds of social dilemmas. Given the pervasiveness of the problem and its importance to all of the social sciences, it is no surprise that thousands of articles and books have been written on the subject. However, little theoretical cumulation of this vast empirical literature has taken place, although important efforts have made headway (Palfrey and Rosenthal 1988; Ledyard 1995; Lichbach 1995). The "Tower of Babel problem" (Ostrom 1997, 156) is particularly severe in the social sciences, where so many disciplines have developed major research programs. The number of variables proposed as affecting the likelihood of collective action is simply astounding. On close examination, some variables with different sounding names turn out to be the same variable. Even after careful sifting and sorting to connect differently named variables to their underlying core concept, however, there are still at least thirty different variables posited to affect the way individuals solve collective-action problems (see, for example, Agrawal 2002). The complexity of this problem exceeds the capacity of any single general theory to encompass a full explanation. A general theory would require that formal modelers, social theorists, experimentalists, and field researchers learn about one another's work to gain substantial cumulation, but communication among theorists and empirical researchers is difficult, even among those who are in the same discipline.

Given the immensity of the corpus of research on this topic, I do not propose to perform a magic trick and bring into being a full general theory of the conditions that facilitate collective action in the confines of this chapter.[1] Instead, I limit myself here to the predictions for social dilemmas made by noncooperative game theory, relying on a particular model of individual choice, and the experimental research related to the general fit between these predictions and the results from many experimental studies.

I review the experimental literature for several reasons. As a researcher with years of experience doing field research, I find the control that one can achieve in experimental studies to be an asset of immense value. The external validity of field research is sometimes simply swamped by the large number of variables that change in unknown ways. In field studies, one is never sure of the exact structure of the incentives nor of how close participants come to reaching an optimal solution. Careful studies in the lab with a precise and controlled focus on a particular aspect of a problem can yield greater confidence in one's ability to understand what is going on in the field under study. Fortunately, many empirical instances of local public-goods and common-pool-resource dilemmas allow for comparison between experimental and field research findings (see Ostrom, Gardner, and Walker 1994). Furthermore, a large number of carefully crafted experimental studies provide substantial evidence about the effect of individual characteristics and structural variables on the likelihood of collective action.

A substantial experimental program on two-person prisoner's dilemma games was initiated more than forty years ago (see Rapoport and Chammah 1965; Rapoport 1974). Three important findings emerged from this research: approximately one-half of the subjects in one-shot prisoner's dilemmas choose to cooperate; *communication* substantially increases the proportion of subjects who select cooperation (Deutsch 1960); and about one-half of the bona fide subjects reciprocates and one-half exploits a partner who adopts a 100 percent cooperative strategy (Rapoport 1968). Because the two-person setting is not as difficult to solve as the N-person setting,[2] I focus in this review on experiments in which $N > 2$. Major experimental programs on N-person social dilemmas began with the work of Peter Bohm (1972), Robyn Dawes, John Orbell, and their colleagues in the 1980s (Dawes, Orbell, and van de Kragt 1984, 1986; Orbell, van de Kragt, and Dawes 1988), David Messick and his colleagues, also in the 1980s (Messick and Brewer 1983; Messick et al. 1983), Gerald Marwell and Ruth Ames (1979), and Vernon Smith (1979, 1980). In the years that have followed, several hundred experimental studies on social dilemmas have been conducted (see Ledyard 1995 for a review of those examining public-goods dilemmas). Thus researchers are at a juncture at which it is possible to examine key theoretical models, place less confidence in those that are not well supported by empirical research, and begin the task of reconstructing an empirically grounded theory.

Theoretical Foundations of Collective Action

In all models of social dilemmas, a group of individuals are involved in a game with a *Nash equilibrium,* or multiple Nash equilibria, for a single iteration of the game that yields less than an optimal outcome

for all involved. The equilibrium is thus Pareto inferior. The optimal
outcome could be achieved if those involved were to cooperate by
selecting strategies other than those prescribed by a subgame-perfect
equilibrium solution to a noncooperative game (Harsanyi and Selten
1988). Besides these assumptions regarding the structure of payoffs
and the presence of inferior equilibria in the one-shot version of the
game, other assumptions made in almost all formal models of social
dilemmas include the following:

• All participants have common knowledge of the exogenously fixed
  structure of the situation and of the payoffs to be received by all
  individuals under all combinations of strategies.
• Decisions about strategies are made independently, often simultaneously.
• No external actor (or central authority) is present to enforce agreements among participants about their choices.

When such a game is finitely repeated, and everyone shares complete
information about the structure of the situation, the predicted outcome for each iteration is still the Nash equilibrium, or equilibria, for
the constituent game. This prediction is based on the concept of *backward induction*.

Social dilemmas are more than an important academic puzzle. A
substantial body of public policy is based on the presumed inability
of individuals to get out of the traps of their own making. This has
been particularly the case in relation to environmental policy since the
publication of Garrett Hardin's (1968) evocative article using the example of herders trapped in the overuse of their common pasture as
a metaphor for the population explosion and other environmental
problems. The grim predictions evoked considerable empirical challenges as well as important theoretical breakthroughs. The predictions
ran counter to so many everyday experiences that many scholars
turned to survey and field studies to examine the level of voluntary
contributions to public goods (see Bromley et al. 1992). Others turned
to the experimental lab and in some contexts confirmed levels of cooperation in one-shot experiments much higher than those predicted.
Game theorists were challenged to rethink their own firm conclusions
and to pose new models in which cooperation might emerge.

The introduction of two kinds of uncertainty into repeated games—
about the number of repetitions and about the types of players participating in a social dilemma—leads to more optimistic predictions. It
is now theoretically well established that when individuals, modeled
as fully rational actors with low discount rates, interact in an indefinitely repeated social-dilemma situation, it is possible for them to

achieve optimal or near optimal outcomes and avoid the predicted strategies of one-shot and finitely repeated games that yield suboptimal outcomes (Fudenberg and Maskin 1986). This is possible when players achieve self-enforcing equilibria by committing themselves to punishing noncooperators sufficiently to deter noncooperation. David Kreps and his colleagues (1982) introduce a second kind of uncertainty related to whether all the players use complete rationality as their guide to action. If there is some uncertainty concerning the presence of some "irrational" player who will reciprocate cooperation with cooperation, then a completely rational player may benefit by cooperating early in a sequence of games and switching to noncooperation at the end. Once either of these two forms of uncertainty is introduced, the number of possible equilibria explodes (Abreau 1988). Everything is predicted: optimal outcomes, the Pareto-inferior Nash equilibria, and everything between.

To generate predictions other than noncooperation, it has been necessary either to assume real uncertainty about the duration of a particular situation or to assume that some players may be "irrational" in their willingness to reciprocate cooperation with cooperation. The prediction for single-shot or finitely repeated games remains the same so long as the theorist assumes that utility is linearly related to a subject's own payoffs. The evidence from single-shot and finitely repeated games strongly contradicts the theoretical predictions for many contexts.

For all of the challenges, we have not yet developed a behavioral theory based on a model of the individual consistent with empirical evidence about individual decisions in social-dilemma situations. This foundation is essential if we are to understand such basic questions as why face-to-face communication so consistently enhances cooperation in social-dilemma experiments or how trust affects the willingness to cooperate. It is also essential for the construction of a coherent explanation of the impact of structural variables such as the size of the group; the heterogeneity of assets, interests, and information; various types of production and payoff functions; monitoring and sanctioning arrangements; and the role of governments in facilitating or retarding collective action.

This has become a particularly challenging puzzle for scholars who are genuinely searching for theoretical frameworks, theories, and models of behavior that integrate understanding across the social sciences. The existence of a single theory that explains how individuals achieve near optimal outcomes in markets but fails to explain why anyone votes or contributes voluntarily to the provision of public goods is an unsatisfactory state of knowledge in the social sciences. Simply assuming that individuals use long-range thinking "to achieve the goal of establishing and/or maintaining continued mutual cooperation" (Pruitt and Kimmel 1977, 375) is also insufficient. Such a theory explains neither the obvious fact that groups often fail to obtain the joint outcomes easily available to them nor the amount of cheating that frequently occurs once an agreement is reached.

I argue that what has come to be called rational-choice theory in the social sciences is instead one model in a family of models useful when conducting formal analyses of human decisions in highly structured physical and institutional settings. As Amartya Sen points out in his presidential address to the American Economic Association, "There are many different conceptions of rational behavior of the individual" (Sen 1995, 2). The model of complete rationality most frequently used in rational-choice explanations is one model of these different conceptions. It is a rather thin model of broader theories of rational behavior.[3] When it has been used successfully, it is largely dependent for its power of explanation on how the structure of the situations involved is modeled (Satz and Ferejohn 1994).

A broader theory of human behavior views humans as fallible cognizers (Clark and Karmiloff-Smith 1993) who attempt to do as well as they can given the constraints of the situations in which they find themselves (or the ones they seek out) (see also Popper 1967). These cognizers learn norms, heuristics, and full analytical strategies from one another, from feedback from the world, and from their own capacity to engage in self-reflection and imagine a differently structured world. They are capable of designing new tools—including institutions—that can change the structure of the worlds they face for good or evil purposes. They adopt both short-term and long-term perspectives dependent on the structure of opportunities they face. Multiple models are consistent with a theory of boundedly rational, norm-learning, and norm-using human behavior, including a model of complete rationality when paired with repetitive, highly competitive situations.

In highly structured and competitive environments such as an open market, predictions generated from the combination of a model of the situation and a model of complete rationality are well supported empirically. As Armen Alchian (1950) has shown, however, entrepreneurs have no alternative other than to seek profits. Those who do not pick profit maximization strategies (by whatever means—including flipping a coin) are eliminated by the selective forces of the market.[4] Furthermore, the market itself generates the limited range of sufficient statistics needed by entrepreneurs to maximize profits (von Hayek 1945). The situation turns the individual into a determinate, calculating machine. Spiro Latsis dramatically describes the situationally determinate status of single-exit or straitjacket situations like the competitive market: "To say that a seller under perfect conditions deliberately chooses a course of action to maximize profits is analogous to saying that a member of the audience is maximizing if he runs out of the single exit available to him in a burning cinema" (Latsis 1972, 210–11).

Although a model of complete rationality provides empirically established predictions about collective outcomes of the decisions of individuals and firms in competitive markets and other highly structured and competitive processes, it does not perform as well when used to analyze less structured situations. In the political world, the models are "most useful where the stakes are high and numbers low" (Fiorina 1995, 88). Rational-choice explanations of the strategies adopted by political parties facing electoral competition are more successful than similar efforts to explain the choices of voters, who do not face strong selection pressures (Satz and Ferejohn 1994). The applications that have been most successful in the social sciences also rely heavily on the structure of the situation.

Thus the institutional structure of a competitive market or of a competitive political process provides the scaffolding that supports the analytical power of thin models of rational choice (Clark 1995). In less structured and less competitive situations, the model of the situation does not lead to a prediction that all who fail to adopt one strategy (by whatever means) will be eliminated. Using a thin model of rational choice in such situations may lead to a prediction of behavior that is repeatedly shown to be empirically false. Those who put the weight of their explanation on a thin model and preclude using models that involve a longer time perspective, and the possibility that humans will adopt norms of reciprocity, fairness, and trust, will not find much empirical support for their predictions in social-dilemma situations. They would predict, for example, that most individuals facing a ten-period, complete-information, public-goods dilemma with opportunities for discussion will contribute zero to the effort over the entire ten rounds. Yet they would be very wrong. Fortunately, many social scientists, game theorists, and biologists are exploring diverse models of the individual that offer considerable promise of providing a better foundation for understanding and explaining social dilemmas (see Selten 1990, 1991; Güth 1995; Crawford and Ostrom 1995; Trivers 1971; Kreps 1990; Ostrom, Gardner, and Walker 1994). Before I get too far ahead of myself, however, let me turn to the question of the general fit of experimental evidence related to one type of social dilemmas—public goods—with theoretical predictions.

The Lack of a General Fit

I begin this discussion exploring six findings about the general fit between the predictions of noncooperative game theory, which use complete rationality for one-shot and finitely repeated social dilemmas, and the behavior observed in *public-goods games*. I focus first on the question of the fit between theory and observed behavior because the predictions are so unambiguously clear and have influenced so much thinking across the social sciences. Experiments conducted on market behavior do fit the predictions closely (see Davis and Holt 1993 for an overview). If one-shot and finitely repeated public-goods experiments strongly supported the predictions of noncooperative game theory, social scientists would have a grounded theory that had close affinities to a vast body of economic theory for which there is strong empirical support. It would then be necessary to turn immediately to the problem of indefinitely repeated situations, in which noncooperative game theory faces an embarrassment of too many equilibria. As it turns out, we have a different story to tell. The six general findings are as follows:

1. High levels of initial cooperation are found in most types of public-goods experiments, but these levels are consistently lower than optimal.

2. Cooperation levels decay toward the predicted Nash equilibrium in repeated public-goods experiments at a rate that is inversely proportional to the number of repetitions.

3. Communication substantially increases cooperation in all types of social-dilemma experiments.

4. Nash equilibrium strategies are not a good predictor at the individual level.

5. Models based on backward induction in finitely repeated public-goods experiments do not predict observed behavior.

6. Individuals solve *second-order social dilemmas* to provide institutional rules that improve outcomes in base social dilemmas.

High Levels of Initial Cooperation

Most experimental studies of public-goods situations have found levels of cooperative actions in one-shot games, or in the first rounds of repeated games, that are significantly above the predicted level of zero (Marwell and Ames 1979, 1980, 1981; Schneider and Pommerehne 1981; Kim and Walker 1984; Isaac, McCue, and Plott 1985; Orbell and Dawes 1991, 1993).[5] "In a wide variety of treatment conditions, participants rather persistently contributed 40 to 60 percent of their token endowments to the [public good], far in excess of the 0 percent contribution rate consistent with a Nash equilibrium" (Davis and Holt 1993, 325). On the other hand, once an experiment is repeated, cooperation levels tend to decline. The individual variation across experiment sessions can be great. In a series of eight experiments conducted by Mark Isaac, James Walker, and Susan Thomas (1984) in which the uniform theoretical prediction was zero contributions even though treatment conditions varied, contribution rates varied from nearly 0 percent to roughly 75 percent of the resources available to participants. Although many researchers have focused on the unexpectedly high rates of cooperation, it is important to note that in sparse institutional settings, cooperation levels never reach the optimum. Thus, though the prediction of zero levels of cooperation can be rejected, cooperation at a suboptimal level is consistently observed in sparse settings.

The Decay of Cooperation Toward Predicted Nash Equilibria

In repeated experiments without communication or other facilitating conditions, levels of cooperation fall (or rise) toward the Nash equilibrium in public-goods (common-pool-resource) experiments. In all repeated experiments, there is considerable pulsing as subjects obtain outcomes that vary as much as 25 percent within short spurts of increasing and decreasing levels of cooperation, but the general trend is toward the *subgame-perfect Nash equilibrium* (Isaac, McCue, and Plott 1985; Ostrom, Gardner, and Walker 1994).[6] For example, in experiments in which contributions produced a relatively large marginal externality for individuals, Isaac and Walker (1988b) found contributions ranging from 50 to 60 percent during the first five rounds but falling to 30 to 40 percent by the ninth and tenth rounds of a ten-round public-goods experiment. Where the positive externalities from marginal contributions were not large, contributions in the initial round ranged from 30 to 40 percent in the initial round and by the tenth round approached zero.

Speculations have been offered that the decay rate simply represents the time it takes subjects to learn the noncooperative equilibrium strategy. James Andreoni (1988) interprets a decay rate that was similar over ten repetitions between strangers (subjects were mixed so they played a different person each time) and partners (subjects continued to play with the same person) as evidence for learning.[7] However, it appears instead that subjects learn something else in repeated experiments. Mark Isaac, James Walker, and Arlington Williams (1994) compare the rate of decay when experienced subjects were explicitly told that an experiment would last ten, forty, or sixty rounds. The rate of decay of cooperative actions is inversely related to the number of decision rounds, as shown in figure 2.1. In the ten-round experiment, contributions ranged from an average close to 50 percent of optimum during the first nine rounds and fell to an average of around 10 percent. In the forty-round experiment, average contributions ranged from 60 percent to 35 percent during the first ten rounds. During the last twenty rounds, contributions did not exceed 40 percent, and they fell below 10 percent on the last round. In the sixty-round experiment, average contributions stayed primarily in the 30 to 65 percent range for the first forty periods. Again, an end effect occurred in the final few rounds.

Instead of learning the noncooperative strategy, subjects appear to have learned how endogenously to stretch out the number of rounds for which the public good was provided at reasonably high levels, even with some subjects free riding. Cooperation rates approached zero only in the last few periods, even when subjects played sixty rounds.

Communication

In cooperative game theory, it is assumed that players can communicate and make enforceable agreements. In noncooperative game theory, players are assumed to be unable to make enforceable agreements (Harsanyi and Selten 1988, 3); thus, whether or not players can communicate is considered irrelevant. Preplay communication is viewed as cheap talk (Farrell 1987). In a social dilemma, self-interested players are expected to try to convince others to cooperate and promise cooperative action but then to choose the Nash equilibrium strategy when they make their private decisions (Barry and Hardin 1982, 381).[8] As Gary Miller expresses it, "It is obvious that simple communication is not sufficient to escape the dilemma" (Miller 1992, 25).[9]

From this theoretical perspective, face-to-face communication should make no difference in the outcomes achieved in social dilemmas, whether they are one-shot, finitely repeated, or indefinitely repeated. Yet a consistent, strong, and replicable finding is that substantial increases in the levels of cooperation are achieved when individuals are allowed to communicate on a face-to-face basis.[10] This holds true across all types of social dilemmas studied in laboratory settings and in both one-shot and finitely repeated experiments. Communication has been found to have a robust and positive impact on cooperation levels even when individuals are not provided with feedback on group decisions after every round (Cason and Khan 1996).

Figure 2.1   Public-Goods Contributions: Varying Time Horizons

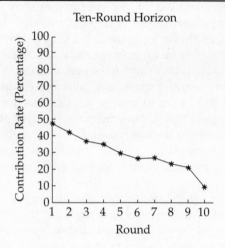

Ten-Round Horizon

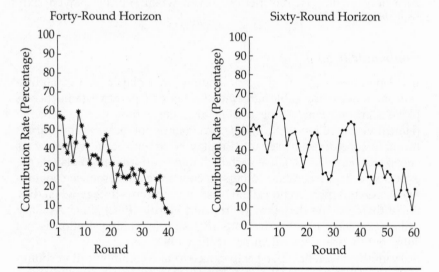

Forty-Round Horizon   Sixty-Round Horizon

Source: Data from Isaac, Walker, and Williams 1994.
Note: Contribution rate is measured by the number of tokens given to the group account. In the ten-round game, contribution rates are averaged over six experiments, and in the forty-round game, over two experiments; the data for the sixty-round game are from a single experiment.

Figure 2.2   Effect of Communication in Public-Goods Experiments: Three Communication Conditions

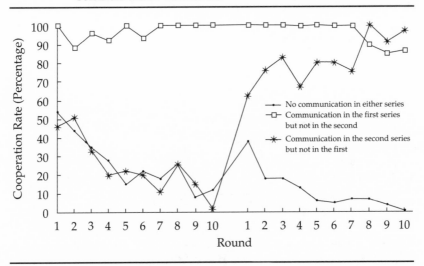

Source: Data from Isaac and Walker 1988a, 1988b.
Note: Cooperation rate is measured as the number of tokens given to the group account.

Isaac and Walker (1988a, 1988b), for example, conducted three designs involving two consecutive series of ten-round public-goods experiments (see figure 2.2). In the first design, subjects had no opportunities for communication in either series. In both series, cooperation levels started relatively high (around 50 percent in the first, at round 1, and around 40 percent in the second series, at round 11) and steadily decayed, fitting the general pattern as described earlier in this chapter. In the second design, subjects were allowed to communicate during the initial series of ten rounds but not in the second series. Cooperation levels varied between 90 and 100 percent of optimum throughout the initial set of ten rounds and remained at close to 100 percent for most of the second set of ten rounds, even though subjects could not communicate at all during these final ten rounds. In the third design, no communication was allowed during the first ten periods (and the normal decay curve was replicated), but communication was allowed in periods eleven through twenty. Cooperation levels jumped during these final ten rounds and approached 100 percent at the end of the final round.

In a series of common-pool-resource experiments, my colleagues and I used a similar design but with two groups rather than three: one design allowed no communication in either series, the other al-

Figure 2.3   Effect of Communication in Common-Pool-Resource
Experiments: Two Communication Conditions

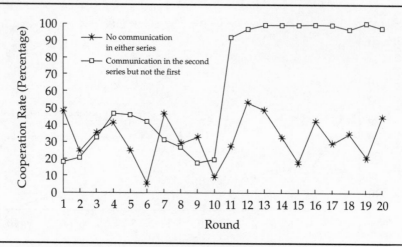

Source: Data from Ostrom, Gardner, and Walker 1994.
Note: Cooperation rate is measured by the number of tokens given to the group account.

lowed communication during the second ten rounds but not the first
ten (Ostrom, Gardner, and Walker 1994) (figure 2.3). With endowments that did not give participants strong capabilities to overutilize
the commons, cooperation levels during the communication rounds
averaged 99 percent, as against an average of 34 percent without
communication (see figure 2.3). When subjects were given sufficiently
large endowments that a small proportion of them could bring joint
returns below opportunity costs, this created a much more fragile environment. Nonetheless, subjects who were allowed to communicate
after the initial ten rounds were able to obtain an average cooperation
rate of 73 percent, in contrast with an average of 21 percent in the
rounds preceding communication.

Exploring the effect of making communication a costly public good
with a provision point, James Walker and I performed an experiment
in which five out of eight subjects had to first provide an opportunity
to communicate through voluntary and anonymous contributions—
that is, they were required to pay for the ability to communicate (Ostrom and Walker 1991). Otherwise, they continued to make independent decisions in the common-pool-resource situation they faced. This
provision mechanism placed subjects in a second-order public-goods
dilemma situation with respect to providing a mechanism for communication. This nontrivial provision problem did, in fact, create a

barrier. Participants did not meet as frequently. On the other hand, all groups succeeded (to some degree) in providing the communication mechanism and in improving their cooperation levels. On average, efficiency in these groups increased from approximately 42 percent (before communication) to 80 percent (after communication) (Ostrom and Walker 1991). Similar results were obtained in the public-goods experiments (Isaac and Walker 1991). It is also the case that providing subjects with one and only one opportunity to communicate before making a series of decisions is not as effective as providing a repeated opportunity to communicate before every round (Ostrom, Gardner, and Walker 1994).

Why does communication increase cooperation? The reasons offered by those doing experimental research on the subject include that it (1) transfers information from those who can figure out an optimal strategy to those who do not fully understand which joint strategy would be optimal, (2) allows the exchange of promises, (3) increases mutual trust and thus affects expectations of others' behavior, (4) adds value to the subjective payoff structure, (5) reinforces prior normative values, and (6) facilitates development of a group identity (Orbell, van de Kragt, and Dawes 1988; Davis and Holt 1993; Ostrom and Walker 1997).

Several scholars have explored whether the effectiveness of communication stems primarily from the first activity—providing information about the optimal strategy. Rob Moir (1995) designed an experiment that followed the basic structure of the common-pool-resource-appropriation game reported in Ostrom, Gardner, and Walker (1994).[11] After an initial five rounds of decisions, Moir specifically told subjects the joint strategy that would yield the highest group outcomes. Telling subjects about the symmetric optimum had no effect on the level of appropriation in the remaining rounds of the experiment, with the exception of the round immediately following this announcement (Moir 1995, 36). Isaac, Walker, and Williams (1994) also overtly told subjects in a public-goods experiment the joint strategy that would maximize their group payoffs and found that this information did not change the level of noncooperation that existed before the exogenous provision of this information.

The importance of communication, then, is not primarily related to the provision of information about optimal strategies. Although this information is indeed discussed in communication rounds, the other reasons appear more important, and they appear to reinforce one another interactively. Summarizing the findings from ten years of research on one-shot public-goods experiments, Orbell, Alphons van de Kragt, and Dawes (1988) stress how many mutually reenforcing processes are evoked when communication is allowed.[12] Unless mutual trust in the promises that are exchanged were to increase, however, expectations of the behavior of others would not change. Thus building trust appears to be a key link in the communication-cooperation connection. It is the central focus of this book.

Furthermore, the efficacy of communication is related to the capability to talk on a face-to-face basis. Jane Sell and Rick Wilson (1991, 1992), for example, developed a public-goods experiment in which subjects could signal promises to cooperate through their computer terminals. The cooperation rates were much lower than those they found in face-to-face experiments using the same design (Isaac and Walker 1988a, 1991). Elena Rocco and Massimo Warglien (1995) replicated all aspects of prior common-pool-resource experiments, including the efficacy of face-to-face communication. (Moir 1995 also replicated these findings.) Norman Frohlich and Joe Oppenheimer (1998) have found that subjects in a prisoner's dilemma situation used face-to-face discussion to stress moral issues and to achieve higher levels of cooperation than they achieved when provided an opportunity to communicate through e-mail—holding other aspects of the experiment constant. Subjects who had to rely on computerized communication, however, did not achieve the same increase in efficiency as those who were able to communicate on a face-to-face basis.[13] Thomas Palfrey and Howard Rosenthal (1988) report that no significant difference occurred in a *provision-point public-goods* experiment in which subjects could send a computerized message stating whether or not they intended to contribute as contrasted to experiments without communication.

The Predictive Capacity of Nash Equilibrium Strategies

From all of the foregoing discussion, it is obvious that individuals in repeated social dilemmas do not tend to use the predicted Nash equilibrium strategy, even though this is a good predictor at both an individual and group level in other types of situations.[14] Although outcomes frequently approach subgame-perfect Nash equilibria at an aggregate level, the variance of individual actions around the mean is extremely large. When groups of eight subjects made appropriation decisions in repeated common-pool-resource experiments of twenty to thirty rounds, the unique symmetric Nash equilibrium strategy was never played (Walker, Gardner, and Ostrom 1990). Nor did individuals use Nash equilibrium strategies in repeated public-goods experiments (Isaac and Walker 1991, 1993; Dudley 1993). In a recent set of thirteen common-pool-resource experiments involving seven players making ten rounds of decisions without communication or any other institutional structure, Walker and colleagues (1997) did not observe a single individual choice of a symmetric Nash equilibrium strategy in the 910 opportunities available to subjects. Kenneth Chan and colleagues also found little evidence to support the use of Nash equilibria when they examined the impact of heterogeneity of income on outcomes. "It is clear that the outcomes of the laboratory sessions reported here cannot be characterized as Nash equilibria outcomes" (Chan et al. 1996, 58).

The Predictive Capacity of Models Based on Backward Induction

In all finitely repeated experiments, players are predicted to look ahead to the last period and determine what they would do in that period. Because in that period there is no future interaction, the prediction is that they will not cooperate in that round. Because that choice would be determined at the beginning of an experiment, players are presumed to look at the second-to-last period and ask themselves what they would do here. Because they would definitely not cooperate on the last period, it is assumed that they would also not cooperate on the second-to-last period. This logic would then extend backward to the first round (Luce and Raiffa 1957, 98–99).

Although backward induction is still the dominant method used in solving finitely repeated games, it has been challenged on theoretical grounds.

> Against this deterministic argument, note that a chooser facing the first play in an iterated prisoner's dilemma can give the other player a contrary signal by cooperating rather than defecting. This wrecks the backwards induction, thus making it rational for the second player to consider cooperation. If the players are able to cooperate for even a few plays in many iterated prisoner's dilemmas, they stand to have a larger payoff than if they defect in all plays. Hence, it may be rational for each player to wreck the backwards induction argument by playing against it. The backwards induction argument is therefore self-contradictory, because it recommends deliberately cooperating in order to wreck its assumptions—if the induction is correct, it is therefore rational to violate it. (Hardin 1997, 29)

Furthermore, as discussed earlier, uncertainty about whether others use norms like *tit-for-tat* rather than following the recommendations of a Nash equilibrium may make it rational for a player to signal a willingness to cooperate on the early rounds of an iterated game and then defect at the end (Kreps et al. 1982).

What is clearly the case, judging from the experimental evidence, is that players do not use backward induction in their decision-making plans in an experimental laboratory. Amnon Rapoport concludes from a review of several experiments focusing on resource dilemmas that "subjects are not involved in or capable of backward induction" (Rapoport 1997, 122). In the experiments in which researchers have clearly stated the number of repetitions, subjects cooperate at a moderate level at the beginning of an experiment. If they can communicate, they may improve their rates of cooperation over time and see no end effect. Without communication, a higher proportion of participants tend to defect in the last round. If they were following the theory, however, they should not have cooperated at all.

Improving Outcomes in Base Social Dilemmas

Changing the rules of a game or using scarce resources to punish or reward those who do not cooperate or keep agreements are not usually considered viable options because these actions create public goods. Thus subjects would face a second-order social dilemma (of equal or greater difficulty) in any effort to use costly sanctions or rewards or change the structure of a game (Oliver 1980). The predicted outcome of any effort to solve a second-order dilemma is failure.

Yet subjects in a large number of different experiments have solved second-order social dilemmas and consequently moved the outcomes in their first-order dilemmas closer to optimal levels (van de Kragt, Orbell, and Dawes 1983; Rutte and Wilke 1984; Sato 1987; Messick and Brewer 1983; Yamagishi 1992; Sefton, Shupp, and Walker 2002; Fehr and Gächter 2000). Toshio Yamagishi (1986), for example, recruited Japanese subjects from a large pool that had been previously tested to determine their levels of trust. In all designs they were asked how much they would contribute to the provision of a bonus provided to the other three players. In two designs, they were asked, in addition, how much they would contribute to a "punishment fund" that would be used to fine the individual who contributed the least to the bonus. As expected, those who had higher levels of trust initially contributed more (about 60 percent of the resources available to them), and those who had less trust contributed about 20 percent less.

The experiment was repeated three times, and contributions decayed to 50 percent in the case of high-trusters and 30 percent in the case of low-trusters. When low sanctions were utilized, both groups allocated some resources to the punishment fund, and the level of cooperation for both groups replicated the pattern established earlier by the high-trusting group. When higher sanctions were utilized, individuals characterized initially by lower trust gave significantly more to the punishment funds but also achieved the highest level of cooperation. In the last round of this experiment, they were contributing 90 percent of their resources to the bonus fund. The high-trusting individuals contributed 70 percent in all three periods. These results, which have now been replicated with subjects in the United States (Yamagishi 1988a, 1988b), show that individuals are willing to contribute to a second-order public good and that sanctioning systems make a difference in the first-order public good. Those who are initially the least trusting are more willing to contribute to sanctioning systems and respond more to a change in the structure of the game.

Walker, Gardner, and I also examined the willingness of subjects to pay a "fee" in order to "fine" another subject (whose actions they could see on their monitors even though they did not know which of seven other players were the computer players on their display) (Ostrom, Walker, and Gardner 1992). Instead of the predicted zero contributions, individuals did significantly use their fees to fine others. Furthermore, they invested more when the fine was lower or when it was more efficacious, and they tended to direct their fines to those who had invested the most on prior rounds—in other words, those who had been the least cooperative. Given the cost of the sanctioning mechanism, subjects tended to overuse it and to end up with a less efficient outcome after sanctioning costs were subtracted from their earnings.[15]

When sanctioning was combined with either a single opportunity to communicate or a chance to discuss and vote on creating their own sanctioning system, results were quite different. With only a single opportunity for communication, subjects were able to obtain an average of 85 percent of the optimal level of investments (67 percent with the costs of sanctioning subtracted). Those subjects who met face-to-face and agreed by majority vote upon a joint strategy and the imposition of a sanctioning system upon themselves achieved 93 percent of optimal yield. The level of defections was only 4 percent; thus the costs of the sanctioning system were low, and net benefits were at the 90 percent level (Ostrom, Walker, and Gardner 1992).

Messick and his colleagues have undertaken a series of experiments designed to examine the willingness of subjects to undertake collective action to change institutional structure when facing common-pool-resource dilemmas (Messick et al. 1983; Samuelson et al. 1984; Samuelson and Messick 1986). In particular, they have repeatedly given subjects the opportunity to relinquish their individual decisions concerning withdrawals from the common resource to a leader who is given the authority to decide for the group. They have found that "people want to change the rules and bring about structural change when they observe that the common resource is being depleted" (Samuelson and Messick 1995, 147). On the other hand, simply having an unequal distribution of outcomes is not a sufficient inducement to affect the decision to change institutional structure (see also Dawes, Orbell, and van de Kragt 1986).

The importance of these experiments is that they show that individuals who are temporarily caught in a social-dilemma structure will invest resources in changing that structure itself to improve their joint outcomes. Thus not only are cooperation levels higher than predicted in many first-order social dilemmas, the prediction that no one would cooperate to solve a second-order social dilemma is also not supported.

Bounded Rationality and Norms

I have discussed six major findings from a large body of experimental research on social dilemmas, but I have not discussed the extensive literature on the structural parameters of a situation, such as the size of the group, the heterogeneity of interests, resources, information, and various types of payoff functions, that affect the level of cooperation achieved.[16] The level of cooperation obtained in experiments varies dramatically and depends systematically on the configuration of many such structural variables. Before beginning an effort to increase the understanding of why particular conditions affect the level of cooperation achieved, I should address one further issue: What is the cumulative impact of these six findings? What do these findings tell us?

In the first place, they tell us that when applied to the context of one-shot and finitely repeated social dilemmas, the currently accepted explanation from noncooperative game theory relying on a particular model of the individual that assumes a close relation between monetary payoffs and utility does not adequately predict or explain findings from N-person laboratory experiments. Cooperative game theory does no better a job explaining the 50 percent or so that do not cooperate when participants have no opportunity to communicate. Cooperative game theory is better at prediction in sparse, symmetric situations in which repeated face-to-face communication is allowed between multiple rounds. Because both cooperative and noncooperative game theory predict extreme values, neither provides explanations for what conditions tend to enhance or detract from cooperation levels.

The quick fix would be to adopt the perspective of indefinitely repeated games. That would allow researchers to draw on the theoretical results that find cooperation to be a feasible equilibrium. Wholesale adoption of this theory has two drawbacks. First, the assumption of indefinite repetition is made about a situation, and the evidence reported in this chapter is from experimental situations that do not meet this assumption. Second, this theory does not say anything about the conditions that are likely to facilitate or deter higher levels of cooperation. The really big puzzle in the social sciences is why cooperation levels vary so much and why specific configurations of situational conditions increase or decrease cooperation. This question is important not only for our scientific understanding but also for the design of institutions to facilitate individuals' achieving higher levels of productive outcomes in social-dilemma situations.

Models of the Individual

There are several steps from theory to the testing of theory in a lab. The first is the development of models of the various working parts of a theory. The second is an adequate operationalization of those models in the design of the experiment. Two factors are essential to all choice theoretic explanations: a model of the individual and a model of the situation. In the laboratory real human beings are the decision makers, so there is no need to construct a model and operationalize this part of the experiment. One is using "the real thing."[17] The models of social dilemmas used in laboratory experiments appear to be quite robust. Researchers are able to create and replicate situations in which there is no cooperation, very high levels of cooperation, or moderate levels of cooperation. The amount of control that can be exercised indicates that the experimental models of dilemma situations are quite good. The model of the individual actor used to explain outcomes appears to be the source of the problem.

It is also the source of heated debates in the social and biological sciences.[18] One particular model of purposive, self-interested, choice-making behavior has proved to be useful in a wide variety of tasks, but it has been confused with a general theory of rational behavior. I consider a complete rationality model to be extremely useful in the explanation of behavior in highly structured, competitive processes, but it is not the only model of rational behavior. I have used and will continue to use this model in situations in which the institutional structure generates sufficient information and incentives to make it a useful and predictive model. At a more general theoretical level, however, I agree with Reinhard Selten (1975) that complete rationality is the limiting case of bounded or incomplete rationality.[19]

Thus I assume that individuals facing social dilemmas in real life and in the lab are rational in a broad sense. I assume that they seek to improve values of importance to them (including what happens to other individuals who are of concern to them); select actions within interdependent situations in which what they do is affected by their expectations of what others will do; use information about the situation and about the characteristics of others to make decisions; and try to do as well as they can given the constraints they face. In addition, I assume that in the course of their lifetimes individuals learn heuristics, strategies, norms, rules, and how to craft rules. Some of life's lessons are applied in a laboratory experiment.

Heuristics, Norms, and Rules

Because I think of individuals as boundedly rational, I do not assume that they always calculate a complete set of strategies for every situation they face. Few situations in life generate information about all actions one could take, all outcomes that could be obtained, and all strategies that others could follow. In a theoretical model of complete rationality, this level of information is simply assumed. In many field and experimental situations individuals tend to use heuristics—rules of thumb—that they have learned over time regarding responses that have, in the past, brought them good outcomes in particular kinds of situations. Over the course of frequently encountered, repetitive situations, individuals learn heuristics that are better tailored to the particular situation. With repetition and sufficiently large stakes, individuals may learn heuristics that approach best-response strategies (Gigerenzer and Selten 2001).

In addition to learning instrumental heuristics, individuals also learn to adopt and use norms and rules. By norms, I mean the internal valuations—positive or negative—that an individual attaches to particular types of action. Sue Crawford and I refer to this internal valuation as a delta parameter that is added to or subtracted from the objective costs of an action (Crawford and Ostrom 1995).[20] Andreoni (1989) models individuals who experience a "warm glow" when they contribute resources that help others more than they help themselves in the short term. Stephen Knack (1992) refers to negative internal valuations as "duty."[21] One can think of the change in preferences from those of the objective payoffs as the internalization of particular moral lessons from life (or from the training provided by one's elders).[22] The strength of the commitment (Sen 1977) made by an individual to take particular types of future actions (telling the truth, keeping promises) is reflected in the size of the delta parameter. After experiencing repeated benefits from other people's cooperative actions, an individual may resolve always to initiate cooperation in the future.[23] Alternatively, after many experiences of being the "sucker" in such situations, an individual may resolve never to initiate unilateral cooperation and to punish noncooperators whenever feasible.

Because norms are learned, they vary substantially across individuals, within individuals across the different types of situations they face, and across time within any particular situation. The behavioral implications of assuming that individuals acquire norms does not substantially vary from the assumption that individuals learn to use heuristics. One might think of norms as heuristics that individuals adopt from a moral perspective in that these are the kinds of actions they wish to follow in living their lives. Once some members of a population acquire norms of behavior, the presence of these norms affect the expectations of other players. When interacting with individuals who are known to use retribution against those who are not fair in the proposals they make, one will do better by making fair proposals. Moreover, once norms are generally shared in a population, expectations can converge to *focal points* (Schelling 1960) such as "Share and share alike."

By rules, I mean the shared understandings groups develop that certain actions in particular situations must, must not, or may be undertaken and that sanctions will be taken against those who do not conform. It is difficult, when doing experimental work, to draw a distinction between internalized, but widely shared, norms for what are appropriate actions in broad types of situations and rules that are self-consciously adopted for use in particular situations. Analytically, individuals can be thought of as learning norms of behavior that are relatively general and fit a wide diversity of particular situations. Rules tend to be self-conscious artifacts related to particular actions in specific situations (Ostrom 1999). Rules are created in both private associations and in more formalized public institutions, where they carry the additional legal weight of being enforced legal enactments.[24]

Reciprocity

That humans learn and use heuristics, norms, and rules is consistent with the lessons learned from evolutionary psychology (see Barkow, Cosmides, and Tooby 1992), evolutionary game theory (see Boyd and Richerson 1988; Güth 1995; Hirshleifer and Rasmusen 1989),[25] and biology (Trivers 1971) and of bounded rationality (Selten 1990, 1991, 2001; Simon 1985). Humans appear to have evolved specialized cognitive modules for diverse tasks including making sense out of what is seen (Marr 1982), inferring rules of grammar by being exposed to adult speakers of a particular language (Pinker 1994), and increasing their long-term returns from interactions in social dilemmas (Cosmides and Tooby 1992). Humans would have dealt with social dilemmas related to rearing and protecting offspring, hunting, and trusting one another to perform future promised actions, millennia before oral commitments could be enforced by external authorities (de Waal 1996).

All reciprocity norms share the common ingredients that individuals tend to react to the positive actions of others with positive responses and to the negative actions of others with negative responses. Many sequences of actions could qualify as a form of reciprocity. Reciprocity is viewed by sociologists, social psychologists, and philosophers as one of the basic norms taught in all societies (see Becker 1990; Ostrom 1997; Gouldner 1960; Thibaut and Kelley 1959; Homans 1961; Blau 1964). The specific reciprocity norms that individuals learn vary from culture to culture and, within a broad cultural milieu, across different types of situations that are confronted repeatedly.

Far and away the most famous reciprocal strategy—tit-for-tat—has been the subject of considerable study from an evolutionary perspective. In simulations, pairs of individuals are sampled from a population who then interact with one another repeatedly in a prisoner's dilemma game. Individuals are modeled as if they had inherited strategies, including the fixed maxims of always cooperate and always defect and the reciprocating strategy of tit-for-tat (cooperate first, and then do whatever the others did on the last round). Robert Axelrod and William Hamilton (Axelrod and Hamilton 1981; Axelrod 1984) have shown that when individuals are grouped so that they are more likely to interact with one another than with the general population, and when the expected repetitions are sufficiently large, reciprocating strategies such as tit-for-tat can successfully invade populations composed of individuals following an all-defect strategy. The size of the population in which interactions are occurring must be relatively small for reciprocating strategies to survive potential errors of players (Bendor and Mookherjee 1987; but see Boyd and Richerson 1988, 1992; Hirshleifer and Rasmusen 1989; Yamagishi and Takahashi 1994).

The reciprocity norms posited to help individuals gain larger cooperators' dividends depend upon the willingness of participants to use retribution at least to some degree. In tit-for-tat, for example, an individual must be willing to "punish" a player who defected on the last round by defecting on the current round. In the grim trigger, an individual must be willing to initially cooperate but then "punish" everyone for the rest of the game if any defection is noticed on the current round. The grim trigger has been used as a support for cooperative outcomes in infinitely (or indefinitely) repeated games (Fudenberg and Maskin 1986). In games in which substantial joint benefits are to be gained over the long term from mutual cooperation, the threat of the grim trigger is thought to be sufficient to encourage everyone to cooperate. A small error on the part of one player or exogenous noise in the payoff function, however, makes this strategy a dangerous one to use in larger groups in which the cooperator's dividend may also be substantial.

When many individuals use reciprocity, there is an incentive to acquire a reputation for keeping promises and performing actions with short-term costs but long-term net benefits. Thus trustworthy individuals who trust others with a reputation for being trustworthy (and try to avoid those who have a reputation for being untrustworthy) can engage in mutually productive social exchanges, even though they are dilemmas, so long as they can limit their interactions primarily to those others with a reputation for keeping promises. A reputation for being trustworthy or for using retribution against those who do not keep their agreements or contribute their fair share becomes a valuable asset. In an evolutionary context, it increases fitness in an environment in which others use reciprocity norms. Similarly, developing trust in an environment in which others are trustworthy is also an asset. Whether reciprocity is advantageous to individuals depends sensitively on the proportion of other individuals who are likely to use reciprocity and on an individual's capacity to judge the likely frequency of reciprocators in any particular situation and over time. When there are many others who use a form of reciprocity that always cooperates first, then even in one-shot situations cooperation may lead to higher returns when a series of diverse situations are considered together.

A theory of bounded rationality and norm-using behavior consistent with the findings of evolutionary game theory and psychology assumes that humans tend to

1. learn from interactions with others about how frequently others use norms such as reciprocity,

2. learn to recognize and remember who are both trustworthy and untrustworthy individuals,

3. cooperate with individuals who are expected (from prior interactions, from information about social history, or from visual and verbal cues) to be trustworthy reciprocators in those risky transactions expected to generate net benefits,

4. build a reputation for being trustworthy by trying to resist temptations to gain short-term gains at the expense of losing opportunities for major long-term benefits,

5. punish those who have cheated or simply not reciprocated in the past, and

6. use a time frame that extends beyond the immediate present.

Fallible human beings facing limits in their cognitive processing do not learn to do all of these perfectly, but they do adopt heuristics that work amazingly well in many settings (see Gigerenzer and Selten 2001). In addition to individuals who adopt various norms of contingent behavior, one can expect to find some individuals who never cooperate with others and a few (but only a few) individuals who always cooperate with others.

As I have indicated, human beings do not inherit reciprocity norms through a biological process (though they may acquire cultural norms through sociological processes). The argument is more subtle. Individuals inherit a capacity to learn and value algorithms that enhance their capacity to increase their own long-term benefits when confronting multiple social-dilemma situations with others who have learned and value similar norms, even though each situation involves different people, payoffs, and levels of uncertainty. The process of growing up in any culture provides thousands of incidents (learning trials) whereby parents, siblings, friends, and teachers provide the more specific content of the type of mutual expectations prevalent in a particular culture. As Dennis Mueller (1986) points out, humans first encounter dilemmas as children. Parents reward and punish them until cooperation is a learned response. In the contemporary setting, a corporate manager tries to gain a reputation for the trustworthiness of his or her company by continuously reiterating and rewarding the use of key principles or norms used by corporate employees (Kreps 1990).

Because reciprocity norms are learned and not biologically inherited, not everyone learns to use reciprocity norms in all situations in which they could be of use. Furthermore, there are multiple types of reciprocity norms that could be used, and some individuals learn norms of behavior that are not so "nice." Some clever and unscrupulous individuals learn how to lure others into dilemma situations and then defect on them. It is possible to gain substantial resources by such means, but to do so one has to hide actions well, to keep moving, or to gain access to great power. Others, not so clever, spend their lives in lonely isolation (either in jail or simply cut off from friends, family, and associates). Should any group be composed of individuals following only reciprocity norms, once they establish cooperative relationships they could lose their skills in detecting and punishing cheaters. Were this to happen, they would be subject to invasion and substantial initial losses by clever outsiders or local deviants who could take advantage of the situation. The presence of untrustworthy participants hones the skills of those who follow reciprocity norms.

It should be noted that reciprocity norms can have a dark side. If the punishment phase learned within one cultural setting or situation is that of escalating retribution, groups who overcome social dilemmas may be limited to tight circles of kin and friends who cooperate only with one another, embedded in a set of hostile relationships with outsiders who are perceived as untrustworthy (Hardin 1995). Energy can then be spent on finding ways of punishing others that continuously escalate into feuds, raids, and overt warfare (Chagnon 1988; Kollock 1993; Boyd and Richerson 1992; Elster 1985). Tight circles of individuals who trust one another may discriminate against others of a different color, religion, or ethnicity to keep them from access to productive opportunities. The focus on the return of favors for favors can also be the foundation of corrupt practices whereby those in official positions do favors for wealthy friends who then return the favors with various forms of financial enrichments. It is in everyone else's interest that some social dilemmas are not resolved, such as those involved in cartel formation, the maintenance of reciprocity relationships that contravene basic moral standards and legal relationships, and those that restrict the opportunities of an open society.

Individuals vary substantially in the probability that they will use particular norms, in the way structural variables affect their level of trust and willingness to reciprocate cooperation in a particular situation, and in the way they develop their own reputations. Some individuals will cooperate in dilemmas only when they have publicly committed themselves to an agreement and have assurances from others that their trust will be returned. Others find it easier to build an external reputation by building their own personal identity as someone who always trusts others until proved wrong. Such an individual will always initiate cooperation in social dilemmas even when there are no explicit agreements. These individuals do not want to spend time and effort, and suffer moral regret, by calculating whether or not they are obliged to cooperate in each and every social dilemma. They simply follow a personal rule to cooperate first when expected net benefits are positive and then react in light of information about what others have done. If trust has not been returned, they stop cooperating and either exit the situation or enter a punishment phase. As Elizabeth Hoffman, Kevin McCabe, and Vernon Smith express it,

> A one-shot game in the laboratory is part of a life-long sequence, not an isolated experience that calls for behavior that deviates sharply from one's reputational norm. Thus we should expect subjects to rely upon

reciprocity norms in experimental settings unless they discover in the process of participating in a particular experiment that reciprocity is punished and other behaviors are rewarded. In such cases they abandon their instincts and attempt other strategies that better serve their interests. (Hoffman, McCabe, and Smith 1996a, 23–24)

Thus, in any population of individuals, one is likely to find at least some individuals who are likely to use one of the following reciprocity norms[26] when they confront a social dilemma that is likely to be repeated more than once.

1. Always cooperate first; stop cooperating if others do not reciprocate; and punish noncooperators if feasible.

2. Cooperate immediately only if you judge others to be trustworthy; stop cooperating if others do not reciprocate; punish noncooperators if feasible.

3. Once cooperation has been established by others, cooperate yourself; stop cooperating if others do not reciprocate; punish noncooperators if feasible.

In addition to these reciprocity norms, one can expect to find at least three other norms.

4. Always cooperate in some contexts.

5. Never cooperate.

6. Mimic norms 1 or 2, but stop cooperating if you can successfully free ride on others.

The proportion of individuals who follow each type of norm will vary from subpopulation to subpopulation and from type of situation to type of situation depending on structural variables. Thus boundedly rational individuals would expect other boundedly rational individuals to follow a diversity of heuristics, norms, and strategies rather than expecting to find others adopting a single strategy—except in those repeated situations in which institutional selection processes sort out those who do not search out optimal strategies. One does not have to assume that others are "irrational" in order for it to be rational to use reciprocity. Investing effort into assessments of other's intentions is thus an important activity that a boundedly rational individual must pursue (see Heiner 2002).

At an earlier juncture, I thought that one would always find that the proportion of individuals who followed the fourth norm—always cooperate—would be small. Since I first wrote portions of this chapter, however, I have read work by Huib Pellikaan and Robert van der Veen (2002), who have conducted extensive survey research on citizens' reactions to a variety of environmental dilemmas. They find a large proportion of the Dutch population that they surveyed reported a willingness to take unconditional, cooperative actions in regard to toxic chemical household waste. Similarly, respondents reported a willingness to save in their household energy consumption—but not to forgo holiday travel, which also consumes a large amount of energy. The importance of their research is both the high level of reported contributions in a large-group dilemma and the difference between the first two dilemmas and the third. Context clearly makes a big difference in the willingness of individuals to contribute.

Individuals following the first norm would be those, along with those following the fourth norm, who cooperate on the first few rounds of a finitely repeated experimental social dilemma without prior communication. Individuals following the second norm would cooperate (immediately) in experiments if they had an opportunity to judge the intentions and trustworthiness of the other participants and expected most of the others to be trustworthy. Those following the third norm would cooperate (after one or a few rounds) in experiments in which others were cooperating.

Evidence of the Use of Reciprocity in Experimental Settings

Laboratory experiments provide evidence that a substantial proportion of individuals use reciprocity norms even in the short-term environments of an experiment. Some of this evidence comes from experiments on *ultimatum games*. In an ultimatum game, two players are asked to divide a fixed sum of money. The first player suggests a division to the second, who then decides to accept or reject the offer. If the offer is accepted, the funds are divided as proposed. If it is rejected, both players receive zero. The subgame-perfect equilibrium is that the first player will offer a minimal unit to the second player who will then accept anything more than zero. This prediction has repeatedly been falsified, starting with the work of Werner Güth, Rolf Schmittberger, and Bernd Schwarze (1982) (see Samuelson, Gale, and Binmore 1995; Roth 1995; Henrich et al. 2001).[27] Subjects assigned to the first position tend to offer substantially more than the minimum unit. They frequently offer the "fair" division of splitting the sum. Second movers tend to reject offers that are quite small. Given that the refusal to accept funds that one could receive contradicts a basic tenet in the complete model of rationality, these findings represent a major challenge to the empirical validity of the complete model of rationality.

Several hypotheses have been offered to explain these findings, in-

cluding a "punishment hypothesis" and a "learning hypothesis."
"The punishment hypothesis is in essence a reciprocity argument. In
contrast with adaptive learning, punishment attributes a motive to
the second mover's rejection of an unequal division asserting that it is
done to punish the first mover for unfair treatment. This propensity
toward negative reciprocity is the linchpin of the argument. Given
this propensity, first movers should tend to shy away from the perfect
equilibrium offer out of fear of winding up with nothing" (Abbink et
al. 1996, 6). Klaus Abbink and his colleagues designed an experiment
in which the prediction of the learning and punishment hypotheses
are clearly different. They find strong support for the punishment hypothesis. "We found that second movers were three times more likely
to reject the unequal split when doing so punished the first mover . . .
than when doing so rewarded the first mover" (Abbink et al. 1996,
15–16).

Kevin McCabe, Stephen Rassenti, and Vernon Smith (1996) have
designed several *extensive-form* games that also examine whether a
substantial number of participants use reciprocity. The experiment begins by asking a first mover to select between two subgames. One
subgame yields fifty points to both players if they use reciprocity. On
the other hand, if players choose the strategy predicted by noncooperative theory, they end up in the second subgame, and each earns
forty points. When the game repeated only once, one-half of the subjects used reciprocity; when repeated for a second time, 58 percent
used reciprocity. When the authors added an option that the first
player could punish a second player who did not return the reciprocity extended by the first player (at a sacrifice in payoff), subjects in
the first position frequently used the costly option to punish nonreciprocators (see chapter 10, this volume).

Two additional findings from one-shot social dilemmas provide
further evidence of the behavioral propensities of subjects. First, those
who intend to cooperate in a particular one-shot social dilemma also
expect cooperation to be returned by others at a much higher rate
than those who intend to defect (Dawes, McTavish, and Shaklee 1977;
Dawes, Orbell, and van de Kragt 1986). As John Orbell and Robyn
Dawes summarize their own work, "One of our most consistent findings throughout these studies—a finding replicated by others'
work—is that cooperators expect significantly more cooperation than
do defectors" (Orbell and Dawes 1991, 519). Second, when there is
choice whether or not to participate in a social dilemma, those who
intend to cooperate exhibit a greater willingness to enter such transactions (Orbell and Dawes 1993). Given these two tendencies, reciprocators are likely to be more optimistic about finding others following
the same norm and disproportionately enter more voluntary social

dilemmas than those who are not reciprocators and assume others are going to defect like they plan to do. Given both propensities, the feedback from such voluntary activities will generate confirmatory evidence that they have adopted a norm that serves them well over the long run. Thus though individuals vary in their propensity to use reciprocity, the evidence from experiments shows that a substantial proportion of the population drawn on by social science experiments (primarily college students in major universities in the United States, Europe, and Japan)—ranging from 50 to 60 percent—do have sufficient trust that others are reciprocators to cooperate with them even in one-shot, no-communication experiments.[28] Furthermore, a substantial proportion of the population is also willing to punish noncooperators (or individuals who do not make fair offers) at a cost to themselves. Norms are learned from prior experience (socialization) and are also affected by situational variables yielding systematic difference among experimental designs. The level of trust and resulting levels of cooperation can be increased by (1) providing subjects with an opportunity to see one another (Orbell and Dawes 1991; Frey and Bohnet 1996);[29] (2) allowing subjects to choose whether to enter a social-dilemma game (Orbell, Schwartz-Shea, and Simmons 1984; Yamagishi 1988c; Schuessler 1989; and Orbell and Dawes 1991, 1993); (3) sharing the costs equally if a minimal set voluntarily contributes to a public good (Dawes, Orbell, and van de Kragt 1986); (4) providing opportunities for distinct punishments of those who are not reciprocators (Abbink et al. 1996; McCabe, Rassenti, and Smith 1996); and, as discussed earlier, (5) providing opportunities for face-to-face communication.

The Core Relationships: Reciprocity, Reputation, and Trust

Behavior in social dilemmas can be better understood if boundedly rational individuals are assumed to enter situations with an initial probability of using reciprocity based on their own prior training and experience. The more benefits they have received in the past from other reciprocators, the higher their own initial inclinations. The more often they have faced retribution, the less likely will they be to see free riding as an attractive option. Their trust that others will also be reciprocators is highly correlated with their own norms but is affected by the information they glean about the reputations of other players and their estimate of the risk of extending trust, given the structure of the particular situation.

Thus at the core of a behavioral explanation are the links between the trust that an individual has in others, the investment others make

Figure 2.4   The Core Relationships in Repeated Social Dilemmas

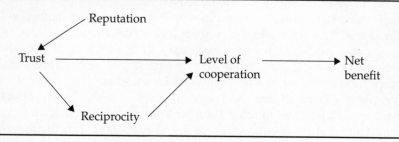

Source: Adapted from Ostrom 1998, 13.

in trustworthy reputations, and the probability of using reciprocity norms (see figure 2.4). This mutually reinforcing core is affected by many structural variables as well as the past experiences of participants. In the initial round of a repeated dilemma, individuals initiate cooperative behavior based on their own norms, how much trust they have that others are reciprocators (based on their own intentions and any information they glean about one another), and how structural variables affect their own behavior and their expectation of others' behavior (see figure 2.5).

If initial levels of cooperation are moderately high, more individuals learn to trust others, and more are more willing to adopt reciprocity norms (norms 1, 2, or 3) or simply cooperate with others. When more individuals use reciprocity norms, gaining a reputation for being trustworthy is a better investment (see figure 2.6). Thus levels of trust and reciprocity and reputations for being trustworthy

Figure 2.5   First Interaction in Series of Repeated Social Dilemmas

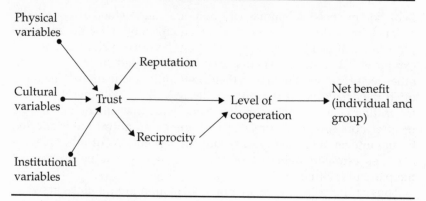

Source: Author's configuration.

Figure 2.6   Feedback in Repeated Social Dilemmas

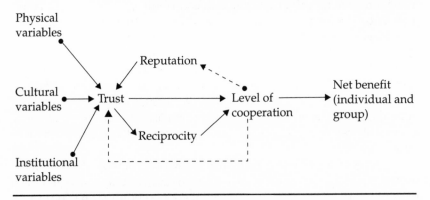

Source: Author's configuration.

are positively reinforcing. This also means that a decrease in any one of these can lead to a downward cascade. Instead of explaining levels of cooperation directly, this approach leads one to link structural variables to an inner triangle between trust, reciprocity, and reputation as these, in turn, affect levels of cooperation and net benefits achieved both by individuals and groups.

With these core relationships, one can begin to explain why repeated face-to-face communication substantially changes the structure of a situation (see the discussion in Ostrom, Gardner, and Walker 1994, 199). With a chance to see and talk with others repeatedly, a participant can assess whether he or she trusts others sufficiently to try to reach a simple contingent agreement regarding the level of joint effort and its allocation. Communication thus allows individuals to increase (or decrease) their trust in the reliability of others. Robert Frank, Thomas Gilovich, and Dennis Regan (1993) have found, for example, that the capacity of subjects to predict whether others would play cooperatively or not was significantly better than chance following a face-to-face group discussion.

These findings were replicated by Masako Kikuchi, Yoriko Watanabe, and Toshio Yamagishi (1996). When successful, individuals change their expectations from their initial probability that others use reciprocity norms to a higher probability that others will reciprocate trust and cooperation. When individuals are symmetric in assets and payoffs, the simplest agreement is to share equally a contribution level that closely approximates the optimum joint outcome. When individuals are not symmetric, finding an agreement is more difficult, but various fairness norms can be used to reduce the time and effort needed to achieve an agreement (see Hackett, Schlager, and Walker

1994; Hackett, Dudley, and Walker 1995). When a contingent agreement is reached, individuals agree to contribute x resources to a common effort so long as at least y proportion of others also contribute. Contingent agreements do not need to include all those who benefit. The benefit to be obtained from the contribution of y others of those affected may be so substantial that some individuals are willing to contribute so long as y others also agree and perform. Pamela Schmitt, Kurtis Swope, and James Walker (2000) show that the effect of heterogeneity is crucially dependent on context and differs in common-pool-resource experiments as contrasted with public-goods experiments.

Contingent agreements may deal with punishment of those who do not cooperate. How to punish noncooperative players, keep one's own reputation, and sustain any initial cooperation that has occurred is more difficult in N-person settings than in two-person settings.[30] In an N-person, uncertain situation, it is difficult to interpret from results that are less than expected whether one person cheated a lot, several people cheated a little, someone made a mistake, or everyone cooperated and an exogenous random variable reduced the expected outcome. If there is no communication, the problem is even worse. Without communication and an agreement on a sharing formula, individuals can try to signal a willingness to cooperate through their actions, but no one has agreed to any particular contribution. Thus no one's reputation (external or internal) is at stake. It is not surprising that even small groups of five to ten individuals in repeated public-goods experiments without communication are unable to do much better on average than the Nash equilibrium, even though some individuals in most experiments start out using cooperation.

Once a verbal agreement in an N-person setting is reached, that becomes the focal point for further action within the context of a particular ongoing group. If everyone keeps to the agreement, no further reaction is needed by someone who is a reciprocator. One simply keeps to the agreement in the future. If, however, the results obtained indicate that the agreement has not been kept, an individual following a reciprocity norm—without any prior agreement regarding selective sanctions for nonconformance—needs to punish those who did not keep their commitment. The most frequently discussed punishment in the game-theory literature is the grim trigger, whereby a participant, once he or she has detected any level of cheating, plays the Nash equilibrium strategy forever. Few subjects use grim triggers, however, in experimental contexts (Ostrom, Gardner, and Walker 1994). A much less drastic punishment strategy is the measured reaction. "In a measured reaction, a player reacts mildly (if at all) to a small deviation from an agreement. Defections trigger mild reactions instead of harsh punishments. If defections continue over time, the measured response slowly moves from the point of agreement toward the Nash equilibrium" (Ostrom, Gardner, and Walker 1994, 199–200).

This makes sense as the initial "punishment" phase in an N-person setting with a minimal institutional structure for several reasons. If only a small deviation occurs, the cooperation of most participants is already generating positive returns. By keeping one's own reaction close to the agreement, one keeps up one's own reputation for cooperation and makes it easier to restore full conformance because cooperation levels are higher. Using something like a grim trigger immediately could lead to the rapid unraveling of the agreement and the loss of substantial benefits over time. To supplement the measured reaction, effort would be expended to determine who is breaking the agreement, to tongue-lash that individual back in line, and to avoid future interactions with that individual. If a sufficiently high level of cooperation is not soon restored, a measured reaction develops into a grim trigger. Subjects in repeated experiments frequently discuss the use of a grim trigger to punish mild defections but reject the idea because it would punish everyone—not just the cheater. They also use their communication opportunities to deliver tongue-lashings to those unknown persons within the group who have failed to keep to an agreement.

In a series of eighteen common-pool-resource experiments, each involving eight subjects in finitely repeated communication experiments, Roy Gardner, James Walker, and I found that subjects kept to their agreements or used measured responses in two-thirds of the experiments (Ostrom, Gardner, and Walker 1994, 215). In these experiments, joint yields averaged 89 percent of optimum. In the six experiments in which some players deviated substantially from agreements and measured responses did not bring them back to the agreement, cooperation levels were substantially lower, and yields averaged 43 percent of optimum (which is still far above zero levels of cooperation).

Thus understanding how trust, reciprocity, and reputation feed one another (or how their lack generates a cascade of negative effects) helps to explain why repeated face-to-face communication can have a major effect. Coming to an initial agreement and making personal promises to one another places at risk each individual's identity as one who keeps his or her word, increases trust, and makes reciprocity an even more beneficial strategy. Tongue-lashing can be partially substituted in a small group for monetary losses, and when backed by measured responses it can keep many groups at high levels of cooperation. Meeting only once can greatly increase trust, but if there are some individuals who do not cooperate immediately, the group never has a further opportunity to hash out these problems. Any evidence of lower levels of cooperation undermines the trust established in the first meeting, and there is no further opportunity to build on that trust or to use verbal sanctioning. The reasons why sending anonymous, computerized messages are not as effective as face-to-face communication are also now clearer. Individuals judge one another's trustworthiness by watching facial expressions and hearing the way something is said. It is hard to establish trust in a group of strangers who will make decisions independently and privately without seeing and talking with one another.[31]

Illustrative Theoretical Scenarios

In this chapter, I have tried to show how a change in the conception of human actors allows for the beginning of a synthesis of what we know from prior research on social dilemmas. Predictions of how individuals will behave in social-dilemma situations based on a complete model of rationality have not been supported by a large body of carefully designed laboratory experiments.

I argue that the particular model of individual choice used in most contemporary analyses of social dilemmas has been and will continue to be a useful model in those settings in which institutions generate strong competitive pressures and those individuals who do not approximate the maximization of some external, short-term payoff function are screened out of the ongoing set of participants. In other words, the model of complete rationality is one model in a family of models that can be used to represent a broader theory of rational behavior. It has, however, been conflated by some scholars with a broader theory of human behavior.

In an effort to contribute to the development of a coherent explanation of human behavior in the pervasive social dilemmas of everyday life, I have tried to draw on what is known about the behavior of boundedly rational individuals who learn to use simple heuristics and norms of behavior reflecting their socialization, their prior experiences, their moral reflections on the type of person they want to be, and the structure and history of the particular situations in which they find themselves. In this chapter, I have not attempted here to develop a specific alternative model; rather, I have tried to stay at the theoretical level and identify the types of attributes of human behavior that should be included in future efforts to formalize specific models. In the efforts of individuals to achieve higher benefits and to do as well as they can given the problems they face, the individual attributes that are particularly important in explaining behavior in social dilemmas include the expectations that individuals have about others' behavior (trust), the norms that individuals learn from socialization and life's experiences (reciprocity), and the identities that individuals create that project their intentions and norms (reputation). There are many different ways that trust, reciprocity, and reputation can be included in models of individual behavior, and scholars who explore evolutionary theory have developed specific models of reciprocity that predict behavior similar to what empirical evidence discussed herein implies (see Güth and Kliemt 1996; Boyd and Richerson 1988).

In addition to using a different theoretical foundation, an important task is to construct theoretical scenarios of how exogenous variables combine to affect endogenous variables that link to the core set of relationships shown in figure 2.4. The obvious candidate variables from the theoretical and experimental literature reviewed in this chapter include the kind of information generated about past interactions, the type of agreements that are developed, the possibilities of settings that encourage the development of jointly held norms, the types of sanctions that are focused on specific individuals, and the sequence in which individuals act. It is not possible to relate all of these variables in one large causal model, given that there are so many variables and that many of them depend for their impact on the values of other variables. It is possible, however, to produce coherent, cumulative, theoretical scenarios that start with relatively simple baseline models. One can then begin the systematic exploration of what happens as one variable is changed. Let me illustrate what I mean by theoretical scenarios.

A Simple and Conducive Scenario

I would first like to embed the core set of mutually reinforcing relationships shown in figure 2.4 in a social-dilemma situation that one would expect to be conducive to achievement of a cooperator's dividend. I start with a small ongoing group—say, ten farmers who own farms of approximately the same size. These farmers share the use of a creek that runs by their relatively flat properties. Each year, they face the problem of organizing one collective workday on which to clear out from the creekbed the fallen trees and brush from the prior winter. All ten expect to continue farming into the indefinite future. They face a linear production function, in that the water supply delivered by the creek varies in direct proportion to how much of this work is completed. Each farmer could spend time on individual activities that would return more than the individual return they would personally receive from their own input into this effort. Thus free riding, hoping the others will contribute their labor, is objectively attractive. The value to each farmer, however, of a successful effort involving a large proportion of them clearing the creek is greater than alternative opportunities.

Given the size of the group, it would be easy for the farmers to engage in face-to-face communication. Because their interests and resources are relatively symmetric, arriving at a fair, contingent agreement regarding how to share the work should not be too difficult. One simple agreement that is easy to monitor is that they all work on the same day but each is responsible for clearing the part of the creek going through his or her property. While engaged in their discussions, they can reinforce the importance of everyone's participation in the workday. In such a face-to-face meeting, they can also gossip about others who may have failed to participate in the past, urge them to change their ways, and threaten to stop all labor contributions if they do not "shape up." If the creek were not to be cleared out for several years in a row, the long-term loss of productive income for each farmer would be substantial. Given the small size of the group, their symmetry, and the relatively low cost of providing the public good, combined with the relatively long time horizon, it can be predicted, with some confidence, that a large proportion of individuals facing such situations will find a way to cooperate and overcome the dilemma. Not only does the evidence from experimental laboratory support that prediction, but substantial evidence from the field is also consistent with this explanation (see Ostrom, Gardner, and Walker 1994).

In this "easy" situation there are four exogenous variables. Three relate to participants: the size of the group, symmetry of interests and resources, and long time horizons. One exogenous variable relates to the physical production function—the low-cost, linear provision of a public good. Given the combination of these four exogenous variables, it is possible to predict the increased likelihood of endogenous variables such as the use of face-to-face communication, a low-cost process of developing an agreement, the development of shared norms related to reciprocity and trust, and the general availability of information regarding past actions. It is these endogenous variables that help to support the potentially positive relationships in this scenario (see figure 2.7). If some unmentioned variable were to prevent the farmers from engaging in face-to-face discussions and building trust in one another's participation, then the situation would be less conducive to collective action.

This is a rough but coherent causal model that connects a model of the situation and a model of the individual to offer an explanation for observed cooperation and to allow identification of the conditions most likely to facilitate collective action. Changes in any of the exogenous variables of this relatively easy scenario tend to increase the

Figure 2.7 A Simple Scenario of Collective Action for Provision of a Public Good

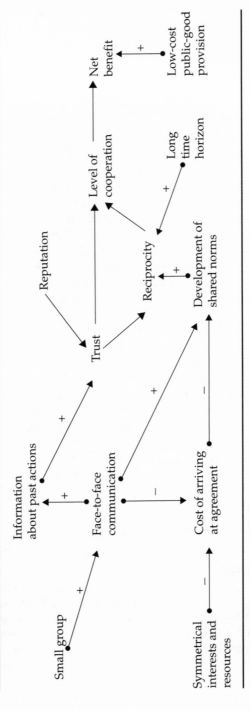

Source: Adapted from Ostrom 1998, 15.

difficulty of achieving successful collective action. For example, suppose a local developer buys five parcels of land to hold for future use as a suburban housing development. The set of actors is now smaller (six instead of ten). The time horizon of one of them—the developer—is extremely short with respect to using the land for farming because the developer has no interest in getting agricultural production from his land. He cannot be seen as a free rider, however, because he sees no benefit to clearing out the creek. Thus the "one" change actually produces several: a decrease in the N of the group, an introduction of an asymmetry of interests and resources, and the presence of one participant who owns half the resources but has a short time horizon. This illustrates how changes in one of the exogenous variables can lead to a cascade of changes in the set of variables and thus how difficult it is to make simple bivariate hypotheses about the effect of one variable on the level of cooperation.

If the developer refuses to help with the spring cleaning, everyone else will have to do double the work to get the same benefit. The smaller subgroup of five might or might not overcome this change in the structure of the situation they face. If the benefit to the farmers of a cleaned-out creek is sufficiently great to make it worth two days of work, they might ignore the developer and simply put in two days each. If they feel he is obliged to follow the norms of the earlier participants from whom he purchased the land, they might not cooperate even though there would be a net benefit from each putting in two days. Here the norm of reciprocity adds an element of uncertainty to the prediction. Whether they cooperate or not depends on both the relationship of benefits to costs and how they interpret the reciprocity norm. Under one interpretation, they are now a group of five. Under another, they are a group of six, one of whom is not cooperating and needs to be punished. That could lead the five farmers to stop their own cooperation.

A Complex and Difficult Scenario

At the other extreme, one can also construct a difficult situation and ask what changes would enhance the likelihood of cooperation. Suppose that a large number of participants—say, fifteen thousand—with differing interests and resources could substantially benefit from developing and using the water resources in a large watershed (see figure 2.8). If the participants are not able to organize their own set of supporting institutions, with just this information one would predict that it would be unlikely that any group could succeed. Given the size of the group, no face-to-face communication could be sustained. No one would know who was cooperating and who was cheating.

Figure 2.8 A Complex Scenario of Collective Action for Provision of a Public Good

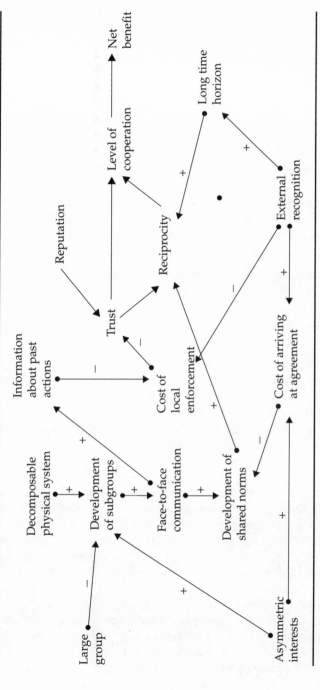

Source: Author's configuration.

Reputations and the use of reciprocity norms would not be of initial help here. If, on the other hand, the participants could start to develop local institutions, the likelihood of success increases. In particular, success would be more likely if the following sequence of events were to occur:

1. The watershed is divided up into major tributaries, tributaries, and subtributaries.

2. Some subgroup of farmers, varying in size from ten to one hundred, sharing water from one of the tributaries is able to organize their own association and agree on how to share the costs of managing their own tributary, including keeping records and using selective sanctions against those who do not contribute resources.

3. Others see the economic advantage to the initial group and begin to develop their own tributary associations.

4. Subgroups begin working together to gain agreement on sharing water and work that spans more than one tributary.

5. Associations federate at several levels to eventually encompass the watershed and all fifteen thousand farmers.

Here the exogenous variables are the size of the group, the heterogeneity of interests and resources, the way the physical system is subdivided into nested units, and the authority to constitute their own associations. The endogenous process would be to break up the organization into smaller local associations in which face-to-face communication about common problems within the smaller unit would be possible. Agreements might be more difficult to achieve than in the easy case (illustrated in figure 2.7), as farmers in this case are heterogeneous, but if the amount of the long-term benefit were substantial and farmers could slowly gain trust in one another's willingness to reciprocate cooperation, they could build up a local association that enabled them to gain a substantial cooperator's dividend on each organized unit. Local associations could also develop low-cost methods for monitoring behavior and sanctioning actions contrary to locally designed rules. If success were achieved in some local units, the process could continue slowly throughout the watershed.

This is a stylized version of a set of exogenous variables that have characterized several experiments—not in an experimental lab, in this case, but in field settings in several different countries including Nepal, the Philippines, and Spain. These field experiments have lasted for at least one hundred years and in one case for more than a thousand years (Yoder 1994; Sengupta 1991; Ostrom 1990). They illustrate that when individuals can break up a large social dilemma into lots of smaller nested dilemmas, they can use face-to-face discussions in much smaller initial associations to eventually solve, through nested organizations, a much larger problem that would be almost intractable for self-organized groups without such a strategy (see Bendor and Mookherjee 1987; Hardin 1982). The key, again, is linking exogenous variables through endogenous processes to the core set of relationships.

One of the important exogenous variables in this type of situation is the relationship of external authorities to such an effort. An essential part of this structure is that the right to engage in self-organization is not challenged by external authorities so long as basic human rights are not violated by local authorities. Without external recognition, someone who broke a local agreement and was threatened with local sanctions could do an end run around the local association to external authorities. If the external authorities supported the aggrieved, then the entire fabric of local agreements to bolster the inner core of reputation and reciprocity interacting to produce higher levels of cooperation could collapse relatively soon. An important aspect of success is allowing groups to impose reasonable sanctions and to expel members who do not contribute agreed-upon inputs after being given several opportunities to participate.

Focusing on this exogenous variable also helps one see where external authorities could provide positive help. Providing technical assistance to find ways of reducing costs or making investments more efficient, helping to enforce local rules when challenges are made to them,[32] encouraging the open exchange of information, and informing participants in one area what others in other regions have accomplished are all conducive to building the productivity of local efforts and increasing trust and reciprocity. There are obviously many other things that external authorities can do to facilitate local collective action, including making low-interest loans available, providing some kinds of basic insurance, and building effective large-scale infrastructures.

This brief description of two alternative theoretical scenarios provides a picture of the type of theoretical development that could be based on a behavioral theory of collective action. I have tried to give a synopsis of theoretical arguments that will need to be developed more thoroughly in future work, but I hope I have also provided at least a glimpse of how a more coherent theory of collective action might be developed by linking exogenous variables to endogenous processes as they, in turn, affect the core relationships of trust, reciprocity, and reputation in their impact on levels of cooperation and outcomes achieved at the individual and group level.

Implications

The implications of developing second-generation models of empirically grounded, boundedly rational, and moral decision making are substantial. Puzzling research questions can now be addressed more systematically. New research questions will open up. The type of research methodologies regularly used in social science will need to be expanded. The level of understanding between those engaged in formal theory, experimental research, and field research across the social and biological sciences will need to be increased (see Costanza et al. 2001).

What the research on social dilemmas demonstrates is a world of possibility rather than one of necessity. We are neither trapped in inexorable tragedies nor free of moral responsibility for creating and sustaining incentives that facilitate our own achievement of mutually productive outcomes. It is our responsibility to build relationships on the basis of trust, reciprocity, and reputation—and to build these three core values themselves. We cannot adopt the smug presumption of earlier group theorists who thought groups would always form whenever a joint benefit would be obtained. We can expect many groups to fail to achieve mutually productive benefits owing to their lack of trust in one another or to the lack of arenas for low-cost communication, institutional innovation, and the creation of monitoring and sanctioning rules (Ostrom 1997). Nor can we simply rest assured that only one type of institution exists for all social dilemmas, such as a competitive market, in which individuals pursuing their own preferences are led to produce mutually productive outcomes. Although new institutions often facilitate collective action, they encounter significant problems in designing new rules, motivating participants to conform to those rules, and finding and appropriately punishing those who cheat. Without individuals viewing rules as appropriate mechanisms to enhance reciprocal relationships, no police force and court system on earth can monitor and enforce all the needed rules on its own. Nor would most of us want to live in a society in which police were really the thin blue line enforcing all rules.

Although I am proposing a further development of second-generation theories of rational choice, theories based on complete but thin rationality will continue to play an important role in our understanding of human behavior. The clear and unambiguous predictions stemming from complete rational-choice theories will continue to serve as a critical benchmark in conducting empirical studies and for measuring the success or failure of any other explanation offered for observed behavior. A key research question will continue to be, What is the difference between the predicted equilibrium of a complete rationality theory and observed behavior? Furthermore, game theorists are already exploring ways of including reputation, reciprocity, and various norms of behavior in game-theoretic models (see Selten 1990, 1991; Güth 1995; Kreps 1990; Rabin 1993; Palfrey and Rosenthal 1988; Abbink et al. 1996). Thus models of bounded and complete rationality may become more complementary in the next decade than appears to be the case today.

For social scientists interested in diverse institutional arrangements, complete rational-choice theories provide well-developed methods for analyzing the vulnerability of institutions to the strategies devised by talented, analytically sophisticated, short-term hedonists (Brennan and Buchanan 1985). Any serious institutional analysis should include an effort to understand how institutions—including ways of organizing legislative procedures, formulas used to calculate electoral weights and minimal winning coalitions, and international agreements on global environmental problems—are vulnerable to manipulation by calculating, amoral participants.[33] In addition to the individuals who have learned norms of reciprocity in any population, there are others who may try to subvert the process so as to obtain substantial returns for themselves while ignoring the interests of others. One should always know the consequences of letting such individuals operate in any particular institutional setting.

The most immediate research questions that need to be addressed using second-generation models of human behavior relate to the effects of structural variables on the likelihood of organizing for successful modes of collective action. Starting with the development of coherent scenarios with relatively simple baseline models, one can proceed to formal models and empirical testing in field and laboratory settings. The kind of theory that emerges from such an enterprise does not lead to global bivariate (or even multivariate) predictions that have been the ideal to which many scholars have aspired. Gerald Marwell and Pamela Oliver have constructed such a series of theoretical scenarios for social dilemmas involving large numbers of heterogeneous participants in collective action. They have come to a similar conclusion about the nature of the theoretical and empirical enterprise. "This is not to say that general theoretical predictions are impossible using our perspective, only that they cannot be simple and global. Instead, the predictions that we can validly generate must be complex, interactive, and conditional" (Marwell and Oliver 1993, 25).

The effort to develop second-generation models of boundedly rational and moral behavior opens up a variety of questions to be pursued that are of major importance to all social scientists and many biologists interested in human behavior. Among these questions are the following: How do individuals gain trust in other individuals?

How is trust affected by diverse institutional arrangements? What verbal and visual clues are used in evaluating other's behavior? How do individuals gain common understanding so as to craft and follow self-organized arrangements (Ostrom 1999)? John Orbell (personal communication) posits a series of intriguing questions that I might add to this list: "Why do people join together in these games in the first place? How do we select partners in these games? How do our strategies for selecting individual partners differ from our strategies for adding or removing individuals from groups?" Some of these questions are successfully addressed in this volume.

This chapter is a substantially modified version of Elinor Ostrom's presidential address to the American Political Science Association, entitled "A Behavioral Approach to the Rational-Choice Theory of Collective Action," which was originally published in the March 1998 *American Political Science Review* 92(1): 1–22. Support from the National Science Foundation (Grant #SBR-9319835 and SBR-9521918) is gratefully acknowledged.

Notes

1. In a major review of the experimental findings in this area, Douglas Davis and Charles Holt note that "the unsettled nature of the experimental literature assessing the various environmental determinants of contributions rates provides a rather unstable backdrop against which the effects of these institutional variations might be evaluated" (Davis and Holt 1993, 333).

2. For example, participants in two-person prisoner's dilemma games are more likely to select cooperative strategies than those in three-person games (Hamburger 1973).

3. The core assumptions of the dominant model of rational behavior used in modern economic theory and in much of classical game theory include fixed, complete, and logically consistent preferences; a perfect correlation between preferences and monetary payoffs (for example, a person will prefer to receive any amount of money over receiving no money at all); full knowledge and analytical calculation of relevant benefits and costs of alternative strategies; and maximization of expected net benefits unconstrained by internal norms of behavior. At the same time that complete rationality makes heroic assumptions about information-processing capabilities, it also presents a thin perception of the capacity of humans for moral reflection and commitment (Sen 1977).

4. The importance of Alchian's results have frequently been misinterpreted. The key result is that the structure of open competitive markets is so strong that few assumptions about individual behavior are needed to generate the existence of competitive equilibria.

5. An exception to this general finding is that when subjects are presented with an experimental protocol with an opportunity to invest tokens in a common-pool resource (the equivalent of harvesting from a common pool), they tend to substantially overinvest in the initial rounds (see Ostrom, Gardner, and Walker 1994, and the comparison of public-goods and common-pool-resource experiments in Ostrom and Walker 1997). John Ledyard (1995) considers common-pool-resource dilemmas to have the same underlying structure as public-goods dilemmas, but behavior in noncommunication experiments is consistently different.

6. The pulsing cannot be explained using a complete model of rationality, but it can be explained as the result of a heuristic used by subjects to raise or lower their investments depending upon the average return achieved on the most recent round (see Ostrom, Gardner, and Walker 1994).

7. The really puzzling finding from Andreoni's study is that the contribution rate among strangers is higher than that among groups held together for the ten periods.

8. In social-dilemma experiments, subjects make anonymous decisions and are paid privately. The role of cheap talk in coordination experiments is considered to be different because there is no dominant strategy. In this case, preplay communication may help players coordinate on one of the possible equilibria (see Cooper, DeJong, and Forsythe 1992).

9. As Robert Aumann (1974) cogently points out, the players are faced with a problem that whatever they agree upon has to be self-enforcing. That has led Aumann and most game theorists to focus entirely on Nash equilibria, which, once reached, are self-enforcing. In coordination games, cheap talk can be highly efficacious. In social dilemmas, there is substantial incentive to cheat on any agreement reached and even to propose agreements with the intention to cheat on them.

10. Among the studies showing a positive effect of the capacity to communicate are Bornstein and Rapoport (1988); Bornstein et al. (1989); Braver and Wilson (1984, 1986); Caldwell (1976); Dawes, McTavish, and Shaklee (1977); Dawes, Orbell, and van de Kragt (1984); Edney and Harper (1978); Hackett, Schlager, and Walker (1994); Jerdee and Rosen (1974); Kramer and Brewer (1986); van de Kragt et al. (1986); Isaac and Walker (1988a, 1991); Orbell, Dawes, and van de Kragt (1990); Orbell, van de Kragt, and Dawes (1991); Ostrom, Gardner, and Walker (1994); Frohlich and Oppenheimer (1998).

11. The average subject payoff in the Moir experiment was $24.22 Canadian dollars. The subject payoff in the Ostrom, Gardner, and Walker experiments varied from $15.00 to $20.00 U.S. dollars.

12. See also Banks and Calvert (1992a and 1992b) for a discussion of communication in incomplete information games. Pamela Schmitt, Kurtis Swope, and Walker (2000) show how trust is undermined if all subjects are not part of the face-to-face discussion.

13. Social psychologists have found that groups who perform tasks using electronic media do much better if they have had an opportunity to work on a face-to-face basis before using electronic communication only (Hollingshead, McGrath, and O'Connor 1993). Rocco (1998) has found that though electronic communication alone did not increase trust and levels of cooperation, computer communication that follows a face-to-face "premeeting" does enhance trust and cooperation.

14. Jacob Goeree and Charles Holt (2001) report on a series of "treasures"— one-shot experiments in which subjects do behave consistently with the predicted Nash equilibrium or subgame-perfect equilibrium. Slight changes of the payoff matrix that do not change the equilibrium prediction can, however, change behavior in the game dramatically, so that the Nash equilibrium no longer predicts outcomes.

15. This finding is consistent with Peter Boyd and Peter Richerson's (1992) finding that moralistic strategies may result in negative net outcomes.

16. In related work, I have summarized similar findings from field research (Ostrom 2001). In future work, I intend to provide a synthesis of these two independent sets of findings and a multilevel theory of institutional choice to complement the behavioral approach to the theory of collective action provided herein.

17. Computer simulations allow comparisons of alternative models of the individual and of the situations. Many simulations using various types of reciprocity strategies have produced outcomes that are similar to those produced in laboratory experiments (see Deadman 1997).

18. See, for example, the debate between Robert Bates and Chalmers in a recent issue of *PS: Political Science and Politics* (Bates 1997 and Johnson 1997).

19. For an update on his views on bounded rationality, see Selten (2001).

20. When constructing formal models, overt delta parameters can be included (see Crawford and Ostrom 1995; Palfrey and Rosenthal 1988). Alternatively, one can assume that these internal delta parameters lead individuals to enter new situations with differing probabilities that they will follow norms such as reciprocity. These probabilities not only vary across individuals, they also increase or decrease as a function of the specific structural parameters of the situation and, in repeated experiments, the patterns of behavior and outcomes achieved in that situation over time.

21. The change in valuations that an individual may attach to an action-outcome linkage may be generated strictly internally or may be triggered by external observation and thus a concern with how others will evaluate the normative appropriateness of actions.

22. Alvin Gouldner considers norms of reciprocity to be universal and as important in most cultures as incest taboos even though the "concrete formulations may vary with time and place" (Gouldner 1960, 171).

23. See Selten (1986) for a discussion of his own and John Harsanyi's (1977) conception of "rule utilitarianism"—the preferences that an individual acquires for following a particular strategy when confronting a situation of a particular type.

24. These issues are discussed in greater depth in Crawford and Ostrom (1995). See also Piaget (1969 [1932]).

25. The evolutionary approach has been strongly influenced by the work of Robert Axelrod (see in particular, Axelrod 1984, 1986; Axelrod and Hamilton 1981; and Axelrod and Keohane 1985).

26. This is not the complete list of all types of reciprocity norms, but it does capture the vast majority of such norms.

27. The results obtained by Hoffman, McCabe, and Smith (1996b) related to *dictator games* under varying conditions of *social distance* are also quite consistent with the behavioral approach of this chapter.

28. Experiments conducted in fifteen small-scale societies located on four continents also challenge current theoretical predictions, but the variation in levels of cooperation is higher and is closely related to cultural norms of each society (Henrich et al. 2001).

29. See also Hoffman, McCabe, and Smith (1996b) on social distance in dictator games.

30. In a two-person situation of complete certainty, individuals can easily follow the famous tit-for-tat (or tit-for-tat or exit) strategy even without communication. When a substantial proportion of individuals in a population do follow this norm, and they can identify with whom they have interacted in the past (either to refuse future interactions or to punish prior uncooperative actions), and when discount rates are sufficiently low, tit-for-tat has been shown to be a highly successful strategy, yielding higher payoffs than are available to those using other strategies (Axelrod 1984). With communication, it is even easier.

31. Seeing one another, however, may induce considerable cooperation. In an ingenious series of experiments, Iris Bohnet and Bruno Frey (1999) conducted both one-shot prisoner's dilemma games and dictator games under three conditions: absolute anonymity, mutual identification, and face-to-face communication. In the mutual-identification condition, the participants in a future game merely stood and looked at one another in a large room. Sixty-three percent of the subjects chose the dominant strategy predicted by noncooperative game theory in the anonymous condition for the prisoner's dilemma game, and 28 percent chose it for the dictator game. The percentages fell to 41 percent when subjects were able to identify one another at a distance before playing a prisoner's dilemma game and to zero when they identified one another before playing a dictator game.

32. This has to be done carefully, however, so that external courts do not entirely substitute for local enforcement.

33. Consequently, research on the impact of institutional arrangements on strategies and outcomes continues to be crucial to future developments. See Alt and Shepsle (1990); Bates (1989); Agrawal (1999); Dasgupta (1993); Eggertsson (1990); Gibson (1999); Levi (1997); Ostrom (1997); Ostrom, Feeny, and Picht (1993); Scharpf (1997).

References

Abbink, Klaus, Gary E. Bolton, Abdolkarim Sadrieh, and Fang Fang Tang. 1996. "Adaptive Learning Versus Punishment in Ultimatum Bargaining." Discussion Paper B-381. Bonn, Germany: Rheinische Friedrich-Wilhelms-Universität Bonn.

Abreau, Dilip. 1988. "On the Theory of Infinitely Repeated Games with Discounting." *Econometrica* 80(4): 383–96.

Agrawal, Arun. 1999. *Greener Pastures: Politics, Markets, and Community Among a Migrant Pastoral People.* Durham, N.C.: Duke University Press.

———. 2002. "Common Resources and Institutional Sustainability." In *The Drama of the Commons,* edited by Elinor Ostrom, Thomas Dietz, Nives Dolsak, Paul Stern, Susan Stonich, and Elke Weber. National Research Council, Committee on the Human Dimensions of Global Change. Washington, D.C.: National Academy Press.

Alchian, Armen A. 1950. "Uncertainty, Evolution, and Economic Theory." *Journal of Political Economy* 58(3): 211–21.

Alchian, Armen A., and Harold Demsetz. 1972. "Production, Information Costs, and Economic Organization." *American Economic Review* 62(5): 777–95.

Alt, James E., and Kenneth A. Shepsle, eds. 1990. *Perspectives on Positive Political Economy.* New York: Cambridge University Press.

Andreoni, James. 1988. "Why Free Ride? Strategies and Learning in Public Goods Experiments." *Journal of Public Economics* 37(3): 291–304.

———. 1989. "Giving with Impure Altruism: Applications to Charity and Ricardian Equivalence." *Journal of Political Economy* 97(6): 1447–58.

Aumann, Robert J. 1974. "Subjectivity and Correlation in Randomized Strategies." *Journal of Mathematical Economics* 1(1): 67–96.

Axelrod, Robert. 1984. *The Evolution of Cooperation.* New York: Basic Books.

———. 1986. "An Evolutionary Approach to Norms." *American Political Science Review* 80(4): 1095–1111.

Axelrod, Robert, and William D. Hamilton. 1981. "The Evolution of Cooperation." *Science* 211(4489): 1390–96.

Axelrod, Robert, and Robert O. Keohane. 1985. "Achieving Cooperation Under Anarchy: Strategies and Institutions." *World Politics* 38(1): 226–54.

Banks, Jeffrey S., and Randall L. Calvert. 1992a. "A Battle-of-the-Sexes Game with Incomplete Information." *Games and Economic Behavior* 4(3): 347–72.

———. 1992b. "Communication and Efficiency in Coordination Games." Working paper. Rochester, N.Y.: University of Rochester, Department of Economics and Department of Political Science.

Barkow, Jerome H., Leda Cosmides, and John Tooby, eds. 1992. *The Adapted Mind: Evolutionary Psychology and the Generation of Culture.* New York: Oxford University Press.

Barry, Brian, and Russell Hardin. 1982. *Rational Man and Irrational Society? An Introduction and Source Book.* Beverly Hills, Calif.: Sage.

Bates, Robert H. 1989. *Beyond the Miracle of the Market: The Political Economy of Agrarian Development in Kenya.* New York: Cambridge University Press.

———. 1997. "Area Studies and the Discipline: A Useful Controversy." *PS: Political Science and Politics* 30(2): 166–69.

Becker, Lawrence C. 1990. *Reciprocity.* Chicago: University of Chicago Press.

Bendor, Jonathan, and Dilip Mookherjee. 1987. "Institutional Structure and the Logic of Ongoing Collective Action." *American Political Science Review* 81(1): 129–54.

Blau, Peter M. 1964. *Exchange of Power in Social Life.* New York: Wiley.

Bohm, Peter. 1972. "Estimating Demand for Public Goods: An Experiment." *European Economic Review* 3(2): 111–30.

Bohnet, Iris, and Bruno S. Frey. 1999. "The Sound of Silence in Prisoner's Dilemma and Dictator Games." *Journal of Economic Behavior and Organization* 38(1): 43–57.

Bornstein, Gary, and Amnon Rapoport. 1988. "Intergroup Competition for the Provision of Step-Level Public Goods: Effects of Preplay Communication." *European Journal of Social Psychology* 18: 125–42.

Bornstein, Gary, Amnon Rapoport, Lucia Kerpel, and Tani Katz. 1989. "Within-Group and Between-Group Communication in Intergroup Competition for Public Goods." *Journal of Experimental Social Psychology* 25(5): 422–36.

Boudreaux, Donald J., and Randall G. Holcombe. 1989. "Government by Contract." *Public Finance Quarterly* 17(July): 264–80.

Boyd, Robert, and Peter J. Richerson. 1988. "The Evolution of Reciprocity in Sizable Groups." *Journal of Theoretical Biology* 132(3): 337–56.

———. 1992. "Punishment Allows the Evolution of Cooperation (or Anything Else) in Sizable Groups." *Ethology and Sociobiology* 13(May): 171–95.

Braver, Sanford L., and L. A. Wilson. 1984. "A Laboratory Study of Social Contracts As a Solution to Public Goods Problems: Surviving on the Lifeboat." Paper presented at the Western Social Science Association meeting. San Diego, California (April).

———. 1986. "Choices in Social Dilemmas: Effects of Communication Within Subgroups." *Journal of Conflict Resolution* 30(1): 51–62.

Brennan, Geoffrey, and James Buchanan. 1985. *The Reason of Rules.* Cambridge: Cambridge University Press.

Bromley, Daniel W., David Feeny, Margaret McKean, Pauline Peters, Jere Gilles, Ronald Oakerson, C. Ford Runge, and James Thomson, eds. 1992. *Making the Commons Work: Theory, Practice, and Policy.* Oakland, Calif.: ICS Press.

Bullock, Kari, and John Baden. 1977. "Communes and the Logic of the Commons." In *Managing the Commons,* edited by Garrett Hardin and John Baden. San Francisco: Freeman.

Caldwell, Michael D. 1976. "Communication and Sex Effects in a Five-Person

Prisoners' Dilemma Game." *Journal of Personality and Social Psychology* 33(3): 273–80.

Cason, Timothy N., and Feisal U. Khan. 1996. "A Laboratory Study of Voluntary Public Goods Provision with Imperfect Monitoring and Communication." Working paper. Los Angeles, Calif.: University of Southern California, Department of Economics.

Chagnon, Napoleon A. 1988. "Life Histories, Blood Revenge, and Warfare in a Tribal Population." *Science* 239(4843): 985–92.

Chan, Kenneth, Stuart Mestelman, Rob Moir, and Andrew Muller. 1996. "The Voluntary Provision of Public Goods Under Varying Endowments." *Canadian Journal of Economics* 29(1): 54–69.

Clark, Andy. 1995. "Economic Reason: The Interplay of Individual Learning and External Structure." Working paper. St. Louis, Mo.: Washington University, Department of Philosophy.

Clark, Andy, and Annette Karmiloff-Smith. 1993. "The Cognizer's Innards: A Psychological and Philosophical Perspective on the Development of Thought." *Mind and Language* 8(4): 487–519.

Cooper, Russell, Douglas V. DeJong, and Robert Forsythe. 1992. "Communication in Coordination Games." *Quarterly Journal of Economics* 107(2): 739–71.

Cosmides, Leda, and John Tooby. 1992. "Cognitive Adaptations for Social Exchange." In *The Adapted Mind: Evolutionary Psychology and the Generation of Culture*, edited by Jerome H. Barkow, Leda Cosmides, and John Tooby. New York: Oxford University Press.

Costanza, Robert, Bobbi S. Low, Elinor Ostrom, and James Wilson, eds. 2001. *Institutions, Ecosystems, and Sustainability*. Boca Raton, Fla.: Lewis.

Crawford, Sue E. S., and Elinor Ostrom. 1995. "A Grammar of Institutions." *American Political Science Review* 89(3): 582–600.

Dasgupta, Partha. 1993. *An Inquiry into Well-Being and Destitution*. Oxford: Clarendon Press.

Davis, Douglas D., and Charles A. Holt. 1993. *Experimental Economics*. Princeton, N.J.: Princeton University Press.

Dawes, Robyn M. 1975. "Formal Models of Dilemmas in Social Decision Making." In *Human Judgment and Decision Processes: Formal and Mathematical Approaches*, edited by Martin F. Kaplan and Steven Schwartz. New York: Academic Press.

———. 1980. "Social Dilemmas." *Annual Review of Psychology* 31:169–93.

Dawes, Robyn M., Jeanne McTavish, and Harriet Shaklee. 1977. "Behavior, Communication, and Assumptions About Other People's Behavior in a Commons Dilemma Situation." *Journal of Personality and Social Psychology* 35(1): 1–11.

Dawes, Robyn M., John M. Orbell, and Alphons van de Kragt. 1984. "Normative Constraint and Incentive Compatible Design." Unpublished paper. University of Oregon, Eugene, Department of Psychology.

———. 1986. "Organizing Groups for Collective Action." *American Political Science Review* 80(4): 1171–85.

Deadman, Peter J. 1997. "Modeling Individual Behavior in Common Pool Resource Management Experiments with Autonomous Agents." Ph.D. diss., University of Arizona.

Deutsch, Morton. 1960. "The Effect of Motivation Orientation upon Threat and Suspicion." *Human Relations* 13(May): 123–39.

de Waal, Frans. 1996. *Good Natured: The Origins of Right and Wrong in Humans and Other Animals.* Cambridge, Mass.: Harvard University Press.

Dudley, Dean. 1993. "Essays on Individual Behavior in Social Dilemma Environments: An Experimental Analysis." Ph.D. diss., Indiana University, Bloomington.

Edney, Julian. 1979. "Freeriders en Route to Disaster." *Psychology Today* 13(3): 80–87, 102.

Edney, Julian J., and Christopher S. Harper. 1978. "The Commons Dilemma: A Review of Contributions from Psychology." *Environmental Management* 2(6): 491–507.

Eggertsson, Thráinn. 1990. *Economic Behavior and Institutions.* New York: Cambridge University Press.

Ekeh, P. P. 1974. *Social Exchange Theory: The Two Traditions.* Cambridge, Mass.: Harvard University Press.

Elster, Jon. 1985. *Sour Grapes: Studies in the Subversion of Rationality.* Cambridge: Cambridge University Press.

Emerson, Richard. 1972a. "Exchange Theory, Part I: A Psychological Basis for Social Exchange." In *Sociological Theories in Progress,* edited by Joseph Berger, Morris Zelditch, and Bo Anderson, vol. 2. Boston, Mass.: Houghton Mifflin.

———. 1972b. "Exchange Theory, Part II: Exchange Relations and Networks." In *Sociological Theories in Progress,* edited by Joseph Berger, Morris Zelditch, and Bo Anderson, vol. 2. Boston, Mass.: Houghton Mifflin.

Farrell, Joseph. 1987. "Cheap Talk, Coordination, and Entry." *Rand Journal of Economics* 18(spring): 34–39.

Fehr, Ernst, and Simon Gächter. 2000. "Fairness and Retaliation: The Economics of Reciprocity." *Journal of Economic Perspectives* 14(3): 159–81.

Fiorina, Morris P. 1995. "Rational Choice, Empirical Contributions, and the Scientific Enterprise." *Critical Review* 9(1–2): 85–94.

Frank, Robert H., Thomas Gilovich, and Dennis T. Regan. 1993. "The Evolution of One-Shot Cooperation: An Experiment." *Ethology and Sociobiology* 14(July): 247–56.

Frey, Bruno S., and Iris Bohnet. 1996. "Cooperation, Communication, and Communitarianism: An Experimental Approach." *Journal of Political Philosophy* 4(4): 322–36.

Frohlich, Norman, and Joe Oppenheimer. 1998. "Some Consequences of E-Mail Versus Face-to-Face Communication in Experiment." *Journal of Economic Behavior and Organization* 35: 389–403.

Fudenberg, Drew, and Eric Maskin. 1986. "The Folk Theorem in Repeated Games with Discounting or with Incomplete Information." *Econometrica* 54(3): 533–54.

Geddes, Barbara. 1994. *Politician's Dilemma: Building State Capacity in Latin America.* Berkeley, Calif.: University of California Press.

Gibson, Clark. 1999. *Politicians and Poachers: The Political Economy of Wildlife Policy in Africa.* Cambridge: Cambridge University Press.

Gigerenzer, Gerd, and Reinhard Selten, eds. 2001. *Bounded Rationality: The Adaptive Toolbox.* Cambridge, Mass.: MIT Press.

72   Trust and Reciprocity

Goeree, Jacob K., and Charles A. Holt. 2001. "Ten Little Treasures of Game Theory and Ten Intuitive Contradictions." *American Economic Review* 91(5): 1402–22.

Gouldner, Alvin W. 1960. "The Norm of Reciprocity: A Preliminary Statement." *American Sociological Review* 25(April): 161–78.

Greif, Avner, Paul Milgrom, and Barry R. Weingast. 1994. "Coordination, Commitment, and Enforcement: The Case of the Merchant Guild." *Journal of Political Economy* 102(August): 745–76.

Grossman, Sanford J., and Oliver D. Hart. 1980. "Takeover Bids, the Free-Rider Problem, and the Theory of the Corporation." *Bell Journal of Economics* 11(spring): 42–64.

Güth, Werner. 1995. "An Evolutionary Approach to Explaining Cooperative Behavior by Reciprocal Incentives." *International Journal of Game Theory* 24(4): 323–44.

Güth, Werner, and Hartmut Kliemt. 1996. "Towards a Completely Indirect Evolutionary Approach." Discussion paper 82. Berlin, Germany: Humboldt University, Economics Faculty.

Güth, Werner, Rolf Schmittberger, and Bernd Schwarze. 1982. "An Experimental Analysis of Ultimatum Bargaining." *Journal of Economic Behavior and Organization* 3(4): 367–88.

Hackett, Steven, Dean Dudley, and James Walker. 1995. "Heterogeneities, Information, and Conflict Resolution: Experimental Evidence on Sharing Contracts." In *Local Commons and Global Interdependence: Heterogeneity and Cooperation in Two Domains*, edited by Robert O. Keohane and Elinor Ostrom. London, England: Sage.

Hackett, Steven, Edella Schlager, and James Walker. 1994. "The Role of Communication in Resolving Commons Dilemmas: Experimental Evidence with Heterogeneous Appropriators." *Journal of Environmental Economics and Management* 27(2): 99–126.

Hamburger, Henry. 1973. "N-Person Prisoner's Dilemma." *Journal of Mathematical Sociology* 3(1): 27–48.

Hardin, Garrett. 1968. "The Tragedy of the Commons." *Science* 162(December): 1243–48.

Hardin, Russell. 1971. "Collective Action As an Agreeable N-Prisoner's Dilemma." *Behavioral Science* 16(5): 472–81.

———. 1982. *Collective Action*. Baltimore: Johns Hopkins University Press.

———. 1995. *One for All: The Logic of Group Conflict*. Princeton, N.J.: Princeton University Press.

———. 1997. "Economic Theories of the State." In *Perspectives on Public Choice: A Handbook*, edited by Dennis C. Mueller. Cambridge: Cambridge University Press.

Hardy, Charles J., and Bibb Latané. 1988. "Social Loafing in Cheerleaders: Effects of Team Membership and Competition." *Journal of Sport and Exercise Psychology* 10(1): 109–14.

Harsanyi, John C. 1977. "Rule Utilitarianism and Decision Theory." *Erkenntnis* 11: 25–53.

Harsanyi, John C., and Reinhard Selten. 1988. *A General Theory of Equilibrium Selection in Games*. Cambridge, Mass.: MIT Press.

Hayek, Friedrich A. von. 1945. "The Use of Knowledge in Society." *American Economic Review* 35(4): 519–30.

Heiner, Ronald A. 2002. "Robust Evolution of Contingent Cooperation in the One-Shot Prisoners' Dilemma." Working Paper 02-01. Fairfax, Va.: James Buchanan Center for Political Economy.

Henrich, Joseph, Robert Boyd, Samuel Bowles, Colin Camerer, Ernst Fehr, Herbert Gintis, and Richard McElreath. 2001. "In Search of Homo Economicus: Behavioral Experiments in Fifteen Small-Scale Societies." *American Economic Review* 91(2): 73–78.

Hirshleifer, David, and Eric Rasmusen. 1989. "Cooperation in a Repeated Prisoner's Dilemma with Ostracism." *Journal of Economic Behavior and Organization* 12(1): 87–106.

Hobbes, Thomas R. 1960 [1651]. *Leviathan, or the Matter, Forme and Power of a Commonwealth Ecclesiasticall and Civil.* Edited by Michael Oakeshott. Oxford: Basil Blackwell.

Hoffman, Elizabeth, Kevin McCabe, and Vernon Smith. 1996a. "Behavioral Foundations of Reciprocity: Experimental Economics and Evolutionary Psychology." Working paper. Tucson, Ariz.: University of Arizona, Department of Economics.

———. 1996b. "Social Distance and Other-Regarding Behavior in Dictator Games." *American Economic Review* 86(3): 653–60.

Hollingshead, Andrea B., Joseph E. McGrath, and Kathleen M. O'Connor. 1993. "Group Task Performance and Communication Technology: A Longitudinal Study of Computer-Mediated Versus Face-to-Face Work Groups." *Small Group Research* 24(3): 307–33.

Holmstrom, Bengt. 1982. "Moral Hazard in Teams." *Bell Journal of Economics* 13(autumn): 324–40.

Homans, George C. 1961. *Social Behavior: Its Elementary Forms.* New York: Harcourt, Brace, and World.

Isaac, R. Mark, Kenneth McCue, and Charles R. Plott. 1985. "Public Goods Provision in an Experimental Environment." *Journal of Public Economics* 26(1): 51–74.

Isaac, R. Mark, and James Walker. 1988a. "Communication and Free-Riding Behavior: The Voluntary Contribution Mechanism." *Economic Inquiry* 26(4): 585–608.

———. 1988b. "Group Size Effects in Public Goods Provision: The Voluntary Contributions Mechanism." *Quarterly Journal of Economics* 103(February): 179–99.

———. 1991. "Costly Communication: An Experiment in a Nested Public Goods Problem." In *Laboratory Research in Political Economy,* edited by Thomas R. Palfrey. Ann Arbor, Mich.: University of Michigan Press.

———. 1993. "Nash As an Organizing Principle in the Voluntary Provision of Public Goods: Experimental Evidence." Working paper. Bloomington, Ind.: Indiana University, Department of Economics.

Isaac, R. Mark, James Walker, and Susan Thomas. 1984. "Divergent Evidence on Free Riding: An Experimental Examination of Some Possible Explanations." *Public Choice* 43(2): 113–49.

Isaac, R. Mark, James Walker, and Arlington W. Williams. 1994. "Group Size and the Voluntary Provision of Public Goods: Experimental Evidence Utilizing Large Groups." *Journal of Public Economics* 54(1): 1–36.

Jerdee, Thomas H., and Benson Rosen. 1974. "Effects of Opportunity to Communicate and Visibility of Individual Decisions on Behavior in the Common Interest." *Journal of Applied Psychology* 59(6): 712–16.

Johnson, Chalmers. 1997. "Preconception Versus Observation, or the Contributions of Rational Choice Theory and Area Studies to Contemporary Political Science." *PS: Political Science and Politics* 30(2): 170–74.

Kikuchi, Masako, Yoriko Watanabe, and Toshio Yamagishi. 1996. "Accuracy in the Prediction of Others' Trustworthiness and General Trust: An Experimental Study." *Japanese Journal of Experimental Social Psychology* 37(1): 23–36.

Kim, Oliver, and Mark Walker. 1984. "The Free Rider Problem: Experimental Evidence." *Public Choice* 43(1): 3–24.

Knack, Stephen. 1992. "Civic Norms, Social Sanctions, and Voter Turnout." *Rationality and Society* 4(2): 133–56.

Kollock, Peter. 1993. "An Eye for an Eye Leaves Everyone Blind: Cooperation and Accounting Systems." *American Sociological Review* 58(6): 768–86.

Kramer, R. M., and Marilyn M. Brewer. 1986. "Social Group Identity and the Emergence of Cooperation in Resource Conservation Dilemmas." In *Experimental Social Dilemmas*, edited by H. A. M. Wilke, David M. Messick, and Christel G. Rutte. Frankfurt am Main, Germany: Verlag Peter Lang.

Kreps, David M. 1990. "Corporate Culture and Economic Theory." In *Perspectives on Positive Political Economy*, edited by James E. Alt and Kenneth A. Shepsle. New York: Cambridge University Press.

Kreps, David M., Paul Milgrom, John Roberts, and Robert Wilson. 1982. "Rational Cooperation in the Finitely Repeated Prisoner's Dilemma." *Journal of Economic Theory* 27(2): 245–52.

Latsis, Spiro J. 1972. "Situational Determinism in Economics." *British Journal of Philosophy of Science* 23: 207–45.

Ledyard, John. 1995. "Public Goods: A Survey of Experimental Research." In *The Handbook of Experimental Economics*, edited by John Kagel and Alvin Roth. Princeton, N.J.: Princeton University Press.

Leibenstein, Harvey. 1976. *Beyond Economic Man*. Cambridge, Mass.: Harvard University Press.

Levi, Margaret. 1997. *Consent, Dissent, and Patriotism*. New York: Cambridge University Press.

Lichbach, Mark Irving. 1995. *The Rebel's Dilemma*. Ann Arbor, Mich.: University of Michigan Press.

Luce, R. Duncan, and Howard Raiffa. 1957. *Games and Decisions: Introduction and Critical Survey*. New York: Wiley.

Marr, David. 1982. *Vision: A Computational Investigation into the Human Representation and Processing of Visual Information*. San Francisco: W. H. Freeman.

Marwell, Gerald, and Ruth E. Ames. 1979. "Experiments on the Provision of Public Goods I: Resources, Interest, Group Size, and the Free-Rider Problem." *American Journal of Sociology* 84(6): 1335–60.

———. 1980. "Experiments on the Provision of Public Goods II: Provision Points, Stakes, Experience, and the Free-Rider Problem." *American Journal of Sociology* 85(4): 926–37.

———. 1981. "Economists Free Ride: Does Anyone Else?" *Journal of Public Economics* 15(November): 295–310.

Marwell, Gerald, and Pamela Oliver. 1993. *The Critical Mass in Collective Action: A Micro-Social Theory.* New York: Cambridge University Press.

McCabe, Kevin, Stephen Rassenti, and Vernon Smith. 1996. "Game Theory and Reciprocity in Some Extensive-Form Bargaining Games." Working paper. Tucson, Ariz.: University of Arizona, Economic Science Laboratory.

Messick, David M. 1973. "To Join or Not to Join: An Approach to the Unionization Decision." *Organizational Behavior and Human Performance* 10(1): 146–56.

Messick, David M., and Marilyn B. Brewer. 1983. "Solving Social Dilemmas: A Review." In *Annual Review of Personality and Social Psychology,* edited by Ladd Wheeler and Phillip Shaver. Beverly Hills, Calif.: Sage.

Messick, David M., Henk A. M. Wilke, Marilyn B. Brewer, Roderick M. Kramer, Patricia E. Zemke, and Layton Lui. 1983. "Individual Adaptations and Structural Change As Solutions to Social Dilemmas." *Journal of Personality and Social Psychology* 44(2): 294–309.

Miller, Gary. 1992. *Managerial Dilemmas: The Political Economy of Hierarchy.* New York: Cambridge University Press.

Moir, Rob. 1995. "The Effects of Costly Monitoring and Sanctioning upon Common Property Resource Appropriation." Working paper. Saint John, New Brunswick, Canada: University of New Brunswick, Department of Economics.

Mueller, Dennis. 1986. "Rational Egoism Versus Adaptive Egoism As Fundamental Postulate for a Descriptive Theory of Human Behavior." *Public Choice* 51(1): 3–23.

Oliver, Pamela. 1980. "Rewards and Punishments As Selective Incentives for Collective Action: Theoretical Investigations." *American Journal of Sociology* 85(6): 1356–75.

Olson, Mancur. 1965. *The Logic of Collective Action: Public Goods and the Theory of Groups.* Cambridge, Mass.: Harvard University Press.

Orbell, John M., and Robyn M. Dawes. 1991. "A 'Cognitive Miser' Theory of Cooperators' Advantage." *American Political Science Review* 85(2): 515–28.

———. 1993. "Social Welfare, Cooperators' Advantage, and the Option of Not Playing the Game." *American Sociological Review* 58(December): 787–800.

Orbell, John M., Robyn M. Dawes, and Alphons van de Kragt. 1990. "The Limits of Multilateral Promising." *Ethics* 100(4): 616–27.

Orbell, John M., Peregrine Schwartz-Shea, and Randy Simmons. 1984. "Do Cooperators Exit More Readily Than Defectors?" *American Political Science Review* 78(March): 147–62.

Orbell, John M., Alphons van de Kragt, and Robyn M. Dawes. 1988. "Explaining Discussion-Induced Cooperation." *Journal of Personality and Social Psychology* 54(5): 811–19.

———. 1991. "Covenants Without the Sword: The Role of Promises in Social Dilemma Circumstances." In *Social Norms and Economic Institutions,* edited by Kenneth J. Koford and Jeffrey B. Miller. Ann Arbor, Mich.: University of Michigan Press.

Ostrom, Elinor. 1990. *Governing the Commons: The Evolution of Institutions for Collective Action.* New York: Cambridge University Press.

————. 2001. "Reformulating the Commons." In *Protecting the Commons: A Framework for Resource Management in the Americas*, edited by Joanna Burger, Elinor Ostrom, Richard B. Norgaard, David Policansky, and Bernard D. Goldstein. Washington, D.C.: Island Press.

Ostrom, Elinor, Roy Gardner, and James Walker. 1994. *Rules, Games, and Common-Pool Resources*. Ann Arbor, Mich.: University of Michigan Press.

Ostrom, Elinor, and James Walker. 1991. "Communication in a Commons: Cooperation Without External Enforcement." In *Laboratory Research in Political Economy*, edited by Thomas R. Palfrey. Ann Arbor, Mich.: University of Michigan Press.

————. 1997. "Neither Markets Nor States: Linking Transformation Processes in Collective Action Arenas." In *Perspectives on Public Choice: A Handbook*, edited by Dennis C. Mueller. Cambridge: Cambridge University Press.

Ostrom, Elinor, James Walker, and Roy Gardner. 1992. "Covenants With and Without a Sword: Self-governance Is Possible." *American Political Science Review* 86(2): 404–17.

Ostrom, Vincent. 1997. *The Meaning of Democracy and the Vulnerability of Democracies: A Response to Tocqueville's Challenge*. Ann Arbor, Mich.: University of Michigan Press.

————. 1999. "Artisanship and Artifact." In *Polycentric Governance and Development: Readings from the Workshop in Political Theory and Policy Analysis*, edited by Michael McGinnis. Ann Arbor, Mich.: University of Michigan Press.

Ostrom, Vincent, David Feeny, and Hartmut Picht, eds. 1993. *Rethinking Institutional Analysis and Development: Issues, Alternatives, and Choices*. 2d ed. Oakland, Calif.: ICS Press.

Palfrey, Thomas R., and Howard Rosenthal. 1988. "Private Incentives in Social Dilemmas." *Journal of Public Economics* 35(April): 309–32.

Pellikaan, Huib, and Robert van der Veen. 2002. *Environmental Dilemmas and Policy Design*. Cambridge: Cambridge University Press.

Piaget, Jean. 1969 [1932]. *The Moral Judgment of the Child*. New York: Free Press.

Pinker, Steven. 1994. *The Language Instinct*. New York: Morrow.

Platt, John R. 1973. "Social Traps." *American Psychologist* 28(August): 641–51.

Popper, Karl R. 1967. "Rationality and the Status of the Rationality Principle." In *Le Fondements philosophiques des systemes economiques textes de Jacques Rueff et essais rediges en son honneur*, edited by E. M. Claassen. Paris: Payot. (Translated as "The Rationality Principle," in *Popper Selections*, edited by David Miller [Princeton, N.J.: Princeton University Press].)

Pruitt, Dean G., and Melvin J. Kimmel. 1977. "Twenty Years of Experimental Gaming: Critique, Synthesis, and Suggestions for the Future." *Annual Review of Psychology* 28: 363–92.

Rabin, Matthew. 1993. "Incorporating Fairness in Game Theory and Economics." *American Economics Review* 83(5): 1281–1302.

Rapoport, Amnon. 1997. "Order of Play in Strategically Equivalent Games in Extensive Form." *International Journal of Game Theory* 26(1): 113–36.

Rapoport, Anatol. 1968. "Editorial Comments." *Journal of Conflict Resolution* 12(2): 222–23.

————. 1974. "Prisoners' Dilemma: Recollections and Observations." In *Game Theory As a Theory of Conflict Resolution*, edited by A. Rapoport. Dordrecht, Netherlands: Reidel.

Rapoport, Anatol, and Albert M. Chammah. 1965. *Prisoners' Dilemma: A Study of Conflict and Cooperation*. Ann Arbor, Mich.: University of Michigan Press.

Rocco, Elena. 1998. "Trust Breaks Down in Electronic Contexts but Can Be Repaired by Some Initial Face-to-Face Contact." In *Proceedings of Computer-Human Interaction 1998*. New York: ACM Press.

Rocco, Elena, and Massimo Warglien. 1995. "Computer Mediated Communication and the Emergence of 'Electronic Opportunism.'" Working Paper RCC13659. Venice, Italy: Universita degli Studi di Venezia.

Roth, Alvin E. 1995. "Bargaining Experiments." In *Handbook of Experimental Economics*, edited by John Kagel and Alvin E. Roth. Princeton, N.J.: Princeton University Press.

Rutte, Christel G., and Henk A. M. Wilke. 1984. "Social Dilemmas and Leadership." *European Journal of Social Psychology* 14(1): 105–21.

Samuelson, Charles D., and David M. Messick. 1986. "Alternative Structural Solutions to Resource Dilemmas." *Organizational Behavior and Human Decision Processes* 37(1): 139–55.

————. 1995. "When Do People Want to Change the Rules for Allocating Shared Resources?" In *Social Dilemmas: Perspectives on Individuals and Groups*, edited by David A. Schroeder. Westport, Conn.: Praeger.

Samuelson, Charles D., David M. Messick, Christel G. Rutte, and Henk A. M. Wilke. 1984. "Individual and Structural Solutions to Resource Dilemmas in Two Cultures." *Journal of Personality and Social Psychology* 47(1): 94–104.

Samuelson, Larry, John Gale, and Kenneth Binmore. 1995. "Learning to Be Imperfect: The Ultimatum Game." *Games and Economic Behavior* 8(1): 56–90.

Samuelson, Paul A. 1954. "The Pure Theory of Public Expenditure." *Review of Economics and Statistics* 36(November): 387–89.

Sandler, Todd. 1992. *Collective Action: Theory and Applications*. Ann Arbor, Mich.: University of Michigan Press.

Sato, Kaori. 1987. "Distribution of the Cost of Maintaining Common Property Resources." *Journal of Experimental Social Psychology* 23(1): 19–31.

Satz, Debra, and John Ferejohn. 1994. "Rational Choice and Social Theory." *Journal of Philosophy* 91(2): 71–82.

Scharpf, Fritz W. 1997. *Games Real Actors Play: Actor-Centered Institutionalism in Policy Research*. Boulder, Colo.: Westview Press.

Schelling, Thomas C. 1960. *The Strategy of Conflict*. Oxford: Oxford University Press.

————. 1978. *Micromotives and Macrobehavior*. New York: W. W. Norton.

Schmitt, Pamela, Kurtis Swope, and James Walker. 2000. "Collective Action with Incomplete Commitment: Experimental Evidence." *Southern Economic Journal* 66(4): 829–54.

Schneider, Friedrich, and Werner W. Pommerehne. 1981. "Free Riding and Collective Action: An Experiment in Public Microeconomics." *Quarterly Journal of Economics* 96(November): 689–704.

Schuessler, Rudolf. 1989. "Exit Threats and Cooperation Under Anonymity." *Journal of Conflict Resolution* 33(4): 728–49.

Sefton, Martin, Robert Shupp, and James Walker. 2002. "The Effect of Rewards and Sanctions in Provision of Public Goods." Working paper. Bloomington, Ind.: Indiana University, Workshop in Political Theory and Policy Analysis.

Sell, Jane, and Rick Wilson. 1991. "Levels of Information and Contributions to Public Goods." *Social Forces* 70(1): 107–24.

———. 1992. "Liar, Liar, Pants on Fire: Cheap Talk and Signaling in Repeated Public Goods Settings." Working paper. Houston, Tex.: Rice University, Department of Political Science.

Selten, Reinhard. 1975. "Reexamination of the Perfectness Concept for Equilibrium Points in Extensive Games." *International Journal of Game Theory* 4(1–2): 25–55.

———. 1986. "Institutional Utilitarianism." In *Guidance, Control, and Evaluation in the Public Sector,* edited by Franz-Xaver Kaufmann, Giandomenico Majone, and Vincent Ostrom. New York: de Gruyter.

———. 1990. "Bounded Rationality." *Journal of Institutional and Theoretical Economics* 146(4): 649–58.

———. 1991. "Evolution, Learning, and Economic Behavior." *Games and Economic Behavior* 3(1): 3–24.

———. 2001. "What Is Bounded Rationality?" In *Bounded Rationality: The Adaptive Toolbox,* edited by Gerd Gigerenzer and Reinhard Selten. Cambridge, Mass.: MIT Press.

Sen, Amartya K. 1977. "Rational Fools: A Critique of the Behavioral Foundations of Economic Theory." *Philosophy and Public Affairs* 6(4): 317–44.

———. 1995. "Rationality and Social Choice." *American Economic Review* 85(1): 1–24.

Sengupta, Nirmal. 1991. *Managing Common Property: Irrigation in India and the Philippines.* London: Sage.

Shepsle, Kenneth A., and Barry R. Weingast. 1984. "Legislative Politics and Budget Outcomes." In *Federal Budget Policy in the 1980s,* edited by Gregory Mills and John Palmer. Washington, D.C.: Urban Institute Press.

Simon, Herbert A. 1985. "Human Nature in Politics: The Dialogue of Psychology with Political Science." *American Political Science Review* 79(2): 293–304.

Smith, Vernon. 1979. "Incentive-Compatible Experimental Processes for the Provision of Public Goods." In *Research in Experimental Economics,* edited by Vernon Smith. Greenwich, Conn.: JAI Press.

———. 1980. "Experiments with a Decentralized Mechanism for Public Good Decisions." *American Economic Review* 70(4): 584–99.

Snidal, Duncan. 1985. "Coordination versus Prisoner's Dilemma: Implications for International Cooperation and Regimes." *American Political Science Review* 79(December): 923–42.

Thibaut, John W., and Harold H. Kelley. 1959. *The Social Psychology of Groups.* New York: Wiley.

Trivers, Robert L. 1971. "The Evolution of Reciprocal Altruism." *Quarterly Review of Biology* 46(March): 35–57.

van de Kragt, Alphons, Robyn M. Dawes, John M. Orbell, Sanford L. Braver, and L. A. Wilson. 1986. "Doing Well and Doing Good As Ways of Resolving Social Dilemmas." In *Experimental Social Dilemmas*, edited by Henk A. M. Wilke, David M. Messick, and Christel G. Rutte. Frankfurt am Main, Germany: Verlag Peter Lang.

van de Kragt, Alphons, John M. Orbell, and Robyn M. Dawes. 1983. "The Minimal Contributing Set As a Solution to Public Goods Problems." *American Political Science Review* 77(1): 112–22.

Walker, James, Roy Gardner, Andrew Herr, and Elinor Ostrom. 1997. "Voting on Allocation Rules in a Commons: Predictive Theories and Experimental Results." Paper presented at the 1997 annual meeting of the Western Political Science Association. Tucson, Arizona (March 13–15).

Walker, James, Roy Gardner, and Elinor Ostrom. 1990. "Rent Dissipation in a Limited-Access Common-Pool Resource: Experimental Evidence." *Journal of Environmental Economics and Management* 19(3): 203–11.

Williams, John T., Brian Collins, and Mark I. Lichbach. 1997. "The Origins of Credible Commitment to the Market." Revised version of paper presented at the annual meeting of the American Political Science Association. Chicago, Illinois (August 31–September 3, 1995).

Yamagishi, Toshio. 1986. "The Provision of a Sanctioning System As a Public Good." *Journal of Personality and Social Psychology* 51(1): 110–16.

———. 1988a. "Exit from the Group As an Individualistic Solution to the Free Rider Problem in the United States and Japan." *Journal of Experimental Social Psychology* 24(6): 530–42.

———. 1988b. "The Provision of a Sanctioning System in the United States and Japan." *Social Psychology Quarterly* 51(3): 265–71.

———. 1988c. "Seriousness of Social Dilemmas and the Provision of a Sanctioning System." *Social Psychology Quarterly* 51(1): 32–42.

———. 1992. "Group Size and the Provision of a Sanctioning System in a Social Dilemma." In *Social Dilemmas: Theoretical Issues and Research Findings*, edited by Wim G. B. Liebrand, David M. Messick, and Henk A. M. Wilke. Oxford: Pergamon Press.

Yamagishi, Toshio, and Karen S. Cook. 1993. "Generalized Exchange and Social Dilemmas." *Social Psychological Quarterly* 56(4): 235–48.

Yamagishi, Toshio, and Nobuyuki Takahashi. 1994. "Evolution of Norms Without Metanorms." In *Social Dilemmas and Cooperation*, edited by Ulrich Schulz, Wulf Albers, and Ulrich Mueller. Berlin, Germany: Springer-Verlag.

Yoder, Robert. 1994. *Locally Managed Irrigation Systems*. Colombo, Sri Lanka: International Irrigation Management Institute.

Chapter 3

Gaming Trust

RUSSELL HARDIN

A LONG-standing and substantial body of work addresses problems of cooperation under several labels, including *collective
action, prisoner's dilemma,* and *social dilemma.* Much of this
work has been experimental. The forms of the games in various experiments vary enormously, but most of them are prisoner's dilemmas involving two or more persons. The literature focuses on isolated interactions as well as on social contexts in which cooperative
(or uncooperative) play evolves over many interactions. Many of the
researchers conducting experimental work have recently shifted their
focus from explaining cooperation to modeling and measuring trust
(also see chapter 8, this volume). Although it would be wrong to say
that the presence of cooperation implies the presence of trust, it is
commonly assumed in much of this work that successful cooperation
indicates some degree of trust among the players. Recent efforts to
introduce extra elements into the games may serve to test not merely
for cooperation but also for trust.

Such work befits the widely held view that trust and distrust are
essentially rational. For example, James Coleman (1990, chapter 5) bases
his account of trust on complex rational expectations. Two central elements are applied in a *rational-choice* account of trust: incentives for
the trusted to fulfill the trust and knowledge to justify the truster's
trust. The second element is the truster's knowledge of the trusted's
incentives or reasons to be trustworthy. It is, of course, the knowledge
of the potential truster, not that of the theorist or social scientist who
observes or analyzes the trust that is at issue. Because my supposed
knowledge of you and your motivations can be mistaken, and because often your incentives might not lead you to cooperate with me

(you might have competing interests that trump your trust), I typically run some risk of losing if I act cooperatively toward you. For present purposes, I assume that knowledge problems are subsumed under such risk assessments and do not analyze them separately, although they play a significant role in the discussions throughout and especially in the discussion of thick relationships in which, by implication, knowledge of potential partners in trust is rich and probably manifold.

There are, of course, many uses of a term as attractive and seemingly good as trust. Some of these uses make it extrarational in some way. For example, in some accounts, trust is held to be founded in emotions or in moral commitments or dispositions (Hardin 2002, chapter 3; evolutionary accounts of such dispositions are discussed in chapters 4 and 5 of this volume). Many of these accounts seem likely to fit some instances of trust or—perhaps more often—of trustworthiness. Little or no experimental work on trust addresses such accounts of trust, although some of the survey and interview work on trust arguably does.

Apart from directly asking people whether they trust, as in surveys, almost all efforts to measure trust involve game experiments in some way. In such experiments the rationality of trusting or distrusting is sometimes de facto assumed. In standard game theory, the players are commonly assumed to be rational, although in experimental games actual players often make quite diverse choices even when they face identical incentives. Therefore, one might suppose either that the subjects make errors or that rationality is not determinately defined in contexts of interactive choice. I think the latter conclusion is correct, and indeed there is no acceptable determinate theory that stipulates a best choice or a best set of choices of strategy in games in general (see further, Hardin forthcoming). Rather, there are many ostensible theories.

In virtually all theories and accounts of trust, there is an element of expectations. Indeed, some accounts seemingly reduce trust to nothing more than expectations, as in such claims as "I trust that it will rain today," although the "it" that I trust has none of the features of a person whom I might trust (see, for example, Barber 1983; Gambetta 1988, 217–18; Dasgupta 1988). Typically, accounts that go further and assume the rationality of trusting are actually accounts of the trustworthiness of others insofar as their trustworthiness is grounded in incentives of some kind that depend on the truster. Hence we may say that rational accounts typically suppose that the truster assumes that the trusted will most likely prove to be trustworthy because it will be in the trusted's interest to act cooperatively with respect to the issues in trust. Nevertheless, the trusted is not guaranteed to be trustworthy, and thus there is some risk in acting on trust.

At least three standard elements are often stated, and two are often entailed by or implicit in the rational accounts of trust. First, the relationship involves a truster, a trusted, and some matter that is at stake in the trust, so that it is a three-part relation. Second, the trusted has some incentive to be trustworthy with respect to the matter at issue in the truster's trust. Third, this incentive might be trumped by other considerations, so that there is some risk of default by the trusted. The two often implicit elements are the claims that trust is cognitive and that it is not a primitive term. To say that trust is cognitive is to say that our trust in another is essentially a matter of relevant knowledge about that other—in particular, knowledge of reasons the other has to be trustworthy. To say that "trust" is not a primitive term means that it must be reducible to other terms, including the terms included in these standard elements. The game models that follow help us to determine what these other terms are.

A full statement of the rational theory, including the incentive and knowledge effects, is roughly as follows. First, you trust me if you have reason to believe it will be in my interest to be trustworthy in the relevant way at the relevant time. Your trust turns, however, not directly on my interests themselves but on whether your own interests are encapsulated in mine—that is, on whether I count your interests as partly my own interests *just because they are your interests* (in philosophers' jargon, I count your interests as my own qua your interests). I might encapsulate your interests in my own for various reasons. Among the most important socially is that I wish to maintain my ongoing relationship with you. I might also consider you my friend, or I might love you, and I might therefore actually take your interests as partly my own because I value you and your well-being sufficiently. Even if we do not directly have a relationship, I might to some extent encapsulate your interests in my own because I value my reputation in dealings with others. Because I encapsulate your interests in my own to some extent, I am likely to be trustworthy to some extent, and therefore you can trust me to that extent.

Not included here are instances in which our interests happen to coincide, so that though I do not take your interests into account I nevertheless act in ways that further your interests. For example, when I drive on the right side of the road in North America, I am not acting out of the interests of other drivers—whom I do not even know and with whom I may have no other relationship than that of having once been near them on a highway—but out of my own direct interests in not being harmed in an accident. In such a case, we may be said to have coincident interests, but we do not encapsulate each other's interest.

Some accounts do not specifically include reference to the trusted's interest in being trustworthy but merely require an expectation that the trusted will fulfill. Adequate reason for such an expectation, however, will typically turn on likely future incentives. My actions in relying or not relying on you will also most likely be tempered by past experience and reputational effects to a large extent, including your reputation for competence. If you never seem to understand the interest you have in future interactions, I will not take significant risks in trying to get you to cooperate.

Note that the encapsulated-interest account backs up a step from a bald expectations account to inquire into the reasons for the relevant expectations. The typical reason for the expectations is that the relationship is ongoing in some important sense. There are two especially important contexts for trust: ongoing or even iterated dyadic relationships and ongoing—or thick—group or societal relationships. The two classes are closely related, and both are subsumed in the encapsulated-interest theory of trust.

These kinds of interaction—dyadic and group—pose incentives to the trusted that are of increasing complexity. The sanction that motivates the trusted person in the one-way trust interaction, if it is to be iterated, is the prospect of future gains from the interaction. The sanction that motivates both parties in the mutual-trust exchange interaction is withdrawal of the other party from a potentially beneficial interaction. The sanction in thick relationships can be withdrawal from the dyadic interaction as well as shunning from the whole community of those who share in the thick relationships, shunning that can be so severe as to exclude one from the community altogether (Cook and Hardin 2001).

Trustworthiness

Any cognitive theory of trust, including but not only the encapsulated-interest theory, makes trust depend on assessments of the trustworthiness of another in the relevant circumstances. If I have reason to think you will be trustworthy, then I trust you. Hence to account for trust we first need an account of trustworthiness. There are two modal conceptions of why one would be trustworthy in a particular context (I take this last phrase for granted hereafter). You may be trustworthy for essentially rational reasons related to your interests or for normative reasons. That is to say, trustworthiness may be incentive based or normatively based.

Your trustworthiness is incentive based if you encapsulate my interests in your own to some extent because, for example, you value the continuance of our relationship, as would be typical of people who are involved in iterated exchange interactions. It is normatively based if you react to my taking a risk on cooperating with you by playing fair with me, being altruistic, or being morally motivated in some other way—perhaps because you have a moral disposition generally to be trustworthy (as in the sometime view of Toshio Yamagishi [chapter 13, this volume] and in the early work of Julian Rotter [1980]). You might be trustworthy for normative reasons even in a context in which we are unlikely ever to meet again. In addition, there is a complex category that might be seen as a mixture of both of these: shared interests. In this complex case, you may share my interests because you love me or you are my close friend and you genuinely encapsulate my interests in yours to some extent.

Trustworthiness that is normative or that is based in such strong shared interests is not at issue in the game experiments reported in this volume. This is not to say that there are no choices that are driven by normative commitments but only that, in the experiments as run, the normative commitments of the potentially trusted person are not at issue when the first player decides whether to be cooperative. Yet these commitments are specifically what defines standard normative accounts of trust, in which the normatively motivated trustworthiness of some people is used to explain the trust that others have in them. The standard theories of trust that make trust depend on the normative commitments of the trusted cannot be tested by experimental games that are played in ignorance of who the other player is. That is the way the experiments typically reported in this volume and the vast bulk of experiments on the one-way trust game are played. The standard theories require a specific judgment of whether the other person is trustworthy. In the standard normative theories of trust, I trust you because, for example, I think you have a moral commitment to being trustworthy or I think you follow a norm of reciprocity. The first mover in a one-shot, one-way trust game with no information on the other player cannot judge that the other player has such a normative commitment or follows such a norm.

Incidentally, the standard normative theories are not related to the commonplace notion of generalized trust, in which I supposedly trust all persons when I first interact with them (see Hardin 2002, chapter 3). Apart from its incoherence for anyone other than a naïf, such a view does not fit the normative theories of trustworthiness, which suppose that I trust those who I think have the relevant commitment to trustworthiness but not those who I think lack such commitment.

The protocols for many experimental games are explicitly intended to block giving the first mover any information about the possible motivations of the second player. In real-world contexts, such devices as reading another's face or actions in another context might give us information about a potential second mover and lead us to presume that that person has a moral commitment or is likely to follow a norm of reciprocity, as in the account of social intelligence presented by Toshio Yamagishi and Riki Kakiuchi (2000) or the reading of faces (chapter 9, this volume). Even in the highly restrictive conditions of the games generally reported here, the second player does have one piece of information about the first player—whether the first player previously acted cooperatively. The second player therefore could act from a normative commitment or norm of reciprocity in response to the first player's action (see chapters 2 and 12, this volume). Your following a norm of reciprocity makes you relatively trustworthy to those who know you follow such a norm. Richer debriefing of subjects in these games might suggest that they are normatively motivated in various ways, but the mere payoff structure of the games and the bald choices cannot tell us why a second player cooperates.

In the current literature on trust, the only view that could bring normative commitments into the first player's decision in a one-shot, one-way trust game is the view that trusting is itself morally required. Almost no one argues for this view (the chief exception is Hertzberg 1988; see further, Hardin 2002, chapter 3). Indeed, this view cannot generally be correct because, for example, it would be immoral and harmful to trust anyone and everyone to baby-sit for one's infant. Trust therefore cannot be strictly moral or morally required. In general, almost all the standard theories of trust, whether incentive based or normatively based, are inherently theories of trustworthiness, a quality that can be morally determined, as it clearly is in some cases.

Mutual Trust

Let us begin with mutual trust, which is game theoretically more complex than one-way trust, but which is better suited to establishing the role of trust in a dyadic relationship. Perhaps the prototypical case of mutual trust at the individual level involves an interaction that is part of a long sequence of exchanges between the same parties. Each exchange is simply the resolution of a prisoner's dilemma (Hardin 1982). A sequence of exchanges is therefore an iterated prisoner's dilemma with, perhaps, some variation in the stakes at each exchange. It is not likely, in real life, to be a game of simultaneous moves; most often it is one of sequential moves, in which you take the risk of doing something for me today in the expectation that I will reciprocate in some way tomorrow. The main incentive that one faces in a particular exchange in which one is trusted by the other is the potential benefit from continuing the series of interactions. The sanction each of us can invoke against the other is to withdraw from

Figure 3.1   Prisoner's Dilemma or Exchange

		Column	
		Cooperate	Defect
Row	Cooperate	20,20	−25,40
	Defect	40,−25	0,0

Source: Author's configuration.

further interaction. In some contexts, this is a substantial sanction because there might be no suitable alternative party for future interactions.

Although this model of mutual trust as based in iterated exchange is not a definition of trust, it is an explanation of much of the trust we experience or see, much of which is reciprocal and is grounded in ongoing relationships. A more limited claim, however, appears to be true: ongoing dyadic relationships of trust typically involve and are often definitive of mutual trust.

Ordinary exchange can be represented as a prisoner's dilemma game, as illustrated in game 1 (figure 3.1). In each cell of the matrix, the first payoff goes to the row player and the second to the column player (in the mnemonic Roman Catholic [R,C] convention). Hence the top left cell (20,20) of the game gives both players their second-best outcomes, which are an improvement over their status quo outcomes (0,0) resulting from mutual failure to cooperate.

Typically, prisoner's dilemma experiments can conclude only that players do or do not cooperate under varied conditions. They cannot directly tell us what the players' motivations are. In particular, they cannot tell us that players trust or distrust each other. Yamagishi and Kakiuchi (2000) and others introduce a move before the play of the prisoner's dilemma. In that prior move, one or both players can alter the stakes of the game, thus increasing the potential winnings from cooperation but also increasing the potential losses from defection. If a player increases the stakes, we might suppose that he or she expresses some degree of trust in the other player by doing so. This is a clever innovation that increases the range of behavior we have to analyze and that may, indeed, commonly reveal degrees of trust. As discussed in the concluding remarks, however, we cannot finally be sure what motivations are at stake in the playing of experimental games.

When set in their strategic structures, several types of behavior often explained as inherently moral can be clearly understood as self-interested (or, in some cases, as overdetermined by both interest and moral commitments). Promise keeping, honesty, and fidelity to others often make sense without any presupposition of a distinctively moral commitment beyond interest. Consider promise keeping, which has been the subject of hundreds of articles and books in moral theory during the past century. David Hume has said, without seeming to think that his statement requires much defense, that the first obligation to keep a promise is interest (Hume 1978 [1739–40], 523). The claim is obviously true for typical promises between close associates who have an ongoing relationship that they want to maintain. If I promise to return your book, I will be encouraged to do so by my desire to have frequent contact with you and to make other exchanges with you. If I generally fail to keep such promises, I can probably expect not to enjoy as many exchanges and reciprocal favors. Promising relationships typically are those in which exchanges are reciprocated over time. Because exchanges are resolutions of prisoner's dilemma problems, promising relationships involving exchange have the incentive structure of the iterated prisoner's dilemma.[1]

The force that generally backs exchange promises is the loss of credibility that follows from breaking them. Without credibility, one loses the possibility of making promises. Why should anyone want the power to make promises? All I really want in my own interest is the power to receive promises. And there's the rub, because promises are generally part of a reciprocal exchange. The real penalty here is not that others will no longer rely on me but that they will not let me rely on them. As is commonly true also of trust relationships, promising typically involves intentions on the parts of two (or more) people.

Coleman implicitly includes the trusted's incentives when he notes that a reciprocal trusting relationship, as in mutual trust in the iterated prisoner's dilemma, is mutually reinforcing for each truster (Coleman 1990, 177–80). Why? Because each person now has an additional incentive to be trustworthy—namely, to give the other person an incentive to be trustworthy. I trust you because it is in your interest to do what I trust you to do. It is in your interest primarily because you want me to continue to be both trusting and trustworthy.

One-Way Trust

In game 2, one-way trust (figure 3.2), the truster must act as though she trusts the trusted—that is, the truster must cooperate—in order

Figure 3.2   One-Way Trust

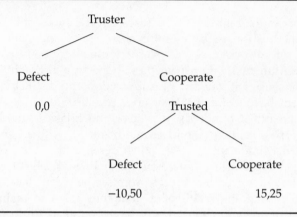

Source: Author's configuration.

to gain from their interaction. Her defection simply entails that there is no interaction, no risk, and no gain. If she acts as though she trusts the trusted, the trusted need then only act in his own interest. It is only the truster whose actions might depend on trusting. The trusted's action does not involve any risk. Hence the trust is genuinely one way. In the game, the truster makes the first move of defecting or cooperating. If she does not choose to take the risk of cooperating, the game ends with payoffs of nothing to both parties. If she takes the risk, then there is a next stage in which the trusted chooses whether to defect or cooperate, with defection being substantially more beneficial than cooperation. The play of the game ends with his choice.

If this game is played anonymously and once only, clearly the trusted's interest is to cheat, and the truster's interest is, therefore, not to risk the initial cooperation. Actual experiments in this game, however, show that many subjects in the role of truster make the risky cooperative move and that many subjects in the role of trusted reciprocate, in a sense, by playing cooperatively and taking a smaller gain than they could guarantee themselves by making a different move (see chapter 10, this volume). If the parties are able to play the game repeatedly, their interests change dramatically, because both can do very well over many plays of the game. If the game is iterated, therefore, it turns into a game that is nearly the mutual-trust game of the iterated prisoner's dilemma discussed earlier.

Note, incidentally, that the one-way trust game of figure 3.2 is a three-part relation. The truster takes a risk on the trusted with respect to a difference of $25 in the payoffs to the truster. We could make an

Figure 3.3   One-Way Trust with High Stakes

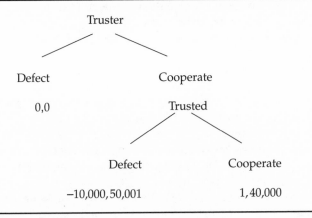

Truster

Defect   Cooperate

0,0   Trusted

Defect   Cooperate

−10,000,50,001   1,40,000

Source: Author's configuration.

analogous claim for the general trust game with whatever parties and stakes. Of course, in a one-way trust game with radically higher stakes, the truster might plausibly decide not to take a risk on the trusted, even though she would take the risk with the stakes at $25. For example, if the final stakes (in the lower left and right outcomes) were (−$10,000, $50,001) and ($1, $40,000), as in game 3 (figure 3.3), we might expect the truster not to take the potentially huge risk of losing $10,000 for the chance of a gain of merely $1.

It is a great strength of the experimental protocol for the one-way trust game that it virtually forces us to be very clear about what is at issue. For example, it is difficult to imagine a reduced analog of the one-way trust game that would represent only a two-part relation unless it allowed the payoffs to be merely ordinal and completely open ended. In such a case, the relevant player would be unable to choose to cooperate at the first move because the loss, if the other party chose to take the noncooperative payoff, could be catastrophic; it could be analogous to the (−$10,000, $50,001) versus ($1, $40,000) outcomes. The potential for a $1 gain is far too trivial to risk even a moderate probability of a $10,000 loss. Players who understood such a game could not, if their own resources were at stake, seriously claim to think it smart to cooperate at the first move. Normally, iteration of a prisoner's dilemma or of a one-way trust game with the same partner might be expected to increase the level of cooperativeness. Even if game 3 were iterated many times, however, it seems unlikely that first movers would take the risk of losing so much for the prospect of so small a gain. After all, it would take ten thousand successful plays of the game to cover the loss incurred in a single unsuccessful play.

The one-way trust game is in a sense only half of many common-place trust relations. In a mutual-trust interaction, for example, both parties are at risk; both might trust or not trust; and both might be trustworthy or untrustworthy. In an ongoing mutual exchange relationship, you and I might both be in a position on occasion to cheat each other. Neither of us would have the restricted role of the truster in game 2, who can take a risk or not but who cannot act on the misplaced trust of the trusted: in that game, the trusted's action does not depend on trust or involve a significant risk.

Unlike the findings of experiments using these games, survey results, such as those on so-called generalized trust, can be based on questions that are vague and even glib and can therefore confuse what is at issue. It is not the respondents to such surveys who are responsible for the glibness, it is the surveyors. For example, the most direct question about trust in the long-running General Social Survey, conducted by the National Opinion Research Center (NORC), is this: "Generally speaking, would you say that most people can be trusted, or that you cannot be too careful dealing with people?" This question appears to make trust a two-part relation. But surely if the payoffs were stipulated as those in the game of one-way trust with high stakes in game 3, the frequency of positive responses would fall radically. Hence respondents take the survey question as elliptical, and they give elliptical answers. Anyone who responds to a question this vague must implicitly restrict its scope to a less significant range of possibilities than those given in game 3. One of the beauties of the experimental paradigm, as represented by many contributions to this volume, is that it imposes sharpness. An experimental protocol for trust must specify players (at least two) and payoffs. Hence it virtually requires that trust be treated as a three-part relation.

The survey question is sometimes taken to describe a two-part relation in another sense. It is supposed that the question stipulates only one party, as if to say I trust virtually everyone or at least certain general categories of people (all Americans, all blacks, all women, all children). The question must be taken as elliptical and incomplete, however, in this sense as well. If we fill in categories and further stipulate characteristics of the individuals in the categories, we must surely again find that respondents differentiate their responses accordingly, perhaps to a very articulate extent. Typically, experiments with the one-way trust game similarly also leave open who the second party is, because players usually do not know who their "partners" are. They do presumably suspect that these partners are others much like themselves, however, so that they are playing against someone from a fairly specific category.

Consider two variations on the one-way trust game: with iteration

Figure 3.4   One-Way Trust with Punishment Option

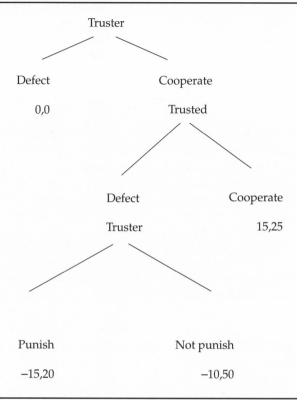

Truster

Defect   Cooperate

0,0   Trusted

Defect   Cooperate

Truster   15,25

Punish   Not punish

−15,20   −10,50

Source: Author's configuration.

and with punishment (figure 3.4). The one-way trust game, when repeated, has some of the quality of the iterated prisoner's dilemma
and therefore of mutual trust. It is not a prisoner's dilemma, however,
because there is no outcome that is best for the truster and simultaneously worst for the trusted. The worst outcome for the trusted in
any given play of the game is analogous to the noncooperation outcome (0,0) in which, in essence, the truster prefers not to risk playing.
If the trusted is the column player, the equivalent of the lower-left cell
payoff (40,−25) of the prisoner's dilemma of game 1 is not possible.
However, there must be some degree of mutual trust if they are to
continue playing because each time he cooperates the trusted must
take a risk that the truster will not continue to make a cooperative
choice at the next play of the game. This is potentially a significant
risk if the payoffs at stake are substantial.

In a punishment variant of the one-way trust game, the first mover
has a chance to make a further choice after the second mover has

defected, as in game 4 (but not if the second mover has cooperated). By choosing the payoff (−15,20), the first mover can punish the second mover for defection. The first mover must bear a cost for the move to punish, and yet many subjects in one-way trust games accept that cost in order to punish the second mover for defection. If there is a second round of play, but with different partners, the availability of the punishment option increases or at least maintains the level of cooperation in the second round. This result follows even though the first mover de facto provides a collective good to the group of first movers on the second round, a collective good from which the first mover does not benefit (see chapter 10, this volume). When there is no punishment available, cooperativeness unravels in repeated play.

In a sense, these two variations introduce more context into the play of the bare one-way trust game. The most important variant of that game would be to introduce still more social context (as in the discussion of the thick-relationships model of trust in the following section). In the general social phenomenon of trust, much of the story is in the larger social context that provides knowledge of others and gives them incentives to behave in trustworthy ways. These are two of the central elements in most theories of trust, especially including the rational accounts, such as the encapsulated-interest theory, and the normative theories. The bulk of all trust relationships may be in ongoing, even thick, relationships.

Thick Relationships

Although the one-way trust game modeled in game 2 represents some real-world instances of choice problems,[2] it does not include all the relevant payoffs in a typical field setting, as contrasted to an experimental setting. For example, so long as she has resources and relationships in the larger community, the truster might be able to inflict eventual costs on the trusted. Almost all real-life games are embedded in a richer array of interactions that influence individuals' decisions. The actual motivations I face in interactions with others are likely to be more clearly self-interested when the effects of reputation, other third-party interactions, and iteration are brought into focus, as they typically must be in real-world contexts. Laboratory experiments are commonly intended to abstract from these and other societal contextual effects. That gives them some of their clarity and resultant power.

It is commonly noted that familiarity and trust are linked. Indeed, as a Tallensi proverb notes, "Familiarity is better than kinship" (quoted in Hart 1988, 186). Why should this be? First, consider the benefits of familiarity. Familiarity with another entails two things. It gives us knowledge about the other—in particular, about the other's trustworthiness (of course, this means that it can give us the knowledge that another is untrustworthy). In addition, it often derives from a relationship that gives the other person incentives to be trustworthy. These are elements that make for rational trust, especially in the encapsulated-interest model.

Now consider the costs of kinship. As Keith Hart notes, "Kinsmen make poor borrowers because they equate their interests with those of the lender" (Hart 1988, 190). Therefore, he says, pretension of familiarity is the normal rhetoric of economic life in the markets of Accra that he studied.

This Tallensi proverb's bit of pragmatic wisdom is merely a more narrowly circumscribed version of trust as encapsulated interest. It implicitly adds to the latter an epistemological assumption that people cannot know enough about their potential partners to trust anyone outside of very close—familiar—communities, which typically generate a lot of knowledge and a number of incentives relevant to trusting someone. I may know my relatives, close friends, and a small number of co-workers and others I regularly deal with well enough to know the limits of their trustworthiness. Among these people I therefore know whom I can trust for what (if my relatives are like Tallensi kin, however, I may be chary of entrusting them with any great stakes).

This can be called the thick-relationships theory of trust. It is a theory in the sense that it gives an explanation of trust. In our community, for example, everyone is involved in ongoing relationships with virtually everyone else. I can expect you to be trustworthy toward me not only because you value further interaction with me but also because you value your reputation, which secures the possibility of continued cooperative interaction with others in our community.

The thick-relationships theory can be illustrated by discussion of trusting political leaders, with whom we generally do not have thick relationships. The philosopher Bernard Williams (1988) views the issue of my trusting political leaders as though it were an exact analog of the more familiar problem of my trusting a close associate. On the thick-relationships theory, because I cannot plausibly know enough about typical political leaders or have enough reciprocal relationships with them to trust them, I do not; hence trust cannot handle these relationships in general (Luhmann 1980). This conclusion is partly misleading. Williams's argument for why trust arises in this context is essentially an account from encapsulated interest, but the latter applies far more generally to contexts other than thick relationships. The conclusion is, however, often correct empirically as a prediction of conditions under which we will find trust.

What I can know reasonably well is that the incentives faced by someone in political office are in the right direction. With respect to my close relations, I may think their incentives are to give various supports to me in particular, and so I can trust them for that reason. The political officeholder might have no particular interest in me, need not even know about me, but may have a strong interest in supporting people in my position in relevant ways. On Williams's account, as well as Geoffrey Hawthorn's (1988) and sometimes Niklas Luhmann's (1980), it is merely a matter of the logic of large numbers and the impossibility of thick relationships with many people that political leaders cannot be trusted. Luhmann says trust is vital in personal relations, but participation in functional systems such as the economy or politics is not a matter of personal relations. It requires confidence but not trust (Luhmann 1980, 22, 30; 1988, 102).

Against the view of Williams, Hawthorn, Luhmann at times, perhaps the anthropologist F. G. Bailey (1988), and others, the role of thick relationships is correctly seen as one possible source of knowledge for the truster about the trustworthiness of another and one possible source of incentives for the trusted to be trustworthy. The first of these is essentially an epistemological role. Obviously, thick relationships yield only a part of the knowledge we have of others; they are merely one among many possible epistemological considerations. Therefore, our understanding should not stop with only the thick-relationships class of epistemological considerations. In practice, this class may often have priority among our sources in our face-to-face interactions, though this descriptive fact does not give it conceptual or theoretical priority. A fully articulated theory will include this class as a part, not as the whole story, of the epistemology of trust. There is unlikely to be any quarrel with the view that knowledge of another's trustworthiness can come from many sources other than thick relationships.

Similarly, a thick relationship with another is only one of many possible ways to give that other the incentive to be trustworthy—for example, in the encapsulated-interest sense of my taking your interests into account because they are your interests. A thick relationship with the truster commonly gives the trusted such incentives through the workings of an iterated prisoner's dilemma of reciprocal cooperation, and this must be an important effect on trustworthiness among familiar relations (Hardin 1991, 2002). One may also have incentive to attend to reputational effects, institutional rewards and sanctions, other third-party effects (Coleman 1990, 180–85), and other considerations. In sum, if there is a general incentive-to-be-trustworthy theory of trust, the thick-relationships theory must be merely a special case of it, a partial theory that cannot be generalized to some contexts. The conditions that lie behind the model are much more general than merely thick relationships. Indeed, the thick-relationships theory is wholly subsumed by the encapsulated-interest theory.

Related to the thick-relationships theory of trust is the quick blurring of individual and institutional problems, which is one of the most common mistakes in all of the writing on trust. It may be more common in the writings of philosophers, least in those of sociologists. Writers in all disciplines, however, occasionally succumb to the easy analogy from individual to institutional issues that abstracts from the institutional constraints. If our theory of trust states simply that trust is grounded in thick relationships, then the conclusion that trust cannot be generalized beyond the small scale follows by definition.

For other theories, it may be easy to see how individual- and institutional-level trust are conceptually related through the same causal mechanism that might work in somewhat different ways in small- and large-scale contexts. For example, the encapsulated-interest theory requires a mechanism by which I come to encapsulate your interests in my own. Earlier, I mentioned three common mechanisms: we are in an ongoing relationship that I want to maintain because it is valuable to me; I love you or consider you my friend; or I value my general reputation, which could be harmed if I am untrustworthy in my dealings with you. The third of these sounds similar to the thick-relationships theory, but it can apply in a much larger array of contexts, including those in which only my reputation with respect to some well defined matter is at issue, not my very general but strictly local reputation for cooperativeness in our small community. Even large corporations and other institutions can sensibly have a concern with their reputations for fair dealing and can therefore sometimes be seen as trustworthy (Dasgupta 1988).

The second of these mechanisms—the trusted's love or friendship for another—is, in general, unlikely to account for institutional-level trustworthiness. A recent president may have said he felt our pain, but we could sensibly doubt that his feelings were specific to us. Different kinds of data or evidence might go into explanations using this theory when it is applied at different levels.

In any theory, the restriction to small-scale thick relationships must follow from other—causal—principles. Going back to those principles is a first step in generalizing the theory. In the theory of Williams (1988), there is a causal reason—iterated interactions—that trust works in thick relationships, and that reason can be seen to apply sometimes in other contexts, such as in urban networks that do not involve the thick relationships of a small community (Cook and Hardin 2001).

Concluding Remarks

Many of the experimental results from trust games show that subjects play them cooperatively even when they are not to be iterated. Hence first movers in the one-way trust game behave cooperatively in the sense of choosing to put themselves at the mercy of the second mover, who could simply choose the (–10,50) outcome in game 2. In one experiment in which the game is played a second time against a different "partner," the rate of risk taking falls significantly, with twice as many first movers choosing to terminate play at the beginning of the first round (chapter 10, this volume). There is no clearly rational account of why first movers should take that initial risk unless, contrary to the experimental protocol, they think that the odds are in favor of their getting a positive payoff (better than the zero payoff they would get from not taking the risk). There is also no clearly rational account of why the second movers often choose the (15,25) outcome when they could do significantly better by defecting and selecting the (–10,50) outcome. When the game is played a second time against a different "partner," the second movers who are offered the chance to cooperate are more likely to defect. Finally, there is also no clearly rational account of why, when they are given the option of punishing the defection of second movers, as in game 4, first movers do so even at cost to themselves.

It is implausible to say that all of these behaviors are motivated by trust as encapsulated interest, and it is also difficult to say that they are motivated by trust in any other sense. For the cooperative first movers, there appears to be either strong normative motivation or, perhaps, a failure to grasp the strategic logic of the payoff structures. The latter possibility is suggested by the fact that, in a second round with changed partners, the level of cooperative play declines substantially, as if to imply that subjects have learned something in their previous play. Of course, they may merely be Bayesian learners who have learned that others are less likely to be trustworthy than they at first assumed. Second movers who make the cooperative choice might be trustworthy in some moral sense; for example, they might be motivated by fairness or honor.

There is a standard argument about the iterated prisoner's dilemma that might be thought to apply immediately to the one-way trust game. By *backward induction* from what it would be rational to do on the final play of a series of prisoner's dilemmas, it is thought by some to be rational to defect on every play. So long as the losses at stake do not threaten bankruptcy and the potential gains are not radically smaller than the potential losses, as they are in game 3 (which is not a prisoner's dilemma), I think this result is simply wrong for the ordinary prisoner's dilemma (see Hardin forthcoming, chapter 2). For the two-move one-way trust game, however, it is relatively compelling. If I assume that, as second mover, your only motivation is your own interest, then I must suppose you will defect if I give you the opportunity to take the second move. Hence it is clearly in my interest in either game 2 or game 3 to defect at the outset to block you from imposing such costs on me. Suppose I understand all of this. Then, if I make the cooperative choice as first mover, it must therefore be true that I suppose you will not act merely from your own interest when you make the second move.

Cooperative play might be motivated by reasons other than trust in the encapsulated-interest or normative accounts. You might act as though you trust me in order to demonstrate to me that you have faith in my morality or character or to give me an opportunity to live up to your hopes even though I may have no incentive to reciprocate your action. Or you may wish not to be the kind of person who acts toward another with distrust that is not based on solid evidence. Such motivations are apt to lead to disappointment in many contexts, but they might be statistically justified in certain milieus. In particular, they might be justified in contexts in which there are rich possibilities of further interactions. In such contexts, however, interest is likely to conspire with your hopes in getting me to reciprocate. One-shot games lack any such context.

Suppose you understand the one-way trust game of game 2 very well and you make the cooperative choice as first mover. We might suppose you act from a relatively generalized trust in the sense that it is not grounded in any relationship that you and I have. Indeed, as the games are typically played in the laboratory, you would not even know my identity or anything else about me, although you might reasonably suppose that I am, for example, another student roughly like yourself. In a one-shot play of the game, you know that I, as the second mover, can choose either to cooperate or to defect at no risk of retaliation from you. I therefore cannot act from an incentive grounded in our relationship. Hence in cooperating on the first move you are offering me a substantial benefit in the hope and maybe even the expectation that I will reciprocate in making the cooperative choice as second mover. If we wish to say that you "trust" in this case, then we must suppose that you trust, for reasons of your expectations, that I will be trustworthy for normative, not self-interest, reasons. More specifically, we must suppose that you judge the general type of person I am likely to be to be trustworthy in that way.

In any one-shot play of any game, such as the one-way trust game, it is not possible to test for trust as encapsulated interest because such trust requires some further relationship between the truster and the trusted. This experimental paradigm therefore rules out a standard form that trust relationships in ordinary life take. This is, of course, a problem of one-shot games that are abstracted from any social context. More generally, the paradigm also rules out testing any theory in which trust depends on an assessment of the potentially trusted person. Such theories presume that we can somehow judge who is and who is not likely to be trustworthy. In a one-shot game with an unknown other, it is impossible that I could be choosing on the basis of any such assessment of the other player. As these games are played, there is no way for the players who, as first movers, are potential trusters to assess the trustworthiness of their partners in the game.

In addition, such games cannot tell us whether a player is trustworthy or takes a risk on the other player out of normative commitments of some kind. The only way to judge the choices of the players as normative is to debrief them and ask leading questions to see what might have motivated them. The mere accounting of the experimental results cannot address this question. One might suppose that many players act from a strong norm of reciprocity, but the mere data on choices in one-shot games cannot tell us this. There are many possible alternative explanations of the behavior, including the player error posited by Kevin McCabe and Vernon Smith. The truth here is that first-mover cooperation in one-shot games is a mystery.

Despite their clarity in many respects, the game representations of various interactions do not unambiguously tell us about trust. The broad range of potential reasons for players' choices is not narrowed to trust, self-interest, normative commitments, or any other motivation. When debriefed after participating in one-way trust game experiments, subjects commonly speak of trust and of the other players as partners. We do not generally know, however, the vernacular implications of these terms. On the evidence of my having asked dozens of people from diverse backgrounds, the vernacular meanings of trust are quite varied. Of course, one might argue that people are often lousy at giving definitions of terms that they nevertheless use very well and in apt contexts. Still, for trust we may go further and say that many people quite clearly mean different things. The variety of academic views of what trust must be is astonishing (see Hardin 2002), although one might expect the philosophical and social scientific literatures to give more and odder meanings than ordinary people give. Academic life, after all, rewards inventiveness. Ordinary people seem less readily inclined to invent meanings—unless, perhaps, to cover the embarrassment of not knowing.

Can we say anything definitively? Perhaps only this: In a one-time play of game 2 between strangers who will not knowingly have any further interactions nor even ever be able to identify each other, it is easy to say what choice maximizes the second mover's payoff: defection. For players who defect at this point we can say that interests have almost surely trumped any other considerations that might have motivated them. This is the only nearly crystal-clear claim we can make about the meaning of any choices in all of these games, although we can probably also clearly say that in the game of one-way trust with high stakes (game 3), it is irrational for the first mover to cooperate if his or her own interests are the only consideration. To my knowledge, no one has had the temerity to inflict an analog of game 3 on real people, so that the claim here is speculative. (One might draw a clear analogy to prisoner's dilemma experiments for cases in which the payoff for cooperating when the other player defects—the so-called sucker's payoff—is extremely bad relative to the payoff from mutual cooperation or mutual defection. In such games, players need not be very risk averse to choose not to cooperate, and typically they do not cooperate.)

A cooperative move by the first mover is still likely to be irrational even if other motivations might be heavily in play. We can only say that these other motivations are easily trumped by self-interest when the game is played at such dramatic stakes, not that they are absent or even weak. Indeed, they might be quite strong, but a first mover with strong normative motivations might still quail in the face of the possibility of a $10,000 loss as the risk for obtaining a trivial $1 gain.

Experimental results show that many players in the position of the second mover of game 2 do not make the individually maximizing choice. The chief reason must be that there is a substantial residue beyond self-interest. Such a residue plays a lesser role in a mutual-trust interaction, in which self-interest is itself likely to be adequate to motivate the players. Some of the confusion over what trust is and, more generally, over what motivates individual choice in varied strategic contexts is played out in these experimental games. By implication, social science is still relatively far from measuring trust experimentally in any definitive or even clear way.

If the experiments on trust are to yield measures of trust as encapsulated interest or any other standard conception of trust, they will have to include more of the social context in the models. For the encapsulated-interest view, they will have to include some analog of the social context that gives people the incentives they normally have to be trustworthy. The experiments reported in this volume are generally too spare to give or to tap any such incentives. Indeed, none of the results presented here allow a test for the thick-relationships view of trust; most of the experiments could accurately be called models of very thin relationships—that is, no relationship at all beyond the immediate interaction. To test the encapsulated-interest or thick-relationships theories requires more context—at a minimum it requires iteration.

To test views that trust depends on an assessment of the character or moral commitments of the trusted, the experiments will have to allow some assessment of these. Playing games completely in ignorance of who the other player is cannot tap motivations grounded specifically in the character of the other. The design of many of the experiments reported in this volume precludes testing any of the standard theories, either interest based or normative, of why people trust. All of the standard theories are grounded in the truster's knowledge or judgment of the motivations, character, or commitments of the trusted, and many of these experiments specifically exclude such knowledge for the first movers. If the standard theories are compelling, what is needed is a trustworthiness game rather than the trust game. Iterated prisoner's dilemmas or iterated versions of the trust game provide de facto tests of the encapsulated-interest theory. Debriefing seems, to date, the only way experimenters have found to assess normative accounts.

Finally, repetition (not strictly iteration in many of these experiments, because it is not repetition with the same partners) of play in some of the experiments suggests that subjects fairly quickly learn or try to figure out what is at issue, so that first plays may tell us little about trust, trustworthiness, self-interest, or any other motivation. Rather, they may chiefly tell us that many subjects do not immediately understand the problems of strategic interaction and cooperation, as modeled by the games.

Notes

1. For more extensive discussion of the strategic variety of promising, see Hardin (1988, 41–44, 59–65). In addition to exchange promises, there can be coordination and gratuitous promises.

2. As is suggested by the example of Trifonov and the Lt. Colonel in Dostoyevsky's (1982 [1880]) novel, *The Brothers Karamazov*, who play out such a game over some years. This example is discussed in Hardin (1991 and 2002).

References

Bailey, Frederick G. 1988. "The Creation of Trust." In *Humbuggery and Manipulation*, by Frederick G. Bailey. Ithaca, N.Y.: Cornell University Press.
Barber, Bernard. 1983. *The Logic and Limits of Trust*. New Brunswick, N.J.: Rutgers University Press.

Coleman, James S. 1990. *Foundations of Social Theory*. Cambridge, Mass.: Harvard University Press.

Cook, Karen S., and Russell Hardin. 2001. "Networks, Norms, and Trustworthiness." In *Social Norms*, edited by Michael Hechter and Karl-Dieter Opp. New York: Russell Sage Foundation.

Dasgupta, Partha. 1988. "Trust As a Commodity." In *Trust: Making and Breaking Cooperative Relations*, edited by Diego Gambetta. Oxford: Blackwell.

Dostoyevsky, Fyodor. 1982 [1880]. *The Brothers Karamazov*, translated by David Magarshack. London: Penguin.

Gambetta, Diego. 1988. "Can We Trust Trust?" In *Trust: Making and Breaking Cooperative Relations*, edited by Diego Gambetta. Oxford: Blackwell.

Hardin, Russell. 1982. "Exchange Theory on Strategic Bases." *Social Science Information* 21(2): 251–72.

———. 1988. *Morality Within the Limits of Reason*. Chicago: University of Chicago Press.

———. 1991. "Trusting Persons, Trusting Institutions." In *The Strategy of Choice*, edited by Richard Zeckhauser. Cambridge, Mass.: MIT Press.

———. 2002. *Trust and Trustworthiness*. New York: Russell Sage Foundation.

———. Forthcoming. *Indeterminacy and Society*. Princeton, N.J.: Princeton University Press.

Hart, Keith. 1988. "Kinship, Contract, and Trust: Economic Organization of Migrants in an African City Slum." In *Trust: Making and Breaking Cooperative Relations*, edited by Diego Gambetta. Oxford: Blackwell.

Hawthorn, Geoffrey. 1988. "Three Ironies in Trust." In *Trust: Making and Breaking Cooperative Relations*, edited by Diego Gambetta. Oxford: Blackwell.

Hertzberg, Lars. 1988. "On the Attitude of Trust." *Inquiry* 31(3): 307–22.

Hume, David. 1978 [1739–40]. *A Treatise of Human Nature*, edited by L. A. Selby-Bigge and P. H. Nidditch. Oxford: Oxford University Press.

Luhmann, Niklas. 1980. *Trust: A Mechanism for the Reduction of Social Complexity*. In *Trust and Power*, by Niklas Luhmann. New York: Wiley.

———. 1988. "Familiarity, Confidence, Trust: Problems and Alternatives." In *Trust: Making and Breaking Cooperative Relations*, edited by Diego Gambetta. Oxford: Blackwell.

Rotter, Julian B. 1980. "Interpersonal Trust, Trustworthiness, and Gullibility." *American Psychologist* 35(1): 1–7.

Williams, Bernard. 1988. "Formal Structures and Social Reality." In *Trust: Making and Breaking Cooperative Relations*, edited by Diego Gambetta. Oxford: Blackwell.

Yamagishi, Toshio, and Riki Kakiuchi. 2000. "It Takes Venturing into a Tiger's Cave to Steal a Baby Tiger: Experiments on the Development of Trust Relationships." In *The Management of Durable Relations*, edited by Werner Raub and Jeroen Weesie. Amsterdam, Netherlands: Thela Thesis Publishers.

PART II

BIOLOGICAL FOUNDATIONS OF TRUST AND RECIPROCITY

Chapter 4

Biological Foundations of Reciprocity

ROBERT KURZBAN

F OR THE past several decades, biologists have struggled with the so-called problem of altruism and the related issue of coopera- tion as these phenomena, at first glance, seem to be in conflict with the principles of natural selection, the cornerstone of modern evolutionary theory. The notion of reciprocity has occupied an impor- tant place in biological thought on these problems.

Robert Trivers (1971) has given an early and classic account of the nature of the problem, based on a discussion by George Williams (1966). Trivers defines altruism as "behavior that benefits another or- ganism, not closely related, while being apparently detrimental to the organism performing the behavior, benefit and detriment being de- fined in terms of contribution to inclusive fitness" (Trivers 1971, 35). Thus an organism behaving altruistically is necessarily one that is en- during a fitness cost. All other things being equal, natural selection eliminates designs that cause organisms to sacrifice reproductive fit- ness and favors designs that do not cause the organism to do so. Given this fact, altruistic designs should not be observed.

This conclusion contrasts with observations of a host of apparently altruistic behaviors in the biological world. Charles Darwin (1871), for example, was puzzled by phenomena ranging from the sterility of certain castes of insects (sterility being ultimate reproductive sacrifice) to the willingness of humans to fight, even die, for their social group. The conflict between the logic of natural selection, according to which genes for altruism should not survive the evolutionary process, and observations of seemingly altruistic behavior has constituted the core of the problem for biologists.

Distinguishing Design and Behavior

It is important, first, to clarify what is and is not in need of explanation. Trivers (1971) phrases his definition of altruism in terms of behavior. However, this conception leads to some difficulties. Consider the case of the insect that inadvertently flies into the spider's web. Clearly, the insect has incurred a net fitness cost. The spider, furthermore, has gained a source of calories, ready to be turned into gametes and fitness gains. Although it conforms to Trivers's definition, we would not really want to classify this behavior as altruism on the part of the insect (after Tooby and Cosmides 1996).

This difficulty can be addressed by couching the definition of altruism in terms of design, or adaptations, rather than behavior (Tooby and Cosmides 1996). To do this, it is useful to consider the organism as a set of integrated systems designed to accomplish particular tasks. Each one of an organism's subsystems has its design by virtue of its ability to solve a particular adaptive problem and thus contribute to reproductive success (Williams 1966). Natural selection is a process that works on designs: genes that code for particular mechanisms are selected for or against by virtue of the behavior that they produce, on average, over evolutionary time (Dawkins 1976). Thus it is not the behaviors in and of themselves that are selected for or against but rather the genes that code for the mechanisms that produce those behaviors. This view, the "adaptationist" view, which emphasizes design (Williams 1966), leads to a slightly but importantly different conception of altruism. John Tooby and Leda Cosmides suggest that altruism, from the adaptationist perspective, ought to be defined in terms of "highly nonrandom phenotypic complexity that is organized in such a way that it reliably causes an organism to deliver benefits to others" (Tooby and Cosmides 1996, 123).

From this perspective, altruistic behaviors are not all that surprising. Organisms entwined in an intricate ecological system might incidentally benefit one another in many circumstances. Furthermore, as an organism's environment diverges from the one in which it evolved, behaviors that generate a fitness cost to an organism become more likely (Symons 1992). For example, each time a moth flies into a candle or electric light, a subsystem designed for a world in which the only source of illumination is the sun (or moon) is "malfunctioning" due to an important change in the environment of the moth.

In contrast, the existence of systems complexly organized and designed for the purpose of conferring benefits on other organisms is (at first glance) surprising. Put another way, (behavioral) altruism that arises as a by-product of mechanisms designed to serve another purpose (flying around to forage or to find a mate, in the case of the unfortunate insect) is not a phenomenon in need of special explanation. Adaptations for altruism—that is, complex phenotypic structures designed to confer benefits on others—require theoretical refinement beyond the basic principles of Darwinian selection (Tooby and Cosmides 1996).

The Solution: The Gene's-Eye View

An explanation of how natural selection could favor designs that deliver benefits to other organisms has been facilitated by the game-theoretical view of the gene (Maynard Smith 1982; Trivers 1971). On this view, genes can be considered as embodying decision rules, or strategies, and the interaction between the strategy specified by a gene and the environment in which the gene exists creates a feedback loop on the gene's replication. That is, a strategy's effectiveness at replicating genes that code for that particular strategy determines the likelihood that the gene will persist in a population. Evolution "chooses" those strategies, or the genes that code for those strategies, that lead to rates of their own replication that are greater than those of alternative strategies. It is in this sense that genes are "selfish": the only factor (in most cases) that determines whether or not they are selected is the effect they have on their own replication. It is also in this sense that genes are "rational": they can be construed as having unidimensional preferences for their own replication and for nothing else.[1]

The fact that genes are selected by virtue only of their fitness consequences led to John Maynard Smith's observation of the irony that "game theory is more readily applied to evolutionary biology than to the field of economic behavior for which it was originally designed" (Maynard Smith 1982, vii). Genes do not have complex utility functions and are not routinely observed to violate the axioms of rational-choice theory, as humans are (see, for example, Camerer and Thaler 1995; Kahneman and Tversky 1982; Hoffman, McCabe, and Smith 1996; Tversky and Kahneman 1981). The "preferences" of genes can always be understood with respect to their own replication.

Biological Algorithms for Cooperation

Natural selection can lead to the accumulation of phenotypic features designed to deliver benefits to other organisms through two well-known pathways: kin selection (Hamilton 1964) and *reciprocal altruism* (Trivers 1971). Kin-selection theory, also known as inclusive-fitness theory, turns on the fact that a gene can increase its rate of replication by facilitating the replication of exact copies of itself, even if the gene that is being replicated resides in a different organism. Indeed, there is no logical difference between a gene replicating itself and a gene replicating a copy of itself.

Because exact copies of a given gene are differentially likely to be found in individuals that are related by descent, selection can favor genes that cause the organism to deliver benefits to genetic relatives (Hamilton 1964). There are, of course, limitations, because a gene that was promiscuously altruistic, even to relatives, would be at a severe disadvantage relative to more selfish alternatives. To be selected for, a gene must act so as to balance its own fitness interests against those of its relatives, weighting its own interests more heavily the more distant the genetic relationship. Specifically, organisms can be designed to incur a cost to deliver a benefit to another organism as long as the cost incurred, C, is less than the product of the magnitude of the benefit delivered, B, and the coefficient of relatedness, r, or the probability that the gene is in the recipient due to common descent. That is, the design must obey the well-known formula, known as Hamilton's rule, $C < rB$.

Take, for instance, a gene that codes for a design feature that causes an organism to deliver benefits to siblings. Because the probability that a full sibling in a sexually reproducing species contains an identical copy of a given gene due to descent is .5, the benefit delivered must be more than twice as great as the cost. It should be noted that, in general, this probability is calculated by virtue of descent, but this does not necessarily have to be the case. If, for instance, there is a cue that correlates with the presence of a particular gene in another organism, benefits can be differentially delivered to organisms with this trait (see, for instance, Richard Dawkins's [1976, 89] discussion of "green beards").

Kin selection has played a major role in the evolution of a vast array of species—most notably, of course, social species, in which contact with conspecifics in general and kin in particular is frequent. (The eusocial insects are a classic example, as the unusual system of inheritance provides a good test of the logic of kin selection [Dawkins 1976].) Humans, of course, fall into this category, and there is abundant evidence that humans have an array of adaptations for cooperative relationships with kin (Daly, Salmon, and Wilson 1997).

The operation of kin selection requires no conscious calculation of costs and benefits; the genes in question must merely embody strategies that obey Hamilton's rule. That is, selection will favor genes that code for the construction of systems that generate behaviors that conform to this rule.

This analysis does not, however, explain how design features that deliver benefits to nonrelatives can emerge. For this, a discussion of reciprocal altruism theory is required (Trivers 1971). Because this analysis has been presented with some frequency, the discussion here is somewhat limited (for detailed discussions, see Axelrod 1984; Axelrod and Hamilton 1981; Trivers 1971; see also Dugatkin 1997 and citations therein).

Trivers (1971) uses the *prisoner's dilemma* to generate a formal account of how cooperation could evolve by the process of reciprocal altruism. The prisoner's dilemma models an environment in which two agents interact with each other. Only two options are available to each, usually referred to as cooperation (C) and defection (D). The payoffs to each are symmetrical and structured so that each agent does better by choosing to defect, regardless of what the other agent does. However, both agents are made worse off if both defect than if both cooperate.[2] The dilemma is that each agent's best move is to defect, but if both do so, they are worse off than if both had chosen to cooperate.

If randomly matched organisms play the prisoner's dilemma game once, organisms that contain genes that code for defection will obtain a higher payoff (that is, fitness benefit) than organisms that contain genes that code for cooperation. Under these conditions, genes that code for the strategy of defection will always outreplicate their more cooperative counterparts.

Now consider a situation in which organisms play the prisoner's dilemma not just once but many times—the so-called repeated (or iterated) prisoner's dilemma. In such a situation, the reproductive success of any given strategy is the sum of the payoffs that strategy receives during all of its repeated interactions. Successive generations come to have a distribution of strategies that is proportional to the reproductive success of each individual strategy in the preceding generation. Over the course of many generations, those strategies that have the greatest reproductive success in comparison with the other existing strategies will come to dominate the population.

This process was simulated in the famous tournament that Robert Axelrod and William Hamilton (1981) ran to determine what strategies would be successful in the repeated prisoner's dilemma environment. As is well known, the winner of this tournament was *tit-for-tat*, a strategy that cooperates on the first move of an iterated prisoner's dilemma and then on subsequent trials does whatever the other player did on the previous move. In this way, tit-for-tat conditionally rewards the other player for cooperative moves by cooperating on the next trial.

Consider a population that consists of two types of organisms: ALL-D, which defects on every round, and TFT, which follows the tit-for-tat strategy on every round. When any two organisms meet for the first time in a repeated sequence, TFTs will cooperate and ALL-Ds will defect. On all subsequent plays, TFTs will cooperate with one another but defect against ALL-Ds. If the game continues for a sufficiently long time, the mutual benefits obtained by TFTs when they play with one another will give them fitness scores higher than ALL-Ds, and over the course of many generations, TFT will come to dominate the population.[3]

This, in essence, is the root of reciprocal altruism theory. Reciprocal altruism relies on one organism's conferring a benefit on another organism, contingent on the second organism's having conferred a benefit on the first. As long as the benefit delivered by each is greater than the cost incurred by each, organisms can mutually benefit one another by what is equivalent to the economic principle of gains in trade.

It is important to be clear about what the game-theoretic analysis of evolution implies. The logic of reciprocal altruism suggests that if organisms live in a world that repeatedly puts them in situations in which they face choices that mirror the payoff structure of the iterated prisoner's dilemma, then genes that embody a rule such as tit-for-tat can, as long as a number of ancillary conditions are met, be selected for. This analysis does not, however, imply that we should expect organisms to be equipped with cognitive machinery that detects when they are in any situation that has the structural properties of the prisoner's dilemma and use a behavioral strategy that corresponds with tit-for-tat. Rather, it suggests that if a particular domain of an organism's social world had the repeated prisoner's dilemma structure over the course of the species' evolutionary history, then cognitive systems designed to play the behavioral instantiation of a strategy similar to tit-for-tat *in that domain* could have emerged.

The distinction here is between the process that creates psychological adaptations and the adaptations themselves (Symons 1992). Unlike individual organisms, natural selection can "see" the fitness outcomes associated with different strategies that emerge through the process of mutation and test them over generations. As a result, organisms come to be equipped with genes that specify decision rules that are successful—that is, rules that contribute to solving a particular adaptive problem. Natural selection is the process by which psychological adaptations are built. The cognitive system of the organism, which executes the strategies that natural selection has chosen, is the adaptation itself.

Thus the process of natural selection obeys the game-theoretic calculus: genes persist only by virtue of their rate of replication. In contrast, the cognitive systems these genes build might or might not function in a way that looks "rational" or consistent with the principles of game theory; they simply have to have been better than any other candidate systems at solving a specific adaptive problem (Cosmides and Tooby 1994; Tooby and Cosmides 1992).

Preconditions for Reciprocal Altruism

Trivers's (1971) analysis illustrates how conditional, or reciprocal, strategies can evolve in a population in which a prisoner's dilemma structure exists. Since then, a voluminous literature has emerged expanding and refining game-theoretical pathways to cooperative behavior (see Dugatkin 1997). It is clear that tit-for-tat is by no means the only possible reciprocal strategy and that the parameters of the environment can have important effects on which strategies are likely to be successful (see, for example, Axelrod 1984; Boyd and Richerson 1990; Nowak and Sigmund 1992).

It is also clear, however, that reciprocally cooperative strategies can emerge only under certain conditions. One important task, then, is to describe the conditions that will facilitate the evolution of reciprocating strategies, because knowing what these conditions are will facilitate our search for reciprocal altruism among nonhuman animals and guide our thinking about the nature of cooperation in humans.

First and foremost, both kin selection and reciprocal altruism work because benefits are delivered contingently, not indiscriminately. In the case of kin selection, the contingency involves a cue to relatedness. In the case of reciprocal altruism, the contingency involves a particular history of interaction.[4] Broadly speaking, for reciprocal altruism to work, at least the following basic minimum requirements must be met.

1. The environment must be one in which there are benefits to be conferred (for example, Trivers 1971).

2. Organisms must have repeated interactions with one another (for example, Axelrod and Hamilton 1981).

3. Organisms must have sufficient information-processing abilities that they are able to distinguish among individuals and remember which ones have and have not delivered benefits in the past (for example, Crowley et al. 1996).

4. Organisms must have sufficient information-processing sophistication and behavioral flexibility that they can interact with other organisms contingent on the history of interaction (for example, Tooby and Cosmides 1996).

The first condition, that there must be the possibility of conferring benefits, might seem obvious, but it is important because it might be relatively rare. Members of any given species make their living in roughly the same way: they consume the same type of food, prefer the same type of territory, and so forth. Thus commodities valuable to one member of a given species are likely to be similarly valuable to another member, limiting the possibility for gains in trade, the engine of reciprocal altruism. Of course, the same resource might be differentially valuable to two members of a given species, depending on their respective current states—a piece of meat is much more valuable to a hungry hunter than to one who is well fed. This implies that we might be more likely to see adaptations for reciprocal altruism in organisms that have more variance in their needs over time (Cosmides and Tooby 1992).

It should also be obvious that reciprocal altruism cannot emerge in organisms that do not interact repeatedly. More precisely, as the probability that one will encounter the same partner in the future decreases, the emergence of cooperation is less likely (May 1981; Michod and Sanderson 1985). Thus reciprocal altruism should be most important in species in which organisms stay in proximity to one another.

The last two constraints on the evolution of cooperation by reciprocal altruism are that the organisms in question must be able to identify other individuals, store and retrieve information about their past actions, and behave appropriately contingent on this history. Although these capacities seem intuitively trivial to humans, there is evidence that they require intricate information-processing systems. The complexity of these operations might pose important barriers to the evolution of cooperation.

These systems are necessary because the reason that tit-for-tat and similar strategies are successful is that they allow those that are willing to cooperate with one another to do so; that is, defectors are excluded from the benefits conferred by cooperation. There are other ways, however, in which this process, known as "assortment," can occur (Michod and Sanderson 1985). David Sloan Wilson and Lee Dugatkin offer the following thought experiment: "Consider an asexual population of two types, A and B, who interact in groups of size N. If individuals can distinguish between types and can choose their associates, the distribution of A and B types into groups may well be nonrandom. In particular, if A types are altruists and B types are freeloaders, then altruists might band together, leaving the freeloaders with each other by default" (Wilson and Dugatkin 1997, 337).

Under these conditions, altruistic As can be successful even though their cooperation is not contingent on the history of interactions. Other models that attempt to explain the evolution of cooperation can also be understood in the context of the assortment of cooperators with cooperators (Frank 1988; Hirshleifer and Rasmusen 1989; Macy and Skvoretz 1998; Michod and Sanderson 1985; Orbell and Dawes 1991; Wilson and Dugatkin 1997). These models succeed because assortment means that by virtue of being a cooperator, one receives the benefits of cooperation. The logic is precisely parallel to that of reciprocal altruism and kin selection: there is a feedback loop on fitness such that being of a particular design increases replication of that design. Assortment models eliminate certain information-processing requirements, such as individual recognition. Other abilities, however, such as the ability to recognize different strategy types, including potential mimics, might be required (see chapter 7, this volume). Two examples from the animal kingdom—predator inspection in fish and food sharing in vampire bats—help to illustrate the principles of reciprocal altruism.

Predator Inspection

In a number of species of fish, including guppies and sticklebacks, the following behavior is observed: individual members of a particular school approach a potential predator, visually "inspecting" it for a brief period of time (Milinski 1987). Doing so puts the inspecting fish at greater risk of being eaten (Dugatkin 1992) but seems to benefit other individuals: groups of fish in which members inspect are less likely to be attacked by predators (Dugatkin and Godin 1992).

Can this behavior be understood in the context of the prisoner's dilemma? There is evidence that the risk to an inspecting (cooperating) fish decreases as the number of other fish accompanying it increases (Pitcher 1992), indicating benefits for mutual cooperation. Moreover, when fish inspect in pairs, a fish that "defects," trailing behind its partner, gains the benefits of the information obtained by the inspection but incurs a much reduced cost in the form of a lower probability of being eaten (Pitcher 1992), suggesting the temptation to defect. These two facts taken together indicate that although there are benefits to mutual cooperation, in any given inspection bout, regardless of what its partner does, an individual fish is better off hanging back, allowing the other to inspect. Although the payoffs in each cell of the payoff matrix have not been precisely quantified, this appears to be a repeated prisoner's dilemma (Dugatkin 1990).

Recognizing that predator inspection might constitute a prisoner's dilemma opened the door to investigating the possibility that these fish use a reciprocal strategy to solve it (Dugatkin 1988; Milinski 1987). Manfred Milinski (1987) developed an ingenious protocol for investigating whether or not sticklebacks play tit-for-tat. He placed a single stickleback in one tank, with a predator in an adjacent tank. In one condition, a mirror was placed alongside the length of the stickleback's tank so that when the fish approached the predator, it appeared as though another fish were accompanying it the whole way (simulating the "cooperate" condition). In a comparison condition, the mirror did not extend the length of the tank but reached only half way and angled away from the path of the inspecting fish, so that it appeared to the inspecting fish as though its "partner" moved further and further away as the inspector got closer to the predator, eventually disappearing well behind the inspecting fish (simulating the "defect" condition).

If these fish play tit-for-tat, we should expect that fish in the cooperate condition would be willing to continue to inspect over subsequent trials but that fish in the defect condition would be less likely to do so. This is precisely what was found in both sticklebacks (Milinski 1987) and guppies (Dugatkin 1988). In addition, some evidence was found that these fish were "forgiving" in the way predicted by tit-for-tat. In the defect condition, fish would "punish" their image on one round by retreating from their inspection once it was clear that their reflection was not following them. However, after the fish had retreated some distance, the mirror made it appear as though its partner was once again nearby. This apparently cooperative move seems to have been sufficient to induce inspection once again.

These experiments do not include an important component of tit-for-tat—namely, that individuals recognize one another and respond according to previous moves. This weakness has been remedied by Dugatkin and Michael Alfieri (1991a, 1991b), who find evidence that sticklebacks respond specifically to the past behavior of a particular partner (see also Milinski, Kulling, and Kettler 1990; Milinski et al. 1990). That is, sticklebacks respond not to the last move in general, but to the move their current partner made the last time they interacted, being less likely to inspect when their partner defected in the previous interaction. Taken together, these experimental findings seem to indicate that predator inspection in fish might be a case of reciprocal altruism.

Blood Sharing

Vampire bats hunt for their food and must obtain blood regularly to survive. Hunting, however, is an uncertain enterprise, and an unlucky bat can find itself in dire need of blood. Conversely, a successful, well-fed bat can sacrifice a small amount of blood and still live to hunt again. Thus hunters who have had success can find themselves in possession of blood whose value is greater to others than to themselves, and they might also occasionally be in the reverse position, placing a high value on others' blood meal when they have none themselves. This creates one of the critical preconditions for reciprocal altruism, the possibility for gains in trade.

In vampire bats, the other conditions hold as well. Bats roost with one another for extended periods of time, can recognize other individuals, and can condition their behavior on past interactions (Wilkinson 1986). Female bats have been observed regurgitating blood to other (only distantly related) bats that are short on blood. Furthermore, the probability that a satiated bat will endure the cost to benefit its neighbor depends on their past interactions. Bats appear to play tit-for-tat, preferentially giving blood to previous donors and withholding it from previously uncooperative partners (Wilkinson 1984). Taken together, there is substantial evidence that vampire bats are engaging in reciprocal altruism.

These two examples are by no means exhaustive, and a large number of putative examples of reciprocal altruism exist.[5] In any case, the same principles should, of course, apply to humans as to any other species, and it is possible to consider reciprocal altruism in the context of human evolution.

Reciprocity in Humans

Of the four requirements for the evolution of cooperation through reciprocal altruism, two refer to the structure of the environment. In particular, organisms must interact with one another repeatedly, and there must be opportunities for gains in trade. These two conditions are met in the two examples above. Is there evidence that this has been the case during human evolution?

Although it is impossible to reconstruct with precision the environment in which humans evolved, anthropological evidence suggests that ancestral conditions did indeed have these features (for example, Boyd 1988; Hawkes 1993). First, there is abundant evidence that our ancestors were extremely social, living in bands that were relatively stable over time (Foley 1987). Thus the probability of repeated interactions in this type of world was high.

The second condition is that there be the opportunity for gains through social exchange. As with bats, hunting, an activity our ancestors were known to do (for example, Lee and DeVore 1968), might be the key to explaining the origins of reciprocal altruism in humans. If lucky hunters shared their food with their less fortunate (and hungrier) band members, each would have been able to smooth consumption, thereby buffering the variability that a hunting lifestyle entails.

The adaptive problems associated with hunting might have created an initial selection pressure leading to adaptations for reciprocal altruism. Of course, other commodities also have the property that their value depends on how much of them one already has. During the course of human evolution, as cognitive abilities to value different types of objects improved, the possible fitness gains that could be achieved would have expanded. The cognitive sophistication of being able to value various types of possible items of exchange, including abstract entities like social support, might have vastly expanded the possibilities for reciprocal altruism in humans (Cosmides and Tooby 1989, 1992). Today, in the complex arena of human social interaction, a wide variety of items are exchanged: tools and other artifacts, land and territory, information, sexual access, and so forth.

Of course, these speculations should be regarded with some caution, as there is limited evidence that can tell us when specific cognitive capacities arose and where these capacities fit with the development of trade and exchange. It is worth noting in this regard intriguing evidence that one of our primate relatives, vervet monkeys, engage in cross-domain reciprocity. Robert Seyfarth and Dorothy Cheney (1984) have found that among unrelated vervets, a request for coalitional support was responded to more favorably if the two monkeys involved had previously been engaged in mutual grooming. Cross-domain reciprocity has been posited to exist among chimpanzees as well (de Waal 1989; chapter 5, this volume).

Beyond the potential for gains in trade, there are other requirements for reciprocal altruism in humans, including distinguishing individuals, behaving contingently on these individuals' past behavior, and, more particularly, discovering and punishing those individuals who do not reciprocate a benefit with a benefit. There is abundant evidence that humans are adept at recognizing and remembering other humans, suggesting the existence of adaptations designed specifically for this purpose (Carey, Diamond, and Woods 1980; Farah et al. 1995). The ability to distinguish faces from nonfaces is precocious, emerging mere moments after birth (Goren, Sarty, and Wu 1975; Johnson and Morton 1991). The ability to distinguish one face from another is subject to specific impairment, as in the case of prosopagnosia, a condition in which the capacity to recognize faces is damaged while other cognitive subsystems are left largely intact (Farah 1990). People's ability to recall faces is much better than for stimuli matched for complexity (Bruce 1988; Roder et al. 1992), and, when unimpaired, the ability to recognize previously seen faces is astounding. In one study, participants were able to correctly recognize 90 percent of photos of former classmates roughly thirty-five years after graduation (Bahrick, Bahrick, and Wittlinger 1975).

In addition, there is a great deal of evidence that humans have a specialized episodic memory system, which stores specific events as opposed to semantic information (Sherry and Schacter 1990). Storing and recalling past episodes with others is obviously crucial for an organism that conditions its behavior on past interactions. Of course, facial-recognition systems and episodic memory systems are likely to serve a number of different functions and might or might not have evolved for the express purpose of keeping social records of others' traits and past behaviors (Klein et al. 2002; chapter 6, this volume).

Finally, Cosmides and Tooby (1989, 1992) have argued that humans have specialized cognitive mechanisms for detecting cheaters. In reasoning tasks, subjects are able to correctly choose a logical violation of a rule in the form of a social contract with greater precision than another rule that has the same formal logical properties but is not in the form of a social contract. This is true even if the social contract is in a context that is unfamiliar to the subjects. Even more striking, if a conditional rule is in the form of a social contract, subjects tend to choose answers that identify potential cheaters even if this conflicts with the logically correct choices (Cosmides and Tooby 1989, 1992). Recent neurophysiological data indicate that, as with facial-recognition systems, cheater-detection systems can be selectively impaired (Stone et al. 1997). Furthermore, there is intriguing evidence for specificity across all three of these domains—Linda Mealey, Christopher Daood, and Michael Krage (1996) have obtained some data that support the idea that people's memory for faces of those who have violated a social exchange is better than for those who have not.

Human ancestral conditions are likely to have had the required structure for the evolution of reciprocal altruism, and there is evidence for the necessary cognitive features in humans as well. It should be noted that the preceding discussion in no way exhausts the cognitive requirements for a sophisticated social-exchange system. Separate subsystems must exist that are capable of calculating costs and benefits of various outcomes and actions for the self; similarly, systems must exist that can calculate the costs and benefits of various actions to other individuals as well. These systems are required so that the potential for gains in trade can be recognized (chapter 6, this volume).[6]

Nonsimultaneous Exchange: Trust and Spite

In the modern world, in which money acts as a medium of exchange, it is easy to overlook the difficulties associated with nonsimultaneous exchanges. There are a number of reasons to believe that, over evolutionary time, nonsimultaneous exchanges were more common than simultaneous ones. For an opportunity for simultaneous exchange to exist, there must be two different objects (artifacts, acts, and the like) in the world: one that organism A has and is valued by organism B more than by organism A, and, at the same time, a second object that organism B has and is valued by organism A more than by organism B. It is impossible to say how frequently this situation has obtained over the course of human evolution, but it is safe to say that if the requirement is lifted that these two objects exist at the same place and at the same time, the opportunities for gains in trade expand.

In simultaneous exchange, one does not have to worry about defection or cheating. In nonsimultaneous exchange, organism A incurs the cost to benefit organism B in the hope that organism B will reciprocate in the future. That is, nonsimultaneous exchange requires trust on the part of the organism that moves first in the transaction. Thus the willingness to enter exchanges in which one organism incurs a cost without the other already having done so facilitates nonsimultaneous exchange and increases the range of possible transactions in which one can take part. Of course, moving first, or trusting, leaves one open to exploitation. In the example presented earlier in this chapter, tit-for-tat can be construed as trusting unknown players on the first move, and tit-for-tat is indeed exploited on initial encounters with ALL-Ds. However, the game-theoretic success of tit-for-tat makes it clear that design for trust in this sense can persist despite the potential for exploitation.

Adaptations to trust, or to move first in a social exchange, require an additional set of adaptations designed to seek retribution for unfulfilled reciprocal exchanges in which one has been the first mover. Thus spite, or the desire to punish (or at least avoid) those who defect or fail to cooperate, is a critical auxiliary system for trust (see Clutton-Brock and Parker 1995 for a discussion of punishment). Hence we should expect to find that humans are willing to incur costs to inflict costs on those who have violated an agreed-upon reciprocal exchange. In addition, we should expect human cognition to be designed to enter into nonsimultaneous exchange, even when doing so exposes them to downside risk, because cognitive systems that did so, when backed by auxiliary punishment systems, would have enabled them to reap otherwise unattainable (fitness) gains.

The precise nature of these cognitive systems designed to trust and punish is, of course, a subject for empirical investigation. In general, these systems should be sensitive to a number of factors, many of which are discussed in this volume, including the potential for future gains in trade (chapter 10, this volume), the history of interaction (chapter 10, this volume), the magnitude of the cost one incurs (chapter 12, this volume), estimations of the probability that the trading partner will reciprocate (chapter 9, this volume), and so forth.

On the Mismatch Between Modern and Ancestral Environments

This analysis does not suggest that humans are rational reciprocal altruists. That is, it does not predict that people will calculate probabilistic costs and benefits and the possibility of punishing defectors in deciding when and whom to trust. Instead, it suggests that the game-theoretical structure of reciprocal altruism has sculpted human cognitive adaptations. In turn, these cognitive systems, built by the process of natural selection, generate modern human behavior (Tooby and Cosmides 1992). The theory of reciprocal altruism is thus a useful guide in looking for cognitive specializations designed to solve the adaptive problem of reaping gains in trade. In contrast, the theory of reciprocal altruism is not in and of itself an appropriate normative theory for predicting human behavior.

Furthermore, it is unreasonable to expect that the specialized cognitive machinery designed to generate adaptive behavior in ancestral environments will necessarily continue to do so in modern ones. To the extent that modern environments differ from ancestral environments, the impact of the operation of particular cognitive systems on reproductive success cannot be predicted (Symons 1989, 1992). In general, systems designed to function well in tight-knit, relatively stable communities might be wholly inappropriate in the modern world, in which encounters with others are frequently one-shot. The operation of mechanisms designed for a different social world can lead to seemingly anomalous behavior.

Our ancestors were probably engaged in a repeated game with virtually everyone in their local environment. In such a situation, an adaptation to desire to punish those who violated the terms of a social contract could easily be selected for: incurring a cost to punish others can be a good evolutionary strategy in repeated games (Boyd and Richerson 1992), especially if it is known that one is committed to a punishment strategy (Frank 1988). Now consider this adaptation in modern environments. Evidence from a large number of experiments indicates that subjects are willing to endure a cost to punish an anonymous other with whom they know they will not subsequently interact if that individual is perceived to have violated an implicit social contract or norm (for example, Hoffman et al. 1996). This apparently "irrational" behavior makes sense when construed as the operation of a psychological system operating in a context for which it was not designed.

Cooperation in Groups

Because cooperation and trust are important political and sociological issues, the question of the nature of the human psychology of group cooperation has been a topic of considerable interest. The logic of the evolution of cooperation in dyadic relationships, however, cannot be straightforwardly generalized from the case of two agents to more complex interactions. The models that can explain the evolution of cooperation in dyads do not necessarily apply to large groups, and separate models for the evolution of cooperation in groups are needed (Boyd and Richerson 1992; Dugatkin 1990; Joshi 1987).

In much the same way that the prisoner's dilemma was used to formalize the analysis of cooperation in dyads, N-person prisoner's dilemma games or *public-goods games* have formed the basis of a number of models of cooperation in groups (Boyd and Richerson 1992; Hirshleifer and Rasmusen 1989). Many evolutionary approaches to the establishment of cooperation in groups have emphasized the punishing of noncontributing group members as a relatively cheap way to induce cooperation. This leads to a higher-order public-goods problem, however, because the provision of punishment itself represents a public good (Boyd and Richerson 1992; Hirshleifer and Rasmusen 1989; Oliver 1980; see also Clutton-Brock and Parker 1995). Although some progress has been made in explaining cooperation in groups (for example, Wilson and Sober 1994), additional models are needed.

An Alternative Route to Reciprocal Benefits

Although kin selection and reciprocal altruism are the most widely known routes to designs for altruism, other evolutionary pathways are possible. Tooby and Cosmides (1996), for example, have proposed an additional model, which they refer to as the banker's paradox (see also Connor 1986). This model bears a resemblance to reciprocal altruism but emphasizes the contingent delivery of benefits from one organism to another rather than the cost to the organism delivering the benefits. Tooby and Cosmides's analysis centers on the fact that by accomplishing their own goals, organisms generate a vast array of externalities: outcomes that are by-products of a mechanism's function. The generation of externalities is a consequence of the interrelationships inherent in any complex ecosystem.

Imagine that some organism A must accomplish some task and that some ways organism A can accomplish the task generate externalities that are more beneficial to some organism B than others. If organism B could develop a system allowing it to reward organism A contingently for operating in one of the ways that benefits organism B, as opposed to hurting it, selection could favor a systematic switch on the part of organism A to perform the task so that it received the contingent benefit.

This analysis translates directly into the complexity of social life. Imagine that there are individuals in the world who, through the course of their normal activities, generate positive externalities with respect to your goals. Because of this fact, these individuals are differentially valuable to you; for this reason, it might be to your advantage to advance their interests so that they stay in the position of being able to emit positive externalities. Because you have a stake in them, they, in turn, might come to value you. Tooby and Cosmides (1996) refer to this process as "runaway friendship" and suggest that it might have led to adaptations designed for friendship distinct from those designed for explicit contingent exchange.

The upshot of this is that adaptations to deliver benefits to others can be selected for not by virtue of the logic of reciprocal altruism but rather because benefit delivery can result in one's being valued. This pathway predicts design features different from those predicted by reciprocal altruism theory and is appealing because this process can begin even under relatively restrictive initial conditions. This pathway might be important to discussions of trust in humans because it suggests that explicit contingent exchange is not the only possible route by which people can obtain reciprocal benefits (see also Fiske 1992). It might therefore be important to distinguish cases of trust, in which a benefit is delivered with the expectation of reciprocity, from cases of engagement, in which agents have a stake in one another's well-being.

Summary and Conclusions

One interesting and important question, from the standpoint of evolutionary theory, is how natural selection could have fashioned adaptations designed to deliver benefits to other individuals. Kin-selection theory and reciprocal altruism theory are two answers to this question. For organisms not closely related by descent, reciprocal altruism is an evolutionary pathway by which the delivery of benefits from one organism to another can lead to enhanced fitness outcomes by virtue of the benefits that an organism receives because of earlier benefit delivery. The threat of cheating can be overcome in these systems either by avoiding interactions with organisms that have failed to reciprocate in the past or through the assortment of cooperators by other means (Michod and Sanderson 1985; Wilson and Dugatkin 1997). Evidence from nonhuman animals suggests that the model of reciprocal altruism is a plausible one, and otherwise puzzling behavior can be explained within this context.

It is probable that the life history of our hominid ancestors, especially the hunting of large game, made possible the gains in trade that are necessary for reciprocal altruism to lead to the emergence of adaptations for conferring benefits on others.[7] Spiraling cognitive complexity, including sophisticated mechanisms for the recognition of individuals and episodic memory storage systems, might well have been important components of the cognitive systems that allowed reciprocal altruism to function. In addition, increasing cognitive capacities for abstracting the costs and benefits of various acts, objects, and states of the world might also have been important for broadening the possible exchanges. With the ability to translate costs and benefits across different types of commodities, possibilities for gains in trade expand considerably.

Because many more exchanges are possible if trade is nonsimultaneous, there are advantages to being willing to enter into an exchange relationship without receiving immediate reciprocation. Such cooperation leaves individuals vulnerable to exploitation, but the threat of punishment, or at least the cutting off of subsequent exchange relationships, might have been sufficient to select for a certain amount of patience in receiving reciprocation. This constellation of adaptations, cognitive systems designed to decide whether and when one ought to enter an exchange as the first mover, led to the phenomenon of trust. A subsystem of this cognitive capacity should include adaptations to detect when one has been cheated, to store the cheating episode, to choose to punish (or at least refuse further interactions with) those who have cheated, and so forth. Evidence for each of these cognitive systems in humans supports the hypothesis that the game-theoretical structure of ancestral environments led to adaptations driven by reciprocal altruism.

Mechanisms designed to deliver benefits to others can misfire by accident or through manipulation. Cuckoo mothers, for example, who are designed to deliver food to their young, sometimes feed chicks of other species placed in their nest because these brood parasites are designed to behave in ways that elicit feeding behavior from their host. In humans, mechanisms designed to trust or deliver benefits can similarly be misled in the presence of cues to which altruistic mechanisms were designed to respond. Because the human social environment differs in important ways from ancestral social environments, it should not be surprising that humans sometimes act in ways that appear overly altruistic by traditional standards of self-interest.

In sum, the evolutionary approach does not imply that humans are "rational" in the traditional economic sense. Rather, it suggests that that the process of natural selection generated cognitive systems and decision rules that led to fitness outcomes greater than those of alternative designs over evolutionary time. If this is the case, the game-theoretic principles developed by biologists and economists represent valuable tools for generating hypotheses about the design of the human mind.

The writing of this chapter was supported by a fellowship from the International Foundation for Research in Experimental Economics. I would like to thank Elinor Ostrom and James Walker, for their valuable comments on earlier drafts, and Kevin McCabe, for his many stimulating discussions on this and other topics.

Notes

1. The teleological language here should be understood as metaphorical shorthand that could be easily translated into properly causal descriptions (Dawkins 1976).

2. There is an additional constraint for the situation to be a prisoner's dilemma—namely, that the sum of the payoffs to each player when one defects and one cooperates be less than twice the payoff to each player when both cooperate. I ignore this here because the purpose of the current discussion is to illustrate the general principles involved in the evolution of reciprocal altruism rather than to present a formal treatment of the prisoner's dilemma.

3. A vast amount has been written on the prisoner's dilemma, and I am ignoring a great deal of this literature, including the problem of how tit-for-tat gets started in a population. Axelrod (1984) provides a more thorough discussion.

4. The distinction between reciprocal altruism and kin selection is the subject of some debate (Rothstein 1980; Rothstein and Pierotti 1988; Wilson and Sober 1994).

5. See Dugatkin (1997) for an array of interesting examples of animal cooperation; see also chapter 5, this volume.

6. See Cosmides and Tooby (1992) for a more thorough and detailed discussion of the cognitive requirements for social exchange.

7. There is not universal agreement regarding the relation between the evolution of reciprocal altruism and hunting (Hawkes 1993).

References

Axelrod, Robert. 1984. *The Evolution of Cooperation.* New York: Basic Books.
Axelrod, Robert, and William D. Hamilton. 1981. "The Evolution of Cooperation." *Science* 211(4489): 1390–96.
Bahrick, Harry P., Phyllis O. Bahrick, and Roy P. Wittlinger. 1975. "Fifty Years of Memory for Names and Faces: A Cross-Sectional Approach." *Journal of Experimental Psychology: General* 104(1): 54–75.

Boyd, Robert. 1988. "Is the Repeated Prisoner's Dilemma a Good Model of Reciprocal Altruism?" *Ethology and Sociobiology* 9(2–4): 211–21.

Boyd, Robert, and Peter J. Richerson. 1990. "Group Selection Among Alternative Evolutionarily Stable Strategies." *Journal of Theoretical Biology* 145(3): 331–42.

———. 1992. "Punishment Allows the Evolution of Cooperation (or Anything Else) in Sizable Groups." *Ethology and Sociobiology* 13(3): 171–95.

Bruce, Vicki. 1988. *Recognizing Faces*. Hillsdale, N.J.: Lawrence Erlbaum.

Camerer, Colin, and Richard H. Thaler. 1995. "Ultimatums, Dictators, and Manners." *Journal of Economic Perspectives* 9(2): 209–19.

Carey, Susan, Rhea Diamond, and Bryan Woods. 1980. "Development of Face Recognition: A Maturational Component?" *Developmental Psychology* 16(4): 257–69.

Clutton-Brock, Tim H., and Geoffrey A. Parker. 1995. "Punishment in Animal Societies." *Nature* 373(6511): 209–16.

Connor, Richard C. 1986. "Pseudoreciprocity: Investing in Mutualism." *Animal Behaviour* 34(5): 1652–54.

Cosmides, Leda, and John Tooby. 1989. "Evolutionary Psychology and the Generation of Culture." Part 2, "Case Study: A Computational Theory of Social Exchange." *Ethology and Sociobiology* 10(1–3): 51–97.

———. 1992. "Cognitive Adaptations for Social Exchange." In *The Adapted Mind*, edited by Jerome Barkow, Leda Cosmides, and John Tooby. New York: Oxford University Press.

———. 1994. "Better Than Rational: Evolutionary Psychology and the Invisible Hand." *American Economic Review* 84(2): 327–32.

Crowley, Phillip H., Louis Provencher, Sarah Sloane, Lee A. Dugatkin, Bryan Spohn, Lock Rogers, and Michael Alfieri. 1996. "Evolving Cooperation: The Role of Individual Recognition." *Biosystems* 37(1–2): 49–66.

Daly, Martin, Catherine Salmon, and Margo Wilson. 1997. "Kinship: The Conceptual Hole in Psychological Studies of Social Cognition and Close Relationships." In *Evolutionary Social Psychology*, edited by Jeffrey A. Simpson and Douglas T. Kenrick. Mahwah, N.J.: Lawrence Erlbaum.

Darwin, Charles. 1871. *The Descent of Man and Selection in Relation to Sex*. London, England: Murray.

Dawkins, Richard. 1976. *The Selfish Gene*. Oxford: Oxford University Press.

de Waal, Frans B. M. 1989. "Food Sharing and Reciprocal Obligations Among Chimpanzees." *Journal of Human Evolution* 18(5): 433–59.

Dugatkin, Lee A. 1988. "Do Guppies (*Poecilia reticulata*) Play Tit for Tat During Predator Inspection Visits?" *Behavioral Ecology and Sociobiology* 23(6): 395–99.

———. 1990. "N-Person Games and the Evolution of Cooperation: A Model Based on Predator Inspection Behavior in Fish." *Journal of Theoretical Biology* 142(1): 123–35.

———. 1992. "Tendency to Inspect Predators Predicts Mortality Risk in the Guppy (*Poecilia reticulata*)." *Behavioral Ecology* 3(2): 124–27.

———. 1997. *Cooperation Among Animals: An Evolutionary Perspective*. New York: Oxford University Press.

Dugatkin, Lee A., and Michael Alfieri. 1991a. "Guppies and the Tit for Tat Strategy: Preference Based on Past Interaction." *Behavioral Ecology and Sociobiology* 28(4): 243–47.

———. 1991b. "Tit for Tat in Guppies (*Poecilia reticulata*): The Relative Nature of Cooperation and Defection During Predator Inspection." *Evolutionary Ecology* 5(3): 300–9.

Dugatkin, Lee A., and Jean-Guy J. Godin. 1992. "Prey Approaching Predators: A Cost-Benefit Perspective." *Annales Zoologici Fennici* 29(4): 233–52.

Farah, Martha J. 1990. *Visual Agnosia: Disorders of Object Recognition and What They Tell Us About Normal Vision.* Cambridge, Mass.: MIT Press.

Farah, Martha J., Kevin D. Wilson, Maxwell H. Drain, and James R. Tanaka. 1995. "The Inverted Face Inversion Effect in Prosopagnosia: Evidence for Mandatory, Face-Specific Perceptual Mechanisms." *Vision Research* 35(14): 2089–93.

Fiske, Alan P. 1992. "The Four Elementary Forms of Sociality: Framework for a Unified Theory of Social Relations." *Psychological Review* 99(4): 689–723.

Foley, Robert 1987. *Another Unique Species: Patterns in Human Evolutionary Ecology.* New York: Longman/John Wiley.

Frank, Robert H. 1988. *Passions Within Reason: The Strategic Role of the Emotions.* New York: W. W. Norton.

Goren, Carolyn C., Merrill Sarty, and Paul Y. K. Wu. 1975. "Visual Following and Pattern Discrimination of Face-Like Stimuli by Newborn Infants." *Pediatrics* 56(4): 544–49.

Hamilton, William D. 1964. "The Genetical Evolution of Social Behavior." *Journal of Theoretical Biology* 7(1): 1–52.

Hawkes, Kristen. 1993. "Why Hunter-Gatherers Work: An Ancient Version of the Problem of Public Goods." *Current Anthropology* 34(4): 341–61.

Hirshleifer, David, and Eric Rasmusen. 1989. "Cooperation in a Repeated Prisoner's Dilemma with Ostracism." *Journal of Economic Behavior and Organization* 12(1): 87–106.

Hoffman, Elizabeth, Kevin McCabe, Keith Shachat, and Vernon Smith. 1996. "Preferences, Property Rights, and Anonymity in Bargaining Games." *Games and Economic Behavior* 7(3): 346–80.

Hoffman, Elizabeth, Kevin McCabe, and Vernon Smith. 1996. "Social Distance and Other-Regarding Behavior in Dictator Games." *American Economic Review* 86(3): 653–60.

Johnson, Mark H., and John Morton. 1991. *Biology and Cognitive Development: The Case of Face Recognition.* Oxford: Blackwell.

Joshi, N. V. 1987. "Evolution of Reciprocation in Structured Demes." *Journal of Genetics* 66(1): 69–84.

Kahneman, Daniel, and Amos Tversky. 1982. "The Psychology of Preferences." *Scientific American* 246(1): 160–73.

Klein, Stanley B., Leda Cosmides, John Tooby, and Sarah Chance. 2002. "Decisions and the Evolution of Memory: Multiple Systems, Multiple Functions." *Psychological Review* 109(2): 306–29.

Lee, Richard B., and Irven DeVore, eds. 1968. *Man the Hunter.* Chicago: Aldine.

Macy, Michael W., and John Skvoretz. 1998. "The Evolution of Trust and Cooperation Between Strangers: A Computational Model." *American Sociological Review* 63(5): 638–60.

May, Robert M. 1981. "The Evolution of Cooperation." *Nature* 292(5821): 291–92.

Maynard Smith, John. 1982. *Evolution and the Theory of Games*. Cambridge: Cambridge University Press.

Mealey, Linda, Christopher Daood, and Michael Krage. 1996. "Enhanced Memory for Faces of Cheaters." *Ethology and Sociobiology* 17(2): 119–28.

Michod, Richard, and Michael Sanderson. 1985. "Behavioral Structure and the Evolution of Cooperation." In *Evolution: Essays in Honor of John Maynard Smith*, edited by Paul J. Greenwood, Paul H. Harvey, and Montgomery Slatkin. Cambridge: Cambridge University Press.

Milinski, Manfred. 1987. "Tit for Tat and the Evolution of Cooperation in Sticklebacks." *Nature* 325(6103): 433–35.

Milinski, Manfred, David Kulling, and Rolf Kettler. 1990. "Tit for Tat: Sticklebacks 'Trusting' a Cooperating Partner." *Behavioral Ecology* 1(1): 7–12.

Milinski, Manfred, D. Pfluger, David Kulling, and Rolf Kettler. 1990. "Do Sticklebacks Cooperate Repeatedly in Reciprocal Pairs?" *Behavioral Ecology and Sociobiology* 27(1): 17–23.

Nowak, Martin, and Karl Sigmund. 1992. "A Strategy of Win-Stay, Lose-Shift That Outperforms Tit-for-Tat in the Prisoner's Dilemma Game." *Nature* 364(6432): 56–58.

Oliver, Pamela. 1980. "Rewards and Punishments As Selective Incentives for Collective Action: Theoretical Investigations." *American Journal of Sociology* 85(6): 1356–75.

Orbell, John M., and Robyn Dawes. 1991. "A 'Cognitive Miser' Theory of Cooperators' Advantage." *American Political Science Review* 85(2): 515–28.

Pitcher, Tony. 1992. "Who Dares Wins: The Function and Evolution of Predator Inspection Behaviour in Shoaling Fish." *Netherlands Journal of Zoology* 42(2–3): 371–91.

Roder, Beverly J., Carey Bates, Shelly Crowell, Thomas Schilling, and Emily Bushnell. 1992. "The Perception of Identity by Six-and-One-Half-Month-Old Infants." *Journal of Experimental Child Psychology* 54(1): 57–73.

Rothstein, Stephen I. 1980. "Reciprocal Altruism and Kin Selection Are Not Clearly Separable Phenomena." *Journal of Theoretical Biology* 87(2): 255–61.

Rothstein, Stephen I., and Raymond Pierotti. 1988. "Distinctions Among Reciprocal Altruism, Kin Selection, and Cooperation and a Model for the Initial Evolution of Beneficent Behavior." *Ethology and Sociobiology* 9(2–4): 189–209.

Seyfarth, Robert M., and Dorothy L. Cheney. 1984. "Grooming Alliances and Reciprocal Altruism in Vervet Monkeys." *Nature* 308(5): 541–43.

Sherry, David F., and Daniel L. Schacter. 1990. "The Evolution of Multiple Memory Systems." *Psychological Review* 94(4): 439–54.

Stone, Valerie E., Simon Baron-Cohen, Leda Cosmides, John Tooby, and Robert T. Knight. 1997. "Selective Impairment of Social Inferences Following Orbitofrontal Cortex Damage." In *Proceedings of the Nineteenth Annual Meeting of the Cognitive Science Society*, edited by M. G. Shafto and Pat Langley. London: Lawrence Erlbaum.

Symons, Donald. 1989. "A Critique of Darwinian Anthropology." *Ethology and Sociobiology* 10(1–3): 131–44.

———. 1992. "On the Use and Misuse of Darwinism in the Study of Human Behavior." In *The Adapted Mind*, edited by Jerome Barkow, Leda Cosmides, and John Tooby. New York: Oxford University Press.

Tooby, John, and Leda Cosmides. 1992. "The Psychological Foundations of Culture." In *The Adapted Mind*, edited by Jerome Barkow, Leda Cosmides, and John Tooby. New York: Oxford University Press.

———. 1996. "Friendship and the Banker's Paradox: Other Pathways to the Evolution of Adaptations for Altruism." *Proceedings of the British Academy* 88: 119–43.

Trivers, Robert L. 1971. "The Evolution of Reciprocal Altruism." *Quarterly Review of Biology* 46(1): 35–57.

Tversky, Amos, and Daniel Kahneman. 1981. "The Framing of Decisions and the Psychology of Choice." *Science* 211(4481): 453–58.

Wilkinson, Gerald S. 1984. "Reciprocal Food Sharing in the Vampire Bat." *Nature* 308(5955): 181–84.

———. 1986. "Social Grooming in the Common Vampire Bat, *Desmodus rotundus*." *Animal Behavior* 34(6): 1880–89.

Williams, George C. 1966. *Adaptation and Natural Selection*. Princeton, N.J.: Princeton University Press.

Wilson, David Sloan, and Lee A. Dugatkin. 1997. "Group Selection and Assortative Interactions." *American Naturalist* 149(2): 336–51.

Wilson, David Sloan, and Elliott Sober. 1994. "Reintroducing Group Selection to the Human Behavioral Sciences." *Behavioral and Brain Sciences* 17(4): 585–654.

Chapter 5

The Chimpanzee's Service Economy: Evidence for Cognition-Based Reciprocal Exchange

Frans B. M. de Waal

B ECAUSE organisms are supposed, first of all, to look out for themselves, biology treats cooperation as a puzzle. Why do animals suffer costs to assist one another, sometimes literally giving their lives so that others may live? Should not such behavior have been weeded out by natural selection? Ever since the 1902 publication of Petr Kropotkin's *Mutual Aid*, the solution to this puzzle has been that one way in which the costs of helping may be offset is through return benefits. It was not until seventy years later that this "You scratch my back, I'll scratch yours" principle was formalized in modern terms by Robert Trivers (1971). Since then it has been central to the explanation of cooperation among unrelated individuals (see chapter 4, this volume).

Reciprocal exchange is an evolutionary argument about how cooperation could have come into existence. As such, it knows no exceptions—that is, it applies to all organisms, from fish to elephants. Our own species is included, and anyone who wants to exclude human behavior would have to come up with extraordinary arguments because in science nothing is more alluring than a unified theory. Thus far, no such argument has been forwarded.

This is not to say that reciprocal help in human society is basically the same as that in fish. This would be a fundamental error: the above

128

theoretical framework deals only with the ultimate reasons for the existence of reciprocal exchange. That is, it hypothesizes why animals engage in such behavior and what evolutionary benefits they derive from it. It says nothing about how it is achieved—that is, it does not offer what is commonly referred to as the proximate explanation. Both fish and humans breathe because their bodies need oxygen for energy production (shared ultimate reason), yet they do so in different ways—fish through gills and humans through lungs (different proximate mechanisms). Similarly, reciprocal exchange may have evolved in many animals for similar reasons yet be achieved in variable ways.

Humans probably have added unique complexities, although, in the larger scheme of things, it is likely that human reciprocity deviates only modestly from that of species with which our species has shared a long evolutionary history, such as the chimpanzee. Chimpanzees, with humans and other apes, are members of the Hominoid family, which sets them apart from monkeys. Genetically, as measured by DNA, an ape is much less like a monkey than like us. The same is true for many of their behavioral and mental characteristics. One notable point of similarity is that apes, like us, have a slow development, reaching adulthood only when they are about fourteen years old. Hence the common dichotomy according to which animal behavior is "instinctive" and our own behavior "learned" really does not apply: both humans and apes go through a long developmental period, and there is probably as little (or as much, depending on one's definition) chimpanzee as human behavior that could be called instinctive.

As for reciprocity, one can easily imagine forms in which the time delay between services is short; hence record keeping is not required, nor, perhaps, is individual recognition. This may be the case for many instances of reciprocity in fish. Even if significant time delays are part of the reciprocal exchange, mutual altruistic action may be based simply on the underlying relationship rather than on contingencies between give and take. The former mechanism has been dubbed symmetry-based reciprocity, and the latter calculated reciprocity.[1] Trust becomes an issue only when expectations regulate reciprocity. Trust requires experience-based predictions of behavior, and in this it is, of course, not unique to our species. We have no trouble recognizing the difference between a trustful or distrustful dog, and we know how long it can take to turn the latter into the former. Trust in cooperative relationships has more specific requirements, however: it is relevant only if cooperation is reiterated, dependent on individual recognition, and contingent on past events.

This is precisely the sort of cooperation addressed in the study examined here. A group of chimpanzees faced with sharable food was observed while engaged in nearly seven thousand interactions; the observations were carefully recorded and entered into a computer according to strict empirical definitions (de Waal 1989). The same had been done with hundreds of grooming interactions before the food trials. The resulting database on spontaneous services exceeds that for any other nonhuman primate (and probably also that for any human society studied) and permits the conclusion that chimpanzees have a capacity for cognition-based reciprocal exchange.

Introduction

Although chimpanzee (*Pan troglodytes*) society has been characterized as a "marketplace" in which services are traded back and forth among individuals (de Waal 1982), hard evidence for a social economy remains meager. For both chimpanzees and other animals, the theory of *reciprocal altruism* (Trivers 1971), one pillar of the evolutionary approach to cooperative behavior, is not nearly as well supported as the theory of kin selection (Hamilton 1964), the other pillar (Wilson 1975).

Reciprocal altruism presupposes that the exchanged acts are costly to the donor and beneficial to the recipient; that the roles of donor and recipient regularly reverse over time; and that except for the first act, donation is contingent upon previous receipt. A significant time delay between given and received services is an additional requirement, which distinguishes reciprocity from so-called mutualism, in which parties benefit simultaneously (Rothstein and Pierotti 1988; Taylor and McGuire 1988). Because reciprocal altruism is expected especially when unrelated individuals regularly work together, monkeys and apes have provided a natural focus for research in this area. In a variety of nonhuman primates, positive correlations have been found between the frequency with which individual A benefits individual B and the frequency with which B benefits A across an entire matrix of group members. Correlational evidence for reciprocity exists for social grooming, food sharing, and agonistic support (de Waal 1989; de Waal and Luttrell 1988; Packer 1977; Seyfarth 1980).

Correlations between given and received acts of assistance across relationships can come about in multiple ways, however, and so before concluding that giving depends on receiving, potentially confounding variables need to be controlled. The most obvious variable to control is time spent in association: if members of a species preferentially direct favors to close associates, the distribution of favors will automatically be reciprocal, owing to the symmetrical nature of association. This mechanism, symmetry-based reciprocity, needs to be distinguished from calculated reciprocity, which is based on mental record keeping of given and received favors (de Waal and Luttrell 1988). In most species for which reciprocal altruism has been reported, including nonprimates such as vampire bats (*Desmodus rotundus*) (Wilkinson 1984) and impala (*Aepyceros melampus*) (Hart and Hart 1992), symmetry-based reciprocity is a likely mechanism. The most convincing evidence that reciprocity persists after association rates have been taken into account concerns chimpanzees. Moreover, only in chimpanzees do reciprocity correlations extend to negative behavior, suggesting retaliation. In earlier work I speak of "revenge" and "punishment" as part of reciprocal exchange in this species (de Waal 1982, 1992), an idea that was later generalized by Timothy Clutton-Brock and George Parker (1995).

Apart from the limitations of a correlational approach, some of the behavior patterns selected for these analyses may not fit the requirement of being costly to the donor. Agonistic intervention on behalf of another individual, for instance, is sometimes risky for the intervener and advantageous for the beneficiary (for example, when a female defends her offspring against an attack by a dominant male), but more often intervention is directed against subordinates and is, hence, relatively risk free (reviewed by Harcourt and de Waal 1992). If all types of agonistic interventions are entered into a single reciprocity analysis, altruistic and nonaltruistic behavior are being inappropriately lumped together. This criticism has been expressed most forcefully in relation to alliances among male baboons in which each victorious ally will try to sneak off with the contested resource, an estrus female. Rather than characterizing these alliances as cooperative, both Frederick Bercovitch (1988) and Ronald Noë (1990) have described them as self-serving and opportunistic. According to Barbara Smuts (1985), however, alliances among older baboon males may be truly reciprocal.

In view of the problems with analyses at the relationship level, there is a need to turn to the interaction level and analyze sequences of behavior over time. The purpose of the present study is to investigate the hypothesis that reciprocal altruism relies on cognitive abilities that make current behavior contingent upon a history of interaction. Does a beneficial act by individual A toward individual B increase the probability of a subsequent beneficial act by B toward A? Preliminary evidence for exchanges of affiliative behavior for agonistic support, and vice versa, exists for cercopithecine monkeys. In previous research (de Waal and Yoshihara 1983), we measured postconflict attraction between previous alliance partners, and Robert Seyfarth and Dorothy Cheney (1984) and Charlotte Hemelrijk (1994) have found that more attention support was given to previous grooming partners engaged in a fight. Experiments on food sharing among capuchin monkeys (*Cebus apella*) further support the possibility of one favor being followed closely in time by another in the opposite direction (de Waal 2000; de Waal and Berger 2000).

The present study investigates sequences of spontaneous grooming and food sharing in a captive colony of chimpanzees to determine how services are affected by previous interaction between the same individuals. The study thereby addresses the issue of partner specificity: does a beneficial act by A toward B affect B's behavior only toward A? The assumption of partner specificity is at the heart of *tit-for-tat* but has thus far not received systematic attention in research on nonhuman animals. In captivity, partner presence and food availability can be held constant, and all social interactions within a particular time window can be recorded. Demonstration of sequential reciprocal altruism under these circumstances would strongly suggest similar exchange mechanisms under natural conditions, such as when wild chimpanzees divide meat (Boesch and Boesch 1989; Goodall 1986; Teleki 1973).

Both easy-to-measure behaviors selected for analysis confer benefits to the partner in terms of nutrition (that is, food) or hygiene and possible calming effects (that is, grooming). In captivity, however, with the abundant food supply and leisure time provided, the cost of these behaviors is rather low. For this reason, I prefer to speak of "social exchange," "services," and "favors" rather than of "altruism," with its connotation of sacrifice. How the economy of low-cost services relates to reciprocal altruism is as yet unclear, but it is reasonable to assume that the two are evolutionarily and psychologically related. Tendencies underlying social exchange may have evolved in the high-risk domain of reciprocal altruism after which they were generalized to interchanges in which there was less at stake. It seems more logical to assume the opposite, however—namely, that the evolution of cooperation started with low-risk exchanges and that costlier forms of cooperation grew out of this (Roberts and Sherratt 1998).

In a previous study I conducted of the same chimpanzee colony, both adult males and females peacefully shared branches and leaves with one another (de Waal 1989). As in other studies of chimpanzees (Teleki 1973), and indeed of primates in general (Feistner and McGrew 1989), the vast majority of these food transfers was of a passive nature: that is, possessors allowed others to remove food from their hands or mouths or to collect food from within arm's reach. The sharing was selective, however, in that possessors were not equally tolerant of all individuals: only about half of the interactions between a possessor and an interested nonpossessor resulted in an actual transfer of food. The ability of a possessor to maintain possession and rebuff approaching individuals was found to be independent of social rank: even the lowest-ranking adult successfully rejected feeding attempts by others. This confirms the remarkable "respect for possession" (Kummer 1991) already noted by Jane Goodall (1971) in her first accounts of food sharing among wild chimpanzees.

Methods

Subjects and Housing Conditions

The study was conducted on a well-established group of twenty chimpanzees, including one adult male and eight adult females. Six of the adult females had been subjects in the previous study; the other two adult females had been juveniles during this study, which took place more than six years earlier (de Waal 1989). The adult male was new to the group, having been introduced a year before the study's onset. Two of the partner combinations among the nine adults were maternal relatives (both mother-daughter pairs); the other thirty-four adult-adult combinations were unrelated. All juveniles and infants in the group had been born to adult females in the group. Group composition during the course of the study was changed only by the birth of three infants into the colony, several temporary removals for veterinary reasons, and the permanent removal of one adult female by the end of 1993.

The colony lived in an outdoor compound of 750 square meters at the field station of the Yerkes Regional Primate Research Center, near Lawrenceville, Georgia. The compound was equipped with climbing structures and visual barriers. At night and when the weather was cold, the group could enter a heated indoor area. Observations took place from a tower with an unobstructed view of the entire compound.

Data Collections

Food trials were conducted approximately twice (maximally thrice) weekly during the springs and summers of a three-year period from 1992 through 1994. At variable prescheduled times, freshly cut branches and leaves were thrown into the enclosure. providing extra food. The plant species most often used were sweet gum (*Liquidambar styraciflua*), sassafras (*Sassafras albidum*), American beech (*Fagus grandifolia*), willow (*Salix spp.*), young blackberry shoots (*Rubus spp.*), bush clover (*Lespedeza repens*), and black oak (*Quercus velutina*), tied together with honeysuckle vine (*Lonicera spp.*) into two large monopolizable bundles.

Interactions were recorded as a spoken account by observers into a tape recorder for half an hour following the introduction of food. A food interaction was defined as an approach by a nonpossessor to within arm's reach of a food possessor. A food transfer occurred when the nonpossessor collected food directly from the possessor's hands or mouth, co-fed on the bundle or pile held by the possessor, or collected food from within easy arm's reach of the possessor.[2]

Food trials, scheduled at ten o'clock in the morning or later, were preceded by a ninety-minute preobservation session. Preobservations ended less than half an hour before the onset of the food trial and were conducted in all three years. In 1992, ninety-minute postobservations were taken immediately following the food trial and in 1993 after a delay of two hours following the food trial. No such postobservations were conducted in 1994. In addition, so-called independent ninety-minute observations were collected throughout the three-year period on days without food trials. Overall, 200 food trials, 282 independent observations, 168 preobservations, and 134 postobservations were conducted.

Data collection outside the food trials included five-minute scan samples of state behaviors, including affiliative contact, play, and point events such as mounting, mating, kissing, embracing, submissive greeting (that is, pant-grunting), intimidation displays, hooting, and aggression. Most important for the present study, grooming bouts were recorded with an all-occurrences sampling technique: groomer, groomee, and bout duration in seconds.

Results

Reciprocity Correlations

A reciprocity correlation is not simply a comparison between the data points above and below the diagonal of a matrix, because such a correlation is not independent of the order in which individuals have been placed. The only result independent of ordering is a correlation between the entire matrix and its transposition. If this procedure is applied to a symmetric matrix, it results in a correlation coefficient of 1. Our procedure tests how closely the data distribution in a matrix approaches symmetry. Because data points in a matrix are mathematically interdependent (that is, there are more data points than individuals), the degrees of freedom of a correlation cannot be specified (Schnell, Watt, and Douglas 1985). The solution used here is free from distributional assumptions: one-tailed probabilities of reciprocity correlation coefficients were evaluated with a quadratic assignment procedure involving one thousand random matrix permutations (Dow, Cheverud, and Friedlaender 1987).

Both social services, grooming, and food sharing showed reciprocal distributions above the nine-by-nine matrix among adults. The Pearson correlation between given and received grooming bouts per hour of observation was $r = .45$ ($p = .006$), and that between given and received food transfers, expressed as a percentage of the possessor's total transfers to other adults, was $r = .26$ ($p = .001$). Reciprocity between these two measures (grooming and food sharing) was positive, as expected, but nonsignificant: $r = .24$ ($p = .09$).

Sharing Following Grooming

Because individuals varied greatly in the number of occasions on which they possessed a sharable quantity of food, the analysis of how grooming affects subsequent sharing could not be based simply on the number of food transfers from A to B. A correction was required for the number of occasions on which A actually had food to share and B had none. The measure used here is food-getting success, defined as the proportion of approaches by B to A followed by B's cofeeding with or obtaining food from A (excluding approaches in which B hardly looked at A's food—for example, when B simply walked by A). Our measure of food receipt thus took into account the inequalities of food possession by comparing food receipt from a particular partner with the interest shown in this partner's food.

Figure 5.1 shows food-getting success based on a total of 6,972 approaches among adults during food trials. For each dyadic direction separately, food-getting success is broken down according to the occurrence of grooming, or not, during preobservations. Thus in the A to B direction, data for food trials preceded by A's grooming of B were pooled to calculate both A's success in obtaining food from B and B's success in obtaining food from A after A had groomed B. The same was done for trials without previous grooming of B by A. As in all analyses, the two conditions were then compared for each dyadic direction separately with a Wilcoxon matched-pairs signed-ranks test (herein referred to as Wilcoxon).[3] Significant results can therefore not be attributed to covariation of grooming and sharing across dyads (that is, some dyads both groom and share more); instead, such results indicate behavioral changes in a majority of dyadic combinations (that is, most dyads share more after grooming than when there has been no previous grooming). Only 10.9 percent of all approaches among adults during food trials followed grooming by the approaching individual, and not all dyadic directions showed approaches under both grooming conditions—that is, following both grooming and no grooming by the approaching individual. Limiting the comparison to those directions in which approaches were observed during both trials with and without previous grooming, it was found that A's

Figure 5.1   The Effects of Grooming on Food Sharing

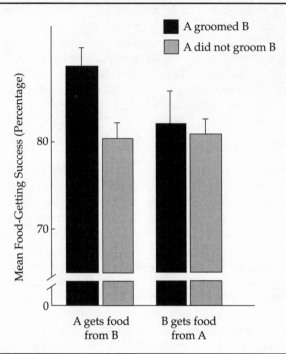

Source: Author's configuration.
Note: N = 6,972 approaches. Mean food-getting success (mean ± SEM) per dyadic direction during food trials. Two conditions are distinguished: either individual A groomed B in the hours preceding the trial, or no previous grooming of B by A occurred. The left-hand side of the graph shows the success of A in obtaining food from B; the right-hand side shows the success of B in obtaining food from A.

food-getting success with B increased when A had groomed B ($z = 3.31$, $p = .0005$, one-tailed), whereas B's food-getting success with A was unaffected by A's previous grooming of B ($z = .36$, ns).

Grooming Effect

If grooming effect is defined as the difference in food-getting success between food trials preceded by grooming of the possessor by the nonpossessor and food trials not preceded by such grooming, dyadic directions involving the adult male showed nearly identical grooming effects (mean ± SEM: = 5.3 percent ± 2.9 percent) as female-female dyads (5.7 percent ± 2.0 percent; Mann Whitney U test: $z = .24$, ns). Across all dyadic directions, grooming effect correlated negatively with the duration of grooming per hour of independent observation (Spearman's rho = -0.33, $n = 43$, $p = .032$, two-tailed), indicating that increased food-getting success owing to grooming was most pronounced in those dyadic directions in which little grooming normally occurred. Nevertheless, increases in food-getting success following grooming were general: thirty-one dyadic directions showed an increase, and only eleven a decrease.

Food trials preceded by grooming were subdivided as to whether A had groomed B for more than or less than 300s. A's food-getting success did not vary across these two conditions $n = 17, T = 69, ns$), suggesting that it is the presence of grooming, rather than its duration, that matters.

Partner Specificity

To investigate whether the increase in sharing following grooming applied specifically to the individual that had done the grooming, A's food-getting success with B was compared across three conditions: after A had groomed B; after one or more adults other than A had groomed B; and after none of the adults had groomed B (figure 5.2). Only the first food-getting success was significantly elevated: A's food-getting success was higher after A had groomed B than after another adult had groomed B (Wilcoxon: $z = 2.00$, $p = .023$, one-tailed).

Rejection

The number of aggressive claims among adults was negligible: only 1.1 percent of transfers involved the use of force. Even the most dominant individuals rarely resorted to aggression and waited patiently, sometimes begging with hand held out, until they could pull a branch out of a bundle or co-feed with the possessor.

The overwhelming majority of food transfers was passive—that is, the food possessor allowed another individual to take food or collect it from nearby rather than give it to the approacher. The possessor could prevent the other from collecting food by walking off, turning its back to the other, pulling the food away, and so on. It was speculated that the effect of grooming on subsequent sharing might be a function of such so-called resistance being shown disproportionately to individuals who had failed to groom the possessor. In support of this hypothesis, the percentage of approaches meeting with resistance was reduced when the approacher had previously groomed the possessor ($z = 3.21$, $p = .0007$, one-tailed) (figure 5.3).

Only a portion of resistance involved agonistic behavior (for example, threat barking, screaming, and gesticulating on the part of the possessor). When tested separately, these agonistic responses, too, oc-

Figure 5.2   Partner Specificity of the Grooming Effect

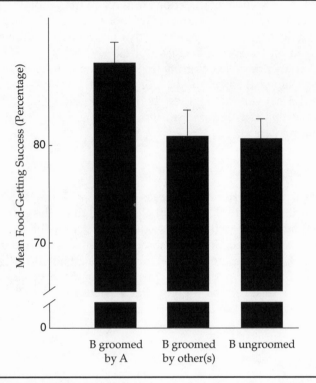

Source: Author's configuration.
Note: N = 43 dyads. Mean food-getting success (mean ± SEM) of individual A in relation to food possessor B under three conditions: A groomed B before the food trial; one or more adults other than A groomed B; and none of the adults groomed B (ungroomed). A's food-getting success was significantly elevated only after A had done the grooming.

curred less often toward a partner who had previously groomed the possessor (mean ± SEM per dyadic direction = 1.0 percent ± 0.6 percent) than when the same partner had not groomed the possessor (3.4 percent ± 0.9 percent; $z = 2.41, p = .008$, one-tailed).

Grooming Following Sharing

After food trials, grooming activity dropped sharply. In 1992, the mean (± SEM) frequency of grooming bouts per hour per adult was 0.63 percent ± 0.17 percent during independent observations but only 0.40 percent ± 0.14 percent during postobservations (comparing grooming output per individual adult: $n = 9, T = 0, p < .01$, two-tailed). When food trials of this period were divided as to whether or not sharing had occurred, a nonsignificant trend was found for

Figure 5.3   Grooming and Resisted Approach

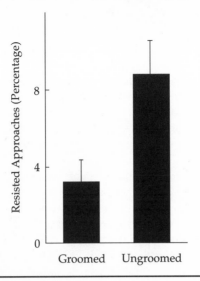

Source: Author's configuration.
Note: N = 177 dyads. Mean percentage of approaches (mean ± SEM) meeting with active resistance from the food possessor when the possessor had not been groomed by the approacher and after the possessor had been groomed by the approaching individual.

grooming in return for received food. Food recipients groomed their benefactors in 6.7 percent ± 1.8 percent of the postobservations compared with 6.2 percent ± 0.9 percent without food receipt from the same partner ($z = 1.33$, *ns*). A stronger effect concerned a reduction of grooming in the sharing individuals themselves. They groomed the beneficiaries of their sharing in 5.5 percent ± 2.0 percent of the postobservations, which was below the rate of 6.3 percent ± 1.0 percent if they had not shared with them ($z = 2.58$, $p = 0.1$, two-tailed).

A less dramatic decrease in grooming was observed in 1993, when postobservations were delayed. The hourly grooming rate dropped from 0.69 percent ± 0.15 percent during independent observations to 0.51 percent ± 0.18 percent during postobservations ($n = 7$, $T = 1$, $p < .05$, two-tailed). No effects on grooming rate, either by the sharing individual or by the recipient, could be demonstrated for the postobservations of this period.

Discussion

In light of the data presented here, it is very likely that the reciprocity correlations previously reported for chimpanzees (de Waal 1989; de Waal and Luttrell 1988) rest on an exchange mechanism in which social services are provided contingent on the services that were received from the same partner. Apart from circumventing the problem of symmetry-based reciprocity, this study addressed two further alternative hypotheses.

According to the first hypothesis, both grooming and food sharing between A and B reflect a common variable, such as the state of the relationship. If this were true, one would expect the most pronounced link between subsequent services to concern the same direction within the dyad. In other words, A's grooming of B should correlate especially with A's sharing with B. Instead, we found that the dyad partners took turns—that is, A's grooming of B specifically increased B's sharing with A. The same hypothesis would predict sharing to be followed by increased grooming in the same direction. The opposite was found, however: previous sharing coincided with reduced grooming of the beneficiary of the sharing. Both effects are consistent with an exchange model, not with a state-of-the-relationship model.

The second alternative hypothesis is that the receipt of a service affects an individual's social attitude toward *all* possible partners, not just the partner who provided the original service (Hemelrijk 1994). This could be called the good-mood hypothesis: that is, the receipt of grooming creates a general benevolent attitude. Our data contradict this hypothesis as well: previous grooming affected the food-getting success of the groomer only, not that of other adults approaching the groomed food possessor.

In sum, the findings of this study are that grooming increases the probability that the recipient of the service will share with its donor and that sharing decreases the probability that the donor of the service will groom its recipient. This is not a matter, therefore, of mere variation across time that causes grooming and sharing tendencies to rise and fall in tandem; rather, what is observed is an exchange mechanism in which donations and receipts of services are stored in memory for at least two hours and exert distinct, partner-specific effects on the subsequent behavior of donors and recipients. In line with this interpretation, food possessors protested more, sometimes aggressively, if approached by a partner who had not groomed them before the trial.

Although it is entirely possible that monkeys, bats, and other nonhuman animals engage in similar exchanges, only for chimpanzees is there evidence for the entire set of features expected if reciprocity is cognition based: partner specificity, selective protest, retaliation, turn taking, and the effect of one service on another. Before concluding that the mechanisms of tit-for-tat are the same in chimpanzees and other animals, more carefully controlled studies will be necessary on other species. At the very least, reciprocal exchange may be most pronounced in chimpanzees.

At the same time, it should be noted that the observed effect on sharing in our study, although significant, was relatively small. Over the years, our chimpanzees seem to have grown increasingly tolerant during food trials, moving from food-getting success among adults of nearly 60 percent (de Waal 1989) to the 81.9 percent of the present study. The majority of approaches between adults occurred without previous grooming between them: if preceded by grooming there was an average increase in the groomer's food-getting success of 5.6 percent. The most dramatic result was perhaps the number of dyadic directions that jumped to 100 percent food-getting success following grooming. Only one of forty-three dyadic directions with approaches under both conditions reached a rate of food-getting success of 100 percent in the absence of previous grooming by the approaching party. If the approacher had groomed the food possessor, on the other hand, no fewer than seventeen dyadic directions reached this high success level.

How these observations of sequential mutual exchange relate to truly costly exchanges, such as those in which one individual risks its life for another, is as yet unclear. The present data are perhaps best interpreted as support for the existence of a service economy among chimpanzees. Reciprocal altruism may be part of this economy and may have been instrumental in its evolution, but the economy covers a much wider range of phenomena than those traditionally defined as "altruistic" (that is, fitness reducing for the donor and fitness enhancing for the recipient). Female sexual proceptivity, for example, is most likely an important currency in the chimpanzee's service economy (Stanford et al. 1994; Yerkes 1941), although no one would argue that a female's willingness to mate reduces her fitness or constitutes cooperative behavior in the usual sense. The concept of "service" or "favor" does cover such behavior and permits a broader perspective on the psychological mechanisms underlying reciprocal exchange in primates.

This chapter has been reprinted, in modified form, from *Evolution and Human Behavior*, vol. 18 (1997): 375–86, with permission from Elsevier Science. The research was supported by grants from the National Institutes of Mental Health (Grant R03-MH49475) and the National Institutes of Health (Grant R01-RR09797), both to the author, and the National Institutes of Health (Grant RR00165) to the Yerkes Regional Primate Research Center. The author is especially grateful to Michael Seres for assistance with data collection and data administration. Thanks are also owed to the animal-care and veterinary staff of the Yerkes Field Station. The Yerkes Regional Primate Research Center is fully accredited by the American Association for Accreditation of Laboratory Animal Care.

Notes

1. For a recent review that includes other possible mechanisms of reciprocity, see Brosnan and de Waal (2002).
2. More detailed descriptions of the behavioral categories can be found in de Waal (1989).
3. Unless otherwise indicated, Wilcoxon terminology is used throughout this analysis.

References

Bercovitch, Frederick. 1988. "Coalitions, Cooperation, and Reproductive Tactics Among Adult Male Baboons." *Animal Behaviour* 36: 1198–1209.
Boesch, Christophe, and Hedwige Boesch. 1989. "Hunting Behavior of Wild Chimpanzees in the Taï National Park." *American Journal of Physical Anthropology* 78: 547–73.
Brosnan, Sarah F., and Frans B. M. de Waal. 2002. "A Proximate Perspective on Reciprocal Altruism." *Human Nature* 13: 129–52.
Clutton-Brock, Timothy H., and George A. Parker. 1995. "Punishment in Animal Societies." *Nature* 373: 209–16.
de Waal, Frans B. M. 1982. *Chimpanzee Politics: Power and Sex Among Apes*. Baltimore, Md.: Johns Hopkins University Press.
———. 1989. "Food Sharing and Reciprocal Obligations Among Chimpanzees." *Journal of Human Evolution* 18: 433–59.
———. 1992. "Coalitions As Part of Reciprocal Relations in the Arnhem Chimpanzee Colony." In *Coalitions and Alliances in Humans and Other Animals*, edited by Alexander H. Harcourt and Frans B. M. de Waal. Oxford: Oxford University Press.
———. 2000. "Attitudinal Reciprocity in Food Sharing Among Brown Capuchins." *Animal Behaviour* 60: 253–61.
de Waal, Frans B. M., and Michelle L. Berger. 2000. "Payment for Labour in Monkeys." *Nature* 404: 563.
de Waal, Frans B. M., and Lesleigh M. Luttrell. 1988. "Mechanisms of Social Reciprocity in Three Primate Species: Symmetrical Relationship Characteristics or Cognition?" *Ethology and Sociobiology* 9: 101–18.
de Waal, Frans B. M., and Deborah D. Yoshihara. 1983. "Reconciliation and Re-Directed Affection in Rhesus Monkeys." *Behaviour* 85: 224–41.
Dow, Malcolm, James Cheverud, and Jonathan Friedlaender. 1987. "Partial Correlation of Distance Matrices in Studies of Population Structure and Genetic Microdifferentiation: Quadratic Assignment." *American Journal of Physical Anthropology* 72: 343–52.
Feistner, Anna T. C., and William C. McGrew. 1989. "Food-Sharing in Primates: A Critical Review." In *Perspectives in Primate Biology*, vol. 3, edited by P. K. Seth and S. Seth. New Delhi, India: Today and Tomorrow's Printers and Publishers.

Goodall, Jane. 1971. *In the Shadow of Man*. Boston: Houghton Mifflin.
————. 1986. *The Chimpanzees of Gombe: Patterns of Behavior*. Cambridge, Mass.: Harvard University Press, Belknap Press.
Hamilton, William D. 1964. "The Genetical Evolution of Social Behaviour, Parts I and II." *Journal of Theoretical Biology* 7: 1–52.
Harcourt, Alexander H., and Frans B. M. de Waal. 1992. *Coalitions and Alliances in Humans and Other Animals*. Oxford: Oxford University Press.
Hart, Benjamin L., and Lynette A. Hart. 1992. "Reciprocal Allogrooming in Impala, *Aepyceros melampus*." *Animal Behaviour* 44: 1073–83.
Hemelrijk, Charlotte K. 1994. "Support for Being Groomed in Long-Tailed Macaques, *Macaca fascicularis*." *Animal Behaviour* 48: 479–81.
Kummer, Hans. 1991. "Evolutionary Transformations of Possessive Behavior." In *To Have Possessions: A Handbook on Ownership and Property*, edited by F. W. Rudmin. Special issue of *Journal of Social Behavior and Personality* 6(6): 75–83.
Noë, Ronald. 1990. "A Veto Game Played by Baboons: A Challenge to the Use of the Prisoner's Dilemma As a Paradigm for Reciprocity and Cooperation." *Animal Behaviour* 39: 78–90.
Packer, Craig. 1977. "Reciprocal Altruism in *Papio Anubis*." *Nature* 265: 441–43.
Roberts, Gilbert, and Thomas N. Sherratt. 1998. "Development of Cooperative Relationships Through Increasing Investment." *Nature* 394: 175–79.
Rothstein, Stephen I., and Raymond R. Pierotti. 1988. "Distinctions Among Reciprocal Altruism, Kin Selection, and Cooperation and a Model for the Initial Evolution of Beneficent Behavior." *Ethology and Sociobiology* 9: 189–209.
Schnell, Gary, Doris D. Watt, and Michael M. Douglas. 1985. "Statistical Comparison of Proximity Matrices: Applications in Animal Behavior." *Animal Behaviour* 33: 239–53.
Seyfarth, Robert. 1980. "The Distribution of Grooming and Related Behaviours Among Adult Female Vervet Monkeys." *Animal Behaviour* 28: 798–813.
Seyfarth, Robert, and Dorothy D. Cheney. 1984. "Grooming, Alliances, and Reciprocal Altruism in Vervet Monkeys." *Nature* 308: 541–43.
Smuts, Barbara B. 1985. *Sex and Friendship in Baboons*. New York: Aldine.
Stanford, Craig B., Janette Wallis, Hamisi Matama, and Jane Goodall. 1994. "Patterns of Predation by Chimpanzees on Red Colobus Monkeys in Gombe National Park, 1982–1991." *American Journal of Physical Anthropology* 94: 213–28.
Taylor, Charles E., and Michael T. McGuire. 1988. "Reciprocal Altruism: Fifteen Years Later." *Ethology and Sociobiology* 9: 67–72.
Teleki, Geza. 1973. *The Predatory Behavior of Wild Chimpanzees*. Lewisburg, Penn.: Bucknell University Press.
Trivers, Robert L. 1971. "The Evolution of Reciprocal Altruism." *Quarterly Review of Biology* 46: 35–57.
Wilkinson, Gerald S. 1984. "Reciprocal Food Sharing in the Vampire Bat." *Nature* 308: 181–84.
Wilson, Edward O. 1975. *Sociobiology: The New Synthesis*. Cambridge, Mass.: Harvard University Press, Belknap Press.
Yerkes, Robert M. 1941. "Conjugal Contrasts Among Chimpanzees." *Journal of Abnormal Social Psychology* 36: 175–99.

PART III

THE LINKS BETWEEN EVOLUTION, COGNITION, AND BEHAVIOR

Chapter 6

A Cognitive Theory of Reciprocal Exchange

KEVIN A. MCCABE

H UMAN RECIPROCITY is a set of behaviors generated by a cognitive strategy that is implemented in the evolved embodied neural circuitry of the central and peripheral nervous system. This means that the study of reciprocity is conducted on at least four different levels.

Reciprocity is studied at the behavioral level by looking at the messages agents send and inferring the behavioral rules that produce these messages. At this level, there are known to be large variations in behavior both within and between individuals. An individual's strategy can be defined as a plan on what behavioral rule to use contingent on available information. Reciprocity is studied at the strategic level by looking at the informational, computational, and equilibrium requirements of the underlying strategy. Many different strategies can explain the observed variation in reciprocity behaviors, and decision-theoretic principles of selection, such as computational simplicity, rational expectations, or utility maximization, are likely to be too simplistic. Reciprocity is studied at the evolutionary level by looking at those strategies that survive under natural selection. Such an analysis critically depends on knowing the evolutionary environment and the path-dependent emergence of a species-specific strategy. Reciprocity is studied at the neural level by looking at how the nervous system actually encodes a particular strategy. However, the complexity of the nervous system requires researchers to have strong prior expectations of the possible strategies that might have been encoded. Although each has both advantages and limitations, taken together the four

147

levels illustrate the benefits to understanding that can be achieved in an interdisciplinary research program called neuroeconomics.

Positive reciprocity can be measured behaviorally using the following definitions. Person 1 shows "trust" for person 2 by taking an action that gives up some amount of immediate benefit in return for a longer-run benefit for both, but in doing so person 1 relies on person 2 to "reciprocate" in the future by taking an action that gives up some benefit in order to make both persons better off than they were at the starting point. In this case, the existence of positive reciprocity makes both persons better off. Positive reciprocity can be contrasted with "negative reciprocity" as follows: person 1 "conciliates" person 2 by taking an action that gives up some amount of immediate benefit to make person 2 better off; but in doing so, person 1 relies on person 2 to refrain from "negative reciprocity" in the future, by which person 2 might take an action that gives up some amount of benefit in order to make person 1 worse off. In this case, the threat of negative reciprocity reduces the ability of person 1 to take advantage of person 2.

Reciprocal behavior can be explored through the use of two classes of games: the *investment game* and the *ultimatum game*. In the investment game, "trust" and "positive reciprocity" come into play, and in the ultimatum game, "conciliation" and "negative reciprocity." The findings from these experiments indicate that reciprocity occurs even in cases in which the game is played only once with anonymously matched subjects. When the game is repeated, there is evidence of a strong tendency for subjects to build reputations as reciprocators, suggesting that they believe there are reciprocators in their cohort.[1]

Trust and conciliation are relatively easy to explain once reciprocity is established, but how does one explain reciprocity? A game-theoretic analysis of reciprocity assumes that subjects will take actions that maximize their self-interest at every stage of the decision process— that they will always act from myopic self-interest. This means that when it comes time to reciprocate, subjects should instead defect in their myopic self-interest. If the subjects moving first know this, then they should not "trust" or engage in "conciliatory" actions. Therefore, reciprocity can be viewed as a form of commitment to a certain course of voluntary action.

There is also evidence that the adaptation of the human mind allows for increasingly more complex commitments to reciprocal actions. The evolutionary psychologists Leda Cosmides and John Tooby (1992) argue that the human mind consists of evolved information-processing mechanisms that are functionally specialized to produce behavior, such as reciprocity, to solve particular adaptive problems, such as personal exchange. Mechanisms that are functionally specialized will be activated by specific environmental content, such as the existence of mutual gains. Within this framework, the argument is made that humans developed mental mechanisms such as "cheater-detection" and "theory-of-mind" modules (see chapter 9, this volume) to enable them to live in close proximity with other humans, thus allowing humans to develop a unique ecological niche as hunters and gatherers of high-density nutrients. According to this line of reasoning, reciprocal behavior first emerged from food sharing and later expanded to many other activities.

The research on delay of gratification suggests the existence in humans of a psychological mechanism for commitment. Janet Metcalfe and Walter Mischel (1999) argue that delay of gratification involves the intervention of cognitively "cool" neural mechanisms to overcome "hot" mechanisms' demand for immediate gratification. In the case of food, "hunger" should lead to neural demands for immediate gratification. Therefore, if humans are to share food, this demand will often have to be overcome by "cool" mechanisms that recognize that others are hungry, too, and that sharing will lead to reciprocity, which will help guarantee against "hunger" in the future. For humans to be able to recognize that sharing may lead to reciprocity requires shared-attention mechanisms (see Baron-Cohen 1995) that allow them to recognize mutual gains and track reciprocal obligations.

A mechanism known as "goodwill accounting" is an enhanced score-keeping strategy that implements delay of gratification in two-person exchange. This strategy satisfies the basic requirements for *reciprocal altruism* as outlined by Robert Kurzban in chapter 4 of this volume. Goodwill accounting (see McCabe and Smith 2000) is a reputation-based scoring mechanism whereby people keep mental accounts of the extent to which potential trading partners can be relied on to establish a trust relationship in exchange settings. Subjects weigh the subjective risk of trusting against the goodwill of their trading partners to decide whether or not to initiate, or reciprocate, an exchange. Not only do people keep goodwill accounts, but they must also be good at reading the level of goodwill they are likely to have with others. A theory-of-mind system has a major impact on the degree of reciprocity attained using goodwill accounting with selected trading partners.

This raises the question of how the brain encodes a strategy like goodwill accounting. Antonio Damasio (1989) introduces the binding problem to explain how the dispersed information about entities and events found in different regions of the brain is integrated to allow decision making. Cooperative behavior requires the binding of contingent information that allows subjects to evaluate the mental states of their counterparts and commit to a stimuli-conditioned reward-motivated choice. Recent brain-imaging experiments suggest that frontal lobe regions associated with "executive control" functions are activated when humans are trying to cooperate with other humans. Because the activations in question control for "executive" functions involved simply in game playing against a computer, the activation of these regions when playing with another person supports the evolutionary psychology hypothesis that humans have evolved content-dependent mechanisms that allow them to overcome their demand for immediate gratification in favor of reciprocal exchange.

Laboratory Evidence for Reciprocity

The laboratory provides researchers with the ability to run controlled experiments and to replicate other researchers' results. As Vernon Smith (1994) points out, this allows researchers to come to an agreement on three basic questions: Do you observe what I observe? Do you interpret what we observe as I interpret it? Do you conclude what I conclude from our interpretation?

In studying reciprocity the basic insight is that both the past (through reputations) and the future (through expectations) matter. It is important to have as a baseline experiment a condition that controls for both these elements. Robert Forsythe and his colleagues (1994) developed such a baseline in the *dictator game*. In this game, player 1 (the dictator) is given an amount of money, say $10, from which he or she can then choose a sum to give to player 2. Clearly, the self-interested strategy for player 1 is to keep all the money, but although player 1s often keep a large share of the money, they still give significant amounts to player 2.

Elsewhere (Hoffman, McCabe, and Smith 1996), I have argued that the findings of Forsythe and colleagues could be explained in terms of the dictators' concern for their reputations and that this reputational effect can be controlled for by varying the *social distance* between the dictator and other persons. Social distance is a measure of the degree to which people feel they are connected either through information about one another or through common social cues. In that paper, we reported that the amount of money dictators in our study were willing to give varied inversely with social distance; the greater the social distance, the less important were individual reputations, resulting in less giving on the part of dictators (Hoffman, McCabe, and Smith 1996). In our replication of the experiment conducted by Forsythe and colleagues (1994), 18 percent of the subject dictators kept all the money, and 32 percent offered $4 or more to their counterparts. We then compared this result to a condition in which subjects' decisions were guaranteed to be double blind: that is, neither their counterparts nor the experimenter could observe subjects' actual decisions. In this condition, 64 percent of the subjects kept all the money, whereas only 8 percent offered $4 or more to their counterparts. From this study we can conclude that the "double-blind" procedure we employed in earlier work (Hoffman et al. 1994) provides a good control condition for a dictator game baseline for laboratory studies of reciprocity.

The investment game (Berg, Dickhaut, and McCabe 1995) provides examples of trusting behavior and positive reciprocity. In this game two subjects are each given an amount of money (say, $10) and then assigned the role of either player 1 or player 2. Player 1 decides how much of the $10 to invest with player 2 and how much to keep. By investing some of the money, player 1 gives up that amount as an immediate benefit. Both subjects know with certainty that the amount invested (in the other player) will increase—say, triple. Thus an investment of $10 will return $30. Player 2 must then decide how much of the tripled amount to keep and how much to send back to player 1 as a return on player 1's investment. By sending back money, player 2 gives up that amount as an immediate benefit. Both subjects know the game will be played only once, and the subjects are guaranteed that no one, including the experimenter, will be able to verify their decisions. Player 1 invests $8 and keeps $2, the $8 triples to $24. Player 2 keeps $14 and sends back $10. Player 1 earns $12 ($2 plus $10) and player 2 earns $24 ($10 plus $14). Player 2 could also decide to keep all $24, in which case player 1 would earn only $2 whereas player 2 would earn $34.

How much should player 1 invest? If player 1 invests nothing, then both players earn $10, which is far less than what they would earn if player 1 could "trust" player 2. If player 1 invests money with player 2, what should player 2 do? The *subgame-perfect-equilibrium* prediction from game theory is that player 2 should keep all the money, but then it is just as obvious that player 1 should not trust player 2 and that both players will earn $10. Deciding whether or not one can trust one's partner is an essential problem encountered in every exchange. Without the costless enforcement of contracts, some degree of trust (and reciprocity) is necessary, but economists all seem to agree that no institution provides costless enforcement. Positive reciprocity can therefore be predicted to play an important role in economic exchange.

In the investment game, player 2 is essentially in the same role as the dictator in the dictator game. Will player 2 behave similarly to the dictators, or will the previous move by player 1 affect player 2's decision? Joyce Berg, John Dickhaut, and I (1995) ran a *one-shot* double-blind investment game with thirty-two pairs of subjects over three sessions. Twenty of the thirty-two player 1s showed high levels of

Figure 6.1   Trust Game

Player 1 •——— (10,10)

Player 2 •——— (15,25)

(0,40)

Source: Author's configuration.

trust by investing $5 or more. Of these twenty, ten player 1s experienced reciprocity, and seven received less than $1. The remaining twelve player 1s invested less than $5 (two player 1s invested nothing). Among those player 1s who exhibited high levels of trust (by investing $5 or more), 40 percent received 40 percent or more of the tripled investment from the player 2s, compared with only 8 percent of the dictators who sent back 40 percent or more (in the double-blind dictator experiment). The higher percentage of amounts sent back in the investment game, compared with the dictator game, suggests that player 2s reciprocate the "trust" shown by player 1s. Past moves do matter (see also chapter 10, this volume).

A reduced-form version of the investment game is the trust game, illustrated in figure 6.1. Player 1 must choose whether to play right, and end the game, or to play down. What will affect player 1's choice? Playing right will result in $10, whereas by playing down player 1 will earn either $15 or nothing. Let U be the utility function for player 1 and p be the probability that player 2 will move right. In terms of standard expected-utility theory, player 1 will move down—that is, will trust—when $pU(15) + [1 - p]U(0) > U(10)$. Let V be the utility function for player 2. When it is player 2's turn to move, he or she must choose between V(25) for playing right or V(40) for playing down. If people are strictly nonsatiated in money—that is, if $U' > 0$ and $V' > 0$, and the game is played only once, then player 1 can reason about player 2 as follows: because V(40) > V(25), player 2 will play down, and thus player 1 should assume $p = 0$; and if $p = 0$, then U(10) > U(0), and player 1 should move right immediately.

When cash-motivated subjects played this game once in a controlled laboratory environment (McCabe and Smith 2000, 50 percent of the player 1s played as predicted and moved right. Fifty percent, however, played down. Furthermore, when player 2s had a chance to play, 75 percent played right—that is, reciprocated—and only 25 percent defect (move down). Why is the game-theoretic analysis presented earlier wrong? One possibility is that player 2 cares about player 1 in the sense that his or her utility function includes player 1's payoff. In this case, we would write $V(25,15) > V(40,0)$. Seventy-five percent of the player 2s might have been altruistic (in that their utility functions included player 1s' payoffs), and 50 percent of player 1s might have expected this level of reciprocity. This explanation has two problems. First, we do not seem to see convergent evidence from other laboratory settings (see chapter 10, this volume), or from field research, for this hypothesis. Second, if giving away money to other people allows them to invest more resources in reproductive success, relative to the givers' investment, why would such a propensity escape invasion from more selfish preferences?

An alternative explanation of the data is that people have evolved cognitive mechanisms for capturing gains from exchange. In this explanation we go back to our self-interested payoffs and note that $U(15) > U(10)$ and $V(25) > V(10)$. Clearly both players can understand they will both be better off with the second-round payoffs (15,25) compared with the payoffs of the first round (10,10). Furthermore, if they succeed, they will both be better off in terms of resources they can invest in reproductive success relative to the rest of the population; but still, what stops player 2 from taking the $40? One possibility is that subjects in the role of player 2 have evolved an ability to delay their immediate gratification (taking $40) in an exchange situation in favor of reciprocity (making the [15,25] split). If, in fact, player 1 could be sure that player 2 had such a mechanism, then player 1, with a high enough value of p, will move down. Appropriately solving the delay of gratification problem allows individuals to solve repeated game interactions without investing in cognitively complex, and costly, repeated game strategies. This means people can cooperate even in one-shot games.

The ultimatum game, first introduced by W. Güth, R. Schmittberger, and B. Schwarze (1982), provides examples of conciliatory behavior and negative reciprocity. In this game, player 1 must decide how to split a fixed amount of money (say, $10). For example, player 1 can propose a split of $8 for player 1 and $2 for player 2 (payoff of [8,2]). However, a proposal of (5,5) would be seen as more conciliatory. Once player 1 proposes a split, player 2 can either accept or reject the offer. If player 2 rejects, then both players earn nothing; otherwise, the players earn the split proposed by player 1.

How should player 1 split the money? A proposal of (9,1) would be better for player 1 than a (5,5) split. But would player 2 be more likely to reject the ($9, $1) proposal—in which case player 1 would end up with nothing? At what level should player 2 reject player 1's offer, given that the rejection of even (9,1) means that player 2 must give up $1? The subgame-perfect-equilibrium prediction is that player 2 should accept any positive offer. Knowing this, player 1 should go ahead and offer (9,1). This means, however, that player 1 has an advantage over player 2. Player 2 can negate this advantage by rejecting player 1's offer, but in that case the gains from exchange will be lost. When Güth, Schmittberger, and Schwarze ran this experiment with cash-motivated subjects, they observed that the modal proposal was to split the money fifty-fifty. This result has now been replicated a large number of times, including by Forsythe and colleagues (1994), who then compare offers in ultimatum games to those in dictator games to determine whether the fifty-fifty proposals in ultimatum games are largely a consequence of player 2's threat to reject.

Forsythe and colleagues find a significant reduction in offers in the dictator game compared with the ultimatum game. They conclude that it is the threat of rejection by player 2 that leads player 1 to follow the conciliatory fifty-fifty split. Because negotiating mutually agreeable splits is essential to every exchange, and because exchange is voluntary and therefore the threat of rejection always looms, it seems clear that negative reciprocity plays an important role in economic exchange.

Following up on the results of Forsythe and colleagues, Hoffman et al. (1994) look at contextual effects that are predicted by social-exchange theory to change subjects' expectations regarding the use of negative reciprocity. According to social exchange theory, subjects form their expectations on the "fairness" of an exchange using three norms: equity, equality, and reciprocity. Equity implies that individuals who contribute more to a social exchange should gain a larger share of the returns. When everyone's contribution is the same, equality implies that everyone should share equally in the benefit. Reciprocity implies that if one individual shares with another individual, the second individual must reciprocate as soon as possible.

Hoffman and colleagues examine two treatments: property rights and social roles. In the property-rights treatment, subjects were assigned the role of first or second mover in one of two ways: either randomly (the RANDOM case)—the standard approach in most ultimatum games—or by winning the right to be first mover in a knowledge contest (the CONTEST case). In RANDOM, the authors predict that the equality norm should be invoked, whereas in CONTEST, being told one has "earned the right" through the contest to be first mover is predicted, by the equity norm, to entitle the first mover to a larger share of the money.

In the social-roles treatment, first movers were referred to either as decision maker 1's (the DIVIDE case) or as sellers (the EXCHANGE case). Second movers were referred to as either decision maker 2's (DIVIDE) or as buyers (EXCHANGE). In DIVIDE, decision maker 1 was asked to divide the $10; in EXCHANGE, a seller was asked to make a price decision against a known buyer's valuation of $10, amounting to an offer to split the money. Second movers were treated similarly. In DIVIDE, decision maker 2 was asked to accept or reject the offer; in EXCHANGE, a buyer was asked to make a decision to buy or not to buy, amounting to a decision to accept or reject the seller's offer. Because sellers are entitled to set prices in most modern retail economies, Hoffman and colleagues predicted that the equity norm may imply a greater share for sellers in the second case. In contrast, the use of neutral terms, such as decision maker, was predicted to invoke the equality norm.

In their resulting two-by-two experimental design, the authors first replicate the results of Robert Forsythe and colleagues; that is, RANDOM-DIVIDE, finding that more than 50 percent of the offers were at fifty-fifty, with a mean offer to decision maker 2s of $4.37. By comparison, in CONTEST-EXCHANGE, which was predicted to have the strongest equity norm effect, fewer than 10 percent of the offers were at fifty-fifty, with a mean offer to decision maker 2s of $3.08. One indication that both groups of decision makers were conforming to social-exchange norms is the relatively low rates of rejection (about 10 percent) in both cases. Furthermore, even though offers to the second mover were much lower in CONTEST-EXCHANGE, rejection rates were at the same level as those in RANDOM-DIVIDE. That rejections did not increase in the CONTEST-EXCHANGE treatment can be explained if second movers had accepted the first movers' right to claim more.

Although social-exchange theory helped motivate and explain the experiments conducted by Elizabeth Hoffman and colleagues (Hoffman, McCabe, and Smith 1996; Hoffman et al. 1994), it does not explain how these norms are formed or how trade-offs are made between them. Whereas the proximate cause of behavior is the embodied brain, the ultimate cause of behavior is the evolutionary process that selected for the current architecture of the brain. The archeological evidence summarized by Richard Klein (1999) suggests that hominid brains underwent a dramatic increase in volume roughly two million years ago and again, more recently, half a million years ago. The best modern example of the environment in which the human brain evolved is the hunter-gatherer society.

The Economic Environment for the Emergence of Reciprocity

According to evolutionary psychology, the human mind consists of a set of evolved information-processing mechanisms and the developmental programs that produce them. These mechanisms are adaptations over evolutionary time to our ancestral environment. Therefore, to understand the function of these mechanisms requires, first, an understanding of the ancestral environment from which they evolved.

What is the environment in which humans evolved? The anthropologist Hillard Kaplan (Nimchinsky et al. 1999) hypothesizes that humans have adapted to an ecological niche involving the hunting and gathering of high-density, protein-rich foods. This niche is likely to have promoted adaptations for food sharing, thus increasing the maximum sustainable group size (see Dunbar 1996) by decreasing the risk of starvation. At the same time, Kaplan points out, adaptation to this niche increased the value of better training in hunting skills. This required a longer adolescence for skills development, creating a role for three-generation families. It also increased the number of dependents in a group, however, which is likely to have increased the minimum sustainable group size as well. One likely consequence of an increasing group size is an increase in specialization, which means more opportunities for trading different goods and services. This, in turn, places much more importance on a person's reputation for trustworthiness and suggests that an appropriate reciprocity strategy will take reputation into account.

How did we get from food sharing to reciprocity? There is evidence that primates have evolved reciprocal mechanisms that extend beyond food sharing. Frans de Waal (1996; see also chapter 5, this volume) argues that chimpanzees can reciprocate across some goods and services. For example, if A grooms B, then the chances increase that B will share food with A later in the day in the form of facilitative taking. This suggests that chimpanzees may be capable of abstractly encoding a favor received from a specific individual, holding that encoding as a reciprocal obligation for at least a short period of time, and choosing an appropriate reciprocal favor for that individual in the future.

Recent neurological evidence has been found of a spindle-cell neuron in the anterior cingulate that seems to occur only in humans and great apes (see Nimchinsky et al. 1999). Interestingly, because it may indicate changes in degree of cognitive function, these cells increase in abundance and begin to exhibit clustering as we move in order from the orangutan, to the gorilla, the chimpanzee, the bonobo, and finally humans. This area of the cortex is hypothesized to act as a supervisory attentional system (see Gazzaniga, Ivry, and Mangun 1998) and is active in tasks involving the inhibition of responses in order to exercise cognitive control. Such inhibitory control would be important for the development of strategies for delaying gratification.

Although increases in brain volume and the presence of spindle cells indicate that important changes have occurred in the hominid brain, these studies do not provide an account of how brain function changed over time. This requires a theory of the origins of the hominid mind. One theory, proposed by Merlin Donald (1991), that is consistent with the evidence presented here is the incremental dominance of successive cognitive mechanisms designed to improve the conscious, voluntary manipulation of hominid's mental models of the world. Donald begins his explanation with primates' capacity for event perception and episodic memory, resulting in a high level of problem-solving skills and the ability to engage in complex social relationships. Primate research enables researchers to delimit the capabilities of this system. In particular, nonhuman primates do not seem to have semantic representational systems that would allow them to mentally reflect on situational similarities or provide systematic pedagogic training to their young.

Donald hypothesizes that the human mind advanced through the development of a number of important neural mechanisms designed to allow new forms of mental representation that support the emergence of a complex human culture. These representations are inherently public forms of knowledge expression leading to the emergence of a "semi-autonomous layer of culture." Donald then summarizes the origins of the human mind as developing through three transitions. The first comprised humans' ability to engage in nonverbal action modeling, or what Donald terms "mimesis." Such an ability would allow individuals to observe others' actions, rehearse them mentally, and then evaluate and refine their own motor skills. The end result is nonverbal communication and shared attention through reciprocal gestures.

Mimesis provides a good starting point for human reciprocity. Shared attention can soon lead to joint recognition, and cooperative effort, for mutual gain. Furthermore, copying another person's actions leads to reciprocal game playing in children and the understanding that if one follows the rules of the game, then another's action should invoke an obligation to perform an expected reciprocating action. However, mimesis is likely to promote reciprocity in kind: I clap, you clap; I share food, you share food.

Once shared attention is possible and reciprocity is expected, development of a "cheater-detection" module sensitive to another person's defection in a personal exchange would allow more generous forms of reciprocity to emerge. This hypothesis is developed and tested in a novel extension of the Wason selection task by Leda Cosmides (1989). Cosmides develops a behavioral framework for testing whether or not a particular mental function is an evolutionary adaptation activated by specific environmental content. It is likely that the propensity for cheater detection, once it had been encoded in humans, supported the development of cognitive strategies such as "goodwill accounting."

Delay of Gratification and Positive Reciprocity

In a typical delay of gratification task, a child is presented with a desirable food item. The child is told that the experimenter will leave the room, and if the child waits until the experimenter returns, then the child will be given two units of the food item. At any time before the experimenter returns, the child can ring a bell, causing the experimenter to return immediately, but then the child will get only one item. The experimenter then measures how long it takes for the child to ring the bell and uses this as a proxy for the child's level of "cognitive control."

Metcalfe and Mischel (1999) summarize a number of behavioral properties involved in the delay of gratification. Two of these stand out in terms of understanding reciprocity. First, when the item in question is visible to the child, then those children who focus their attention on the reward tend to delay for a shorter period of time than those children whose attention is focused elsewhere. Second, cognitive control—as indicated by how long they wait—increases with age. Metcalfe and Mischel propose a framework they call the hot-cool system for explaining these properties.

According to this framework, the brain can be divided into "hot" systems that react automatically to stimuli triggers and "cool" systems that are primarily narrative in nature. These two systems are interconnected in such a way that the "cool" system somehow mediates the reward-contingent brain activations associated with hot systems' demand for immediate gratification. The cool system does this by "weaving knowledge about sensations and emotions, thoughts, actions, and context into an ongoing narrative that is coherent, goal sensitive, and strategic" (Metcalfe and Mischel 1999, 6). But how does the brain's narrative ability allow for delay of gratification?

Within this framework, the ability to exert cognitive control is closely linked to one's ability to divert attention away from the "hot" arousal-based features of the reward. For example, children are better able to control their immediate demand for a treat if they are distracted by playing a game. Alternatively, the item in question can be mentally placed in another context that reduces the level of "hot" systems activation. For example, children who are told that when the experimenter returns they will have a party where the treats will be eaten appear able to exert better cognitive control.

What is the linkage between the delay of gratification paradigm and the investment game described earlier? Player 1 must decide how much of the $10 to keep and how much to send. First, will dollars activate the "hot" system? Evidence from brain imaging suggests that the presence of monetary rewards causes dissociable activations in the brain's reward systems. There is also evidence of activation in the orbitofrontal cortex for monetary gains and losses, even when subjects are not actually paid. The ability of abstract monetary rewards to activate this region, where reward-contingent responses are learned, suggests that action responses pursuant to these rewards are likely to be under the influence of the brain's "hot" systems. Thus the temptation to keep the $10 and walk away, rather than to wait for the possibility of getting even more money, fits the delay of gratification paradigm.

The cool system can intervene for player 1 by invoking a narrative of trust and reciprocity and thus exerting control over the immediate desire to keep the money and end play. Thus player 1 may reason, "Player 2 will surely understand that if I send player 2 the $10 and it triples to $30 I will expect player 2 to send me back something more than the $10 I invested." However, whether or not this narrative is invoked will most likely depend on the context and also on player 1's beliefs about the likelihood that player 2 will reciprocate. Player 2's choice to reciprocate can also be understood as delay of gratification, even in a one-shot game, if cognitive control is learned in the context of repeat interaction and activated unconsciously by cues occurring in the one-shot games. For example, player 2 may think, "It is only right that I send player 1 back more than $10, given that it was player 1 who made it possible for me to have the money to make this decision."

If trust and positive reciprocity can be seen as part of the cognitively cool narrative to allow cooperation through delay of gratification, then this behavior should exhibit the general characteristics associated with delay of gratification. For example, people better able to distract themselves, perhaps in the form of personal or social obligation, will be better cooperators, and cooperation should improve with age. The framework of the hot-cool system does not provide any demonstration that the delay of gratification in a social context will actually make someone better off, because it increases the likelihood of being cheated. What strategy might implement this mechanism?

Goodwill Accounting and Positive Reciprocity

Although an exchange can be measured in terms of the usual who, what, when, where, and how, the subjective value to the participants can at best be inferred. For example, one inference that is often made about why an exchange occurs is that both parties in a voluntary exchange must have been made better off—that is, the value of voluntary exchange is always positive. However, the inability to know how much the other player values the exchange means that "reciprocity" probably does not depend on a cost-benefit type of analysis; instead, these behaviors are initiated by specific informational stimuli within the exchange context.

Can we identify a strategy that may have emerged through natural selection to produce a particular behavior like reciprocity? A strategy like *tit-for-tat* (see Axelrod 1997) shows how cognitively simple the implementation of reciprocal altruism can be, but it is not the only, nor necessarily the best, strategy for implementing reciprocity. The optimal strategy depends on the environment in which the strategy operates. For example, Robert Axelrod points out that a three-state contrite tit-for-tat strategy performs better in a noisy environment.

Figure 6.2 illustrates how the trust game in figure 6.1 can be extended to include "goodwill" decisions. Player 1's evaluation of the game results in the real-valued vector $(g_t^{12}, h_t^{21}, x^1, y_t^{12})$ where g_t^{12} is the amount of goodwill player 2 has with player 1, h_t^{21} is player 1's expectation of the amount of goodwill player 1 has with player 2, x^1 is player 1's evaluation of the subjective risk of playing the game with an unknown counterpart, and y_t^{12} is player 1's expectation of player 2's subjective risk evaluation. Player 1 moves down if and only if $g_t^{12} > x^1$ and $h_t^{21} > y_t^{12}$. When player 1 moves down, player 2 faces a similar calculation and will move right if and only if $g_t^{21} > x^2$ and $h_t^{12} > y_t^{21}$. Given the sequential nature of the game, however, player 2 can infer that $h_t^{12} > y_t^{21}$, resulting in the need to determine only whether $g_t^{21} > x^2$. It is an open (and interesting) question whether the calculations should be made in terms of expected value, replacing h_t and y_t^{12} with distribution functions and then calculating the expected value to player 1 of playing down, given that player 2 is following the same goodwill accounting rule. Such a calculation would recognize trust as a calculated cost-benefit analysis that would be influenced by the size of the payoffs.

The effect of h_t^{ji} is that agent I can now form some expectation about agent j's likely behavior. If, for example, $h_t^{II} < x^I$, then agent I would realize that agent j is very likely to defect in these circumstances because i does not yet have enough goodwill with j for the

Figure 6.2   Goodwill Accounting in the Trust Game

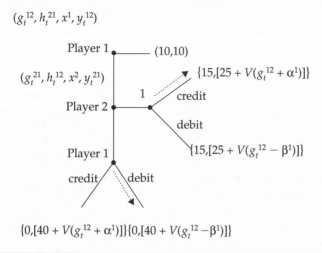

Source: Author's configuration.

degree of risk in the current situation. If agent i can avoid the situation, then agent i can avoid the resulting mutual loss of goodwill. This helps explain the experimental work by John Orbell and Robyn Dawes (1993), which finds that individuals cooperate much better in *prisoner's dilemma games* when each participant can decide whether or not to participate in the game before play begins.

The role of mind reading in goodwill can explain why researchers observe differences in behavior between *normal-form* (simultaneous play) and *extensive-form* (sequential play) *games* even though theory predicts isomorphic behavior (Schotter, Weigelt, and Wilson 1994; Rapoport 1997; McCabe, Smith, and LePore 2000). For example, in the trust game shown in figure 6.1, when player 1 moves down player 2 knows for sure that $g_t^{12} \geq x^1$. If, however, player 2 had to move simultaneously with player 1, player 2's choice would be based on the relationship, $h_t^{12} \geq x^2$, which has greater potential for error.

Once players 1 and 2 have made their decisions and an outcome is reached, the trust game is modeled as extended to include decision nodes to update goodwill accounts. These decisions are made simultaneously, and for space reasons only player 1's decision is shown in figure 6.2 (player 2's decision is similar). If player 2 reciprocates, player 1 can choose either to credit player 2's goodwill with the calculation $g_t^{12} + \alpha^1$ or to debit player 2's goodwill with the calculation $g_t^{12} - \beta^1$. Similar updating decisions are possible if player 2 defects. The goodwill accounting strategies will always credit a counterpart's goodwill if he or she behaves cooperatively and debit goodwill if he or she behaves noncooperatively (when cooperation was possible). Player 2 will have an incentive to cooperate if the increased payoff from defection is less than the value of future interactions with higher goodwill, that is, if $(40 - 25) < V(g_t^{12} + \alpha^1) - V(g_t^{12} - \beta^1)$.

Why isn't this the whole story? Because, logically, in one-shot games $V(g_t + 1^{12}) = 0$. Therefore, the fact that people reciprocate in one-shot, anonymous games supports the hypothesis that goodwill accounting is invoked automatically as an adaptation for an environment in which most trading is repeated—that is, the agent does not mentally alter the computation conditional on the anonymous interaction being a one-shot event. Suppose the interaction is face-to-face, and not anonymous, but still "one shot" or unrepeated. Now each player sees the other, knows that they might meet again outside the experimental laboratory, and should invoke the reputational norm much more strongly than in anonymous matching.

In a series of tournaments organized by Robert Axelrod, well-known game theorists were asked to submit their favorite strategies for playing the repeated prisoner's dilemma. Axelrod (1984) found that the simple behavioral strategy known as tit-for-tat often won these tournaments. A person who plays tit-for-tat always cooperates in the first period and then in subsequent periods plays whatever his or her partner played in the previous period. Why was tit-for-tat so successful? Axelrod notes that all of the successful strategies, including tit-for-tat, were "nice"—that is, players were never the first to defect—and were reciprocal—that is, they always met cooperation with cooperation and defection with defection.

The goodwill accounting strategy is nice when it starts with a high initial level of goodwill, g_0^{ij}, relative to the distribution of subjective risks, x^i. The goodwill accounting strategy is reciprocal but only indirectly, through the updating of goodwill. Depending on the goodwill updating parameters, α and β, (see figure 6.2) the goodwill accounting strategy will be more or less contrite and generous, attributes found to be important in strategies that must cope with noisy play in the repeated prisoner's dilemma (see Axelrod 1997). Generosity allows a certain number of defections to go unpunished. The goodwill accounting strategy accomplishes this by decreasing goodwill-slowly—that is, with a relatively small β.

In earlier work Vernon Smith and I simulate the goodwill accounting strategy in an ecology of prisoner's dilemma games (McCabe and Smith 2001). In this simulation, twenty-five agents are initialized with goodwill and updating parameters. They then play their immediate

Figure 6.3   Trading Partners

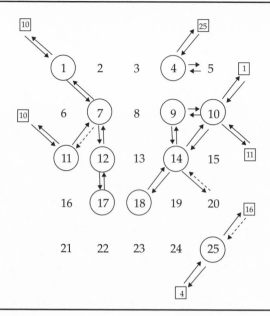

Source: Author's configuration.

neighbors over two hundred iterations of randomly selected instantiations of the prisoner's dilemma game. After the two hundredth iteration, the amount of goodwill between neighbors is determined, and trading partners are defined as those neighbors who have built up at least 90 percent of maximum (solid arrows) or 50 percent of maximum (dotted arrows) goodwill, as shown in a new simulation in figure 6.3. Owing to the random draws and resulting updating, different patterns of trading networks spontaneously emerge, with certain individuals (such as 7, 10, 14, and 25) playing central roles.

In addition, we performed an extreme test of the robustness of the goodwill accounting strategy by making every odd-numbered agent play a noncooperative (defection) strategy (McCabe and Smith 2001). As shown in figure 6.4, the defectors initially do better than the nice types, who are using the goodwill strategy with randomly distributed parameters. However, by period 112, the nice types have updated their goodwill accounts sufficiently to avoid the defectors and deal only with other nice types. The nice types are now in possession of a theory-of-mind capacity to read their goodwill (although imperfectly) with other players. With this ability, the nice types can now more easily avoid the defectors and break even much earlier in the play. As

Figure 6.4   Average Cumulative Payoffs, by Agent Type

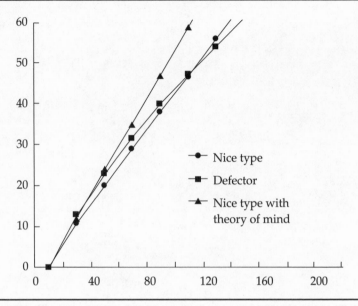

Source: Author's configuration.

their theory-of-mind capacity improves, the break-even point is even further reduced.

In studying the behavior generated by goodwill accounting, an additional relevant parameter is how much goodwill player 1 gives a player 2 who he or she has met for the first time. In general, this will most likely be a function of player 2's reputation and characteristics (such as group affiliation). Clearly, if player 1 gives to player 2, then player 1 will cooperate with player 2 in a greater number of risky exchange situations. However, player 1 is thereby left more vulnerable to defection. This may help explain why, in minimal group experiments, in-group members are more likely to punish other in-group members. In terms of goodwill accounting, the point of an in-group interaction is that each player starts with higher initial goodwill, but it is thus all the more important to punish defections. This also makes it clear that personal exchange relationships based on goodwill accounting are exclusionary by nature. As such, they can, in fact, become counterproductive as the potential for gains from exchange becomes more widespread. This raises the question, How can goodwill accounting be augmented to allow more inclusive exchange?

The Neural Correlates of Reciprocity

Most economics experiments study subjects' choices through the messages sent to the institution during the exchange process. Subject beliefs are inferred indirectly from these messages, and learning is studied by varying the information available and examining the changes in messages that occur over time. In addition to the more traditional study of the message-sending behavior of subjects in an experimental laboratory, a study of brain activation during the decision-making process can now be conducted, to see whether the cognitive model of exchange is implemented in humans in circumscribed brain areas.

P. C. Fletcher and colleagues (1995) use position emission transaxial tomography (PET scans) of regional cerebral blood flow to study brain activation of normal subjects as they performed story comprehension tasks. In theory-of-mind stories, subjects answered questions that required them to infer the mental states of a person in the story. These stories were compared with physical stories that involved people and from which subjects were required to infer an implicit element of the story. In physical stories, however, the implicit state did not include mental states. Both stories were then compared with an unrelated sentences task that did not require integration of the sentences into a story structure nor require inference to answer the follow-up questions.

The main area of difference is Broadmann's area 8 (BA8), which is significantly more active in comprehension tasks associated with theory-of-mind stories. Fletcher and colleagues conclude that their experiments "allow us to make the surprising inference that the attribution of mental states is particularly associated with the function of a highly circumscribed brain system" (Fletcher et al. 1995, 118).

In a recent paper my colleagues and I hypothesize that reciprocal behavior requires the binding of contingent information that allows subjects to evaluate the mental states of their counterparts and commit to a stimuli-conditioned reward-motivated choice (McCabe et al. 2001). The medial prefrontal cortex may serve as an important convergence zone in this decision problem because it exhibits a pattern of connectivity that would enable the binding of game and counterpart entities to a mutual-gains event.

To test this hypothesis, pairs of subjects were recruited to participate in a paid magnetic resonance imaging (MRI) experiment. The subject in the scanner played a trust game, a punishment game, or a mutual-advantage game through an interactive display system in the scanner, while the other subject made decisions from a computer in the control room that was connected to the scanner system. Subjects played seventy-two games, in six blocks of twelve, presented in ran-

Figure 6.5   Brain Activation in Cooperators

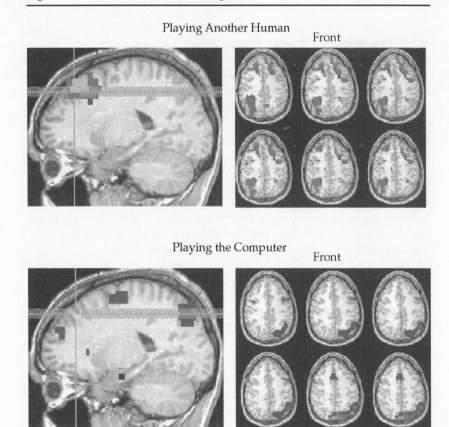

Playing Another Human

Front

Playing the Computer

Front

Source: Author.

dom order. In half of these games, it was common knowledge that subjects played each other (human-human), whereas in the other thirty-six games, the subject who was in the scanner played a computer following a fixed, and known, probabilistic strategy (human-computer).

Behavioral data show that seven of the twelve subjects in our experiment consistently attempted cooperation with their human counterparts. Within this group, we find that the medial prefrontal cortex was more active when the seven cooperators were playing a human than when they are playing a computer following a fixed (and known) probabilistic strategy. Within the group of noncooperators, we find no significant differences in medial prefrontal activation between the computer and human conditions. Figure 6.5 shows the activation differences for a typical cooperator when he or she played a human versus the computer. The difference in frontal activation is evident.

One possible explanation for our results is that within this class of games, subjects learn to adopt game-form-dependent rules of thumb when playing the computer or when playing noncooperatively with a human counterpart. In comparison, cooperation requires an active convergence zone that binds joint attention to mutual gains with sufficient inhibition of immediate reward gratification to allow cooperative decisions.

Conclusion

Reciprocity can best be understood by exploring the phenomenon at many different levels and by building theories that allow us to integrate knowledge across levels. At the behavioral level, both trust and conciliatory behavior, and the underlying positive and negative reciprocity that support them, are observed in one-shot games. Goodwill accounting is an example of a robust strategy for dealing with positive reciprocity. The efficiency of this strategy can be improved with a theory-of-mind module that allows individuals to better identify likeminded cooperators and to avoid defectors. Theory of mind also allows subjects to share attention on mutual gains, thus providing a potential mechanism for the observed activation of executive systems that inhibit actions that would result in immediate gratification in favor of cooperative rewards.

Note

1. Further analysis of strategic behavior can be found in chapter 10 of this volume.

References

Axelrod, Robert. 1984. *The Evolution of Cooperation*. New York: Basic Books.
———. 1997. *The Complexity of Cooperation*. Princeton, N.J.: Princeton University Press.
Baron-Cohen, Simon. 1995. *Mindblindness*. Cambridge, Mass.: MIT Press.
Berg, Joyce, John Dickhaut, and Kevin McCabe. 1995. "Trust, Reciprocity, and Social History." *Games and Economic Behavior* 10: 122–42.
Cosmides, Leda. 1989. "The Logic of Social Exchange: Has Natural Selection Shaped How Humans Reason? Studies with the Wason Selection Task." *Cognition* 31(3): 187–276.

168   Trust and Reciprocity

Cosmides, Leda, and John Tooby. 1992. "Cognitive Adaptations for Social Exchange." In *The Adapted Mind*, edited by Jerome H. Barkow, Leda Cosmides, and John Tooby. New York: Oxford University Press.

Damasio, Antonio. 1989. "The Brain Binds Entities and Events by Multiregional Activation from Convergence Zones." *Neural Computation* 1: 123–32.

de Waal, Frans. 1996. *Good Natured.* Cambridge, Mass.: Harvard University Press.

Donald, Merlin. 1991. *Origins of the Modern Mind: Three Stages in the Evolution of Culture and Cognition.* Cambridge, Mass.: Harvard University Press.

Dunbar, R. I. M. 1996. "Determinants of Group Size in Primates: A General Model." In *Evolution of Social Behaviour Patterns in Primates and Man,* edited by W. G. Runciman, J. Maynard Smith, and R. I. M. Dunbar. New York: Oxford University Press.

Fletcher, P. C., F. Happe, U. Frith, S. C. Baker, R. J. Dolan, R. S. J. Frackowiak, and C. D. Frith. 1995. "Other Minds in the Brain: A Functional Imaging Study of 'Theory of Mind' in Story Comprehension." *Cognition* 57: 109–28.

Forsythe, Robert, Joel Horowitz, N. Eugene Savin, and Martin Sefton. 1994. "Replicability, Fairness, and Pay in Experiments with Simple Bargaining Games." *Games and Economic Behavior* 6(3): 347–69.

Gazzaniga, Michael, Richard Ivry, and George Mangun. 1998. *Cognitive Neuroscience: The Biology of the Mind.* New York: W.W. Norton.

Güth, W., R. Schmittberger, and B. Schwarze. 1982. "An Experimental Analysis of Ultimatum Bargaining." *Journal of Economic Behavior and Organization* 3: 367–88.

Hoffman, Elizabeth, Kevin McCabe, Keith Shachat, and Vernon Smith. 1994. "Preferences, Property Rights, and Anonymity in Bargaining Games." *Games and Economic Behavior* 7: 346–80.

Hoffman, Elizabeth, Kevin McCabe, and Vernon Smith. 1996. "Social Distance and Other-Regarding Behavior." *American Economic Review* 86: 653–60.

Klein, Richard. 1999. *The Human Career.* 2d ed. Chicago: University of Chicago Press.

McCabe, Kevin, D. Houser, L. Ryan, Vernon Smith, and T. Trouard. 2001. "A Functional Imaging Study of 'Theory of Mind' in Two-Person Reciprocal Exchange." *Proceedings of the National Academy of Sciences* 98: 11832–35.

McCabe, Kevin, and Vernon Smith. 2000. "A Two-Person Trust Game Played by Naïve and Sophisticated Subjects." *Proceedings of the National Academy of Sciences* 97(7): 3777–81.

———. 2001. "Goodwill Accounting in Economic Exchange." In *Bounded Rationality: The Adaptive Toolbox,* edited by Gerd Gigerenzer and Reinhard Selten. Cambridge, Mass.: MIT Press.

McCabe, Kevin, Vernon Smith, and Michael LePore. 2000. "Intentionality Detection and 'Mindreading': Why Does Game Form Matter?" *Proceedings of the National Academy of Sciences* 97: 4404–9.

Metcalfe, Janet, and Walter Mischel. 1999. "A Hot/Cool-System Analysis of Delay of Gratification: Dynamics of Willpower." *Psychological Review* 106(1): 3–19.

Nimchinsky, Esther, Emmanuel Gilissen, John M. Allman, Daniel P. Perl, Joseph M. Erwin, and Patrick R. Hof. 1999. "A Neuronal Morphologic Type

Unique to Humans and Great Apes." *Proceedings of the National Academy of Sciences* 96: 5268–73.

Orbell, John, and Robyn Dawes. 1993. "Social Welfare, Cooperators' Advantage, and the Option of Not Playing the Game." *American Sociological Review* 58: 787–800.

Rapoport, Amnon. 1997. "Order of Play in Strategically Equivalent Games in Extensive Form." *International Journal of Game Theory* 26: 113–36.

Robson, Arthur, and Hillard Kaplan. Forthcoming. "The Evolution of Human Life Expectancy and Intellegence in Hunter-Gatherer Economies." *American Economic Review*.

Schotter, Andrew, Keith Weigelt, and Chuck Wilson. 1994. "A Laboratory Investigation of Multiperson Rationality and Presentation Effects." *Games and Economic Behavior* 6: 445–68.

Smith, Vernon. 1994. "Economics in the Laboratory." *Journal of Economic Perspectives* 8: 113–31.

Chapter 7

Conflict, Interpersonal Assessment, and the Evolution of Cooperation: Simulation Results

JAMES HANLEY, JOHN ORBELL, AND TOMONORI MORIKAWA

H OW COOPERATIVE dispositions might have evolved among social animals has, for many years, been productively addressed within the *prisoner's dilemma* paradigm. That game
captures the intuition that by cooperating, individuals can often produce more than is possible by their separate efforts and also that self-
interest can lead individuals to undermine their cooperative efforts.[1]
The structure is robust, with only minor elaborations necessary to
show how populations can realize their cooperative opportunities.
The best-known such elaboration is iteration of the game; simply requiring players to interact in a sequence of prisoner's dilemmas can
lead them to adopt cooperation-inducing strategies such as *tit-for-tat*
(see, for example, Axelrod 1984; Nowak and Sigmund 1992) and win-
stay, lose-shift[2] (Nowak and Sigmund 1993, see also Schuessler 1989
and Vanberg and Congleton 1992).

Nevertheless, studying the prisoner's dilemma in isolation from
the full complexity of a subject's social life might have led researchers
to miss important processes that bear on the evolution of cooperation.
In particular, natural societies make it possible for individuals to engage in conflictual games with one another as well as cooperative
ones;[3] and the fact that choices must be made *among* these two types
of games as well as within them raises the possibility that the evolu-

tion of cooperativeness has been critically influenced by the fact that those "prior" between-game choices are necessary. Notably, individuals intending cooperation and defection might differ in their willingness to play cooperative games, moving disproportionately into conflictual games and, thus, altering the proportion of cooperators and defectors in the cooperative games that are consummated. As Robert Trivers (1971) classically points out, anything that alters the probability that cooperators will enter into play with one another also alters the probability that cooperation will survive (see also Orbell and Dawes 1991), and adding the option to play a conflictual game might have just that effect.

We address that possibility in the present chapter. To do so, we developed an evolutionary simulation—the Anticipatory Interactive Planning Simulation—that gives agents the option of playing both cooperative and conflictual games with one another but in which choices must be made among such games. To make those choices, individuals are equipped with capacities that give them some control over the information that others receive about their intentions and also over the accuracy of the information that they receive about others' intentions. These mechanisms are subject to evolution by natural selection, as is the disposition to cooperate, although not cooperating or defecting behaviors as such. In these terms, we arrive at two conclusions: First, among populations in which individuals have only such cooperative games available—in which the option of fighting does not exist—there is no selection on the capacity to accurately recognize others' intentions, and cooperativeness itself is negatively selected, under some parameters such that the society itself dies. Second, when individuals within populations do have the option of fighting among themselves, positive selection on the capacity accurately to recognize others' intentions does happen, and it becomes possible also for cooperative dispositions to evolve in a positive direction.

Theoretical Background

Our study is developed from the "Machiavellian" or "social-intelligence" hypothesis. In essence, that hypothesis proposes that the human brain has been, in substantial part, designed by natural selection for negotiating a complex social space comprising conspecifics. Historically, group living provided improved defense against predators, better success as predators, more-ready access to mates, and (sometimes) assistance in raising children. Group living also brought members into competition with one another, however, with some being more successful in that competition than others, and whatever genes contributed to that success were disproportionately passed on to successive generations. By this hypothesis, three critical cognitive mechanisms were subjected to such selection: those facilitating quick and accurate assessment of others' capacities and intentions; those facilitating successful manipulation of information received (and believed) by other such individuals; and those that would translate information received (and believed) into adaptively appropriate actions.

These ideas underlie the notable paradigmatic convergence that has been happening in recent years between developmental and comparative psychology, cognitive ethology, theory of mind, and human intentionality. They have also proved fertile for developing hypotheses—some of them now well supported by laboratory work—about the cognitive processes underlying cooperative social transactions ("social contracts").[4] For present purposes two themes need emphasis: First, social transactions are complex (Humphrey 1976) and manipulative (Dawkins and Krebs 1978), with humans' capacity for language only making them more so (Dunbar 1996). Adaptive social decision making requires the individual to assess the intentions and capacities of particular protagonists. However, because one individual's assessment of another can have critical implications for the target as well as for the judge, individuals who know they are being assessed (and that means everyone in an even moderately tight-knit group) will attempt to control the information that others have about them (Marler, Karakashian, and Gyger 1991; Savage-Rumbaugh and McDonald 1988; Whiten and Byrne 1988). This means, in turn, that judges must take the likelihood of deceit into account, that the target must take account of the judge's such efforts, and so on.

Second, the huge information demands of success in such a complex and manipulative world translate into strong adaptive pressures on information-gathering and information-processing (cognitive) mechanisms. For some animals, of course, stereotyped responses will be sufficient. When the environment is complex and manipulative, a more developed structure will be advantageous, and mutations supporting it will be favored. Development in this case, however, implies modularity. As is increasingly accepted (Cosmides and Tooby 1994; Gigerenzer 1997; Sperber 1994), a general-purpose information processor is at a serious disadvantage in competition with a bundle of modules, each specialized to gathering information of a particular type (domain specific) and only of that particular type (special purpose). Theorists differ about the extent of modularity, with some arguing for a combination of general purpose and modular structures (for example, Mithen 1996) and others arguing that the logic of modularity implies modules essentially "all the way down" (for example, Sperber 1994). Nevertheless, a consensus is emerging that (at least) major functional problems confronted in the ancestral past are likely to have produced cognitive structures specialized to addressing those problems.

Two implications follow for the evolution of cooperative behavior. First, studying the evolution of cooperative behavior in an environment in which only cooperative games are possible seriously distorts the nature of the social environment in which cooperative behavior—to whatever extent it does exist—actually did evolve. Although it may be analytically convenient to do so, and excluding the full complexity of social life beyond cooperative games might be argued as an appropriate move toward simplifying an otherwise intractable problem, cooperative behavior necessarily evolved in an ecology of many different, and often excruciatingly difficult, social games—with the full complexity of that ecology most likely having left its imprint on the evolution of cooperation, as on the evolution of all other social behaviors.

Second, studying the evolution of cooperative behavior requires simultaneous attention to the evolution of cognitive mechanisms specialized for playing social games—and not just cooperative games. The tradition, of course, is to focus on the evolution of cooperation as against defection in itself, or perhaps on the evolution of strategies in which the act of cooperation (or defection) is contingent on some prior condition having happened, and this is no doubt defendable, again, as a move toward simplification.[5] As the paradigm suggests, however, behavior is necessarily a function of information that is gathered from the environment, and if cognitive evolution has not made certain kinds of information accessible, behaviors in response to such information should not be expected to happen. In particular, if cognitive evolution has made it difficult to access information about others' cheating intentions, then cheating will be likely to prosper and cooperation to erode. Conversely, if cognitive evolution has made it easy—or at least cost-effective—to detect cheaters, then cooperators will be able to avoid exploitation, and cooperation is likely to flourish—at least, that is, if playing other social games is not more attractive to would-be cooperators than playing cooperative ones.

Within this framework, "trust" is an expectation about another's future cooperation, should a prisoner's dilemma game be consummated (see, for example, Orbell, Dawes, and Schwartz-Shea 1994; see also chapter 3, this volume). Assigning a protagonist a high probability of cooperating means that one is trusting of that individual, whereas assigning a low such probability means that one is mistrustful of that individual. Note, however, that being trusting does not necessarily entail entering (or offering) a prisoner's dilemma, just as being mistrustful does not necessarily entail rejecting (or refusing) such a game. The game that one prefers will depend on the magnitude of the payoffs from the alternative games that are available, in conjunction with the expected performance of a protagonist in those alternatives. With appropriate game parameters, an individual might reject a prisoner's dilemma in favor of an alternative game, even when he or she assigns a protagonist a high probability of cooperating, or accept a prisoner's dilemma in preference to an alternative, even when assigning such a protagonist a low probability of cooperating.

Furthermore, this framework distinguishes between protagonists' behavior in particular games; their choices among different kinds of games; their expectations about others' behavior in particular games— in the case of prisoner's dilemma games, their degree of "trust"; the algorithms by which they compute which among several game alternatives they should play; and the information-processing or cognitive mechanisms that provide them with information as input to those calculations. From an evolutionary perspective, the latter two are critical, being the product of aeons of natural selection, but the Anticipatory Interactive Planning Simulation we describe distinguishes among all these various levels of analysis.

Simulating Complex Social Ecologies: The Anticipatory Interactive Planning Simulation

Our interest in the evolution of cooperativeness within a complex ecology of diverse games, and in the role played in that evolution by cognitive mechanisms that are themselves subject to evolution, clearly precludes analysis by conventional observational methods; the relevant events have been gone for perhaps hundreds of thousands of years.[6] Furthermore, the possibility of complex interactions among game structure, game parameters, and cognitive and behavioral evolution makes employing deductive methods premature, at least. Computer simulation, however, is a practical means by which hypotheses about how evolution actually happened can be developed, and we adopt that method here. In our simulation, therefore, the following conditions obtain:

First, there is a population of agents living in a world that offers them an ecology of opportunities for both cooperative and conflictual games. Cooperative games are modeled in standard prisoner's dilemma terms, and conflictual games are modeled as *hawk-dove games*.[7] Players calculate the expected value of playing the respective games with each other individual they encounter, preferring whichever offers the highest expected value but choosing to play no game at all if both expected values are zero or less. Operationally, one player (Alpha) makes this calculation first, offering the game that it prefers to a second player (Beta). Should Alpha want a hawk-dove game, it challenges with hawk, obliging Beta to choose between taking up the challenge (hawk) and rejecting it (dove). Should Alpha wish a prisoner's dilemma game, it offers one to Beta, who can then either accept or reject that offer. Should Alpha want no game at all, it simply "walks on by," leaving Beta no alternative but to accept that "nonsocial" outcome.[8]

Second, agents have "attributes" that determine how they will play cooperative and conflictual games. With respect to cooperative (prisoner's dilemma) games, each individual has, throughout its life, a fixed probability of cooperating (p^c) and thus of defecting ($1 - p^c$). The actual choice between cooperation and defection in a particular game is determined by sampling from a probability distribution, so defined.[9] The outcome for such a game is, therefore, determined by the two agents' respective such samples. With respect to conflictual (hawk-dove) games, each individual is characterized by "strength," an integer greater than zero that is, throughout its life, its actual fighting ability should a hawk-hawk conflict be joined. When two agents join in a fight, the outcome is determined probabilistically by relative strength. Specifically, Alpha's probability of winning is Alpha's strength / (Alpha's strength + Beta's strength), and Beta's probability of winning is one minus that amount.

Third, agents have the capacity to lie about their cooperativeness and their fighting strength. Because it makes no strategic sense for an individual to assert, for example, "I have a 70 percent probability of cooperating with you," all are assumed to assert, "I will *certainly* cooperate with you"—or, expressed in operational terms, "My p^c is 1.0." Thus, there are two components to messages conveyed about cooperative intentions: the truth (the actual p^c) and a lie (one minus the actual p^c). Similarly, each individual is capable of issuing a "bluff" of some magnitude about its fighting strength, operationalized (like strength) as an integer of some value greater than zero. As with cooperative intentions, therefore, there are two components to messages conveyed about fighting strength: the truth (actual strength) and a lie (the bluff). If believed, both such lies can contribute significantly to the liar's welfare, persuading a protagonist to play a prisoner's dilemma game when it is likely to get suckered or not to issue a hawk challenge when, had it done so, it probably would have provoked a dove response and, thus, have captured v (the gain from winning a fight) without opposition. The question, however, is whether such lies will be believed.

Fourth, agents have at least some capacity to make the "lie" component of messages that they transmit believable—to be good liars. These information-manipulating capacities, one for lies about cooperativeness (persuasiveness^{PD}) and one for lies about strength (persuasiveness^{HD}), are defined as integers greater than zero. Note that we have modeled these as distinct capacities. Quite plausibly they are not distinct in real brains; perhaps we have only a single capacity for lying, one that works quite adequately across domains. The modularity argument discussed earlier, however, raises the possibility that there are domain-specific capacities—that the manipulative capacities required for lying about cooperativeness are different from those required for lying about strength. We have kept them separate in the simulation, allowing us to observe whether, in our simulated world, these capacities diverge throughout an evolutionary sequence. Their failure to diverge would be consistent with only a single mechanism being required.

Fifth, agents have at least some capacity to penetrate protagonists' lies about their cooperativeness and their fighting strength. These information-processing capacities, one for lies about cooperativeness (perceptiveness^{PD}) and a different one for lies about fighting strength (perceptiveness^{HD}), are defined as integers greater than zero. Once again, we define two functionally distinct such capacities; agents in this simulation have not just a single "truth detector" but two, each specialized for detecting the truth about a different claim protagonists make. Russell Hardin (in chapter 3, this volume) points out the importance of gathering relevant knowledge about another when making decisions about whether or not to trust that person. Whereas he subsumes the knowledge problem under the risk assessment problem, we specify them separately in the simulation such that these perceptive capacities provide the knowledge that agents use to assess the expected value of playing particular games with one another. Once again, our brains might or might not contain such separate capacities for distinct games; but, again, the conservative modeling strategy is to assume domain specificity and to observe separate trajectories through evolutionary sequences.

In the natural world, of course, humans (and no doubt other social animals) employ a wide range of processes for gathering information about the intentions and capacities of others. We gossip, learning "on the cheap" what others have experienced with particular individuals (Dunbar 1996). We employ stereotypes and other heuristics (Rothbart and Taylor 1992), perhaps organizing new information within existing categories (Orbell, Zeng, and Mulford 1996). We use our capacity for "theory of mind" (Baron-Cohen 1995; Carruthers and Smith 1996). We model others' mental processes from what we know—believe we know—of our own (Orbell and Dawes 1993). And, of course, when the individuals in question are not strangers, we rely on our own past experience through iterated sequences of social games (Axelrod 1984). Indeed, it would be surprising if such a fundamental business as anticipating others' social behavior were not addressed by such a diversity of mechanisms. It is simply too important a function to be dependent on only one, or even a few.

In the simulation, nevertheless, we make no attempt to capture this diversity of mechanisms, making only the one distinction between those that are employed for predicting others' cooperation and defection choices in prisoner's dilemma games and those that are employed for assessing whatever strength others can bring to bear in hawk-dove games. "Perceptiveness" is a summary term for all the particular mechanisms and processes that have been supported by evolution for addressing the problem of information gathering with respect to the two types of games, and it is well beyond our present purpose to attempt an analysis of their separate importance or how they might interact.

Sixth, agents are assumed to accept the truth component in a protagonist's messages but must try to penetrate the lie component.[10] Among real people, the extent to which one individual's lies are penetrated by another depends on the message sender's capacity to be persuasive and the message receiver's capacity to penetrate lies, with the receiver's eventual assessment depending on the relative strength of these two capacities. Operationally, therefore, the proportion of the lie that is actually believed is

$$\text{sender's persuasiveness}^{PD} / (\text{sender's persuasiveness}^{PD} + \text{receiver's perceptiveness}^{PD}),$$

in the case of prisoner's dilemma games, and

$$\text{sender's persuasiveness}^{HD} / (\text{sender's persuasiveness}^{HD} + \text{receiver's perceptiveness}^{HD}),$$

in the case of hawk-dove games. The receiver's actual assessment is the real truth plus the proportion of the sender's lie that is actually believed.

Seventh, agents evaluate the probable returns from entering the respective games with a particular protagonist, making a value-maximizing choice among those games and the third option of playing no game at all (which always returns zero). Agents are assumed to know their own fighting strength and whether they will cooperate or defect should a prisoner's dilemma game be consummated, and they are also assumed to know the payoffs for the respective games.[11] They

must use the assessments they have made about a protagonist, however, to calculate the expected value of playing the respective games,
and those assessments are likely to contain at least some error. Agents
are, in other words, boundedly rational (Simon 1955, 1956), basing
choices between playing and not playing particular games with particular individuals on information that is likely to be imperfect. For
those agents, as for real humans negotiating the natural world, there
is no alternative but to use such information if they are to reap the
very considerable benefits of social life.

Emotions, of course, are the stuff that subjective social life is made
of, and people generally experience emotions as being proximate
causes of their actions—as distinct from the kind of expected-value
calculus being modeled here. Consistent with Robert Wright (1994)
and others (for example, Lane and Nadel 2000), however, we see
emotions as the "executors" of behavior, certainly a product of evolution but one whose function is to promote behaviors that are (or
were) adaptive in particular circumstances identified by the individual's cognitive apparatus. In the present context, therefore, we assume that an individual who assesses a hawk challenge as having a
positive expected value will be motivated to issue such a challenge by
operationally appropriate emotions (for example, anger) and that one
who assesses a dove response as superior is motivated to take that
action by a different set of emotions (such as fear). Similarly, we assume that an individual who assesses a prisoner's dilemma game as
most advantageous will be motivated to enter such a game by a different, but functionally similar, set of appropriate emotions—perhaps
greed, if intending defection, or friendliness, if intending cooperation.
For modeling purposes, however, we can proceed by omitting the
emotional link between such assessments and behavior.[12]

Eighth, outcomes from such encounters determine each agent's
probability of surviving and reproducing, thus of passing its various
attributes on to the next generation. Payoffs from the two games—
which might be positive or negative[13]—may be thought of as units of
reproductive fitness or, consistent with John Hartung, "any arbitrarily
bestowable resource, ability, or status that might enhance the reproductive success of its possessor" (Hartung 1976, 607). The simulation
proceeds through a succession of synchronous generations,[14] each
agent accumulating (or losing) wealth as a consequence of its fortunes
in social life. Agents survive only one generation. Although agents'
wealth is allowed to recover should it fall below zero in the course of
their lifetimes, any agent who has negative wealth at the end of a
generation dies without reproducing.

Consistent with the idea of genetic competition among group
members, at the end of each generation there is a selection process by

which the number of offspring an agent produces is a function of its relative success in social game playing. Specifically, agents whose wealth is below the median do not reproduce at all; those whose wealth is between the median and twice the median have one offspring; those whose wealth is between twice and three times the median have two offspring, and so on. Their lives are defined by the reproductively important social games that they play, and—if they have been sufficiently successful in playing those games—by the act of producing some number of offspring.[15]

Ninth, offspring inherit their parents' behavioral and cognitive attributes, but because natural selection builds from variation, those attributes are subject to mutation on being transmitted from a parent to a child. As in standard evolutionary models, mutation is random with respect to adaptive value; a mutation might prove useful in the environment into which a child is born, but it might instead be damaging to that child's ability to prosper there. Operationally, mutations on particular parental attributes are defined by the parameters' frequency and magnitude. The former is the probability that an attribute will be subject to mutation. The latter is the number of integers by which a particular attribute will change—positively or negatively.[16] Although the magnitude of possible mutations is finite, the possibility of mutation means that, after many generations, mean population attributes might diverge substantially from those of the founding population.[17]

In these terms, our interest is in how mean population values for agents' cognitive attributes and for their cooperativeness evolve through successive generations as a function of their opportunity to play conflictual hawk-dove games as an option to their opportunity to play (potentially) cooperative prisoner's dilemmas with one another.

Findings: A World in Which Only Cooperative Games Are Possible

To analyze the role that the option of fighting might play, we begin with a world in which fighting is not possible. If cooperation prospers, we will conclude that the option of fighting is not a necessary condition for that to happen. We also design this initial world so that everything is stacked in favor of cooperation's surviving and prospering. Most analyses of how cooperation might evolve begin from the assumption that cooperation must first find a toehold in a hostile world and then look for ways by which that toehold might be expanded. If cooperation does not survive and prosper in a world that is initially "cooperation friendly," then we can conclude that it would not do so in one that was initially more hostile. In the terms developed here, therefore, a "cooperation friendly" world would be one in which two conditions obtain: First, agents in the initial generation are more likely than not to cooperate. With most agents most of the time intending cooperation, most interactions will be among cooperators, meaning that cooperators will, most of the time, capture the mutual-cooperation payoff—and be spared the sucker's payoff from playing a game with a defector.

Second, players have high levels of perceptiveness^{PD} relative to persuasiveness^{PD}—that is, they have well developed capacities for penetrating lies about cooperative intentions relative to others' capacities for telling persuasive lies. In a world of mostly cooperation-inclined agents, of course, the few who were inclined toward defection would have easy pickings and, absent others' capacity to recognize and avoid them by successful "scrutiny" (Frank 1988, 61), would rapidly grow in number and eventually dominate the ecology.[18] If the former had a well-developed capacity for such scrutiny, they might be able to recognize and avoid the latter and thus stay ahead in the evolutionary race.[19] Note that agents in this world are not necessarily characterized by "trust" or "mistrust." They are rather—for the most part—well equipped to accurately determine whether or not they should be trusting.

Yet cooperation does not prosper in this cooperation-friendly world absent the option of fighting. To illustrate, we use the case in which the probability of cooperating (p^c) is set at .6 for all members of the initial population;[20] persuasiveness^{PD} is set at 50; and perceptiveness^{PD} is set at 75.[21] Prisoner's dilemma games available to agents in this simulation (and the ones to come) all have the same payoff parameters: free riding (t) = 20; mutual cooperation (c) = 10; mutual defection (d) = -10; and being "suckered" (s) = -20. Figure 7.1 reports the incidence of the four possible outcomes to encounters—mutual cooperation, mutual defection, cooperation and defection, and no play—by generation.[22] Most striking is the steady increase of mutual defection and the corresponding decrease of mutual cooperation and the mixed defect-and-cooperate outcome.[23]

To understand the declining incidence of mutually cooperative relationships, selection must first be understood at two progressively "lower" levels of analysis—agents' cooperative dispositions and their capacities to penetrate to the truth underlying others' claims to perfect cooperativeness. Figure 7.2 addresses the former, showing a steady decline in mean cooperativeness (p^c) from the initial .6 to a value somewhat below .2 just before the society crashes (at generation 281). This change is more than sufficient to explain the decline in mutually cooperative relationships and the increase in mutually defecting ones recorded in figure 7.1 As p^c declines, the frequency of

Figure 7.1   Evolution of Cooperation in a Cooperation-Friendly World, Absent Conflictual Games, by Generation

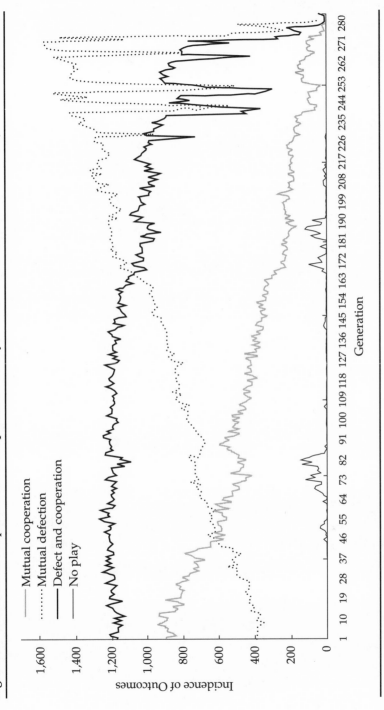

Source: Authors' configuration.
Note: Propensity to cooperate (*c*) is 75; propensity to defect (*d*) is 50; thus, the probability of cooperation (*p^c*) is .6. Capacity for telling persuasive lies (persuasiveness^PD) is 50; capacity for penetrating lies (perceptiveness^PD) is 75.

Figure 7.2   Evolution of Cooperativeness in a Cooperation-Friendly World, Absent Conflictual Games, by Generation

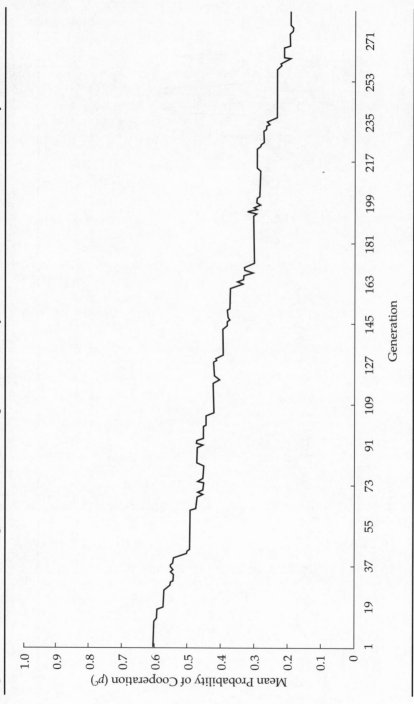

Source: Authors' configuration.
Note: Propensity to cooperate (*c*) is 75; propensity to defect (*d*) is 50; thus, the probability of cooperation (p^c) is .6. Capacity for telling persuasive lies (persuasiveness^{PD}) is 50; capacity for penetrating lies (perceptiveness^{PD}) is 75.

encounters between two cooperators diminishes, while the frequency of encounters between two defectors increases.

Figure 7.3 addresses agents' capacity to penetrate the truth underlying their protagonists' claims to fully cooperative intentions. Although a protagonist's capacity to tell a persuasive lie (persuasiveness[PD]) and the agent's capacity for penetrating such a lie (perceptiveness[PD]) both have an independent effect on the agents' ability to make an accurate assessment of the protagonist's cooperative intentions, the critical issue is the relative magnitude of these two values.[24] Figure 7.3 records that relative magnitude, with positive values indicating that agents are, on average, more perceptive than persuasive and negative values indicating that persuasiveness has gained the advantage. As can be seen, this value moves from .2 at the outset (as defined by the starting parameters in this cooperation-friendly world) to less than − .4 at the time the society eventually crashes. Through time, selection is making agents relatively more able to issue persuasive lies about their cooperative intentions than to penetrate to the truth underlying such lies.

This increase in relative persuasiveness can damage uncooperative agents by increasing the probability that they will be persuaded to enter relationships with other similarly uncooperative agents. By the same token, it can help cooperative agents by increasing the probability that they will enter relationships with one another. But the damage that relative persuasiveness can do to cooperative agents by getting them into relationships with defectors is (by definition in the prisoner's dilemma) greater than the damage it can do to defectors who make the same mistake.[25] Similarly, the benefit that cooperators gather by being persuaded to enter relationships with other cooperators is (also by definition in the prisoner's dilemma) less than the benefit that defectors gather from being persuaded to do the same thing.[26] The selective pressures against cooperativeness recorded in figure 7.2 are, therefore, readily understood in terms of the increase of relative persuasiveness recorded in figure 7.3.[27] The final question is what accounts for the increase of relative persuasiveness.

The answer lies in the opportunities that are provided by unit changes in perceptiveness[PD] and persuasiveness[PD]. An upward mutation on the former will certainly increase an offspring's capacity to avoid damaging play with defectors, but—in this world in which playing prisoner's dilemma games is the only way to gain wealth— successfully avoiding a defector can return only the zero payoff from not playing.[28] A gain of zero is certainly better than taking a loss, but it leaves the agent with no fitness gain and, at the outset at least, perilously close to negative fitness. On the other hand, although both cooperators and defectors can be damaged by being persuaded to play with defectors, an upward mutation on persuasiveness[PD] can

Figure 7.3 Relative Magnitude of Perceptiveness[PD] to Persuasiveness[PD] in a Cooperation-Friendly World, Absent Conflictual Games, by Generation

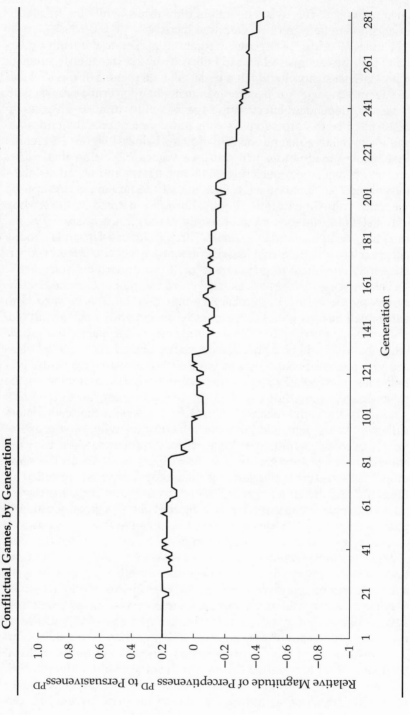

Source: Authors' configuration.
Note: Propensity to cooperate (c) is 75; propensity to defect (d) is 50; thus, the probability of cooperation (p^c) is .6. Capacity for telling persuasive lies (persuasiveness[PD]) is 50; capacity for penetrating lies (perceptiveness[PD]) is 75.

also lead to profitable interactions with other agents and consequent fitness gains. With only prisoner's dilemma games possible, perceptiveness^{PD} can prevent losses but can never return gains, whereas persuasiveness^{PD} can sometimes return quite substantial gains.

To summarize: when playing prisoner's dilemma games is the only way by which agents can make a living, and when the society is initially cooperation friendly, relative persuasiveness is favored because persuasiveness^{PD} makes such gains possible whereas perceptiveness^{PD} makes possible only the avoidance of losses. Increases in relative persuasiveness, in turn, favor agents with low p^c values, and that increases the incidence of mutual defection and lowers the incidence of mutual cooperation. The next question is what happens when agents have other ways of making a living—specifically, when they can make gains by fighting with one another.

Findings: A World in Which Cooperative and Conflictual Games Are Both Possible

To assess the affect of having an alternative, conflictual, game, we begin with a world that is initially cooperation unfriendly, populated at the outset by agents with a low probability of cooperating (p^c) and with high persuasiveness^{PD} relative to perceptiveness^{PD}—that is to say, with agents who are both defection prone and not particularly good at recognizing others' true intentions, substantially similar to those populating the prior run near its uncooperative end. Absent the option of fighting, cooperation rapidly decays in such worlds. Should cooperation now flourish, we will, accordingly, have reason to believe that the option of fighting is, somehow, making the difference.

In the illustrative case used this time, p^c for all agents in the initial population is set at .33,[29] perceptiveness^{PD} at 25, and persuasiveness^{PD} at 50. Agents have only a .33 probability of cooperating in any given prisoner's dilemma game, and relative perceptiveness leaves them able to penetrate only .33 of a protagonist's lie about being perfectly cooperative.[30] Prisoner's dilemma games are played on the same matrix as in the earlier case ($t = 20$; $c = 10$; $d = -10$; and $s = -20$), and hawk-dove games are played with v (the gain from winning a fight) set at 30 and l (the loss from losing a fight) set at -20.[31] Perceptiveness^{HD} and persuasivenesss^{HD} are both set at 50, meaning that agents penetrate .5 of their protagonists' bluff with respect to fighting strength. Fighting strength and bluff are both set at 50. Together, these hawk-dove settings mean that agents in the first generation overestimate one another's strength as $50 + (.5 \times 50) = 75$.

With the availability of hawk-dove games, even these initially cooperation-unfriendly societies normally survive indefinitely (well beyond the 30,000 or so generations that can be conveniently handled). Furthermore, the relatively stable patterns that do persist through these extended periods become established quite rapidly—granted some fluctuations that are inevitable, given the stochastic elements of the simulation—allowing us to "zoom in" on the first 750 generations in order to demonstrate what is happening. As figure 7.4 shows, at the outset in the cooperation-unfriendly world only prisoner's dilemma games are played, and they remain substantially the most frequent way for agents to interact with one another in this ecology, even though hawk-dove games and the no-play option are also available. Within about fifty generations, however, hawk-dove games are played with at least some regularity. The question that concerns us is whether the availability of hawk-dove games, despite the relative infrequency with which they are played, influences the pattern of choices that develops throughout successive generations in the far more frequent prisoner's dilemma games.

Certainly, the pattern of outcomes to prisoner's dilemma games is very different from the case in which agents do not have the option of playing hawk-dove games (the situation illustrated in figure 7.1). Figure 7.5 shows that at the outset mutual defection is far more frequent than mutual cooperation (about 1,100 instances of the former compared with about 250 of the latter). Of course, something like this is to be expected when all agents in the first generation have a p^c of .33. The trend now, however, with the option of conflictual games, is toward an increase in mutual cooperation and a decrease in mutual defection—to the point at which, by the time 750 generations have passed, the situation has roughly reversed (with about 1,000 mutually cooperative outcomes compared with about 200 mutually defecting ones). Furthermore, this basic pattern of outcomes, once achieved, persists indefinitely.

Moving one step "lower" to the behavioral dispositions that underlie this pattern of outcomes, figure 7.6 shows a steady upward movement of p^c from the initial .33 to a relatively stable 0.70 by 750 generations. Despite the fact that this world started off with conditions hostile to cooperativeness, cooperative dispositions are clearly positively selected—in sharp contrast with what happened in the initially cooperation-friendly world absent the option of playing hawk-dove games. This trend is sufficient to explain the increasingly cooperative outcomes illustrated in figure 7.5, but the more fundamental question concerns the reasons for such positive selection on cooperativeness in this world with the option of fighting.

Figure 7.7 shows that relative perceptiveness increases in this world from its initially low point of $-.33$ to around .25 by the end of the first 750 generations. In fact, this is not too surprising; we

(Text continues on p. 191.)

Figure 7.4   Incidence of Cooperative and Conflictual Games in an Initially Cooperation-Unfriendly World, by Generation

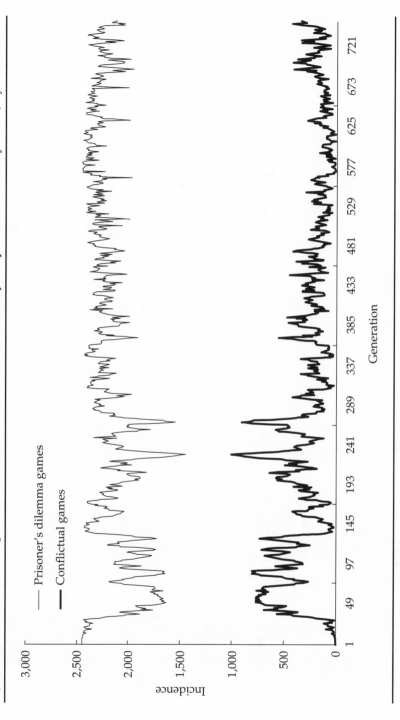

Source: Authors' configuration.
Note: Propensity to cooperate (c) is 50; propensity to defect (d) is 100; thus the probability of cooperation (p^c) is .33; capacity for telling persuasive lies (persuasiveness^{PD}) is 50; capacity for penetrating lies (perceptiveness^{PD}) is 25.

Figure 7.5   Evolution of Outcomes to Prisoner's Dilemmas in an Initially Cooperation-Unfriendly World, with Conflictual Games, by Generation

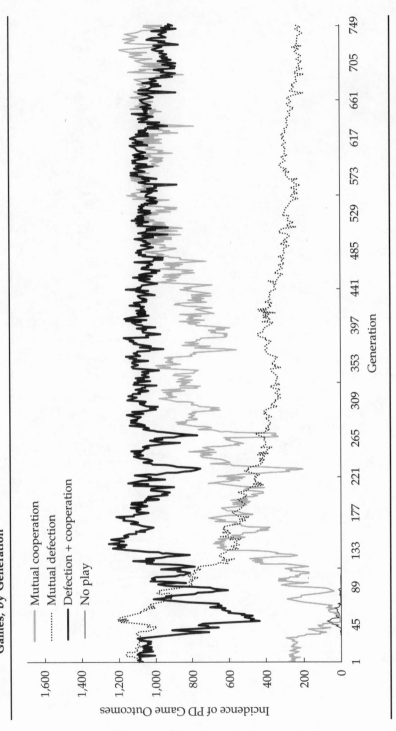

Source: Authors' configuration.
Note: Propensity to cooperate (*c*) is 50; propensity to defect (*d*) is 100; thus the probability of cooperation (*p^c^*) is .33. Capacity for telling persuasive lies (persuasiveness^PD^) is 50; capacity for penetrating lies (perceptiveness^PD^) is 25.

Figure 7.6 Evolution of Cooperativeness in an Initially Cooperation-Unfriendly World, with Conflictual Games, by Generation

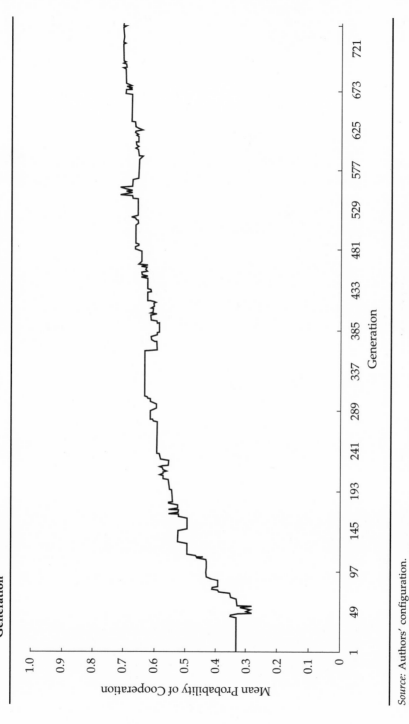

Source: Authors' configuration.
Note: Propensity to cooperate (c) is 50; propensity to defect (d) is 100; thus the probability of cooperation (p^c) is .33. Capacity for telling persuasive lies (persuasiveness^{PD}) is 50; capacity for penetrating lies (perceptiveness^{PD}) is 25.

Figure 7.7 Relative Magnitude of Perceptiveness^{PD} to Persuasiveness^{PD} in an Initially Cooperation-Unfriendly World, with Conflictual Games, by Generation

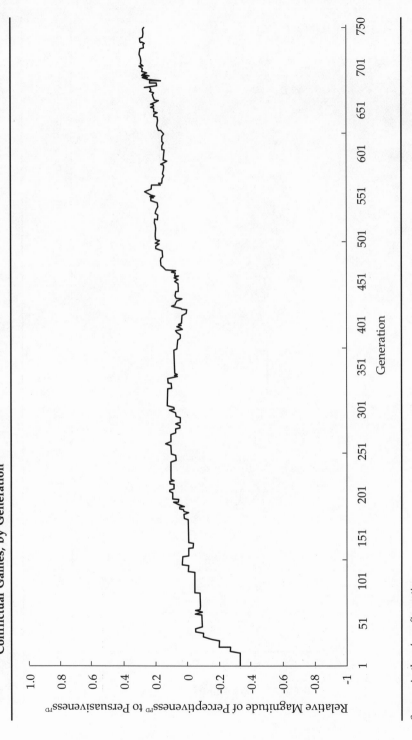

Source: Authors' configuration.
Note: Propensity to cooperate (*c*) is 50; propensity to defect (*d*) is 100; thus the probability of cooperation (p^c) is .33. Capacity for telling persuasive lies (persuasiveness^{PD}) is 50; capacity for penetrating lies (perceptiveness^{PD}) is 25.

should expect perceptiveness[PD] to be advantageous, and persuasiveness[PD] to be disadvantageous, in a society that is populated substantially by agents who have a low probability of cooperating.

More interesting is the apparent ease with which this population
moves in a cooperation-friendly direction from its initially cooperation-unfriendly character. Whereas the earlier society, initially cooperation-friendly, became less cooperative and less relatively perceptive
and showed no signs of recovering once it became cooperation-unfriendly—in the particular example, in fact, it collapsed—the initially
cooperation-unfriendly society recovers rapidly from initially low
such values and achieves what appears to be an equilibrium not too
different from the starting parameters that were set for the earlier
population. Because the major difference between the two simulations
is the availability of the hawk-dove option in the second and its absence in the first, it appears that the option of fighting is critical to the
evolution of a stable, cooperative society. By what process, then, does
the option of fighting support the evolution of a cooperation-friendly
society?

How the Option of Fighting
Supports Cooperation

There are two critical facts: First, an agent in the second simulation
who comes to believe that a protagonist is not particularly cooperative, and thus that playing a prisoner's dilemma game with that individual would not be a very good deal, has a potentially quite profitable alternative beyond simply opting out of engagement with this
individual altogether. Second, such agents are likely to be disproportionately inclined toward cooperation.

In a cooperation-unfriendly world absent the option of fighting, an
agent who estimates a positive but fairly low expected value from
entering a particular prisoner's dilemma will, nevertheless, rationally
enter. Entering might produce a gain; the protagonist in question
might be more cooperative than the assessment, or perhaps the assessment is correct but, on this particular occasion, that agent happens (with a low probability) to "sample" a cooperative choice. Entering might also produce a loss, however. Although the positive
expected value implies that entering is a good bet, good bets can go
wrong, and the lower the expected value the greater the probability of
that happening.

In a cooperation-unfriendly world with the option of fighting,
however, an agent who makes such an estimate must then assess the
expected value of making a hawk challenge and will enter the prisoner's dilemma only if the estimate for that challenge is still lower

than the estimate for the prisoner's dilemma.[32] Otherwise, rationality dictates that the hawk challenge be issued instead. The availability of the hawk-dove option, in other words, provides a possibly quite useful alternative for agents facing an unpromising prisoner's dilemma game with a protagonist of questionable cooperativeness.[33]

This option of fighting will, ceteris paribus, be more attractive for intending cooperators than for intending defectors. This is a straightforward consequence of the fact that cooperation is always a less rewarding choice than defection—that, by definition in the prisoner's dilemma, defection dominates cooperation. In other words, with the assessment of a protagonist's probability of cooperating constant, the expected value of entering a prisoner's dilemma game will always be lower for an agent who intends cooperation than for one who intends defection. Thus intending cooperators (more generally, agents with high p^c values) will be more likely to abandon the prisoner's dilemma option in favor of the hawk-dove option than will intending defectors (generally, agents with *low* p^c values).

This relative exodus to the fighting option of agents who would otherwise cooperate has two consequences for the success of cooperative dispositions in the population. First, it means that agents intending defection will be more likely to end up playing one another and taking the loss from mutual defection than they would be if cooperators were not "escaping" in this manner. Because agents intending defection are disproportionately likely to have low p^c values, therefore, the selective exit of intending cooperators from prisoner's dilemma games to hawk-dove games creates selective pressures against dispositions to defect (d).

Second, it means that intending cooperators will be disproportionately protected from the perils of playing only marginally attractive prisoner's dilemma games. Absent the hawk-dove option, such individuals would play low-expected-value games and often suffer losses, but with that option they need no longer take that risk and will enter prisoner's dilemmas only when the expected value of doing so is quite high—presumably, because a protagonist is assigned a higher probability of cooperating. The availability of the hawk-dove alternative, therefore, increases the probability that intending cooperators will avoid being exploited by defectors and will capture the comfortably positive mutual-cooperation payoff—thus creating selective pressures in favor of cooperative dispositions (c). Together, these two effects are sufficient to produce the continuing positive selection on the probability of cooperation (p^c) recorded in figure 7.6 and the consequent continuing increase of mutually cooperative game outcomes (and decline in mutually defecting outcomes) recorded in figure 7.5.[34]

The argument also depends on intending cooperators' being perceptive enough to recognize with reasonable accuracy when a protagonist intends defection—sufficiently so, that is, to penetrate at least a substantial portion of a protagonist's "I am perfectly cooperative" lie. If agents were, in general, more persuasive than perceptive, intending defectors should be expected to frequently "pull the wool over the eyes" of intending cooperators, with the result that the latter would be dissuaded from abandoning prisoner's dilemmas when they should abandon them, thus losing any advantage that they could otherwise reap from the hawk-dove alternative. In fact, in this simulation agents start off with such relative persuasiveness, but—as figure 7.7 indicates—in this initially cooperation-unfriendly world there are strong selection pressures in favor of relative perceptiveness.[35]

As was suggested earlier, one reason for such pressures is simply that, in this unfriendly world, increments of perceptiveness^{PD} are substantially more adaptive here than are increments of persuasiveness^{PD}. When one is surrounded by relatively uncooperative people, random selection of partners will mean disaster, and the ability to identify the minority who are relatively cooperative is critical to one's survival and prosperity. Another, more fundamental, reason, however, is that, with the option of playing hawk-dove games now available, increments of perceptiveness^{PD} can do a lot more than simply help an agent avoid the loss of playing a prisoner's dilemma with a defector, getting zero as opposed to taking a loss of some magnitude. In particular, they can bring a cooperative agent the quite substantial benefit (v) from winning a hawk-hawk fight—or, better still, of getting the same amount by scaring off a protagonist without a fight.

In summary, therefore, when hawk-dove games are an option for agents, five conditions result. The benefits available from playing hawk-dove games increase the selective pressures on perceptiveness^{PD} relative to persuasiveness^{PD}. Increases in relative perceptiveness increase the capacity of intending cooperators (as well as intending defectors) to recognize and successfully avoid intending defectors as partners in prisoner's dilemma games. The fact that intending cooperators abandon prisoner's dilemma games in favor of hawk-dove games more readily than intending defectors "protects" cooperative dispositions from the damage that consummated games with defectors would bring. That same fact provides positive benefits to agents with cooperative dispositions by increasing the probability that they will consummate prisoner's dilemma games—when they do play them—with one another. Finally, increasing cooperativeness in the population increases the incidence of mutually cooperative outcomes in general and reduces the incidence of mutually defecting ones.[36]

Raising the Bar for Staying in Prisoner's Dilemma Games

By the argument just outlined, intending cooperators who find playing a hawk-dove game more attractive than playing a prisoner's dilemma game with a particular protagonist can gain significantly by making a hawk challenge. We have illustrated the dynamics by introducing a hawk-dove game in which v is set at 30 and c is set at -20, but should the attractiveness of hawk-dove games be increased by raising the stake (or, of course, by making losing less costly), intending cooperators will have a still more attractive alternative to entering a prisoner's dilemma game with a dubiously cooperative protagonist. That is to say, with a still more attractive hawk-dove game as an alternative, intending cooperators will, all else being equal, be in a position to be still more particular about those with whom they enter prisoner's dilemma games, at least sometimes rejecting such a game even if the expected value of playing is substantially positive.

By "raising the bar" for staying in prisoner's dilemma games, such more attractive hawk-dove games should—up to a point, at least—increase positive selective pressures on cooperative dispositions, thus increasing the number of mutually cooperative outcomes to the prisoner's dilemmas that are joined. There is strong support for that prediction. If all other starting parameters are kept as they were in our cooperation-unfriendly world but v is raised to 35, the probability of cooperation now equilibrates at around .8 within a few hundred years (from .7), and the mutually cooperate outcomes equilibrate at around 1,200 per generation (from around 1,000 per generation).

As hawk-dove games become progressively more attractive, of course, there will be an increase in fighting among agents in the population. In fact, hawk-dove games can become so attractive that they substantially crowd out prisoner's dilemma games, making the world one of frequent fighting and only infrequent cooperative games[37]— perhaps the kind of nasty and brutish world that Thomas Hobbes imagined as the state of nature. "Warlike" worlds in which there is frequent fighting, however, are not necessarily populated by substantially uncooperative individuals. And worlds populated by substantially cooperative individuals are not necessarily more peaceful worlds.[38] The point, nevertheless, is that progressively more attractive hawk-dove games will increase (in particular) cooperators' ability to be particular about their partners for prisoner's dilemma games— and will contribute thereby to the evolution of cooperative dispositions.

Conclusions

Our argument has been developed with hawk-dove games as an alternative to prisoner's dilemmas, but the more general point is that some alternative way of making a living other than participation in prisoner's dilemma games has the potential to support positive selection on cooperative dispositions. In fact, of course, game theorists have studied a wide variety of "stand-alone" games, and any one of them might—in both natural and simulated worlds—be a viable alternative for individuals confronting possible prisoner's dilemma play.[39] Neither does the alternative have to involve social interaction at all. Although humans are usually not very impressive on their own, it is possible sometimes for them to make a quite adequate living without social interaction of any kind, and our conclusions are quite compatible with that possibility, as well.[40] In fact, we can demonstrate this by setting the no-play payoff at values higher than the zero previously used in reporting these results; when that is the case, cooperators are still selectively benefited—and increasingly so (up to a point) as the value of that no-play payoff increases. We have used the hawk-dove game to make the more general point simply because cooperation and conflict are so frequently accepted as basic dichotomies of social life.

Neither is our analysis incompatible with the long-standing idea that conflict between groups—more generally, external threat—has contributed to the evolution of cooperative relationships within them (for example, Brewer 1981; Campbell 1965, 1975). In fact, it complements that idea. As pointed out earlier, we do not address how cooperation might evolve in a world populated exclusively by egoists, and in both simulations agents have at least some disposition to cooperate at the outset. Our analysis does identify one process by which mechanisms that support such "starting" dispositions can be positively selected through an extended sequence of generations, and external threat is certainly one such mechanism (Caporael et al. 1989).

We have made a methodological point, an epistemological point, and a substantive point. The methodological point is that studying behavior in one kind of game in isolation from behavior in other kinds of games can lead analysts to miss important processes that bear on the particular behavior that interests them. All social animals live in an ecology of diverse games (Long 1958) that are available as alternative ways for individuals to relate to one another, and the possibility of choice between such games can influence the pattern of choices within them. Our analysis has illustrated this with respect to the long-standing discussion about how cooperation might have evolved, but it is, of course, a general point that is just as relevant to behavior in other social games.

The epistemological point—closely related—concerns the evolutionary framework within which we have conducted our analysis. We have addressed "trust" as a subjective expectation that a protagonist will act in a cooperative manner, employing the concept to address agents' choices among prisoner's dilemma and hawk-dove games. At the level of information processing, however, such expectations are a function of the information that agents can retrieve about others' likely behavior—which, in turn, is a function of agents' own information-processing or cognitive structures, themselves a product of evolution over thousands of generations. At a "higher" level, expectations about others' cooperative behavior have consequences for the incidence of diverse kinds of behaviors, which, in turn, influence the welfare of whole societies. Our point is not the truism that "everything is connected to everything." It is that, precisely because these various levels of analysis are clearly interdependent, it is critical for analysts to find some set of terms—a paradigm, perhaps—within which all such levels can be addressed. We hope to have illustrated how evolutionary psychology and, more generally, evolutionary epistemology are promising candidates in those terms (see also chapter 6, this volume).

The substantive point is that conflict and cooperation might not be as diametrically opposed as is often believed. It is no doubt true that divided houses cannot stand—or, in more prosaic terms, that constant fighting among members of a group is likely to undermine the cooperative behavior that is necessary for the group itself to prosper, even survive. We are not saying that there must be constant fighting for cooperation to evolve; in fact, as we have pointed out, if the incentives for individuals to fight among themselves are particularly strong, fighting will overwhelm cooperative behavior. The analysis shows only that if individuals have the option of fighting with one another there will be selective pressure on relative perceptiveness—making agents progressively more able to tell whether protagonists can be trusted—and that cooperative dispositions will then grow through an evolutionary sequence.

The option of fighting does not mean that members of a population will necessarily fight very often. It does mean, however, that cooperative dispositions will be more likely to evolve, and cooperative dispositions are the basis on which cooperative behavior is built.

This work was funded by the National Science Foundation (Grant SBR-9808041). Cian Montgomery (Intel) wrote the program on which our analysis is based and helped in many other ways. The chapter has bene-fited from the authors' collaboration with Nicholas Allen, Department of Psychology, University of Melbourne; and from valuable suggestions by Deborah Baumgold and Misha Myagkov, members of the Operations and Game Theory Seminar and the Methodology Institute Seminar at the London School of Economics, and members of the Institute of Cognitive and Decision Sciences at the University of Oregon.

Notes

1. The prisoner's dilemma is a choice problem in which a dominant alter-native (better for the choosing individual regardless of what others do) is associated with an outcome at the aggregate level that is deficient, yield-ing outcomes worse than had everyone chosen otherwise (Dawes 1975). In its standard two-person variant, individuals' payoffs for the pris-oner's dilemma are $t > c > d > s$, when $2c > (t + s) > 2d$ (c is the co-operator, d the defector, t the free rider, and s the sucker).

2. Win-stay, lose-shift means to repeat the previous strategy if the other player cooperates, and to change strategy if the other player defects.

3. More generally, societies offer individuals an "ecology of games" (Long 1958) that they might play with one another, including not only many different cooperative and conflictual games but also the full range of games that theorists have analyzed on a stand-alone basis.

4. Important works across this range of fields include Baron-Cohen (1995); Barton and Dunbar (1997); Byrne (1995a, 1995b); Cheney and Seyfarth (1991); Cosmides (1989); Cummins (1998, 1999); Dawkins and Krebs (1978); Dukas (1998); Dunbar (1996); Gigerenzer (1997); Gigerenzer and Hug (1992); Goody (1995); Harcourt and de Waal (1992); Humphrey (1976); Jolly (1966); Kummer et al. (1997); Mithen (1996); Ristau (1991); and Whiten and Byrne (1997).

5. It is certainly true that much work in this tradition implies ongoing cog-nitive processing. Tit-for-tat, for example, is said to be attractive, among other reasons, because it is "simple," allowing players to economize on such processing, with protagonists rapidly coming to understand what is going on and to adjust appropriately (Axelrod 1984; cognitive economy is also invoked in Orbell and Dawes 1991). The evolution of cognitive mechanisms in themselves, however, is seldom addressed.

6. Steven Mithen (1996), however, has demonstrated that the fragmentary fossil record can be used for productively piecing together plausible hy-potheses about the course of cognitive evolution.

7. In a hawk-dove game, two players encounter a resource v that can be consumed by either player. A hawk choice indicates a willingness to fight; the dove choice is to back off, leaving the resource in the undis-puted control of the other. If both play hawk, a fight ensues, with a winner capturing v and a loser being obliged to pay the cost, l. If both play dove, both move away from the resource, and neither gains nor

loses. The classic enunciation of the hawk-dove game is by John Maynard Smith (1974a, 1974b, 1982; Maynard Smith and Price 1974); see also Smith and Winterhalder (1992) and Weibull (1995).

8. An asymmetry exists between the two games insofar as a hawk challenge from Alpha, if issued, obliges Beta to choose between hawk and dove—effectively, to play the hawk-dove game—but an offer of a prisoner's dilemma game by Alpha might be rejected by Beta. This is, we believe, consistent with most natural situations in which an individual who is challenged to a fight must either accept or reject that challenge, but in which cooperative games require agreement from both parties before they are joined.

9. The reasons for an individual's choice of cooperation or defection in the particular case, and thus for its probability of cooperating in general, are exogenous to the model; the simulation specifies only that agents will cooperate with some probability, for some reason. The simulation may be thought of, therefore, as addressing the evolution through time of whatever mechanisms support cooperativeness.

10. Communication among protagonists also involves the problem of believing the true component of a message that is sent; the entire message must be assessed for its truthfulness. We are presently developing a simulation that incorporates this more complex model.

11. Payoff parameters for both games are set at the outset of a run and are constant for all games played throughout that run.

12. Cognitive evolution, of course, has molded the algorithms by which animals process information as well as the mechanisms by which they retrieve information from others and emit it to others, but our simulation does not address that particular process. Whatever the particular "wet" mechanisms by which information processing happens, however, they must be "adaptively rational" (Cosmides and Tooby 2001), and expected value algorithms capture precisely that necessary requirement.

13. In the hawk-dove game, the gain from winning a fight, v, is always positive and the loser's cost or loss, l, is always negative. In the prisoner's dilemma game, mutual cooperation and the free rider's payoff are always positive, meaning that playing with a cooperator always returns a gain, albeit a greater gain for a defector than for another cooperator; and mutual defection and the sucker's payoff are always negative, meaning that playing with a defector always returns a loss. We adopt this convention to sharpen the evolutionary consequences of the capacity to distinguish defectors from cooperators in prisoner's dilemma games.

14. A generation consists of one round of interactions in which each agent initiates one interaction with each other agent. Thus each agent plays twice with each other agent in its generation, one as initiator (Alpha) and once as responder (Beta).

15. If agents produce more offspring than the carrying capacity, n, a sample of n is chosen randomly to populate the ecology in the next generation.

16. For all runs reported, frequency was .04 and magnitude was randomly selected from the range -5 to $+5$. Our experience, however, is that changing either or both values does not have a substantial impact on the ways in which the population changes but affects only the speed at which such change occurs.

17. Defined in these terms, mutation would not work in a similar manner for the probability term p^c as for the other attributes that are defined as open-ended integers. Accordingly, p^c is constructed by two integer attributes, d and c, the former being the propensity to defect and the latter being the propensity to cooperate, both subject independently to mutation. These integers are then used to define p^c using $c/(c + d)$.

18. This is not to say they would thereby prosper. Obviously, in an ecology dominated by defectors, most interactions will be among such defectors, with the result that most agents will repeatedly capture only the low (in our set of parameters, negative) mutual-defection payoff.

19. Having set up this cooperation-friendly world for analytic purposes, we are absolved from the need to explain how such a world might have evolved in the first place—but, for the sake of argument, it is not impossible that social perceptiveness, at least, could have evolved as an adaptive response to some other problem (say, predation or predator avoidance) and then have been co-opted to social purposes.

20. Operationally, c is set at 75 and d at 50—which, by the algorithm $c/(c + d)$, produces a p^c of .6.

21. Because the simulation has many stochastic elements, no two runs with the same initial parameters will produce exactly the same results. However, while the figures we use are drawn from single runs, they are typical examples of stable patterns that emerged over five hundred runs with these and similar parameters. In the present case, note that the initial settings for persuasiveness^{PD} and perceptiveness^{PD} do not preclude agents who intend defection from having some success in convincing protagonists that they intend cooperation. Agents in this first generation accept $50/(50 + 75) = .4$ of the lie portion of the protagonist's claim to being perfectly cooperative. Because, for all agents in the initial generation, $p^c = .6$, the lie portion itself is $1.00 - .6 = .4$, and so the accepted value of the lie is $.4(.4) = .16$. The estimate individuals in this initial generation make of each other's cooperativeness is, therefore, $.6 + .16 = .76$, a figure that will be built into their calculations of the expected value of playing a prisoner's dilemma game with any particular individual—a figure that is an overestimate but that will lead agents to enter into games that will most often give them positive returns.

22. In the case illustrated, the whole population survives only 281 generations. "Population death" of this kind is quite frequent in simulations with these parameters, but given the stochastic elements in the simulation it is not inevitable. The choice of starting parameters, of course, has some bearing on whether or not the society survives. With starting p^c set

still higher and with perceptiveness^{PD} still higher relative to persuasiveness^{PD}, the population is more likely to survive. The critical issue, however, is not whether the society itself survives; it is what happens to cooperativeness during the period that it does survive.

23. With the game parameters adopted, the defection plus cooperation outcome—which also declines—does return one individual (the defector) 20 while costing the other (the cooperator) -20, meaning that, in net, each time this outcome happens no social or aggregate wealth is either created or lost. Note that, in this simulation, agents do sometimes protect themselves by choosing no play, but that neither produces social gain nor private gain to either of the individuals.

24. Specifically, (perceptiveness^{PD} $-$ persuasiveness^{PD})/(perceptiveness^{PD} $+$ persuasiveness^{PD}).

25. That is to say, the sucker's payoff (s) is worse than the mutual-defection payoff (d).

26. That is to say, the free rider's payoff (t) is greater than the mutual-cooperation payoff (c).

27. We are not suggesting that relative persuasiveness will always evolve; in fact, the next simulation to be reported shows that exactly the opposite can happen. Generally, a society that is populated at the outset by agents with low p^c values will place a premium on perceptiveness^{PD}, and relative perceptiveness is likely to evolve; in such a world, persuasiveness^{PD} will be likely to get agents (cooperators and defectors alike) into trouble by promoting relationships with defectors, and perceptiveness^{PD} will be much more useful. The point of the present analysis is to show that, when prisoner's dilemma games are the only way of making a living, selective pressures work against cooperation, and it is not to say anything general about selective pressures on relative persuasiveness.

28. Perceptiveness^{PD} does not actually help agents recognize cooperators and thus capture gains from playing more often with them because in the absence of such perceptiveness all agents are believed to be cooperators. Only if the default were that all others were believed to be defectors would perceptiveness help agents to recognize cooperators. To use such a default in the simulation, we would have to eliminate the attribute of persuasiveness^{PD}, the capacity to make others believe one is cooperative. We believe it crucial to include both of these competing capacities because, as Catherine Eckel and Rick Wilson note, the "ability to read intentions has evolved along with the mechanisms for displaying intentions" (chapter 9, this volume).

29. Operationally, c is set at 50 and d is set at 100, which by the algorithm $c/(c + d)$ produces a p^c of .33.

30. Meaning that agents at the outset of this cooperation-unfriendly world accept $50/(50 + 25) = .67$ of the lie portion of the protagonist's claim to being perfectly cooperative. Because, for all agents in the initial generation, $p^c = .33$, the lie portion itself is $1.00 - .33 = .67$, and so the ac-

cepted value of the lie is $.67(.67) = .45$. The estimate individuals in this initial generation make of one another's cooperativeness is, therefore, $.33 + .45 = .78$—a highly inaccurate estimate that will fool both cooperators and defectors into games that are likely to give them negative returns.

31. Setting v at 20 and l at -20 would make all fights effectively zero sum. Given that individuals have the capacity to bluff, and that only some portion of such bluffs is likely to be penetrated, the expected value of entering such a zero-sum game would normally be negative, making it rational for agents to reject fighting in favor of the no-play payoff of zero (or, of course, of playing a prisoner's dilemma game, should the expected value of that kind of game be positive). The present settings are designed to make hawk-dove games at least sometimes attractive, even if a protagonist's bluff is substantially successful, but not so attractive that they overwhelm any appeal that playing a prisoner's dilemma might have.

32. In the present simulation, both Alpha and Beta have the option of rejecting a prisoner's dilemma game, whereas only Alpha has the option of making a hawk challenge; Beta can only accept or reject such a challenge (by playing hawk or dove, respectively). Alpha, therefore, is the only agent in a position to act on a comparison between the expected values of playing a prisoner's dilemma and of fighting. In the simulations reported here, however, each agent plays both the Alpha and Beta roles with each other agent once in a generation, meaning that this asymmetry cannot bias our findings.

33. The situation, of course, works in the other direction, as well: agents who assess the expected value of fighting with a particular protagonist as only marginally positive might find the expected value of entering a prisoner's dilemma significantly more attractive and offer such a game, accordingly. In other words, agents who assess themselves as having low fighting strength relative to that of a protagonist are likely to be particularly enthusiastic would-be prisoner's dilemma players, presumably with a particular interest in persuading the relatively powerful individual of their cooperative dispositions. Our present focus, however, is on the implications of the hawk-dove alternative for how prisoner's dilemma games are played, and we do not develop these issues any further here (but see Orbell, Morikawa, and Allen forthcoming).

34. This is a special case of Trivers's principle that the distribution of benefits from cooperation must be nonrandom and biased toward those who cooperate (Trivers 1971, 37).

35. The present argument depends on there being no negative correlation between cooperativeness (p^c) and fighting ability: cooperators are not necessarily worse fighters. If there were such a negative correlation, then intending cooperators could often find fighting to be no more attractive an alternative than entering a prisoner's dilemma game. Correspondingly, intending defectors could often find that fighting is just as attrac-

tive (or even more attractive) for themselves as for intending cooperators. We see no evidence of that from the simulations we have run, however.

36. One of the reasons for the continuing interest in cooperation is that
(within a prisoner's dilemma paradigm, at least) the mutual-cooperation
outcome provides the highest aggregate or social payoff. Although we
share this reason for being interested in how mutual cooperation can
evolve, we point out that in a more complex "ecology of games"—which
we are introducing here—mutual cooperation might not be the socially
most productive outcome to the set of "games people play." Notably in
the present context, if the stake in a hawk-dove game (v) is sufficiently
high relative to the cost of losing a fight (l) and also relative to available
prisoner's dilemma payoffs, then such games could produce more
wealth than prisoner's dilemma games, even if one individual does lose
a fight and is forced to pay l. Of course, hawk-dove games presume the
existence of a resource (v) that is worth fighting over (manna from
heaven?), whereas the definition of prisoner's dilemma games includes
the idea that wealth is somehow created by individuals successfully cooperating with one another.

37. This might happen in the natural world, for example, should resources
that are critical to survival and reproductive success (for example, food,
water, and mates) be in short supply within the population and should
individuals be generally able to gather other important resources on
their own, absent cooperative relations with others. With the current parameters, the relevant threshold is reached with $v = 40$, beyond which
prisoner's dilemmas become only infrequent ways by which agents relate to one another. There is, nevertheless, still positive selection on p^c,
although by a process somewhat different from that being explored here
(Orbell, Morikawa, and Allen forthcoming).

38. This point has been obscured, we believe, by the frequency with which
the Hobbesian state of nature has been modeled in prisoner's dilemma
terms as involving a choice between a dominant incentive to act in a
predatory manner and a suboptimal equilibrium at the "war of every
man with every man" (Hobbes 1962 [1651], 100; for example, see
Gauthier 1969, 1986; Hampton 1986). Although the prisoner's dilemma
surely does capture at least some part of what Hobbes was arguing, it
does not provide an adequate general model of the logic of fighting. In
particular, it does not capture the obvious fact that picking a fight is not
always a dominant incentive—something we are confident that Hobbes,
too, would have recognized.

39. Anatol Rapoport, Melvin Guyer, and David Gordon (1976), for example,
distinguish seventy-eight two-by-two games (including the prisoner's
dilemma), each with a distinctive incentive structure, and that list does
not include the still wider set of possible n-person games.

40. In fact, as Kristen Hawkes (1993) shows, foraging and hunting for small
game provides a larger proportion of the diet for some hunter-gatherers

than does large game hunting—which frequently requires more cooperative effort.

References

Axelrod, Robert. 1984. *The Evolution of Cooperation*. New York: Basic Books.

Baron-Cohen, Simon. 1995. *Mindblindness: An Essay on Autism and Theory of Mind*. Cambridge, Mass.: MIT Press.

Barton, Robert A., and Robin I. M. Dunbar. 1997. "Evolution of the Social Brain." In *Machiavellian Intelligence II: Extensions and Evaluations*, edited by Andrew B. Whiten and Richard W. Byrne. Cambridge: Cambridge University Press.

Brewer, Marilynn B. 1981. "Ethnocentrism and Its Role in Interpersonal Trust." In *Scientific Inquiry in the Social Sciences*, edited by Marilynn B. Brewer and Barry E. Collins. San Francisco: Jossey-Bass.

Byrne, Richard W. 1995a. "The Ape Legacy: The Evolution of Machiavellian Intelligence and Anticipatory Interactive Planning." In *Social Intelligence and Interaction: Expressions and Implications of the Social Bias in Human Intelligence*, edited by Esther N. Goody. Cambridge: Cambridge University Press.

———. 1995b. *The Thinking Ape: Evolutionary Origins of Intelligence*. New York: Oxford University Press.

Campbell, Donald T. 1965. "Ethnocentric and Other Altruistic Motives." In *Nebraska Symposium on Motivation*, edited by David LeVine. Lincoln, Nebr.: University of Nebraska Press.

———. 1975. "On the Conflict Between Biological and Social Evolution, and Between Psychology and Moral Tradition." *American Psychologist* 30(12): 1103–26.

Caporael, Linnda, Robyn Dawes, John Orbell, and Alphons van de Kragt. 1989. "Selfishness Examined: Cooperation in the Absence of Egoistic Incentives." *Behavioral and Brain Science* 12(4): 683–99.

Carruthers, Peter, and Peter K. Smith. 1996. *Theories of Theories of Mind*. Cambridge: Cambridge University Press.

Cheney, Dorothy L., and Robert M. Seyfarth. 1991. "Truth and Deception in Animal Communication." In *Cognitive Ethology: The Minds of Other Animals*, edited by Carolyn A. Ristau. Hillsdale, N.J.: Lawrence Erlbaum.

Cosmides, Leda. 1989. "The Logic of Social Exchange: Has Natural Selection Shaped How Humans Reason?" *Cognition* 31(3): 187–276.

Cosmides, Leda, and John Tooby. 1994. "Origins of Domain Specificity: The Evolution of Functional Organization." In *Mapping the Mind: Domain Specificity in Cognition and Culture*, edited by Lawrence A. Hirschfeld and Susan A. Gelman. Cambridge: Cambridge University Press.

———. 2001. "The Evolution of Adaptations for Decoupling and Metarepresentation." In *Metarepresentation*, edited by Dan Sperber. New York: Oxford University Press.

Cummins, Denise Dellarosa. 1998. "Social Norms and Other Minds." In *The*

Evolution of Mind, edited by Denise D. Cummins and Colin Allen. New York: Oxford University Press.

———. 1999. "Cheater Detection Is Modified by Social Rank: The Impact of Dominance on the Evolution of Cognitive Functions." *Evolution and Social Behavior* 20(4): 229–48.

Dawes, Robyn. 1975. "Formal Models of Dilemmas in Social Decision-Making." In *Human Judgment and Decision Processes*, edited by Martin F. Kaplan and Steven Schwartz. New York: Academic Press.

Dawkins, Richard, and John R. Krebs. 1978. "Animal Signals: Information or Manipulation?" In *Behavioral Ecology: An Evolutionary Approach*, edited by John R. Krebs and Nick B. Davies. Oxford: Blackwell Scientific.

Dukas, Reuven, ed. 1998. *Cognitive Ecology: The Evolutionary Ecology of Information Processing and Decision Making*. Chicago: University of Chicago Press.

Dunbar, Robin. 1996. *Grooming, Gossip, and the Evolution of Language*. Cambridge, Mass.: Harvard University Press.

Frank, Robert. 1988. *Passions Within Reason*. New York: W. W. Norton.

Gauthier, David. 1969. *The Logic of "Leviathan": The Moral and Political Theory of Thomas Hobbes*. Oxford: Clarendon.

———. 1986. *Morals by Agreement*. New York: Oxford University Press.

Gigerenzer, Gerd. 1997. "The Modularity of Social Intelligence." In *Machiavellian Intelligence II: Extensions and Evaluations*, edited by Andrew B. Whiten and Richard W. Byrne. Cambridge: Cambridge University Press.

Gigerenzer, Gerd, and Klaus Hug. 1992. "Domain-Specific Reasoning: Social Contracts, Cheating, and Perspective Change." *Cognition* 43(2): 127–71.

Goody, Esther N., ed. 1995. *Social Intelligence and Interaction: Expressions and Implications of the Social Bias in Intelligence*. Cambridge: Cambridge University Press.

Hampton, Jean. 1986. *Hobbes and the Social Contract Tradition*. New York: Cambridge University Press.

Harcourt, Alexander H., and Frans B. de Waal, eds. 1992. *Coalitions and Alliances in Humans and Other Animals*. New York: Oxford University Press.

Hartung, John. 1976. "On Natural Selection and the Inheritance of Wealth." *Current Anthropology* 17(4): 607–22.

Hawkes, Kristen. 1993. "Why Hunter-Gatherers Work: An Ancient Version of the Public Goods Problem." *Current Anthropology* 34(4): 341–61.

Hobbes, Thomas. 1962 [1651]. *Leviathan*. New York: Collier Books.

Humphrey, Nicholas K. 1976. "The Social Function of Intellect." In *Growing Points in Ethology*, edited by Patrick P. G. Bateson and Robert A. Hinde. Cambridge: Cambridge University Press.

Jolly, Allison. 1966. "Lemur Social Behavior and Primate Intelligence." *Science* 153(3735): 501–6.

Kummer, Hans, Lorraine Daston, Gerd Gigerenzer, and Joan B. Silk. 1997. "The Social Intelligence Hypothesis." In *Human by Nature: Between Biology and the Social Sciences*, edited by Peter Weingart, Sandra D. Mitchell, Peter J. Richerson, and Sabine Maasen. Mahwah, N.J.: Lawrence Erlbaum.

Lane, Richard D., and Lynn Nadel, eds. 2000. *Cognitive Neuroscience of Emotion*. Series in Affective Science, edited by Richard J. Davidson, Paul Ekman, and Klaus Scherer. New York: Oxford University Press.

Long, Norton. 1958. "The Local Community As an Ecology of Games." *American Journal of Sociology* 64(3): 251–61.

Marler, Peter, Stephen Karakashian, and Marcel Gyger. 1991. "Do Animals Have the Option of Withholding Signals When Communication Is Inappropriate? The Audience Effect." In *Cognitive Ethology: The Minds of Other Animals*, edited by Carolyn A. Ristau. New York: Lawrence Erlbaum.

Maynard Smith, John. 1974a. *Models in Ecology.* Cambridge: Cambridge University Press.

———. 1974b. "The Theory of Games and the Evolution of Animal Conflicts." *Journal of Theoretical Biology* 47: 209–21.

———. 1982. *Evolution and the Theory of Games.* Cambridge: Cambridge University Press.

Maynard Smith, John, and G. R. Price. 1974. "The Logic of Animal Conflict." *Nature* 246(November): 15–18.

Mithen, Steven. 1996. *The Prehistory of the Mind: The Cognitive Origins of Art, Religion, and Science.* London: Thames and Hudson.

Nowak, Martin, and Karl Sigmund. 1992. "Tit for Tat in Heterogeneous Populations." *Nature* 355(6357): 250–53.

———. 1993. "A Strategy of Win-Stay, Lose-Shift That Outperforms Tit-for-Tat in the Prisoner's Dilemma Game." *Nature* 364(6432): 56–58.

Orbell, John, and Robyn Dawes. 1991. "A 'Cognitive Miser' Theory of Cooperators' Advantage." *American Political Science Review* 85(2): 515–28.

———. 1993. "Social Welfare, Cooperators' Advantage, and the Option of Not Playing the Game." *American Sociological Review* 58(6): 787–800.

Orbell, John, Robyn Dawes, and Peregrine Schwartz-Shea. 1994. "Trust, Social Categories, and Individuals: The Case of Gender." *Motivation and Emotion* 18(2): 109–28.

Orbell, John, Tomonori Morikawa, and Nicholas Allen. Forthcoming. "The Evolution of Political Intelligence: Simulation Results." *British Journal of Political Science.*

Orbell, John, Langche Zeng, and Matthew Mulford. 1996. "Individual Experience and the Fragmentation of Societies." *American Sociological Review* 61(6): 1018–32.

Rapoport, Anatol, Melvin J. Guyer, and David G. Gordon. 1976. *The 2 × 2 Game.* Ann Arbor, Mich.: University of Michigan Press.

Ristau, Carolyn A. 1991. *Cognitive Ethology: The Minds of Other Animals.* Hillsdale, N.J.: Lawrence Erlbaum.

Rothbart, Myron, and Marjorie Taylor. 1992. "Category Labels and Social Reality: Do We View Social Categories As Natural Kinds?" In *Language, Interaction, and Social Cognition*, edited by Gün R. Semin and Klaus Fielder. London: Sage.

Savage-Rumbaugh, Sue, and Kelly McDonald. 1988. "Deception and Social Manipulation in Symbol-Using Apes." In *Machiavellian Intelligence: Social Expertise and the Evolution of Intellect in Monkeys, Apes, and Humans*, edited by Richard W. Byrne and Andrew B. Whiten. Oxford: Clarendon.

Schuessler, Rudolf. 1989. "Exit Threats and Cooperation Under Anonymity." *Journal of Conflict Resolution* 33(4): 728–49.

Simon, Herbert. 1955. "A Behavioral Model of Rational Choice." *Quarterly Journal of Economics* 69(1): 99–118.

————. 1956. "Rational Choice and the Structure of the Environment." *Psychological Review* 63(2): 129–38.

Smith, Eric Alden, and Bruce Winterhalder, eds. 1992. *Evolutionary Ecology and Human Behavior.* New York: Walter de Gruyter.

Sperber, Dan. 1994. "The Modularity of Thought and the Epidemiology of Representations." In *Mapping the Mind: Domain Specificity in Cognition and Culture,* edited by Lawrence A. Hirschfeld and Susan A. Gelman. New York: Cambridge University Press.

Trivers, Robert. 1971. "The Evolution of Reciprocal Altruism." *Quarterly Review of Biology* 46(March): 35–57.

Vanberg, Viktor J., and Roger D. Congleton. 1992. "Rationality, Morality, and Exit." *American Political Science Review* 86(2): 418–31.

Weibull, Jörgen W. 1995. *Evolutionary Game Theory.* Cambridge, Mass.: MIT Press.

Whiten, Andrew, and Richard W. Byrne. 1988. "The Manipulation of Attention in Primate Tactical Deception." In *Machiavellian Intelligence: Social Expertise and the Evolution of Intellect in Monkeys, Apes, and Humans,* edited by Richard W. Byrne and Andrew Whiten. Oxford: Clarendon.

————, eds. 1997. *Machiavellian Intelligence II: Extensions and Evaluations.* Cambridge: Cambridge University Press.

Wright, Robert. 1994. *The Moral Animal.* New York: Random House.

PART IV

EXPERIMENTAL EVIDENCE

Chapter 8

Experimental Studies of Cooperation, Trust, and Social Exchange

KAREN S. COOK AND ROBIN M. COOPER

T RUST HAS become a central topic of discussion in the social sciences during the past decade. Francis Fukuyama (1995), Robert Putnam (1993, 2000), Niklas Luhmann (1988), and others argue that trust is an essential social lubricant; it facilitates cooperation and contributes to the maintenance of social order at the micro level as well as at the societal level. Social order might exist without trust if supported by strong institutions that ensure commitments, provide for sanctioning and monitoring, and enforce contracts (see Barber 1983; Hardin 1999; Luhmann 1988). The capacity to engage in mutually beneficial relationships based on trust and reciprocity extends the reach of institutionally supported activities, however, and enables a range of interactions that would not be possible in the absence of such institutions. The contributors to this volume explore the microfoundations of trusting relationships, primarily using the experimental method. This work produces a more fine-grained analysis of the structure of trust relationships and the motivations for engaging in cooperative behavior that is the hallmark of social order in any society. The primary focus of the micro-level work is the behavior George Homans (1974 [1961]) likes to call "sub-institutional."

Social psychologists since the 1960s have investigated the conditions that facilitate social cooperation. The central research question addressed in this work has been, "What makes cooperation in society possible?" To study this question at the micro level, experimentalists developed specific paradigms (for example, experimental games) with which to analyze the determinants of cooperative behavior in the laboratory. Limitations to this work led researchers to attempt to develop survey measures of trust that could be used outside the laboratory. Since then, most of the research on trust, cooperation, and social exchange has relied on these two methodologies.

This chapter provides a broad overview of the research that contributes to our understanding of the role of trust at the micro level of society. In particular, we investigate the role of trust as a facilitator of spontaneous cooperation and informal social exchange. An overarching theme of this chapter is that the experimental research on trust must eventually provide a richer sense of the effects of social context if it is to inform our understanding of the role of trust in society at large.

Prisoners Fail to Cooperate; Do We?

Game theory has become the primary tool for investigating the incentive structures and related factors that facilitate or inhibit cooperation. The paradigmatic case is the analysis of cooperation (and noncooperation, usually called defection) in the *prisoner's dilemma* (Luce and Raiffa 1957). The prisoner's dilemma became the foundation for the analysis of cooperation, in part, because the game structure so clearly represents the nature of the conflicting incentives involved in certain social situations—namely, those in which the individual incentives to defect (for example, turn state's evidence) overshadow the collective benefit that might be obtained from jointly cooperating (for example, not squealing and going free).

Some would argue that the issue at the center of this dilemma is one of trust. Did the separately jailed prisoners trust that their partner in crime would not be tempted to turn state's evidence to gain a lighter sentence? Oddly, the real-world dilemma was more complex than that represented in most experimental versions, which do not allow for prior interaction between the players. In fact, only recently (see chapter 12 and others in this volume) have researchers begun to examine trust in the context of repeated play with the same partners over time. The typical *one-shot* prisoner's dilemma represents a two-person mixed-motive situation in which each actor has only two options: to cooperate or to defect. Neither actor knows at the time he or she makes the decision what the other actor will do. The outcomes vary depending on the actor's own choice and the choice of his or her partner.

Briefly, the structure of the payoffs in the prisoner's dilemma can be explained as follows.[1] In this discussion, C refers to a cooperative action and D to a noncooperative action. A combination of the two letters indicates the joint actions for both parties, as typically represented in matrix form. Thus CD is the outcome when person 1 cooperates and person 2 defects;. CC represents the situation in which both individuals cooperate; DD represents mutual defection; and DC represents defection by person 1 and cooperation by person 2. The prisoner's dilemma is defined as a situation satisfying two incentive conditions: CC > DD (mutual cooperation is more beneficial to both parties than mutual noncooperation); and DC > CC and DD > CD (but each party is better off not cooperating than cooperating, regardless of the other person's action).

In the classic case, individuals fail to cooperate to achieve a positive outcome because it is in each actor's interest (narrowly defined in terms of the maximization of payoffs) to defect if the other cooperates. If both individuals reason in the same way, then both will defect; and when both individuals defect, the outcome is less desirable than if both individuals were to cooperate. Thus when both individuals employ the dominant strategy (to defect), the joint outcome they reach is socially deficient in the sense that mutual cooperation would be better for all. The central question in this research is what happens when the individually dominating strategies (in this case, to defect) converge on this deficient equilibrium (Dawes 1991) and what factors mitigate this outcome. The outcome of the prisoner's dilemma is predicated not only on the motivational assumption of egoism on the part of each actor but also on a set of structural conditions concerning repeated play, information availability, communication possibilities, pregame interaction. and so forth that have been studied experimentally (see reviews by Dawes 1980; Messick and Brewer 1983; Yamagishi 1995).

In one of the earliest experimental investigations of cooperation and trust (using the prisoner's dilemma), Morton Deutsch (1960) claims that individuals must develop "mutual trust" if they are to cooperate with one another. One factor that affects the development of mutual trust is the individual's "orientation" to his or her partner. Here Deutsch foreshadows later research that focuses on the actors' motivations as well as features of the social situation that might facilitate the development of mutual trust. Deutsch argues that mutual trust emerges (and positively affects cooperation) when individuals are positively oriented to one another's welfare. In one experiment, he manipulated "orientation" by using different experimental instructions in each of three conditions to create three types of players: cooperative, individualistic, and competitive.[2]

Deutsch predicted that subjects with a cooperative orientation (those who were positively oriented to their partners' welfare) would develop relationships characterized by mutual trust and would engage in cooperative behavior. He found that a cooperative orientation led individuals to make cooperative choices that resulted in mutual gain, whereas the competitive orientation led individuals to make noncooperative choices resulting in a mutual loss (Deutsch 1960).

In this study, Deutsch examined not only the effects of orientation on cooperation but also the role of certain situational conditions on cooperation. These include the opportunity to know what the other person will do once the subject cooperates, the opportunity to communicate a system of role obligations or mutual responsibilities that ensure cooperation and that also provide for sanctioning, and the power to influence the other's behavior and hence to reduce any incentive he or she might have to engage in uncooperative behavior. Deutsch discovered that the effects of these situational conditions varied depending on the orientation of the subjects (cooperative, individualistic, and competitive). Subjects with a cooperative orientation, for example, did not need the opportunity to communicate to choose cooperatively, whereas subjects with a competitive orientation exhibited motives that made it difficult for them to engage in "trustworthy" communication (Deutsch 1960).

Deutsch's work represents one of the earliest experimental efforts using the prisoner's dilemma setting to examine the nature of the relationship between trust and cooperation. However, there are both conceptual and methodological limitations to this study. Deutsch theorizes early on in the article that mutual trust facilitates cooperation. He then says that mutual trust develops as a result of orientation (cooperative, individualistic, and competitive). One is left wondering what the real role of "mutual trust" is in his argument. If cooperative orientation leads to cooperative behavior, why do we need the concept of trust to understand that relationship? Moreover, Deutsch later adds that when the subjects did cooperate, they were making a "trusting choice," treating cooperation as the indicator of trust. Thus trust seems to be both a feature of the relationship (mutual trust instigates cooperation by way of orientation) and a feature of a particular behavior (a trusting choice is a choice to cooperate). Yet "trust" was not actually operationalized or measured in this experimental study. Instead, Deutsch theorized about the relatively indirect role of trust in producing cooperation. Essentially, this early work on cooperation and trust served to highlight certain factors (orientation and even social-context factors such as communication) that are important for the development of trust and also for the initiation of cooperation. The exact nature of the relationship between cooperation and trust, however, is far from clear in this work (as in some of the subsequent experimental work that used this paradigm) and deserves further attention.

As interest in the problem of trust grew, experimenters continued to use the fairly standard protocols for studying cooperation (such as prisoner's dilemma games) to investigate trust, often, like Deutsch, simply using cooperative behavior as an indicator of trust. The main problem with this work was that it confounded trusting behavior and cooperation. If trust plays a part in easing the way to cooperation, treating cooperative behavior in the laboratory as a measure of trust makes the experimental evidence circular. Does trust lead people to cooperate, or does cooperation lead people to trust one another? One way out of this conundrum was for investigators to measure trust by using a separate set of questionnaire items for classifying subjects before their participation in the experiment. Trust measured this way is treated as an individual difference factor on which individuals may vary, like a personality trait (and not as a feature of the relationship). Moreover, measuring trust using items on a survey represents a strictly attitudinal measure of trust. Such measures could be obtained and subsequently correlated with behavior in the game setting (or indicators of intended behavior on surveys). Julian Rotter (1967) was a pioneer in the survey work on trust that he instigated, in part, as a reaction to the limitations of the experimental work using the prisoner's dilemma paradigm.

Attitudinal Measures

One of the earliest attitudinal measures of trust is Rotter's (1967) interpersonal trust scale. Rotter defined trust as a "generalized expectancy held by an individual that the word, promise, oral or written statement of another individual or group can be relied on" (Rotter 1967, 653). This definition of trust is quite different from the mutual trust mentioned in Deutsch's work and in more recent treatments of the topic by experimentalists, including the exchange theorists, who focus on trust as a feature of a social relationship. Rotter's definition addresses the confidence aspect of trust (in the more colloquial usage of the term, referring to confidence in the absence of uncertainty, as implied in statements such as "I trust that the sun will rise tomorrow").

Using a Likert format, Rotter included items in his trust scale requesting subjects to express their trust in a variety of social objects such as parents, teachers, physicians, politicians, and classmates.[3] The scale was constructed as an additive scale in which a high score would show trust in a great variety of social objects. In addition to these specific items, the scale includes a few questions that were intended to measure a broader conception of trust or a more general optimism regarding society.[4] Finally, Rotter added several filler items intended to disguise the purpose of the scale. The survey comprises approximately twenty-five measures of trust and fifteen additional items that were considered filler items. Rotter's interpersonal trust scale, the first of its kind, was developed primarily as an attitudinal measure of trust that might be predictive of a wide range of social behaviors, including cooperation.

One of Rotter's (1971) rationales in pursuing survey work on trust was his dissatisfaction with the focus of other social psychologists at the time on prisoner's dilemma games. His primary purpose was to investigate the extent to which trust is a general personality factor that can be used as a predictor of socially oriented cooperative behavior in a wide range of settings. He argued that because prisoner's dilemma and other games might produce relatively specific reactions more characteristic of competitive situations, they cannot be generalized to other types of interpersonal interactions. One of his main concerns was the extent to which the existing measures of trust were valid. He worked for almost two decades on measurement issues, and others investigated the validity of the scale he developed. Some of the validation studies tried to determine the nature of the correlations of the interpersonal trust scale with other factors viewed as possible predictors of levels of trust (for example, social class, age, Machiavellianism, belief in human benevolence). In this survey work, conducted from 1960 until 1980, Rotter explored the differences between high-trusters and low-trusters and the relation between trust and trustworthiness. His work reveals an overall positive correlation between trust and trustworthiness and also a positive correlation between low trust and untrustworthy behavior (indicators included self-reported cheating and lying). High-trusters are more trustworthy, find it difficult to lie, and are generally more likable. They are also more likely to contribute to the provision of *public goods* through (self-reported) volunteering and engagement in other socially valuable behaviors. In addition, results suggest that high-trusters are more likely to have the capacity to differentiate whom to trust from whom not to trust on the basis of fairly specific cues. These data come from surveys in which the level of risk at stake in the decision to trust is implicit. In fact, precisely what actors are being trusted about is not specified in typical survey items like Rotter's or in items used subsequently in the General Social Survey.

Rotter's survey evidence also indicates that high- and low-trusters clearly differ in their approach to strangers. High-trusters are more likely to trust a stranger than are low-trusters.[5] The difference is captured in the following stylistic quotes. The high-truster says, "I will trust a person until I have clear evidence that he or she can't be trusted." The low-truster, in contrast, says, "I will not trust a person until there is clear evidence that he or she can be trusted" (Rotter 1980). The divide is reflected in their levels of cautiousness. This finding is replicated in the survey data collected by Toshio Yamagishi and Midori Yamagishi (1994) comparing high- and low-trusters in the United States and Japan. The low-trusters in both cultures are more cautious than the high-trusters when dealing with strangers, though those in Japan are more cautious than those in the United States, reflecting, in part, the overall differences in levels of trust in the two cultures. General trust levels are higher in the United States than in Japan.

Other researchers have developed scales to measure variations in trust among individuals. David Thornton and Paul Kline (1982), for example, developed a scale known as the Belief in Human Benevolence Scale. Toshio Yamagishi created a composite scale referred to simply as the trust scale (Yamagishi 1986; Yamagishi and Yamagishi 1994).[6] Trust measures included in the General Social Survey and the National Election Studies and their limitations are discussed more fully in Margaret Levi and Laura Stoker (2000). Trust measured with one of these scales typically represents a general belief in human benevolence (Yamagishi and Yamagishi 1994). Use of these scales has been combined with experimental work such that subjects are selected into the experimental studies based on variations in their levels of trust as measured before their research participation. Comparisons are then made between high- and low-trusters in their game behavior or rates of cooperation.

Measures of trust in this context are, again, strictly attitudinal. They are of interest here primarily because they often correlate with behavioral differences between actors in various settings, including experimental games, but what these items actually measure is still under investigation by survey researchers in several fields (see Levi and Stoker 2000). However, the use of such items in experimental settings was one way out of the difficulty of confounding behavioral measures of trust and cooperation. In addition, it helped with the problem of determining causation because trust (treated as an individual difference factor, as Rotter conceived of it) was measured before engagement in the experiment.

Survey work can get at only self-reported intentions to behave in specific ways or self-reported estimates of the frequency of a behavior such as volunteering. The significant role that experimental work has played in the development of theories of trust and trustworthiness is in clarifying the behavioral implications of trust and specifying the conditions under which mutual trust emerges.

Behavioral Measures

Subsequent to the work of Deutsch and others in the 1960s, experimentalists made various modifications in the standard experimental protocols for studying cooperation to generate distinct behavioral measures of trust and cooperation. By obtaining separate behavioral measures of both concepts, rather than relying solely on responses to survey items as indicators of trust,[7] direct questions concerning the nature of the relation between trust (and trustworthiness) and cooperation can be answered more fully. Furthermore, if trust is conceived as a feature of a relationship between actors, then experiments allow for investigation of the relational aspects of trust. Survey work (for example, the national probability samples from the General Social Survey and the National Election Studies survey) does not, because the respondents are rarely in relationships with one another.

One of the modifications made to the standard game setting to solve the problem of confounding behavioral measures of trust and cooperation involved a fairly minor change in the experiment. As John Orbell, Peregrine Schwarz-Shea, and Randy Simmons (1984) argued, trust can be examined not only in the standard prisoner's dilemma setting but also in the setting in which subjects are allowed to exit the game (that is, they are permitted to choose to play or not to play). When actors are given the more realistic option of not playing the game at all (that is, the exit option), the results become more relevant to the analysis of trust. Initially, the choice to cooperate in such situations was treated as an indicator of trust (or, more precisely, trustfulness). As Deutsch's (1960) study demonstrates, however, in this case cooperation and trust are confounded, and causation is unclear. However, when the choice to play or not to play is allowed, then the choice to play is considered to be a behavioral indicator of trust, whereas the choice to cooperate is simply the behavioral indicator of cooperation (Orbell, Schwarz-Shea, and Simmons 1984). Several studies use this modified prisoner's dilemma paradigm, including those by Orbell and Robyn Dawes (1993), Yamagishi (1988), and Michael Macy and John Skvoretz (1998).

Although altering the standard prisoner's dilemma game to include the decision to exit proved fruitful in investigating the nature of the link between trust and cooperation, progress was stimulated further by the development of what is now called the trust game, or the trust-honor game, designed specifically for the purpose of studying trust in experimental settings. This experimental protocol is currently being used widely for research on trust, especially in economics and psychology (for example, Snijders and Keren 1999), even though Russell Hardin (chapter 3, this volume) argues that risk taking is a better term than trust for the behavior investigated in these game situations. The trust-honor game (referred to in chapters 2 and 3, this volume, as the "one-way" trust game) differs in a significant way from the standard prisoner's dilemma protocol.

The trust-honor game is essentially a sequential version of a modified prisoner's dilemma game. That is, first one subject has to decide whether or not to cooperate without knowing what his or her partner will decide. The second subject, with knowledge of the first player's decision, then gets to decide whether to cooperate in return. In the case of cooperation, the second subject can react only by either exploiting the other player or honoring the trust placed in him or her and reciprocating with a cooperative response. That is, the second subject can either cooperate or defect, receiving the higher payoff and taking advantage of the "trust" placed in him or her. It is called the trust-honor game for this reason. First, I decide whether or not to "trust" you (or take a risk on you) and cooperate on the first play of the game, then you must decide whether or not to "honor" that trust by cooperating in return. Clearly, this behavior can be viewed as risk taking by the first player.

For the second player there is virtually no risk because he or she knows exactly what the first mover has decided to do. The decisions are not made simultaneously, as in the standard prisoner's dilemma. The second player just has to decide whether or not to defect and keep the profits by doing so or to return the "trust" by not engaging in exploitation. To the extent that this is the first of a set of interactions between two players in the same game, being trustworthy pays off in the form of the possibility of developing a mutual-trust relationship. In the more typical one-shot games (or repeated games with random matching on every play of the game) this possibility does not exist. In those cases, defection is the predicted response, although more players cooperate than would be expected on the basis of strict maximization of profit logic.[8]

The incorporation of the exit decision into the prisoner's dilemma and the development of the trust-honor game allowed researchers to examine more closely the nature of the relation between trust and cooperation. In addition, some experimentalists have now developed new variants of the trust game to examine in greater detail the factors that facilitate or inhibit the emergence of trust under different social conditions. For example, Toshio Yamagishi has developed a variant of the trust game in which subjects can choose to raise or lower the amount that is at stake in the subsequent decision to cooperate or not. The initial choice to raise or lower the stakes involved, then, is used as a distinct indicator of the level of trust in the partner (or, more precisely, an assessment of the partner's trustworthiness). In this scenario subjects can "invest" in the trust of their partners as well as signal their degree of trust in their partners. This experimental setting allows for the analysis of factors that enhance and erode trust in developing relationships among individuals in networks of varied size when repeated play is allowed. In addition, because the experiment has been conducted in different cultural contexts, it may provide new insights into distinct cultures of trust.

Experimental Evidence on Trust

In the experimental literature on cooperation and trust there are three core elements: the motivational assumptions regarding the actors, incentive structures of the game and the related strategies actors employ in the experiment in response to incentives, and the conditions or features of the social context in which the actions are embedded (such as communication between actors, size of group to which the actor belongs, and the like). Clearly, these elements address different levels of analysis. In dealing with motivations, the focus is on the actor. When investigating the incentive structure, the focus is on the rules of the experimental protocol (or game). The strategies actors employ are connected to the incentive structure operationalized in the experiment.[9] Emphasizing social context moves the discussion beyond the actor and the rules of the game to a consideration of the situations in which the individuals and the game are embedded. All three elements have been the focus of experimental work.

Motivations

A simple motivational assumption of egoism (or self-interest) is typically the basis for predictions about behavior in *noncooperative game theory*. Social psychologists, however, have expanded the set of potential motivations in a variety of studies of cooperation and trust (for example, Liebrand 1986; Liebrand et al. 1986).

An early study by two psychologists, Fred Arnstein and Kenneth Feigenbaum (1967), contrasts two motivational orientations: cooperativeness and competitiveness.[10] Before participating in twenty-four trials of a prisoner's dilemma, subjects wrote briefly about their conscious thoughts and motivations. Their written responses were then scored for "cooperativeness-competitiveness," "trust-mistrust," and degree of economic rationality. Here, motivational orientation was manipulated by the experimenter in the same way that Deutsch manipulated it, but the sample was divided on this variable first. Arnstein and Feigenbaum (1967) found that behavior yielding maximum joint earnings was strongly influenced by both cooperativeness and trust, but behavior yielding maximum individual earnings did not have as strong a relation to competitiveness and mistrust. Early on, then, researchers concluded that the different responses (maximizing joint earnings and maximizing own earnings) were linked to (but not perfectly correlated with) specific motivational orientations such as cooperativeness-trust and competitiveness-mistrust, respectively.

Extending this line of work, Charles McClintock's (1972) influential research outlined four principal social motives: individual gain maximization (individualism or egoism), relative gain maximization (competition), joint gain maximization (cooperation), and others' gain maximization (altruism). In simplest terms, egoists maximize their own payoffs, competitors maximize the difference between their own and others' payoffs, cooperators minimize the difference between their own and others' payoffs, and altruists maximize others' payoffs.[11] In a subsequent article on the broader topic of social values, McClintock (1976) included a fifth motive, which he termed others' gain minimization or aggression. This fifth motive is rarely included in the experimental work on cooperation and trust.

The work of McClintock and others on various "social orientations" posits the existence of different social motivations among the actors in any setting. According to Yamagishi, social orientation is defined as "an attitude taken toward self and an interdependent other" (Yamagishi 1995, 322). As mentioned earlier, actors can be classified using this scheme as individualists (egoists), altruists, competitors, or cooperators.[12] These distinct social motivations can be viewed either as more or less enduring individual differences or as motivations that vary across both individuals and situations. In response to the traditions of social orientation and motivation, John Kuhlman, Curt Camac, and Denise Cunha (1986) contend that the differences in social motivations between groups of individuals defined in the social-orientation tradition as competitors or cooperators may reflect differences in social expectations rather than in motivation. What differs, for example, between those classified as cooperators and those classified as competitors in these games of cooperation is really the nature of their expectations about the behavior of others in the setting. Along these same lines, trust is viewed in this context as the positive expectation of the level of cooperativeness of others.

Kuhlman, Camac, and Cunha call their approach the strategic-cognitive view of social orientation. In Richard Arneson's (1982) terms, both "reluctant cooperators" and "nervous cooperators" recognize the importance of mutual cooperation in the prisoner's dilemma situation, but they are hesitant to cooperate when others are not cooperating or are not expected to cooperate. In essence, if they cannot trust others to cooperate, they will not cooperate (Yamagishi 1995). It is their expectations about the behavior of others that allow them to be classified as cooperators or competitors. Competitors are less likely to expect others to cooperate and generally tend to see others as competitive. In contrast, cooperators are more likely to view others as sometimes cooperative and sometimes competitive (not as uniformly cooperative). This is what makes them more cautious. This difference also means that cooperators, unlike competitors, are more likely to differentiate between situations in which it "pays" to cooperate and those in which it does not. "Even egoists are willing to cooperate," Yamagishi concludes, "if they understand the long-term consequences of non-cooperative behavior and, at the same time, trust others" (Yamagishi 1995, 330).

The social-orientation tradition that distinguishes actors in terms of motivations (and defines these motivations as enduring attitudes) does not differ in its predictions from Kuhlman, Camac, and Cunha's approach distinguishing actors in terms of motivations defined as expectations. In fact, Kuhlman, Camac, and Cunha (1986) and Yamagishi (1995) have both argued that motivations can be seen as including expectations of the behavior of others, thus mitigating the need to distinguish between a motivational approach and a strategic-cognitive approach to orientations. Whether we distinguish between actors according to attitudes (social-orientation tradition), expectations of others' behavior (strategic-cognitive view), or in line with Russell Hardin's (1993) distinction between optimistic and pessimistic individuals,[13] researchers who study trust and cooperation are concerned with the motivational (or social) orientation of individuals because it is one basis for making behavioral predictions under varying circumstances.

Closely related to differences in motivation and expectations of others' behavior is the research that investigates the differences between high- and low-trusters, deriving, in part, from the earlier work of Rotter (1967) and others. In several recent experiments, Yamagishi (2001) has found that high-trusters (as measured with the six-item general trust scale developed in Yamagishi and Yamagishi 1994) are more accurate in estimating their partners' behavior than either low-trusters or medium-trusters. Participants held a group discussion on garbage-collection issues before participating in the experiment. The subjects were told that the discussion was a part of another study and that the nature of the conversation was independent of the subsequent experiment. The real purpose of the discussion was to give participants a forum in which to ascertain information and cues to predict their partner's choices in the prisoner's dilemma. Yamagishi (2001) finds that, following the discussion, high-trusters were more accurate predictors of the behavior of their partners (either cooperation or defection in a one-shot prisoner's dilemma game) than either low-trusters or medium-trusters. Along the same lines, Yamagishi, Masako Kikuchi, and Motoko Kosugi (1999) consistently find that high-trusters are more sensitive than low-trusters to information potentially revealing the lack of trustworthiness in others. Taken together, these two sets of experiments suggest that high-trusters have a more fine-grained and accurate set of expectations about others. In addition, because high-trusters make more accurate predictions, they tend to cooperate more than low-trusters. Here, the link between a trusting orientation and cooperation is evident. Moreover, Yamagishi links the classification of subjects based on motivations to trust along a second underlying dimension concerned with behavioral expectations of others. Taken in this light, the distinction between high and low trust is connected to underlying motivations that help explain behavior under various conditions. There is now a significant amount of experimental evidence regarding the behavioral differences between high- and low-trusters. One example of this can be found in another experiment, conducted by Yamagishi, Karen Cook, and Motoki Watabe (1998), in which the researchers find that in the face of social uncertainty, high-trusters tend to form committed relations less frequently than do low-trusters.[14]

Another study conducted in Japan by Nahoko Hayashi (1995) provides further evidence concerning the differences between high- and low-trusters. In a computer simulation of groups with different average levels of trust, Hayashi finds that higher levels of trust benefited the actors when substantial opportunity costs existed. Moreover, the actor's cooperativeness (not the overall rate of cooperation of the group members) was dependent upon the actor's level of trust. Consistent with previous evidence, high-trusters were more cooperative when they expected others to be cooperative. This study, along with the others we have discussed, provides a growing body of evidence to support the contention that in many settings the behavior of high-trusters differs from that of low-trusters, often to their benefit. Contrary to earlier anecdotal evidence but consistent with Rotter's early survey work, high-trusters are not more gullible. Instead, they appear to be expert readers of social signals, knowing when it pays to cooperate and when it does not.

Orbell and Robyn Dawes's (1993) findings provide additional evidence of the behavioral differences between high- and low-trusters. Because high-trusters are more likely than low-trusters to interact with strangers, at least on first encounter, they are more likely to have their expectations confirmed concerning the other's trustworthiness. This "risk taking," or lower level of cautiousness, provides them with the opportunity for more profitable interactions over time, given that those lower in trust are less willing to engage strangers at all.[15]

Additional insights into the behavioral differences between high- and low-trusters come from earlier research on low-trusters using a completely different experimental paradigm. Thomas Wright, Pamela Maggied, and Mary Palmer (1975) conducted what they term an "unobtrusive experiment" to examine the hypothesis that low-trusters are more suspicious of strangers than are high-trusters. The authors note that the previous research on Rotter's interpersonal trust scale, indicating that low-trusters are more suspicious than high-trusters, was based on evidence from self-reports (obtained from surveys) and laboratory experiments. This previous research illustrates specifically that low-trusters are more suspicious of experimenters (Roberts 1967) as well as peers (Wright 1972) in prisoner's dilemma games.

At the beginning of the academic year, these researchers had students enrolled in introductory psychology courses at the University of Connecticut and Ohio University complete the interpersonal trust scale and give their phone numbers to the experimenters. Students scoring in the top third of the scale (high-trusters) and those scoring in the bottom third of the scale (low-trusters) were then called and asked to participate in an experiment. The caller categorized the students' questions (asked during this telephone call) as either logistical questions or suspicious questions. Logistical questions consisted of questions about the place and time of the experiment, and suspicious questions consisted of questions as to the nature of the study and the means by which the caller received the name of the subject. In both locations, high-trusters not only asked significantly fewer questions than the low-trusters but also asked significantly fewer suspicious questions than did the low-trusters. Wright, Maggied, and Palmer (1975) found further evidence for the relation between level of trust and level of suspicion. These findings are consistent with later results concerning differences between high- and low-trusters in cautiousness and expectations concerning the trustworthiness of others.

A related study, conducted more recently, examines the differences between high- and low-trusters in their responses to fear. Craig Parks and Lorne Hulbert (1995) hypothesize that in the presence of fear, high-trusters will cooperate more frequently than low-trusters, and when fear is absent, high- and low-trusters will cooperate at the same rate. These hypotheses are motivated indirectly by two findings. First, Amnon Rapoport and Dalit Eshed-Levy (1989) have found that fear (of being cheated) does affect the level of contribution made in iterated *public-goods games*. Second, Yamagishi and Kaori Sato (1986) have found that high-trusters tend to be less fearful than low-trusters. Based on the results of an experiment with ninety-four undergraduates participating in public-goods games and resource dilemma games in which fear was manipulated, Parks and Hulbert (1995) find support for their hypothesis. The findings held across both games, suggesting that low-trusters are more risk averse under conditions that activate fear.

Incentive Structures and Strategies

Individual differences in motives and orientations are only one source of the variation in cooperative behavior and the emergence of mutual trust under various conditions. Another major factor in the social setting is the incentive structure and the strategies actors employ under varying incentives. The incentive structure of the game is intimately connected to the strategies employed by actors in the game. As such, these two topics are intertwined in our discussion. Work using the trust-honor game illustrates clearly the effect of the incentive structure (manipulated by the researchers). Kevin McCabe and his colleagues (McCabe, Rassenti, and Smith 1998; chapters 10 and 6, this volume), along with other economists and social psychologists, have recently used the trust-honor game to examine the relation between trust, reciprocity, and cooperation. In an effort to show how reciprocity supports more cooperation than game theory predicts, these researchers designed an experiment to compare the game-theoretic hypotheses concerning low levels of predicted cooperation with the culturally and biologically derived hypothesis that reciprocity supports cooperation. McCabe, Rassenti, and Smith (1998) find strong support for cooperation under complete information in trust games in which cooperation was not reinforced by the prospect of punishment for defection from reciprocity. They claim that "only under private information do we observe strong support for noncooperative game theory" (McCabe, Rassenti, and Smith 1998, 10).[16]

Joyce Berg, John Dickhaut, and McCabe (1995) designed an experiment to study trust and reciprocity in an investment setting. Once again, the trust-honor game was used. By experimental design the authors attempted to control for alternative explanations of cooperative behavior such as the effects of repeated-game reputation and punishment threats. The results of this experiment show that "reciprocity exists as a basic element of human behavior and that this is accounted for in the trust extended to an anonymous counterpart" Berg, Dickhaut, and McCabe 1995, 122). Their current work investigates the sources of the biological and evolutionary roots of these findings. McCabe's and Smith's research on trust and reciprocity is an example of some of the research making use of the trust-honor game to examine how changes in the structure of the game affect trust (see chapters 10 and 6, this volume). The strategies of *tit-for-tat* and hostage posting are employed by actors in response to such structural variations in the game.

Tit-for-Tat   Much of the work in the general game-theoretic tradition deals with the effectiveness of different strategies in maximizing cooperative play under varying incentives. The early work was not explicitly linked to trust. Strategies are considered to be "decision rules prescribing when to cooperate and when to defect" (Yamagishi 1995, 320). Robert Axelrod's (1984) classic work, for example, on the tit-for-tat strategy addresses the effectiveness of such a strategy in two-person iterated prisoner's dilemma games. The tit-for-tat strategy represents the following rule: cooperate on the first trial, and then do what your partner does on each subsequent trial; that is, cooperate if your partner does, and defect if he or she fails to cooperate. Compared with other conceivable strategies, such as always defect, always cooperate, or "tit-for-two-tats," this strategy works best for maximizing payoffs to the players involved as well as rates of cooperation. In Yamagishi's (1986) terms, action interdependency is introduced between the partners' actions when the tit-for-tat strategy is used. The interdependence of actions is the critical feature of the strategy. This interdependence also creates the possibility for the emergence of mutual trust over time.

Research by Samuel Komorita, J. A. Hilty, and Craig Parks (1991) sheds more light on the nature of the tit-for-tat strategy investigated by Axelrod. These researchers assert that two important properties of the tit-for-tat strategy are based on the reciprocity norm: First, it is a "provocable" strategy, as the individual immediately retaliates if his or her partner defects. Second, it is a "forgiving" strategy, as the individual immediately reciprocates cooperation if his or her partner returns to cooperation after defection.

Komorita, Hilty, and Parks (1991) conducted two experiments to examine the effects of the delay of reciprocity for two types of tit-for-tat strategies. In the first experiment, the reciprocation was immediate; in the second, reciprocation was delayed by one trial. Subjects (undergraduate male students) were led to believe that they were playing a two-person prisoner's dilemma with another student, but they were actually playing against a computer-programmed strategy. The results of both experiments demonstrate a significant negative effect for the delay of reciprocity. The mean proportion of cooperative choices was greater when cooperative overtures were reciprocated immediately than when they were delayed (Komorita, Hilty, and Parks 1991). The delay may signal to the partner a lower willingness to be cooperative.

Jonathan Bendor's (1987) research also provides some insight into the conditions under which use of the tit-for-tat strategy is optimal for generating cooperation.[17] He asserts that Axelrod's claim that tit-for-tat is an extremely robust strategy assumes perfect monitoring, such that players can either directly see or infer their partners' choices. Such monitoring, of course, obviates the need for trust. Bendor notes that many real-life dilemmas have outcomes that are functions of exogenous events, and the difference between intended and unintended effects is hard to discern with certainty. His point is noted here because it further substantiates our claim that research on cooperation and trust needs to acknowledge more fully the effects of variations in social context. Effects of uncertainty on trust and interpersonal commitment have been examined by exchange theorists more recently. The specific role trust plays in the selection of strategies, however, has not been fully investigated. In addition, the role that strategies play in building trust, as implied in the work of Komorita, Hilty, and Parks (1991), also needs further study.

Hostage Posting   Experiments have recently been conducted in which the subjects in the standard trust-honor game in psychology and economics (see, for example, Prosch and Petermann 1998) can offer part of their eventual payoff as an inducement to their partners to return the trust placed in them (often referred to as "posting a hostage"). This commitment mechanism alters the underlying incentive structure of the game, increasing the payoff to the player for engaging in mutual trust and increasing the cost to the partner for betraying that trust (Snijders 1994). For example, I might accept your necklace as a "bond" that you will repay the loan I make you today. If you fail to return the money, I have at least gained a necklace for the cost of my loan (and you have lost it). "Hostage posting" is a type of commitment mechanism or means by which the incentive structure can be altered to realize the *Pareto-optimal* state of mutual trust.

Bernard Prosch and Soren Petermann (1998) demonstrate how, even under difficult conditions, cooperation can emerge through credible commitments. They examine the role of commitment in *chicken-game* settings, in which the failure to mutually cooperate is especially costly. Hostage posting is also discussed by Werner Raub (1990) in some detail. Raub analyzes hostage posting as a mechanism for stabilizing social and economic relations in situations in which mutual cooperation is Pareto optimal but difficult to achieve owing to incentive problems. In these circumstances, as noted earlier, hostage posting can be used as a self-enforcing commitment device.

Raub presents a game-theoretic model of hostage posting. Simultaneously and independent of one another, players decide whether to post a hostage and also whether to cooperate. Raub asserts that an individually rational strategy would go as follows: on the first move, post a hostage; on the second move, cooperate if the partner has also posted a hostage but refuse to cooperate if the partner has not posted a hostage. The beauty of this strategy is that it contains both a promise to cooperate and a threat not to cooperate. It also provides a signal of one's willingness to trust, though in the absence of the chance to post a hostage (or some similar mechanism), cooperation is unlikely when the stakes are high. Raub uses experimental games to test his model, and his results suggest that the credibility of promises and threats is a necessary condition for hostage posting, which promotes cooperation when it otherwise might not occur.

In an extensive study Chris Snijders (1996) conducts a series of experiments using what he calls the "hostage trust game," a variant of the trust-honor game that includes the option of posting a hostage (or giving something to signal cooperativeness or trustworthiness). In these experiments variations in degree of "bonding," level of compensation, and temptation to defect are investigated. The major results include the following:

- All actors who decide to post a hostage also generally decide to trust their partners.

- Trust decreases with increasing risk (for example, when the payoffs are increased and the value of the bond that is posted is decreased).

- As the temptation to defect increases there is a decrease in the extent to which trust is honored.

- Contrary to expectation, refusing to post a hostage does not seem to have much effect on the honoring of trust.

Subsequent research on hostage posting in relation to trust in the modified trust-honor game has arrived at similar results in terms of how the use of signaling reduces some of the uncertainty that a partner is willing to be trustworthy. More recently, Michael Bacharach and Diego Gambetta (2001) have provided a fairly complex theory of signaling as it applies to trust and the determination of trustworthiness or what they refer to as the *second-order social dilemma* of trust—the decision of whom to trust. More empirical research on signaling mechanisms and the role they play under conditions of uncertainty and risk to facilitate the emergence of trusting behavior would be useful in developing dynamic models of behavioral trust.

Social Context

Given that one of our goals is to focus more attention on the social context in which trust behaviors are embedded, we shift our attention now to the experimental work that varies the social conditions under which trust and cooperation are expected to occur. Here, we move beyond the simple "rules" of the game and the concomitant incentive structures to factors that are external to the game, such as the social identities of the actors, the size of the group to which the individual belongs, the degree of communication, the existence of time pressure, and third-party effects, among others. A fairly large number of studies has been conducted focusing on the social factors that affect cooperation (see reviews by Yamagishi 1995; Dawes 1980; Messick and Brewer 1983). In the cooperation literature, some of the social factors that have been studied fairly extensively include communication, identity, group formation, pregame interaction, and cultural differences. Fewer experimental studies actually examine the social factors that inhibit or produce trust (see also chapter 12, this volume). We focus primarily on the latter.

Research on in-group favoritism illuminates a widespread mechanism that fosters trust for those on the inside of the circle as well as distrust for outsiders. This significant body of experimental work presents challenges to those concerned about ethnic identity and intergroup conflict. Experimental research on this topic links directly to macro-level work on trust by political scientists, sociologists, economists, and anthropologists and clarifies some of the micro-level processes involved. An example of this research is found in David De Cremer and Mark Van Vugt's recent study of the positive effect of social identification on promoting cooperation in *social dilemmas.* These researchers conducted a number of experiments to examine two alternative explanations of this effect: an increase in the value assigned to the collective good (goal-transformation hypothesis) and an enhancement of trust in the cooperation of other group members (goal-amplification hypothesis). Their findings provide support for both explanations and suggest that "selfish" individuals can be encouraged to cooperate by increasing the salience of their group membership (De Cremer and Van Vugt 1999). Here, we see how the effects of social context, such as group identity, can alter the motivation to cooperate in the situation. Common group membership may also increase the within-group mutual trust that could mediate the level of cooperation. Intergroup trust and cooperation is a complex phenomenon.[18]

Another experiment examines the effect of group size on trust. Kaori Sato (1988) predicted that because strategic considerations are less relevant in larger groups, the effect of trust on cooperation would diminish as group size increases. The results support this hypothesis. The interaction effect of trust by group size was significant, but the simple main effect of trust was significant only in three-person groups. Taking both of these studies together, we find that the size of the group matters. If it is large, it can diminish the effect trust has on cooperative behavior (Sato 1988). Yet if it is large and the individual identifies with the group, group size can enhance the effect trust has on cooperative behavior (De Cremer and Van Vugt 1999).

Michael Macy and John Skvoretz (1998) conducted a simulation study to examine the effect of "neighborhood" size on trust.[19] Using computer simulation, they investigated three main factors: the relative cost of exit from the group, the size of the neighborhood, and the "embeddedness of the interaction."[20] They arrive at two findings: First, when the exit option was relatively costly, players generally chose to trust one another, regardless of the "type" of partner (neighbor or stranger).[21] Second, neighborhood size and embeddedness of the interaction combined to determine the probability of exchanging with any given neighbor and, by extension, the probability of the emergence of trust. Following the modification of the prisoner's dilemma game described by Orbell, Schwarz-Shea, and Simmons (1984) and used by Orbell and Dawes (1993) to include the exit option, Macy and Skvoretz were able to investigate how the costs of exiting, as well as other structural features such as embeddedness, affect the emergence of trust.

Communication is yet another social-context factor that can affect both trust and cooperation. In an early study, Donald Granberg, Scott Stevens, and Sandra Katz examined the effect of communication on cooperation. They find that in the prisoner's dilemma, in the absence of communication (in the form of structured prewritten messages sent after trials fifteen, thirty, and forty-five in a sixty-trial game), cooperation tended to decrease over trials (Granberg, Stevens, and Katz 1975). Twenty years later, Kumiko Mori explored the effects of communication but did so with a focus on trust, not just cooperation. Mori conducted an experiment to examine the role of preexperimental communication in the development of two types of interpersonal trust—general trust and specific trust.[22] Results reveal that the two types of trust were contingent upon the opportunity for communication and also that communication strongly affected specific trust toward the partner with whom communication had occurred (Mori 1996). Other researchers have demonstrated the significance of pregame communication, especially that entailed in face-to-face interaction, as a facilitator of cooperation (Caldwell 1976; Dawes, McTavish, and Shaklee 1977; Edney and Harper 1978; Orbell, van de Kragt, and Dawes 1988).

Treating time pressure as a social-context variable, William Ross and Carole Wieland varied both time pressure and levels of trust to examine the responses of individuals allegedly settling a dispute. Individuals could choose between several responses during the interaction; two of these were inaction and sending rapport-building messages. The mediators in the dispute chose "inaction" less frequently when time pressure was high and chose to send more rapport-building messages when trust was low (Ross and Wieland 1996). These findings suggest ways in which situational factors interact with standard variables in experimental situations (for example, level of trust). They also provide some clues as to how situations involving low trust might be handled, especially when conflict resolution is important.

Another social context factor examined by researchers studying trust is referred to as third-party effects. Ronald Burt and Marc Knez assert that although the simplest social context for trust is an isolated dyad, the more usual context is two people surrounded by various close friends, enemies, or simply acquaintances. They argue that third-party gossip, for example, enhances both the positive and the negative in a relationship, making both parties more certain of their trust (or distrust) in each other. Moving outside the experimental laboratory, these researchers analyzed network data obtained from a probability sample of three thousand senior managers. They determined that trust is significantly amplified by third parties, who have a positive effect on trust within strong relations and a negative effect within weak relations (Burt and Knez 1995). The terms strong and weak, in this context, refer to the intensity of the relationship.[23]

In a unique experimental study, Anat Anshel and David Kipper investigated the effects of two components of group singing (music and activity) on trust and cooperation. Subjects ($N = 96$) participated in a single session of one of the following activities: group singing (music with activity), listening to music (music with no activity), poetry reading (activity with no music), and film viewing (no music and no activity). They predicted that group singing (requiring coordination and joint effort) would yield the highest trust and cooperation scores. The subjects played a standard prisoner's dilemma game and then completed a trust differential questionnaire at the end of the study. The results confirmed the predictions concerning the positive effects of music on trust and of activity on cooperation (Anshel and Kipper 1988).

Culture or nationality has also been considered in the study of trust as a social context factor. Yamagishi (1988), for example, compares the tendencies of American and Japanese subjects to desert (or exit) a group that contains free riders (those who receive benefits without making contributions).[24] He examines the relatively common view that American society is characterized by individualism and Japanese society by collectivism. Such a view implies that Japanese subjects will be more likely than American subjects to remain in the group (and not exit). Yet the results did not support this hypothesis.

Yamagishi discovered that the tendency to remain in the group was much stronger among the American subjects than it was among the Japanese when exit would have been costly for the individual. Specifically, American subjects exited the group in approximately one out of twenty trials, despite incurring monetary costs for leaving, whereas Japanese subjects exited the group much more frequently (an average of eight out of twenty trials). (As discussed earlier, exit, in this paradigm, involves the choice of not participating at all on a particular decision trial.) These results illustrate that though neither group of subjects wanted to remain in the group when the cost of staying was low, Americans were more likely to stay when the exit response was costly, whereas Japanese subjects were more willing to pay the high cost of exit.

If the Japanese are collectivist (and prefer to be a part of a group rather than be independent from it) and Americans are individualistic (and prefer the opposite), then the American subjects should have exited more frequently than the Japanese. In this study, the fact that Americans were more willing to remain in a group suggests that they are more trusting of others than the Japanese. These counterintuitive findings suggest that our surface images of complex societies may not hold up under closer examination.

Other studies have considered this national difference as well. Hayashi and colleagues argue that there are two bases for the expectation of a partner's cooperation in one-shot prisoner's dilemmas: general trust and a sense of control. They hypothesized that Japanese and American subjects would differ as to which basis they used. These researchers find that whereas Japanese subjects rely on the sense of control over their partners' action, American subjects rely on general trust when forming expectations of their partners' cooperation (Hayashi et al. 1999). Social context, conceived of in this way (as country of origin), is an important factor influencing both trust and cooperation, but the effects are not simple main effects, and the issue requires more theoretical and empirical work.

Orienting our review to three key theoretical elements—motivations, incentive structure and strategies, and social context—has allowed us to identify persistent themes in the literature as well as topics for further research. Some of the work on trust has used the motivational (or social) orientations of individuals (for example, ego-

istic, cooperative, competitive, and altruistic) to make predictions regarding trusting behavior and cooperation. Both Kuhlman (in Kuhlman, Camac, and Cunha 1986) and Yamagishi (1995) eventually argued that these motivations can be seen as differences in the nature of
the expectations of others' behaviors (initially treated as distinct from
motivation in the strategic-cognitive approach to social orientation).
These underlying motivations can be seen as directly linked to the
distinction between high-trusters and low-trusters. A review of research on the differences (both attitudinal and behavioral) between
high-trusters and low-trusters confirms this point. Future research
could investigate specifically how high-trusters and low-trusters differ in their responses to certain social-context variables such as group
identity, communication, and third-party effects, among others.

In our review of the research on incentive structures and strategies
(such as tit-for-tat and the use of commitment devices like hostage
posting), we have examined ways in which these strategies induce or
inhibit cooperation and the emergence of trust. In the future the use
of these strategies could be examined as they relate to particular
group-level factors such as embeddedness and level of communication. Finally, the work on social-context factors and their effects on
trust addresses issues surrounding both dyadic and multiparty trust
relationships. Group identity, group size, communication, time pressure, third-party effects, and even country of origin matter in trust
formation and cooperation. Future research should develop more
fully the work on social context to include and attend to variation in
motivational orientation and incentive structures and strategies in relation to group-level factors, both theoretically and empirically.

Trust and Social Exchange

The main experimental research tradition in sociology that focuses on
trust grows out of the experimental work on social-exchange relations
and networks. The focus is on exchange (as a form of cooperation)
and the role that trust plays in various types of social exchange (for
example, restricted or dyadic exchange versus generalized exchange,
negotiated versus nonnegotiated exchange; see Molm and Cook
1995). In this discussion we shift the focus from the conditions of the
particular game to analyzing exchange settings in which cooperation
entails the contingent act of trading resources of value or mutually
arriving at a negotiated agreement between two or more parties.

Some authors argue that trust is implicated in some forms of exchange and not in others (for example, Seligman 1997). In interactions
characterized as generalized exchange, in which one person must
give without the assurance of an immediate return or the confidence

provided by explicit negotiations over the terms of trade, trust is usually required. Trust also comes into play in what Linda Molm (1997) refers to as reciprocal (or nonnegotiated) social exchange for the same reasons. Reciprocal exchanges involve contributions that are separately performed and nonnegotiated. One person initiates the process (with a small act or gift) without knowing whether or when the other person will reciprocate (Molm and Cook 1995). However, implicit in the initial "gift" offered to initiate an exchange relation is the assumption that at some later point the other person will honor the implied obligation to offer something in return. (This act is to be distinguished from what must be classified as a "pure gift" with no expectation of return, but this category may actually be quite rare empirically.)

Trust and Negotiated Exchange Relations

Peter Kollock conducted an experiment to examine how different exchange conditions lead to different levels of trust among trading partners. His results suggest that different levels of trust emerge when uncertainty (in the form of information asymmetry) is varied. Specifically, reported trust was significantly higher on average in the condition of uncertainty (involving less information) than in the condition of certainty (in which more information about the quality of the goods to be exchanged was provided). The second main finding regarding trust was the relation between the exchange partners' commitment to each other and trust. Subjects rated their most frequent exchange partners (the partner to which a subject was more committed) as more trustworthy than their least frequent exchange partners in both the certain and the uncertain conditions. This suggests that increasing the frequency of positive interactions between partners (that is, increasing commitment) facilitates trust even under conditions of certainty, in which mutual trust is less crucial (Kollock 1994). This finding is consistent with more recent results reported by Edward Lawler and Jeongkoo Yoon (1998) indicating a positive link between exchange frequency and relational commitment, perhaps a precursor to mutual trust.

Kollock's work identifies an important question for scholars studying trust and negotiated exchange: What effects do various levels of uncertainty have on trust in exchange relationships?[25] Hayashi and colleagues (1999) present the findings of an experiment that examined a set of hypotheses concerning the relation between levels of social uncertainty and two types of trust: particularistic (as a sense of control) and general. Simulating a market involving negotiated transactions between sellers and buyers, in an experiment similar to Kollock's, the researchers found support for their main hypotheses. Their results support the following claims: greater uncertainty leads to commitment formation; committed partners have higher levels of particularistic trust; greater social uncertainty improves particularistic trust; and the tendency to form commitments in a socially uncertain situation is weaker among those whose level of general trust is high. The last finding is consistent with results reported by Yamagishi, Cook, and Watabe (1998) indicating that commitment varies inversely with level of general trust: low-trusters are more likely than high-trusters to form commitments, especially under uncertainty.

Trust and Other Forms of Exchange

Although most of the research on social exchange has focused on negotiated exchange (see Cook and Emerson 1978; Markovsky, Willer, and Patton 1988; Molm and Cook 1995), various studies have been conducted on power, commitment, and the role of trust in other forms of exchange. Yamagishi and Cook (1993), for example, initiated experimental research on generalized exchange, comparing univocal reciprocity in a chain-generalized exchange structure (similar to a Kula ring) with net-generalized exchange, which has the structure of a standard social dilemma in which actors must give to the group in exchange for a collective benefit that is obtained only if all make contributions. They find that cooperation rates were higher in the chain-generalized structure, in which there was no assurance of a return but in which each actor had the opportunity to give to one person they were connected to in the circle of exchange, than in the net-generalized exchange structure, in which free riding was more likely to occur. The results also demonstrate that high-trusters were more likely than low-trusters to exchange under both structures, and this effect was more pronounced in the generalized-exchange network. In this work trust was treated as an individual difference factor, not as an emergent behavioral process in the exchange situation. In Kollock's (1994) experimental work trust was treated as a dependent variable, measured in a postexperimental questionnaire.

Subsequent research has begun to investigate more closely the role of trust in the process of establishing and maintaining exchange relations. Trust is examined in this work as an outcome of the exchange process. Molm, Nobuyuki Takahashi, and Gretchen Peterson (2000), for example, compare negotiated exchange and reciprocal exchange with respect to the intensity of the interpersonal commitments that emerge between exchange partners and the emergence of trust (more precisely, perceptions of trustworthiness in their partners). As noted in Cook and Rice (2001), the form of the exchange, whether the relationship can be characterized as negotiated or reciprocal exchange, is what, according to Molm, Takahashi, and Peterson (2000), affects actors' feelings of trust and their positive evaluations of their partners. Rewards from exchange are not guaranteed in reciprocal exchange because acts of giving need not be reciprocated. The uncertainty this generates allows actors to establish their trustworthiness by the continued reciprocation of valued resources. Positive evaluations of one's exchange partners are higher in reciprocated exchange than in negotiated exchanges, in part, because in negotiated exchange the rewards are typically assured as a result of the binding nature of such agreements. Moreover, Molm, Takahashi, and Peterson argue, actors' positive evaluations of their partners will increase as behavioral commitment between the parties to the exchange increases as a result. Frequent exchanges enhance positive feelings (as Lawler and Yoon [1998] also argue), and effective commitment increases. Mutual trust in this work is viewed as a by-product of commitment.

More work on the emergence of trust in social-exchange relations and networks is now under way as investigators begin to learn more about the ways in which different forms of exchange affect the underlying social dynamics. Different forms of exchange result in different types of uncertainty and create different interactional structures, some more enduring than others. These factors have clear implications for the emergence of mutual trust and the impact of distrust when it exists under different exchange conditions (for example, in the way distrust undermines commitment). Results of this research will help to clarify the role of social structures (a context factor) and power asymmetries in those structures (where they exist) in facilitating and inhibiting the emergence of trusting relationships in certain social contexts that extend beyond those often examined in the experimental literature in psychology and economics. Unfortunately, the contexts explored in psychology and economics are more often than not one-shot interactions in which trust plays a minimal role, if it plays a role at all (see also chapter 3, this volume). Continued experimental work on cooperation and social exchange has the potential to provide significant extensions of the existing theoretical and empirical research on trust (and insights into the mechanisms for facilitating trust) in social settings outside the laboratory.

Conclusion

Experimental research on cooperation and trust provides insights into the ways in which cooperation is fostered in social situations. Trust may be a by-product of cooperative relations (as Kollock's 1994 work tends to suggest), or it may be an essential factor that makes cooperation possible when social constraints and institutional safeguards are not in place. Experimental data allow researchers to delve more deeply into the theoretical structure of trusting relations and to illuminate the precise conditions under which such relations emerge or decay. Notwithstanding the many isolated findings regarding the role of trust in producing social order by making cooperation possible where it might not easily be achieved, we do not yet have a fully developed theory of trust in social relations that codifies and explains these findings.

Although there are suggestive hypotheses about the bases of trust (for example, reciprocity), we need a more complete theory of the nature of the causes of trust. Why does trust emerge when it does? What are the social structural features of the situations in which trust emerges or fails to emerge? Why do individuals differ in their capacities for trust? What are the social consequences of the failure of the production of trust? Some of these questions can be answered by further experimental work using the paradigms that have been developed for laboratory work that are described in the early part of this chapter and in the discussion of social exchange.

Continued work using these basic paradigms will be central to the development of a cumulative body of research on the sociology of trust. As we have argued, however, to provide insights into the role of trust in the larger society, experimental work will need to include a more complete treatment of the effects of social context factors (that is, network factors, group size, group identity, cultural context, and characteristics of the situation in which the actors are embedded—for example, the potential for sanctioning, the existence of informal monitoring, and reputational effects). Moving in this direction will provide experimentalists fertile ground for further research using existing paradigms or modifications of them and holds the promise of producing more systematic work on both the antecedents and consequences of trust.

Notes

1. This description comes from Yamagishi (1995).

2. In the cooperative condition, subjects were led to believe that the welfare of the other person as well as the subject's own welfare was of concern to the subject and that the other person felt the same way. In the individualistic condition, the subject was led to believe that the subject's only interest was in doing as well as possible for himself or herself, regardless of how well the other person did (and that the other person felt the same way). In the competitive condition, the subject was led to believe that the

subject wanted to do as well as possible for himself or herself by defeating the other person, and that the other person felt the same way. These conditions were operationalized by inserting different paragraphs at the end of the instructions that explained the mechanics of the game.

3. One of the items reads as follows: "Parents usually can be relied upon to keep their promises" (Rotter 1967, 654).

4. One such item reads as follows: "In dealing with strangers one is better off to be cautious until they have provided evidence that they are trustworthy" (Rotter 1967, 654). Items like this one were later incorporated into the General Social Survey.

5. In a study of delinquent adolescents, Bernard Fitzgerald, Richard Pasewark, and Sally Noah (1970) find that Rotter's interpersonal trust scale fails to differentiate between delinquent and nondelinquent groups of both males and females.

6. Yamagishi and Yamagishi (1994) also make a distinction between general trust (measured by this scale) and particularistic trust. Whereas general trust is trust of human beings in general, including strangers, particularistic trust is trust in a specific interaction partner. This distinction is utilized in Hayashi et al. (1999) (reviewed later in this chapter).

7. Here, by "survey items," we mean items in which respondents are asked to report their behavior, not survey items aimed at gathering information about the attitudes of respondents, discussed earlier. However, survey items are notoriously bad indicators of general behavioral tendencies. We tend to report our own behavior in biased ways. For example, sometimes we overestimate positive behaviors and underestimate negative behaviors.

8. See chapter 6, this volume, on reciprocity and goodwill accounting.

9. The discussion on motivations addresses an actor's "state" preceding participation in the experiment; the discussion on incentive structure and strategies, although it examines actors' behavior, is focused primarily on the strategies actors employ as a result of the game structure, not as a result of their motivations or orientation.

10. Later, Barbara Meeker (1983) contrasted these same two motivational orientations (cooperative and competitive) in an investigation of the role of trust and reciprocity in producing cooperative behavior. Two experiments were designed to test two related processes hypothesized to mediate the effect of cooperative orientation on cooperative behavior: the development of trust and the development of reciprocity. Meeker finds support for her prediction regarding the effect of cooperative orientation on cooperative behavior through reciprocity but not through trust.

11. Few subjects fit the category "maximize other's gain" (pure altruism) in these studies; thus we focus here on the other three motives that are more frequently observed.

12. Some researchers, however, have recently attested to the existence of a new "type" of individual. Alphons van de Kragt, Dawes, and Orbell (1988) use the term "rational altruists" to describe individuals who act to the benefit of others even at considerable cost to themselves. They propose that "rational altruists" base their decisions on the magnitude of the external benefit as well as on the personal costs. These researchers conducted two experiments using the prisoner's dilemma paradigm to test their proposition. Yet they did not find support for the rational-altruist explanation of cooperation: whether external benefit is measured in terms of number of individuals benefiting from a cooperative choice or the total monetary benefit produced, its increase does not bring about higher levels of cooperation (van de Kragt, Dawes, and Orbell 1988). Although these researchers examined only cooperation (and not trust), their theory of the "rational altruist" could be examined using the trust game. As yet, this has not been done.

13. Hardin (1993) would not view the mere positive expectation of cooperation as an adequate conception of trust. Instead he outlines what he terms "optimistic trust," asserting that optimistic people overestimate the probability of the trustworthiness of others for various reasons. Furthermore, he claims that these optimistic overestimates precipitate greater cooperation in *social-dilemma* situations. Jane Mansbridge (1999), however, does not distinguish between Hardin's (1993) "optimistic trust" and Yamagishi and Yamagishi's (1994) "cognitive bias." She writes: "What Hardin calls 'optimistic trust' Toshio and Midori Yamagishi (1994) call 'cognitive bias'" (Mansbridge 1999, 295).

14. Yamagishi, Cook, and Watabe conducted two experiments with college students in the United States (Seattle, Washington) and Japan (Sapporo). They hypothesized that social uncertainty would promote commitment formation between particular partners and that when facing social uncertainty high-trusters would form committed relations less frequently than low-trusters. Both predictions received empirical support. The researchers suggest a theory of trust emphasizing the role of general trust in freeing individuals from the confines of safe (and closed) relationships (Yamagishi, Cook, and Watabe 1998). This theory helps explain behavioral differences between high- and low-trusters previously attributed to cultural differences. Low-trusters in both cultures are less willing to take the risk of locating a more profitable opportunity in an uncertain environment. They are more concerned with avoiding the possibility of exploitation.

15. Using the exit-option protocol explained earlier, Orbell and Dawes conducted an experiment to examine how the option to play or not play in a prisoner's dilemma can affect social welfare as well as the relative gains and losses of individuals who intend to cooperate or defect. Subjects were led into a room with five other individuals. The subjects then entered a field of two-person prisoner's dilemma games, one game with

each of the five individuals present. The researchers varied the decision rule with which the subjects were presented. Under the binary-choice rule, subjects played a single prisoner's dilemma game with five other individuals. They had only two options: to cooperate or to defect, as in the standard setting. Under the trinary-choice rule, however, subjects were given the option of playing a prisoner's dilemma game with the five individuals and were offered three alternatives: to cooperate, to defect, or to exit (not play at all). Orbell and Dawes (1993) discovered that the aggregate payoff (social welfare) from decision making in the trinary-choice condition was significantly higher than in the binary choice condition. Moreover, by using a two-by-two design to compare the estimated payoffs for intending cooperators and intending defectors in the binary-choice situation with the estimated payoffs for intending cooperators and intending defectors in the trinary-choice situation, Orbell and Dawes found that intending cooperators in the trinary-choice situation had the highest payoffs. Such a finding allows them to conclude that the increase in aggregate payoff (social welfare) in the trinary-choice game occurred because "intending cooperators are more willing to enter into such games than are intending defectors, which increases the probability of socially productive cooperate-cooperate relationships" (Orbell and Dawes 1993, 798). In this experiment, Orbell and Dawes highlight the important advantages (increased social welfare) that are obtained when individuals are given the choice to cooperate, defect, or not play at all. Again, whereas choosing to cooperate has been viewed in the past as an indicator of trust, by including the option to exit in the prisoner's dilemma, one can see how the mere act of playing is an indicator of trust. In this way, cooperating does not signal trust; playing does.

16. For a more complete discussion of the game and the general argument, see chapters 3 and 6 in this volume.

17. David Kreps, Paul Milgrom, John Roberts, and Robert Wilson (1982) assert that an individual has an incentive to maintain a reputation for consistently using the tit-for-tat strategy because if an opponent were convinced that the individual played tit-for-tat, the opponent would respond by cooperating in the future. In response to this work, Len-Kuo Hu (1995) uses forward induction (instead of *backward induction*) to suggest that a player's selection of tit-for-tat is based not on concern for reputation but rather on the player's assessment of the other player's future strategy type.

18. See work by Miles Hewstone on intergroup cooperation—for example, van Oudenhoven, Groenewood, and Hewstone (1996).

19. The use of the word "neighborhood" requires explanation. Macy and Skvoretz assume that exchanges are embedded in a social network and that players experience two types of interactions. They can interact with "neighbors," insofar as the partners the player encounters are likely to encounter one another and to reencounter the player. Or, they can interact with strangers insofar as they are unlikely to encounter associates of

their partner and unlikely to encounter that partner again. In the simulation, the researchers experiment with neighborhoods ranging in size from ten to fifty members.

20. "By 'embeddedness of interaction' we mean the extent to which interaction with prospective partners is limited to those in a player's neighborhood. If embeddedness equals 1, its maximum, all interactions are limited to neighbors. If embeddedness equals 0, all interactions are with those outside the neighborhood. If embeddedness equals .5, then a player is just as likely to interact with a neighbor as with a stranger" (Macy and Skovertz 1998, 646). The researchers experimented with embeddedness ranging from .5 to .9 in their simulations.

21. In using the prisoner's dilemma with exit option, Macy and Skovertz define trust behaviorally, just as Orbell, Schwarz-Shea, and Simmons (1984) and Orbell and Dawes (1993) do. Trust is the willingness to participate in a risky venture. Hence trust applies to both cooperators and defectors. "Playing" the game indicates trust, and "not playing" indicates distrust.

22. This distinction is similar to the one made by Yamagishi and Yamagishi (1994) (and also Hayashi et al. 1999) between generalized and particular trust. See note 6.

23. However, David Krackhardt (1996) criticizes this study, claiming that people's perceptions of their networks are more important than the reality of those networks. The study of perceived networks, Krackhardt concludes, will offer better predictions of trust than a study focusing on actual networks.

24. Chapter 13 in this volume gives a more thorough treatment of this study.

25. Negotiated exchange involves a joint decision process to determine the terms of the exchange, and the benefits received by both participants are easily identified as paired events, called a transaction (Molm and Cook 1995).

References

Anshel, Anat, and David A. Kipper. 1988. "The Influence of Group Singing on Trust and Cooperation." *Journal of Music Therapy* 25(3): 145–55.

Arneson, Richard J. 1982. "The Principle of Fairness and Free-Rider Problems." *Ethics* 92(4): 616–33.

Arnstein, Fred, and Kenneth D. Feigenbaum. 1967. "Relationship of Three Motives to Choice in the Prisoner's Dilemma." *Psychological Reports* 20(3): 751–55.

Axelrod, Robert. 1984. *The Evolution of Cooperation.* New York: Basic Books.

Bacharach, Michael, and Diego Gambetta. 2001. "Trust in Signs." In *Trust in Society,* edited by Karen S. Cook. New York: Russell Sage Foundation.

Barber, Bernard. 1983. *The Logic and Limits of Trust.* New Brunswick, N.J.: Rutgers University Press.

Bendor, Jonathan. 1987. "In Good Times and Bad: Reciprocity in an Uncertain World." *American Journal of Political Science* 31(3): 531–38.

Berg, Joyce, John Dickhaut, and Kevin A. McCabe. 1995. "Trust, Reciprocity, and Social History." *Games and Economic Behavior* 10(1): 122–42.

Burt, Ronald S., and Marc Knez. 1995. "Kinds of Third-Party Effects on Trust." *Rationality and Society* 7(3): 255–92.

Caldwell, Michael. 1976. "Communication and Sex Effects in a Five-Person Prisoners' Dilemma Game." *Journal of Personality and Social Psychology* 33(3): 273–80.

Cook, Karen S., and Richard M. Emerson. 1978. "Power, Equity, and Commitment in Exchange Networks." *American Sociological Review* 43(5): 721–39.

Cook, Karen S., and Eric R.W. Rice. 2001. "Exchange and Power: Issues of Structure and Agency." In *Handbook of Sociological Theory*, edited by Jonathan Turner. New York: Kluwer.

Dawes, Robyn M. 1980. "Social Dilemmas." *Annual Review of Psychology* 31: 169–93.

———. 1991. "Social Dilemmas, Economic Self-interest, and Evolutionary Theory." In *Frontiers of Mathematical Psychology: Essays in Honor of Clyde Coombs*, edited by Donald R. Brown and J. E. Keith Smith. New York: Springer-Verlag.

Dawes, Robyn M., Jeanne McTavish, and Harriet Shaklee. 1977. "Behavior, Communication, and Assumptions About Other People's Behavior in a Commons Dilemma Situation." *Journal of Personality and Social Psychology* 35(1): 1–11.

De Cremer, David, and Mark Van Vugt. 1999. "Social Identification Effects in Social Dilemmas: A Transformation of Motives." *European Journal of Social Psychology* 29(7): 871–93.

Deutsch, Morton. 1960. "The Effect of Motivational Orientation upon Trust and Suspicion." *Human Relations* 13(2): 123–39.

Edney, Julian, and C. S. Harper. 1978. "The Commons Dilemma: A Review." *Environmental Management* 2(4): 491–507.

Fitzgerald, Bernard J., Richard A. Pasewark, and Sally J. Noah. 1970. "Validity of Rotter's Interpersonal Trust Scale: A Scale of Delinquent Adolescents." *Psychological Reports* 26(1): 163–66.

Fukuyama, Francis. 1995. *Trust: The Social Virtues and the Creation of Prosperity*. New York: Simon & Schuster, Free Press Paperbacks.

Granberg, Donald, J. Scott Stevens, and Sandra Katz. 1975. "Effect of Communication on Cooperation in Expanded Prisoner's Dilemma and Chicken Games." *Simulation and Games* 6(2): 166–87.

Hardin, Russell. 1993. "The Street-Level Epistemology of Trust." *Politics and Society* 21(4): 505–29.

———. 1999. "Do We Want Trust in Government?" In *Trust in Government*, edited by Mark Warren. Cambridge: Cambridge University Press.

Hayashi, Nahoko. 1995. "Emergence of Cooperation in One-Shot Prisoner's Dilemmas and the Role of Trust." *Japanese Journal of Psychology* 66(3): 184–90.

Hayashi, Nahoko, Nobuyuki Takahashi, Motoki Watabe, and Toshio Yamagishi. 1999. "Reciprocity, Trust, and the Sense of Control: A Cross Societal Study." *Rationality and Society* 11(1): 27–46.

Homans, George C. 1974 [1961]. *Social Behavior: Its Elementary Forms.* New York: Harcourt Brace Jovanovich.

Hu, Len-Kuo. 1995. "Cyclical Cooperation and Noncooperation." *Academia Economic Papers* 23(1): 57–93.

Kollock, Peter. 1994. "The Emergence of Exchange Structures: An Experimental Study of Uncertainty, Commitment, and Trust." *American Journal of Sociology* 100(2): 313–45.

Komorita, Samuel S., J. A. Hilty, and Craig D. Parks. 1991. "Reciprocity and Cooperation in Social Dilemmas." *Journal of Conflict Resolution* 35(3): 494–518.

Krackhardt, David. 1996. "Comment on Burt and Knez's Third-Party Effects on Trust." *Rationality and Society* 8(1): 111–16.

Kreps, David M., Paul Milgrom, John Roberts, and Robert Wilson. 1982. "Rational Cooperation in the Finitely Repeated Prisoner's Dilemma." *Journal of Economic Theory* 27(2): 245–52.

Kuhlman, John, Curt R. Camac, and Denise A. Cunha. 1986. "Individual Differences in Social Orientation." In *Experimental Social Dilemmas*, edited by Henk A. M. Wilke, David M. Messick, and Christel G. Rutte. Frankfurt, Germany: Verlag Peter Lang.

Lawler, Edward J., and Jeongkoo Yoon. 1998. "Network Structure and Emotion in Exchange Relations." *American Sociological Review* 63(6): 871–94.

Levi, Margaret, and Laura Stoker. 2000. "Political Trust and Trustworthiness." *Annual Review of Political Science* 3: 475–507.

Liebrand, Wim B. G. 1986. "The Ubiquity of Social Values in Social Dilemmas." In *Experimental Social Dilemmas*, edited by Henk A. M. Wilke, David M. Messick, and Christel G. Rutte. Frankfurt, Germany: Verlag Peter Lang.

Liebrand, Wim B. G., Ronald W. Jansen, Victor M. Rijken, and Cor J. Suhre. 1986. "Might over Morality: Social Values and the Perception of Other Players in Experimental Games." *Journal of Experimental Social Psychology* 22(3): 203–15.

Luce, R. Duncan, and Howard Raiffa. 1957. *Games and Decisions.* New York: Wiley.

Luhmann, Niklas. 1988. "Familiarity, Confidence, Trust: Problems and Alternatives." In *Trust*, edited by Diego Gambetta. Oxford: Blackwell.

Macy, Michael W., and John Skvoretz. 1998. "The Evolution of Trust and Cooperation Between Strangers: A Computational Model." *American Sociological Review* 63(5): 638–60.

Mansbridge, Jane. 1999. "Altruistic Trust." In *Democracy and Trust*, edited by Mark E. Warren. Cambridge: Cambridge University Press.

Markovsky, Barry, David Willer, and Travis Patton. 1988. "Power Relations in Exchange Networks." *American Sociological Review* 53(2): 220–36.

McCabe, Kevin A., Stephen J. Rassenti, and Vernon L. Smith. 1998. "Reciprocity, Trust, and Payoff Privacy in Extensive-Form Bargaining." *Games and Economic Behavior* 24(1–2): 10–24.

McClintock, Charles G. 1972. "Social Motivation: A Set of Propositions." *Behavioral Science* 17(5): 438–54.

———. 1976. "Social Values: Their Definition, Measurement, and Development." *Journal of Research and Development in Education* 12(1): 121–37.

Meeker, Barbara F. 1983. "Cooperative Orientation, Trust, and Reciprocity." *Human Relations* 37(3): 225–43.

Messick, David M., and Marilyn B. Brewer. 1983. "Solving Social Dilemmas: A Review." In *Review of Personality and Social Psychology*, vol. 4, edited by Ladd Wheeler. Beverly Hills, Calif.: Sage.

Molm, Linda D. 1997. *Coercive Power in Social Exchange*. Cambridge: Cambridge University Press.

Molm, Linda D., and Karen S. Cook. 1995. "Social Exchange." In *Sociological Perspectives on Social Psychology*, edited by Karen S. Cook, Gary Alan Fine, and James S. House. Boston: Allyn and Bacon.

Molm, Linda D., Nobuyuki Takahashi, and Gretchen Peterson. 2000. "Risk and Trust in Social Exchange: An Experimental Test of a Classical Proposition." *American Journal of Sociology* 105(5): 1396–427.

Mori, Kumiko. 1996. "Effects of Trust and Communication on Cooperative Choice in a Two-Person Prisoner's Dilemma Game." *Japanese Journal of Experimental Social Psychology* 35(3): 324–36.

Orbell, John M., and Robyn M. Dawes. 1993. "Social Welfare, Cooperators' Advantage, and the Option of Not Playing the Game." *American Sociological Review* 58 (6): 787–800.

Orbell, John M., Peregrine Schwarz-Shea, and Randy T. Simmons. 1984. "Do Cooperators Exit More Readily Than Defectors?" *American Political Science* 78(1): 147–62.

Orbell, John M., Alphons J. C. van de Kragt, and Robyn M. Dawes. 1988. "Explaining Discussion-Induced Cooperation." *Journal of Personality and Social Psychology* 54(5): 811–19.

Parks, Craig D., and Lorne G. Hulbert. 1995. "High and Low Trusters' Responses to Fear in a Payoff Matrix." *Journal of Conflict Resolution* 39(4): 718–30.

Prosch, Bernhard, and Soren Petermann. 1998. "The Chicken and the Hostage: Cooperation and Commitments in Experimental Settings." Paper presented at the International Sociological Association meetings.

Putnam, Robert D. 1993. *Making Democracy Work: Civic Traditions in Modern Italy*. New York: Basic Books.

———. 2000. *Bowling Alone: The Collapse and Revival of American Community*. New York: Simon & Schuster.

Rapoport, Amnon, and Dalit Eshed-Levy. 1989. "Provision of Step-Level Public Goods: Effects of Greed and Fear of Being Gypped." *Organizational Behavior and Human Decision Processes* 44(3): 325–44.

Raub, Werner. 1990. "Cooperation via Hostages." Paper presented at the American Sociological Association meetings, Washington, D.C. (August 11–15).

Roberts, M. D. 1967. "The Persistence of Interpersonal Trust." Master's thesis, University of Connecticut.

Ross, William H., and Carole Wieland. 1996. "Effects of Interpersonal Trust and Time Pressure on Managerial Mediation Strategy in a Simulated Organizational Dispute." *Journal of Applied Psychology* 81(3): 228–48.

Rotter, Julian B. 1967. "A New Scale for the Measurement of Interpersonal Trust." *Journal of Personality* 35(4): 651–65.

———. 1971. "Generalized Expectancies for Interpersonal Trust." *American Psychologist* 26(5): 443–50.

———. 1980. "Interpersonal Trust, Trustworthiness, and Gullibility." *American Psychologist* 35(1): 1–7.

Sato, Kaori. 1988. "Trust and Group Size in Social Dilemmas." *Japanese Psychological Research* 30(2): 88–93.

Seligman, Adam B. 1997. *The Problem of Trust*. Princeton, N.J.: Princeton University Press.

Snijders, Chris. 1994. "Cooperation via Hostage Posting: The Impact of Incomplete Information." Paper presented at the International Sociological Association's meeting, Bielefeld, Germany (July 19–23).

———. 1996. *Trust and Commitments*. Utrecht, Netherlands: Interuniversity Center for Social Science and Research.

Snijders, Chris, and Gideon Keren. 1999. "Determinants of Trust." In *Games and Human Behavior: Essays in Honor of Amnon Rapaport*, edited by David V. Budesco and Ido Erev. Mahwah, N.J.: Lawrence Erlbaum.

Thornton, David, and Paul Kline. 1982. "Reliability and Validity of the Belief-in-Human-Benevolence Scale." *British Journal of Social Psychology* 21(1): 57–62.

van de Kragt, Alphons J. C., Robyn M. Dawes, and John M. Orbell. 1988. "Are People Who Cooperate 'Rational Altruists'?" *Public Choice* 56(3): 233–47.

van Oudenhoven, Jan Pieter, Jan Tjeerd Groenewood, and Miles Hewstone. 1996. "Cooperation, Ethnic Salience, and Generalization of Interethnic Attitudes." *European Journal of Social Psychology* 26(4): 649–61.

Wright, Thomas L. 1972. "Situational and Personality Parameters of Interpersonal Trust in a Modified Prisoner's Dilemma Game." Ph.D. diss., University of Connecticut.

Wright, Thomas L., Pamela Maggied, and Mary L. Palmer. 1975. "An Unobtrusive Study of Interpersonal Trust." *Journal of Personality and Social Psychology* 32(3): 446–48.

Yamagishi, Toshio. 1986. "The Provision of a Sanctioning System As a Public Good." *Journal of Personality and Social Psychology* 51(3): 110–16.

———. 1988. "Exit from the Group As an Individualistic Solution to the Public Good." *Journal of Experimental Social Psychology* 24(6): 530–42.

———. 1995. "Social Dilemmas." In *Sociological Perspectives on Social Psychology*, edited by Karen S. Cook, Gary Alan Fine, and James S. House. Boston, Mass.: Allyn and Bacon.

———. 2001. "Trust As a Form of Social Intelligence." In *Trust in Society*, edited by Karen S. Cook. New York: Russell Sage Foundation.

Yamagishi, Toshio, and Karen S. Cook. 1993. "Generalized Exchange and Social Dilemmas." *Social Psychology Quarterly* 56(4): 235–48.

Yamagishi, Toshio, Karen S. Cook, and Motoki Watabe. 1998. "Uncertainty, Trust, and Commitment Formation in the United States and Japan." *American Journal of Sociology* 104(1): 165–94.

Yamagishi, Toshio, Masako Kikuchi, and Motoko Kosugi. 1999. "Trust, Gullibility, and Social Intelligence." *Asian Journal of Social Psychology* 2(1): 145–61.

Yamagishi, Toshio, and Kaori Sato. 1986. "Motivational Bases of the Public Goods Problem." *Journal of Personality and Social Psychology* 50(1): 67–73.

Yamagishi, Toshio, and Midori Yamagishi. 1994. "Trust and Commitment in the United States and Japan." *Motivation and Emotion* 18(2): 129–66.

Chapter 9

The Human Face of Game Theory: Trust and Reciprocity in Sequential Games

CATHERINE C. ECKEL AND RICK K. WILSON

T HE HIGH degree of initial cooperation among strangers is a fascinating empirical regularity. This is not to say that all individuals begin by behaving cooperatively, nor is it the case that a given individual always begins by behaving cooperatively. Humans tend to be conditional cooperators, basing their decision to cooperate on initial expectations about their counterparts. How are these expectations formed? Our view is that humans share a capacity to read one another's intentions through a set of cues such as facial expressions, body language, and tone of voice. The ability to read intentions has evolved along with the mechanisms for displaying intentions.

The cues from which intention is inferred come from many sources. People use all of the information available to them in forming expectations about others' play, including information about individual characteristics (such as sex or race) as well as many forms of verbal and nonverbal communications. The most obvious of these is the human face.

Reading Intention

Game theory has provided a successful model for the social sciences. In many settings it fares very well as a predictive model—particularly where there are many actors, their interactions are anonymous, and the underlying institutional mechanisms are disciplining (see Ostrom

1998; Smith 1998). However, in face-to-face bargaining, where the actors are not anonymous, and under relatively weak institutional mechanisms, standard game theory is much less successful in predicting behavior (see chapter 2, this volume).

A large body of empirical research demonstrates that in bargaining situations laboratory subjects often choose strategies that appear to be cooperative, in contrast with the individual-payoff-maximizing play predicted by game theory. Much recent research is centrally concerned with whether and how actors look beyond their own payoffs and to the payoffs, actions, and judgments of those with whom they interact. This "other-regarding" behavior is pronounced in two-person bargaining games in which subjects split a fixed pie, including *ultimatum* and *dictator games* (Camerer 2003; Eckel and Grossman 1996, 1998; Forsythe et al. 1994; Hoffman et al. 1994). Such behavior is even more pronounced in situations in which there are gains to cooperation, such as *public-goods games* (Ledyard 1995), investment trust games (Berg, Dickhaut, and McCabe 1995), and *gift-exchange games* (Fehr, Kircksteiger, and Reidl 1993). These results are neither random nor haphazard; on the contrary, behavior inconsistent with game-theoretic predictions based on pure monetary payoffs is routine and patterned.

Consider the game illustrated in *extensive form* in figure 9.1. It represents a two-person sequential game with perfect and complete information. In this game the payoffs are given in dollars (for convenience), and by convention player A's payoffs are in the first position. Player A makes the first choice—either to end the game, taking $10 and leaving player B with $0, or to pass the decision to play to player B. If the money is passed, it is immediately tripled. Player B then decides between two allocations. In the first, player B takes the entire amount, in the second both players get something ($20 for A and $10 for B).

Conventional game theory has player A ending the decision at the first move. However, what makes this game interesting is other options are available by which both players can be made better off. For player A to choose to pass, however, the second player must be trusted. Similarly, player B must reciprocate that trust by choosing the (20,10) allocation. The problem for player A is difficult, because to risk trusting B, A must draw some inference about the trustworthiness of B. How can trust and trustworthiness be communicated if the players are strangers? Any attempt to answer this question involves an understanding of both the importance and difficulty of signaling and reading intentions.

Figure 9.1   Sample Sequential Game

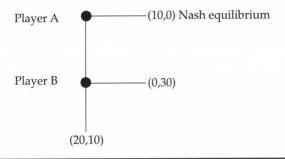

Player A ●————————(10,0) Nash equilibrium

Player B ●————————(0,30)

(20,10)

Source: Authors' configuration.

Theory of Mind

The idea of directly reading another's intentions is appealing, but of course it is not possible to do so. A fascinating branch of research on autistic persons sheds considerable light both on the importance of the ability to read intentions and the extent to which people routinely engage in social signaling and mind reading. This research suggests that individuals generate and read a raft of signals that betray their intentions, even if attempts are made to mask them (see Baron-Cohen 1995; O'Connell 1998). Persons with autism lack the ability to interpret facial expressions and other social signals, a condition that causes them a great deal of difficulty in social interaction. Autistic persons must learn social exchange by rote—categorizing signals and remembering their meaning—and as a result they frequently make mistakes.[1]

Psychologists have identified the mechanism that autistics lack: the ability to put themselves in the place of others, referred to as having a "theory of mind" about another person. A theory of mind requires that a person be able to separate what he or she knows from what another might know. In a simple test of this concept, a child is shown a box for a familiar brand of candy and is asked to guess its contents. The child typically guesses that candy is in the box; the experimenter then reveals that the box contains pencils. The child is asked to predict what another person coming into the room will think is in the box. Most children over the age of three believe that the response will be "candy"; they are able to put themselves in another person's shoes, imagining what it is like to be the other. By contrast, autistic children invariably predict that others will think the box contains pencils; they are unable to disentangle what they know from what the other might know or to understand the mental state of the other. A theory of mind appears to be a necessary precondition for negotiating complex social spaces. For complex decisions, simply observing a signal is not enough. Instead, the signal must be interpreted by imagining the mental state of another, drawing an inference about that other's likely strategy, and then reasoning about an appropriate response. As a consequence, an autistic person's inability to pick up on the intentions of others leads to serious difficulties in social interaction. The problem is not one of social ineptness but rather a cognitive failure to imagine the mental state of another person.

A theory of mind has three components (Baron-Cohen 1995, chapter 4). The first is characterized as an intentionality detector. Psychologically, this amounts to the ability of individuals to impute purpose and cause to another's actions. In part this means an ability to recognize that others have goals and to derive hypotheses about how actions will be related to attaining those goals. Children as young as seven months old can distinguish between events that have a clear cause, such as a hand picking up a doll, and events with no apparent cause, such as a doll being lifted by an invisible wire (see the discussion by O'Connell 1998, 41–42). The second component involves an eye-direction detector, which enables an individual to recognize the focus of attention of another person and to draw inferences about the intentions of that person. As Sanjida O'Connell notes, "The evolutionary reason why you should take very good care to detect eye gaze is because when another animal is looking at you it can mean one of the three 'F's. Either that animal wants to fight you, feed on you, or mate with you" (O'Connell 1998, 47).

The final component involves a shared-attention detector. Again, the eyes are important for what is communicated. In its most mentally complex form, a shared-attention detector can be characterized as a mechanism that recognizes a relationship among two individuals and an object. If there is a bottle of Chardonnay on a table, and Rick follows Cathy's gaze to the bottle, and Cathy returns her gaze to Rick, who in turn looks between Cathy and the wine bottle, then a complex representation can be inferred: Rick sees that Cathy sees the wine (and Cathy sees that Rick sees her see the wine). Her request is communicated, and Rick pours her a glass of wine. Such a complex mental concept can occur only with joint mental attention. This in turn provides an interesting guarantee of the "common-knowledge" assumption crucial for game theory.

Simon Baron-Cohen argues that a general "theory-of-mind mechanism" ties together these volitional, perceptual, and epistemic mental-state concepts. Such a mechanism enables people to draw inferences about the intentions of others by going outside themselves. Contending that autistics lack the ability to read another's mind, Baron-Cohen asks the reader to imagine how difficult life would be without that ability:

> This is what it's like to sit round the dinner table. . . . Around me bags of skin are draped over chairs, and stuffed into pieces of cloth, they shift and protrude in unexpected ways. . . . Two dark spots near the top of them swivel restlessly back and forth. A hole beneath the spots fills with food and from it comes a stream of noises. Imagine that the noisy skin-bags suddenly moved toward you, and their noises grew loud, and you had no idea why, no way of explaining them or predicting what they would do next." (Gopnik 1993, quoted in Baron-Cohen 1995, 5)

The difficulty that autistics experience in negotiating normal social interaction illustrates the importance of being able to imagine the mental state of another. The heuristic for trusting (or being perceived as trustworthy) is complicated and depends heavily on imagining a counterpart's mental calculations. People ordinarily have a number of mechanisms on which they rely when considering whether to trust. They may have reputational information about their counterparts, or they may have recourse to institutions that will protect them if someone proves untrustworthy. Yet quite often we trust strangers, and we do so by making a simple assessment of the mental state of the other. This is quite different from making a decision about O'Connell's three Fs and relying on simple signals of anger or lust. Trust, like cooperation, requires an understanding that there are joint gains to be had from non-Nash behavior, requires that the counterpart understands the same thing (shared attention), and requires that an individual be able to read the counterpart's intention.

Emotion

It might be argued that the rational agents in standard game-theoretic models are themselves autistic: those models require only that the other is assumed to be seeking the same advantage as one's self, and as a consequence there is no need to go beyond one's self. Although some game-theoretic models of reputation formation and one-sided signaling offer greater complexity, theorists usually do not model the possibility that actors read the intentions of their counterparts (and perhaps signal something about themselves) to coordinate on a *Pareto-superior* but nonequilibrium outcome. It seems clear that this sort of communication can greatly facilitate coordination.

It would be convenient if intention could be simply signaled and credibly read. However, strategic actors are capable of sending false signals. When Cathy walks onto the lot, the car salesman's smile does not necessarily signal that he is pleased to see her; more likely, he or she is trying to put her at ease and allay her suspicions (and sell her a car at a price that is advantageous to the salesman). For a signal of intention to be credible, it must be easily interpretable and costly to fake, and the recipient must be able to imagine the mental state of the signaler. Do such credible signals exist?

Robert Frank argues that emotions have the capacity to add credibility to a signal of intention. A reputation for vengefulness, for example, enhances a bargaining position, but a credible commitment to revenge requires a powerful emotional display. The display of anger, which cannot easily be simulated, makes credible the threat of (irrational) revenge. Emotions act as commitment devices—as incentives to behave (or not behave) in a particular manner. For example, guilt is unpleasant and acts as a kind of tax on cheating. Furthermore, Frank argues, people form judgments about the emotional states of others on the basis of observable cues, such as "the pitch and timbre of the voice, perspiration, facial muscle tone and expression, and movement of the eyes. . . . Some people we sense we can trust, but of others we remain forever wary" (Frank 1988, 8).

In a related paper, Frank, Thomas Gilovich, and Dennis Regan present experimental evidence that subjects accurately predict cooperation by others, although the authors do not explore the mechanism by which this occurs (Frank, Gilovich, and Regan 1993, 137–43). One possibility is that facial expressions, among other factors, provide telltale cues to the underlying emotional state of a person. Expressions that require muscles that are not (or not typically) under conscious control are likely to be more effective communicators of intentions. These "reliable" cues can be used to predict cooperation or reciprocity.

The idea that one agent can understand the mental state of another; central to Frank's argument, is missing in standard models of game theory. In experimental environments in which subjects do not observe one another, there is a surprising amount of trust and reciprocity (Berg, Dickhaut, and McCabe 1995; Falk and Fischbacher 1998; Fehr and Schmidt 1999; Güth 1995; McCabe, Rassenti, and Smith 1998). Kevin McCabe, Stephen Rassenti, and Vernon Smith (1998) claim that subjects draw inferences about the disposition of the population based on their past experience. Although subjects may condition their behavior on their expectations about tendencies in a population (see also Fahr and Irlenbusch 2000), our interest is primarily in settings in which people have the opportunity to observe one another and to exhibit behavior that is conditional on an individual partner's intentional and unintentional signals.

Social Signals

Emotionally charged signals may be credible. However, it seems unlikely that anyone can afford (either psychically or physically) constantly to display extreme emotion. Other shortcuts, then, are used to gauge signals. Clearly, the context in which signals are presented is important—especially for imagining the mental state of another. This context, of course, is culturally derived. For example, in our interactions with strangers we often form quick impressions based on sex, socioeconomic status, or ethnicity. The meaning read into these observable signals may vary across cultures, within a culture, and over time. Even so they are likely to affect subsequent interactions.

Evidence from experimental economics confirms the importance of these traits in strategic interaction. Actors may treat a subject's external characteristics as a signal of expected play. Several studies investigate differences in the behavior of women and men in games involving fairness and cooperation. The argument common to these studies, drawn from theories and evidence from social psychology, is that women are expected to be more "cooperative" than men. In the ultimatum game, for example, women are expected to reject an offer of a given size less frequently than men. If players anticipate this behavior, then both men and women would offer less to women than to men. Catherine Eckel and Philip Grossman (2001) find some evidence of both conjectures—women do reject less frequently, and all players offer (slightly) more to men than to women. If women are more cooperative, they also should make higher allocations to others in the dictator game; this hypothesis is investigated by Eckel and Grossman (1998, 1999) and by James Andreoni and Lise Vesterlund (2001) and confirmed in nearly every setting.[2]

Another factor that might be expected to affect strategic play is social status. Sheryl Ball and colleagues (Ball et al. 2001; Ball and Eckel 1998) examine the effect of artificially induced, observable status differences on play in market and bargaining settings. Their procedure awards gold stars to a subset of the players, who then wear the stars while playing a subsequent game. In general they find that subjects who have been awarded higher status have higher earnings in subsequent games. In a game designed to test trust and reciprocity, Edward Glaeser and colleagues (2000) find that subjects with higher socioeconomic status are more likely to have their trust reciprocated. Eckel and Grossman (1996) investigate another sort of status difference. Examining the effect of a credible signal of neediness, they find that in a dictator game setting, individuals are more generous to needy subjects. Status differences appear to affect the expectations of both high-status and low-status players. Players make inferences about the intentions of their counterparts based on the status differential.[3]

People send and receive many signals in their interactions with one another. Some signals are beyond the control of the signaling actor and are constant across environments (for example, sex); others are largely involuntary but contingent on the environment (for example, emotional displays); still others are quite deliberate. An obvious device for signaling intentions is the human face. Human facial expressions are only partially controlled by the expresser, which gives these signals credibility. There is extensive research on human facial expressions and what they mean to observers, beginning with Charles Darwin's (1998 [1872]) provocative treatise, which argues that humans, like animals, have evolved patterns of signaling behavior, including facial expressions.

Facial Expressions

A small academic industry has grown up around the study of facial expressions. Much of the research has followed the lead of Paul Ekman (1972, 1982) and focuses on confirming the idea that there is a common, universal set of facial expressions. It is assumed that many of these expressions are involuntary and reveal the underlying emotional state of the expresser. If facial expressions are the result of this emotional leakage, and if everyone shares the same universal repertoire of expressions, then a person's emotional state will be easily inferred by others.

There is some support for this position. Researchers find that subjects label certain expressions of emotion in the same way, regardless of culture (see reviews in Ekman 1982; Fridlund, Ekman, and Oster 1987). This research has uncovered six distinct emotions that are read with ease across cultures: anger, disgust, happiness, sadness, fear, and surprise. Alan Fridlund, Paul Ekman, and Harriet Oster (1987, 159) note that the emotions of happiness, anger, disgust, sadness, and combined fear and surprise have been validated in both literate and preliterate societies. Typically, subjects are shown photographs of posed expressions, in which the poser is from a different culture and often a different ethnic group. Subjects are then asked to match an emotion with each photograph. These results are robust, though not unassailable (see Russell 1994).

Smiles

The smile represents the emotion that is the most easily recognized: happiness. True smiles tend to be symmetric and involve the muscles at the corners of the eyes as well as the mouth. Typically, about 80 percent of members of different populations agree that smiling photographs signal happiness. However, though a smile generally yields a clear emotional meaning, this does not imply that it sends a clear message about the intention of the signaler. A number of experiments suggest that "false" smiles may be difficult to judge from still photographs. In an early paper, Ekman and Wallace Friesen (1982) argue that false smiles tend to be asymmetric, usually do not involve the "crinkly-eye" effect, occur at inappropriate times, and have excessively long duration.

Much of the subsequent literature has had a difficult time uncovering precise differences between genuine and false smiles. For example, Ekman, Wallace Friesen, and Maureen O'Sullivan describe an experiment designed to test whether individuals can mask their emotions. Student nurses viewed two videotapes, one of pleasant nature scenes and the other of unpleasant surgical procedures and burns. While viewing the tapes, they were asked to describe to an unseen interviewer their reactions to these images. However, they were instructed to act while viewing the unpleasant tape as if they were viewing the pleasant tape, masking their true reactions. Using the authors' system of facial-action coding, coders checked types of smiling expressions. In their analysis, the authors found subtle differences among forms of smiling, depending on the condition to which subjects were exposed, primarily involving the muscular activity around the eyes. If movements of the mouth alone were analyzed, on the other hand, no difference was found between truthful and deceptive behavior (Ekman, Friesen, and O'Sullivan 1988).

Ekman and Maureen O'Sullivan (1991) used these videotapes in a further experiment. Ten equal-length segments of the tape were used; on half of the tapes, nurses had been told to lie about what they were seeing; on the other half, they were instructed to respond truthfully. These videotape clips were shown to subjects who were asked to judge whether the speaker was "honest" or "deceptive." For two of the ten clips, these individuals also were asked briefly to explain their judgments. The viewers ranged from members of the Secret Service to polygraph examiners to college students. Interestingly, members of the Secret Service were best able to differentiate between the honest and deceptive video clips. More generally, those who are best able to detect liars report that they rely heavily on nonverbal behavior as well as subtle facial expressions.

James Carroll and James Russell (1997) find that subjects are better able to interpret the meaning of a smile within a well-defined context. Similarly, José-Miguel Fernández-Dols and Maria-Angeles Ruiz-Belda (1995, 1997) argue that smiling is the result of an interaction between an emotional state and a social context. Smiles are an important means for communicating a signal to others and within clear social situations. Their 1995 study of Olympic gold medalists analyzes the expressions of winners coming to the podium to receive their medals. Within a five-minute period there was a marked change in facial expressions—even though those gold medalists were presumably very happy—with smiles recorded the most during a period of social interaction and the least during periods of individual isolation. Smiling appears as an expression of happiness only when it is useful to communicate that happiness to others. This reinforces the notion that facial expressions act as social signals.

The discussion suggests that facial expressions unfold in a context. Although emotional leakage may provide the basis for a facial expression and may be necessary for facial expressions to be read as credible, the social context and the mental state of the other are also crucial for social signaling. Our question is whether a smile can be a signal of trustworthiness.

Experiment 1: A Pilot Test

We conducted a pilot experiment using photographic stimuli of two models, one male and one female, with several posed facial expressions. The models were instructed to exhibit three distinct facial expressions: happiness, neutrality, and anger. This experiment has two goals: first, we want to know whether subjects read the posed expressions in the same way; second, we want to know whether these expressions have any effect on the behavior of subjects.

Initial Survey of Facial Expressions

A total of 154 subjects in two large introductory economics classes at Virginia Polytechnic Institute and State University were asked to judge the emotional content of six photographs.[4] Each image was presented to the subjects for fifteen seconds; subjects then were asked to rate a series of statements about the image, using a five-point Likert scale ranging from 1 (strongly agree) to 5 (strongly disagree). The statements included a set of emotion and behavior items, only two of which are analyzed here: "This person is happy" and "I could trust this person." The order of presentation of expressions was rotated, although the male model was always presented first.

Figure 9.2 presents the average ratings of emotional content for the pairings of smiling and neutral images. The obvious finding is that subjects are quick to pick out happiness as the emotion portrayed by the smiling models. Moreover, there is a slight difference between the male and female images, with the female ratings bracketing the male

Figure 9.2   Mean Ratings of Happiness and Trust in Smiling and Neutral Faces

Male, smiling		Male, neutral	
Happy	1.70 (.67)	Happy	3.38 (.83)
Trustworthy	3.00 (.67)	Trustworthy	2.98 (.74)

Female, smiling		Female, neutral	
Happy	1.54 (.64)	Happy	3.82 (.52)
Trustworthy	3.81 (.62)	Trustworthy	3.74 (.69)

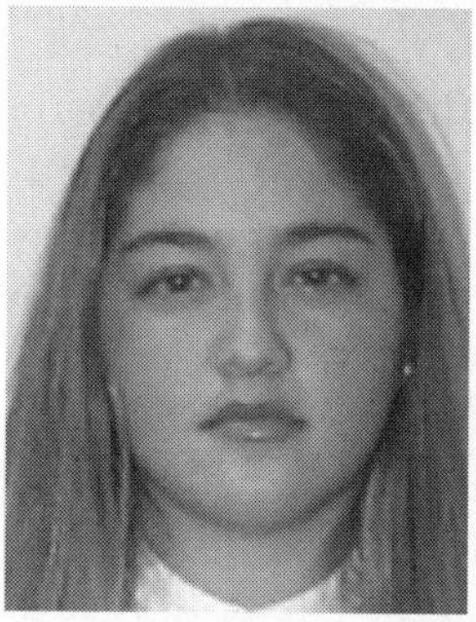

Source: Authors.
Note: Subjects rated two statements about the images on a five-point scale (1 = strongly agree, 5 = strongly disagree): "This person in happy," and "I could trust this person." Standard deviations are in parentheses.

ratings for the "happy" item and significantly higher for the "trust" item.[5]

These results show that subjects are adept at reading something about the emotional state of the models in the photographs. In general this finding is consistent with previous research on facial expressions: basic emotions such as happiness are easily interpreted from photographs. If we were to stop here we might conclude that trust is affected by both the expression and the sex of the signaler. However, these results tell us nothing about a behavioral response to a setting with financial stakes.

Game Experiment

In the second component of the pilot experiment, we examined the effect of facial characteristics on strategic play in the two-person sequential game illustrated in figure 9.1 We asked whether the perceptions revealed in the survey data would carry over into a decision-making environment. A total of 408 students in five large introductory economics classes at Virginia Tech were used. In four of the classes, one of the images presented in figure 9.2 was shown. The remaining class was a control group to which no image was displayed. The experiment is a between-subjects design.

Subjects were shown one of the images projected on a screen. A sheet was handed out to each subject with the decision problem shown in figure 9.3, including check boxes at all nodes of the decision tree. All subjects were assigned the position of the first decision maker, whose choice was to move left or right. Once subjects had made the first choice, the experiment was halted, and five of the subjects were randomly selected to leave the room to complete the experiment and receive payment in private. The rest of the subjects completed a brief questionnaire and manipulation check, including several questions about the characteristics of the image. After all materials were collected, subjects were debriefed on the design and purpose of the experiment.

Analysis

Summary data on the decisions of the subjects are shown in table 9.1. Overall, a little more than 40 percent of the subjects chose a left-branch move, indicating trust of the imaged counterpart. Even in our control group, with access to no facial stimulus, subjects chose the left branch 39.5 percent of the time. This proportion is close to the result found by McCabe, Rassenti, and Smith (1998), in which 43 percent of the subjects chose left moves.

We do not find that smiles in general lead to greater trusting be-

Figure 9.3   Game Used in Experiment 1

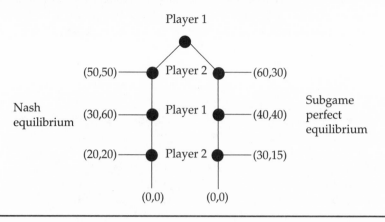

Player 1

(50,50) —— Player 2 —— (60,30)

Nash
equilibrium   (30,60) —— Player 1 —— (40,40)   Subgame
perfect
equilibrium

(20,20) —— Player 2 —— (30,15)

(0,0)   (0,0)

Source: Authors' configuration.

havior. Although the smiling male model is trusted more than the smiling female, the neutral female image generates far greater trusting behavior than any of the other images.

What is surprising is that even though 51 percent of subjects fail to take a trusting move when faced with the smiling female photograph, a majority still regard that image to be both friendly and cooperative. The postdecision questionnaire completed by the subjects included a series of statements of the form, "My counterpart [in this experiment] was _____" and offered subjects three choices: for the "friendly" item, they could choose friendly, neutral, or unfriendly; for the "cooperative" item, they could choose cooperative, neutral, or uncooperative. Although these ratings are consistent with the images, they do

Table 9.1   Subjects' Responses to Facial Images (Percentage)

Response	Blank	Male, Smiling	Male, Neutral	Female, Smiling	Female, Neutral
Left move (trust)	39.5 (30)	45.7 (42)	28.4 (31)	38.7 (24)	53.6 (37)
Image is friendly	59.2 (45)	51.1 (47)	10.1 (11)	69.4 (43)	7.5 (5)
Image is cooperative	63.2 (48)	52.2 (48)	15.6 (17)	53.2 (33)	21.7 (15)

Source: Authors' compilation.
Note: Number of responses is given in parentheses.

not help explain the opposite results for the male and female images. For example, the "friendliness" ratings of the female neutral image are the lowest of all of the images, and yet the number of subjects choosing the left branch is the highest in response to that image.

Discussion

Although we anticipated that subjects' behavior would not support the strict game-theoretic prediction, we did not anticipate the mixed effect of a smile. Based on the survey data, we expected a smile to invite trust. Indeed, for the male model this was the case. That finding is reversed, however, for the female image. The female smiling image was apparently considered trustworthy but neither friendly nor cooperative. It is as if subjects regarded the male model's smile as genuine but not the female model's smile. All in all, we find weak and somewhat puzzling behavioral effects on strategic choice in this trust game. Moreover, the results are not consistent with conjectures about the emotional content of visual images and what those images should do for reading the intention of a counterpart. These results led us to believe that characteristics of the face other than the smile itself might have a significant effect on the tendency of others to trust that face. Facial expressions are complex, and our pilot design may have inadvertently introduced some confounding factor into the experimental test. These results led to important modifications of our design.

Experiment 2: Multiple Smiling Faces

In response to puzzling results from the pilot experiment, we expanded the number of models used to sixty, each of whom provided two posed facial expressions. In addition, all subjects involved in the decision-making part of the experiment were paid for their participation. The instructions and the game were markedly simplified, and participants were recruited for the decision-making component from a different subject pool.[6] The second experiment has two components, similar to those of the first: a set of subjects first assess a facial expression, using a survey instrument; then a different set of subjects engage in a decision-making task in a controlled laboratory setting.

Survey of Facial Expressions

Concerned with the limitations of our first survey instrument, we markedly redesigned our second instrument to provide more detailed information on subjects' interpretations of the facial expressions. In the new instrument, each subject received a black-and-white photograph and was asked first to rate the face on a series of twenty-five word pairs of opposite meaning, then to answer an additional five items relating to trust. The word pairs were taken from Norman Anderson (1968), and the pairs were matched using extreme ratings on his listing.[7] The additional five items, designed to elicit a more precise measure of the perceived trustworthiness of the photographic image, placed subjects in hypothetical trusting situations with the photographic image. In each case respondents were asked whether the person represented by the image would carry out some action at a personal cost (returning a wallet, doing a favor, contributing to a group project, or reciprocating friendship). Subjects answered using a six-point, Likert-like scale with no neutral category. The five questionnaire items are presented in appendix A9.1 of this chapter.

Two poses from each of sixty photographic models were used: a smile and a neutral expression. The 120 photographs were coded as either smiling or not smiling relative to one another. There is a good deal of variation in the "smiling" expressions—ranging from broad, genuine smiles to smirks to very nearly neutral expressions. For any given model, it is clear which is the smiling photograph, but a comparison of smiles across subjects reveals considerable heterogeneity. The photographs were taken from the Psychological Image Collection at Stirling (PICS), University of Stirling Psychology Department, Stirling, Scotland.[8] The PICS images database is a collection of images that has been used in psychological research concerned with visual perception and memory.

Two hundred twenty-eight students from Virginia Tech participated in the questionnaire study. The photographic images were assigned randomly to subjects; the order of the word pairs was the same for all subjects. Two different groups were used. In the first group, made up of 202 subjects, each subject viewed only a single image. In the second group, made up of 26 subjects, each subject viewed 5 images that were chosen and ordered randomly.[9] In all, there are 337 evaluations, with each face evaluated by 2 to 4 different subjects.[10]

Results

Analysis of the five "trust" questions indicates that four of the items scale well together (Cronbach's alpha = .85). The item asking the subject whether he or she would accept a ride home late at night with the model is only weakly related to the other items. This is not surprising in that the item measures a judgment about personal danger that is quite different from the other items and is correlated with the sex of the respondent. We built a trustworthiness score for each image by reversing the order of the items, summing the scores, and then taking the average.[11] The resulting values ranged from 1.9 to 4.9, with low values indicating low trustworthiness.

Early in this chapter we argue that a smile might induce trust. In this experiment we find support for that argument: the trustworthiness score is positively related to whether the image is smiling. A matched-pairs t-test for differences between the values of the scale for smiling and neutral expressions is statistically significant ($t = 3.83$, $df = 59$, $p < .001$). Smiles appear to convey trustworthiness. Figure 9.4 presents the some of the trustworthiness ratings for a sample of eight images. The horizontal axis indicates the values along the trustworthy scale. The figure plots the distribution of scores on this scale, separating smiling and neutral expressions. Smiling faces are scored in the bottom panel of the figure, neutral faces at the top. For this figure we selected images associated with extreme values on the trustworthy scale. The photographs on the upper left, categorized as neutral, held low values on the scale; and, as can be seen, they do not exhibit particularly welcoming expressions. The four photographs on the bottom right, categorized as smiling, score very high on the trustworthy scale. Our results strongly suggest that smiles invite trust. At the same time we find a modest effect for female images that, regardless of the expression, are deemed somewhat more trustworthy ($t = 1.97$, $df = 33.3$, $p = .06$; corrected for unequal variances).

These data illustrate a connection between smiles and the expectation that trust will be reciprocated. However, they are collected for hypothetical settings. We next ask whether this pattern of responses carries over to a decision-making setting with financial stakes. The set of subjects for this experiments consisted of 120 graduate students and staff from a variety of Oxford University departments and colleges, solicited by e-mail and by posters distributed to departments and colleges within the vicinity of the Department of Zoology.

Decision-Making Experiment

The decision-making experiment is a three-factor design (a two-by-two-by-two matrix), the factors being the sex of the subject, the sex of the photograph subject, and whether the photograph subject is smiling. In this discussion we focus on the impact of two of these three factors—the sex of the image and whether its subject is smiling—in addition to the trustworthiness measure developed from the survey data.[12]

Each subject was randomly assigned one of the photographic images as a "counterpart" in a simple bargaining game. The subjects were led to believe that they would be playing against the pictured

Figure 9.4 Distribution of Trustworthiness Scores, by Facial Expressions

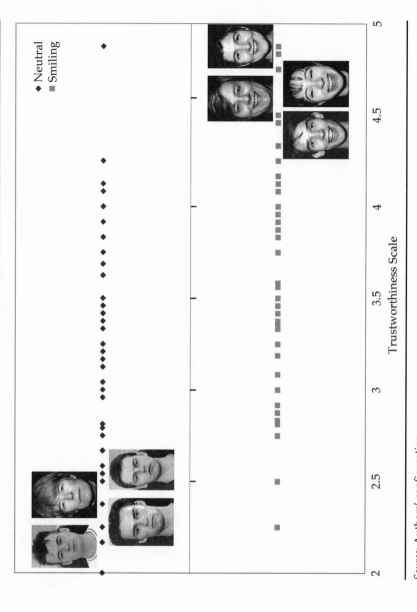

Trustworthiness Scale

Source: Authors' configuration.
Note: A sample of images are displayed near their scores on the scale. Low values indicate low levels of perceived trustworthiness.

Figure 9.5   Game and Parameters Used in Experiment 2

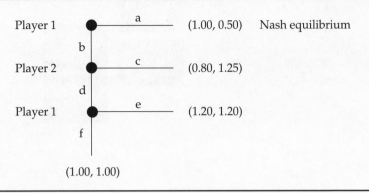

Player 1	•———a———	(1.00, 0.50)	Nash equilibrium
Player 2	b •———c———	(0.80, 1.25)	
Player 1	d •———e———	(1.20, 1.20)	
	f		
	(1.00, 1.00)		

Source: Authors' configuration.

subject, but in fact they were playing against a preprogrammed strategy.[13] Subjects, seated at a computer terminal for the duration of the experiment, participated in a variation of the trust game developed by Joyce Berg, John Dickhaut, and Kevin McCabe (1995) and shown in figure 9.5. All payoffs are in British pounds. The game was structured as follows: At the first node of the decision tree, the subject chose between two alternatives. A move to the right ended the experiment: the subject earned £1.00, and his or her counterpart £0.50. A downward move passed the choice to the second player, who then faced a similar choice to end the experiment (giving the second player £1.25 and the first player £0.80) or to pass the move back to player 1. The first player then had a choice between £1.00 and £1.20 for each of the players. The unique *Nash equilibrium* for this game has the first mover terminating the game at the first node. However, trust and reciprocity return gains to both players. An initial trusting move is problematic because the second player has an incentive to quit at the second node, leaving the first player worse off; but if that trusting move is reciprocated, then both players are better off than they would have been at the Nash equilibrium.

At the outset, subjects were photographed to heighten the sense that they were playing against a counterpart at another computer in a separate room. After being given detailed on-screen instructions, each subject was then shown a black-and-white photograph of his or her apparent counterpart. The image remained visible as a smaller side picture while the game was being played. When the game was finished the subjects completed an on-screen questionnaire.

In this game, all subjects were first movers. The first move was the most interesting, as it indicates whether a subject decided to trust his or her counterpart. A subject who chose to pass was told to wait for his or her counterpart to make a decision. The computer was pre-programmed so that the counterpart always chose to reciprocate and then passed the final choice to the subject.[14]

Based on our previous discussion, we offer several predictions:

- Prediction 1: Subjects will immediately choose to quit, reaching the *subgame-perfect Nash equilibrium* (the game-theoretic prediction).
- Prediction 2: Images coded as smiling will invite greater trusting behavior;
- Prediction 3: Images that score highest on the trustworthy scale will invite greater trusting behavior.

We rely on our survey results that suggest subjects assess the trustworthiness of the images in a systematic manner. We expect these attitudinal assessments to be related to behavior.

Summary results are shown in table 9.2.[15] First, it is clear that the first prediction can be rejected: subjects chose the trusting move 61.7 percent of the time. This is contrary to the game-theoretic hypothesis predicting that subjects will chose the subgame-perfect equilibrium.

The second prediction is supported by the data. Subjects trusted smiling counterparts in 68.3 percent of decisions and nonsmiling counterparts in 55 percent of decisions. Using a one-tailed proportions test for paired samples, we can reject the hypothesis that the smiling and nonsmiling counterparts are trusted equally ($t = 1.66$, $p = 0.051$).[16] The third prediction, using ratings based on the trustworthiness index, is weakly supported. Subjects tend to trust partners who are rated higher on our index. The relationship is significant at the .07 level ($t = 1.49$, $df = 119$, $p = .07$).

Table 9.2   Perceived Trustworthiness of Facial Images, by Sex and Facial Expression (Percentage)

Facial Image	Neutral	Smiling	Total
Male	57.4	68.1	62.8
Female	46.2	69.2	57.7
All	55.0	68.3	61.7

Source: Authors' compilation.
Note: The table gives the percentages of sample subjects who made trusting moves in simulated play with each subset of facial image.

Table 9.3   Probit Regression Results: Perceived Trustworthiness

Variable	Model 1	Model 2	Model 3	Model 4
Intercept	0.348	−0.143	0.210	−0.334
	(0.212)	(0.462)	(0.222)	(0.479)
	$p = .101$	$p = .758$	$p = .344$	$p = .485$
Smile	**0.361**		**0.378**	
	(0.236)	—	(0.239)	—
	$p = .063^a$		$p = .057^a$	
Trustworthiness scale		**0.269**		**0.298**
	—	(0.177)	—	(0.181)
		$p = .064^a$		$p = .050^a$
Female image	−0.116	−0.248	0.608	0.468
	(0.287)	(0.297)	(0.482)	(0.492)
	$p = .685$	$p = .405$	$p = .207$	$p = .341$
Female subject	−0.379	−0.331	−0.132	−0.092
	(0.236)	(0.238)	(0.266)	(0.266)
	$p = .102$	$p = .164$	$p = .619$	$p = .729$
Female image and female			**−1.248**	**−1.232**
subject	—	—	(0.621)	(0.632)
			$p = .045$	$p = .051$
Log likelihood function	−77.35	−76.92	−75.21	−74.91

Source: Authors' compilation.
Note: The dependent variable is the trust move. Standard errors for coefficients are in parentheses. Values in boldface type are significant at $p \leq 0.10$.
[a]One-tailed test.

In the analysis of the first (pilot) experiment, the sex of the image subject appeared to affect the decision. We expect a similar pattern in this second experiment and estimate a series of probit models to test for these relationships while controlling for other factors (see table 9.3). Model 1 estimates the decision by a subject (whether or not to take the trust move) as a function of whether the image subject was smiling, the sex of the image subject, and the sex of the decision maker (both dummy variables, with female coded as 1). The coefficient for the smiling condition is positive and at the margin of statistical significance under a one-tailed test. Female subjects were less likely to take a trusting move, and subjects in general were less likely to trust a female image. This latter parameter estimate is weak, with considerable variation. The sex of the subject produces a stronger effect and approaches the $p = .10$ level of significance.

Model 2 is estimated in much the same way. However, rather than using a dummy variable for whether or not the photographed image was smiling, we use the trustworthiness scale value for the image.

Again we find a positive effect that is statistically significant at the .07 level for a one-tailed test. Simply put, the higher an image was rated on the trustworthiness scale (as assessed by an independent population), the more likely a subject was to pick a trusting move. When the sex of the image and the sex of the subject were controlled for, we find results similar to those in Model 1; female images are less likely to be deemed trustworthy, and female subjects are less likely to choose to trust.

Models 3 and 4 repeat the first two models but add an interaction term for the sex of the image and sex of the subject. This interaction term takes on a value of 1 when female subjects were paired with a female photographed image. Once again we find that both the smiling condition and the trustworthiness scale have a positive and strong effect on making a trusting choice. The coefficients for the sex of the image switch signs, now becoming positive, although still without statistical significance. This indicates that a female image may be more likely to be trusted, except by other women. The interaction term provides most of the explanatory power, with a large, statistically significant, negative effect on choice. In short, female subjects are less likely to trust these female images. This is true in both models, and the magnitude of the effect is almost identical in both. Likelihood ratio tests indicate that the unrestricted estimates in models 3 and 4, which allow the effect of the sex of the image to differ by the sex of the subject, are significantly different from the restricted models (model 1 = model 3, χ^2 (1) = 4.28, p = .039; model 2 = model 4, χ^2 (1) = 4.02, p = .044): men and women respond differently to the sex of their counterparts.

Discussion

The main results of this second study are that smiling, at the margin, positively affects trust among strangers; subjects draw inferences about the trustworthiness of their partners based on a photographed image of that partner and act on that basis; and other features, extending beyond simple smiles, affect trusting behavior. Smiling increases trust among strangers; subjects were more likely to trust people when images presented them as smiling than when they were presented as not smiling. The result is significant in a one-tailed, matched-pairs proportions test, as well as in regression analysis.

Our second finding is derived from subjects' responses to questionnaire items that were designed to measure people's sense of the trustworthiness of the photographed model. An independent population assessed these images, and we calculated a score for each photograph. This trustworthiness scale predicts whether or not subjects are likely to take a trusting move in a game with financial stakes. Of course, because the two are correlated, we are unable to disentangle whether it is the smile or the assessment of trustworthiness that drives the observed pattern of behavior. Notwithstanding the link between smiles and trustworthiness, we interpret this to mean that subjects are able to detect a difference in facial expressions and that those expressions affect subjects' beliefs about the trustworthiness of their counterparts. Thus smiling appears to serve as an informative stimulus to elicit trusting behavior.

Finally, we find important differences in the assessments and behavior of women and men. Female subjects were significantly less likely to trust their female counterparts in this game. These findings join those by many others in pointing out that males and females may respond differently to a given environment. This leads us to believe that the sex of the participants will have an impact on face-to-face negotiations and other settings in which one's sex is difficult to mask.

Conclusion

This research leads us to a methodological point and a theoretical observation. The methodological point is that there can be a mismatch between attitudes and action. In both experiments we found that individuals are adept assessing the emotional content of the facial expression of a photographed image. At the same time we found that subjects easily (and readily) draw inferences about the trustworthiness of the individual in the photograph. However, when we ask subjects to select a strategic action contingent on the photographed counterpart, behavior and attitudes are only weakly correlated.

This weak correlation is especially evident in our first experiment. Subjects could easily identify the emotional expression and could also read differences in trustworthiness across the different expressions. However, when asked to choose an action contingent on the photographed expression, subjects' decisions were not consistent with expectations derived from assessments of the image by an independent sample.

The results of the first experiment allowed us to identify and correct potential design problems. In the second experiment we were able to improve the clarity of the instructions, and our puzzling results led us to expand the set of images and improve the precision of our attitudinal survey instrument. We are far more confident of the results of this attitudinal survey and experiment. Here we find that smiling and trustworthiness are perceived as related; that is, subjects who view a smiling image appear to read the smile as a marker of trustworthiness. Our behavioral results also tend to support this point: subjects are more likely to trust smiling images and images that are rated high on the trustworthiness scale.

It is not surprising that attitudes and behavior differ. Subjects find it easy to claim they will trust others when trust carries no costs; a costly behavioral expression of trust, however, is not as readily forthcoming. Additional work is needed to construct instruments that link both attitudes and behavior in predictable ways.

Our more general point is that subjects are willing to trust even when standard game-theoretic models predict they should not. The root cause of this trusting behavior is not that people are hardwired for cooperation. We do not think people come into the world with a fixed orientation toward trusting others. Instead, we think that people are conditional in their choice of strategies. People quickly assess their partners and then play appropriate strategies. This implies that the same person may trust some and not others.

We argue that people do not naïvely trust; rather, they make decisions based on observations about their counterparts. Trust with strangers is possible and is rooted in the ability to read nonverbal signals and to imagine the mental state of another. When there are potential gains for trusting and trustworthy behavior, individuals turn to a variety of cues to build beliefs about strangers. Social status, sex, and ethnicity are common cues, and the latter two are difficult to hide in face-to-face bargaining situations. At the same time, the face itself is a rich set of cues. Some of those cues may be involuntary and, in that, reveal the emotional state of another. Other cues, such as the perceived attractiveness or maturity of the face, may trigger quite different responses. Finally, there are intentional facial expressions that provide convenient shorthand in well-understood social settings (for example, the hostile stare used to punish inappropriate behavior).

The standard game-theoretic model would argue that facial expressions could not be credible. There is nothing to bind a smile, for example, to the promise of trustworthy action. In a sense a smile should be no more than another form of cheap talk. Smiles can be as empty as promises—especially from strangers. However, this is not what we find.

We find that subjects are attuned to the smiles of their counterparts. This is not an accident but part of evolved human cognition. Humans (and many other animals) are adept at reading nonverbal signals. Evolutionary processes have designed us to pay attention to others (recall O'Connell's three Fs). The ability to recognize whether another individual wants to fight or mate is critical in evolutionary terms. Whether more complex social behavior can be credibly signaled is another question. We contend that reading a signal is one thing, imagining the intention of a counterpart is quite another.

Like game theorists, evolutionary theorists wonder whether non-verbal signals can be credible. If they can be mimicked (costlessly imitated), then they have no value for signaling. If a signal does have value, then there should be evolutionary pressures to display the signal falsely. Smiles certainly have this characteristic—they can easily be imitated. We do not find that smiles always lead to trust, nor would we want to suggest that the secret to understanding trust is hidden behind a smile. For complex social behavior we think that the capacity to imagine the other's intention is essential. It is this aspect of cognition that prevents the "arms race" of displaying and mimicking signals. People use a good deal of information about strangers to quickly make an assessment about how to proceed. Because the benefits from trust can be high, it is often worth trusting. This must be done conditionally, however, and only if the intention of the partner is clear. A smile has signal value and certainly provides an invitation to trust. The central lesson, however, is that humans are adept at reading not just signals but also the intention behind a signal, and it is this capacity that smoothes the path toward social trust.

Appendix

Appendix A9.1   Questionnaire Items Used in Second Experiment

The following questions were asked after subjects had rated the faces using twenty-five word pairs: At this point we have some different questions to ask you about the image.

If this person found your wallet on the street, how likely is it this person would return it to you?
1. Very Likely
2. Likely
3. Somewhat Likely
4. Somewhat Unlikely
5. Unlikely
6. Very Unlikely

How likely is it that you would accept a ride home from this person at night?
1. Very Likely
2. Likely
3. Somewhat Likely
4. Somewhat Unlikely
5. Unlikely
6. Very Unlikely

How likely do you think you would make friends with this person?
1. Very Likely
2. Likely
3. Somewhat Likely
4. Somewhat Unlikely
5. Unlikely
6. Very Unlikely

How likely would you be to ask this person to do you a favor?
1. Very Likely
2. Likely
3. Somewhat Likely
4. Somewhat Unlikely
5. Unlikely
6. Very Unlikely

If you were assigned to do a group project with this person, how likely is it that this individual would do his/her share?
1. Very Likely
2. Likely
3. Somewhat Likely
4. Somewhat Unlikely
5. Unlikely
6. Very Unlikely

Source: Authors' compilation.

The paper on which this chapter is based was prepared for the Trust Working Group Meeting, sponsored by the Russell Sage Foundation, February 19 and 20, 1999, in New York. Valuable assistance for the classroom experiments conducted at Virginia Polytechnic Institute and State University was provided by Fatma Aksal, Robert Bowles, Tony Dziepak, Rob Gilles, Cathleen Johnson, Mark McLeod, and Randall Verbrugge. Special thanks go to Jorn Scharlemann and Alex Kacelnik. Finally, we spent some time bending the ears of Betsy Hoffman, Kevin McCabe, and Vernon Smith.

Notes

1. Temple Grandin (1996), a high-functioning autistic, provides a moving account of this process.

2. Eckel and Grossman (forthcoming) survey results on ultimatum, dictator, and public-goods games.

3. In addition to the experimental work in economics, there is a large literature in sociology on status characteristics and influence. See, for example, Ridgeway et al. (1998) and Webster and Hysom (1998).

4. Although we intended to test all three posed emotional expressions—happiness, neutrality, and anger—in the game experiment (the second component), we were unable to conduct a condition with the female angry face. To keep a balanced design we omit the discussion of the male angry face.

5. These findings are supported under ANOVA (analysis of variance) models of both happiness and trusting ratings. The main effects for smiling are very strong (and statistically significant at the .001 level). For the happiness rating there is also a significant interaction between the sex of the image and the smile. For the trust rating there is a significant interaction between the sex of the model and the sex of the subject, with females more likely to trust the male image.

6. In the first experiment almost 36 percent of the subjects complained that the instructions were unclear. By contrast, in this second experiment, fewer than 6 percent of the subjects found the instructions unclear.

7. The word pairs were pretested with twelve subjects under a different task. The word-pair items have also been used by Eckel and Rick Wilson (1999) and by Jorn Scharlemann and colleagues (2001) and are discussed fully there.

8. The URL for this website is: *pics.psych.stir.ac.uk*.

9. The first group of subjects completed this task as part of an in-class exercise; the second group of subjects was paid. In the second group subjects were allotted thirty minutes to complete the task. Analysis not

presented here indicates no significant difference between the two groups with respect to their ratings.

10. Jorn Scharlemann and colleagues (2001) evaluated the same images. However, in that setting each image was evaluated by a single subject. As the authors note, this introduced a good deal of noise into the analysis. By increasing the number of evaluations of these images, we are more confident of the scales developed on the basis of these images.

11. This scale is correlated at .683 with an additive scale of two items related specifically to trust taken from the semantic differential word pairings discussed in Scharlemann et al. (2001).

12. These experiments were conducted by Jorn Scharlemann. We thank him for the use of these data. Extensive analysis of differences by sex pairing can be found in Scharlemann et al. (2001).

13. Experimental control over the content of the images necessitated some degree of deception. Our protocol conforms to American Psychological Association guidelines.

14. The last choice, between terminal branches e and f in figure 9.5, tests whether subjects make *rational choices*—that is, whether they are able to differentiate between payoffs of £1.20 (branch e) and £1.00 (branch f). Any subjects making the irrational choice of branch f were excluded from the analysis.

15. Of the 131 subjects participating in the study, 3 were excluded because of incomplete pairing (that is, only one of the pair of faces was shown), 4 because of technical problems (computer or camera crashed), and another 4 because they made the irrational choice (branch f) (3 percent of subjects reacted irrationally). Of the remaining 120 subjects used for analysis, 7 (6.2 percent) reported that the instructions were unclear. The average duration of experiment, including instructions and on-screen questionnaire, was about 8 minutes. Of the 50 subjects who commented on the game, only 4 (8 percent) stated that they believed their counterparts were not real persons.

16. Although the paired-sample test is rare, such a test is entirely appropriate in this setting. Each model presents two different images, one smiling and one not smiling. Thus we can pair the responses to the two images. This finding shows that smiles affect "trust" in this experiment. A standard t-test gives a similar result. See Kimmel (1957) on the use of one-tailed tests.

References

Anderson, Norman H. 1968. "Likableness Ratings of 555 Personality-Trait Words." *Journal of Personality and Social Psychology* 9(3): 272–79.

Andreoni, James, and Lise Vesterlund. 2001. "Which Is the Fair Sex? Gender Differences in Altruism." *Quarterly Journal of Economics* 116(1): 293–312.

Ball, Sheryl, and Catherine C. Eckel. 1998. "The Economic Value of Status." *Journal of Socio-Economics* 27(4): 495–514.

Ball, Sheryl, Catherine C. Eckel, Philip Grossman, and William Zame. 2001. "Status in Markets." *Quarterly Journal of Economics* 116(1): 161–88.

Baron-Cohen, Simon. 1995. *Mindblindness: An Essay on Autism and Theory of Mind*. Boston: MIT Press.

Berg, Joyce, John W. Dickhaut, and Kevin A. McCabe. 1995. "Trust, Reciprocity, and Social History." *Games and Economic Behavior* 10(1): 122–42.

Camerer, Colin. 2003. "Social Preferences in Dictator, Ultimatum, and Trust Games." In *Behavioral Game Theory: Experiments in Strategic Interaction*, Princeton, N.J.: Princeton University Press.

Carroll, James M., and James A. Russell. 1997. "Facial Expressions in Hollywood's Portrayal of Emotion." *Journal of Personality and Social Psychology* 72(1): 164–76.

Darwin, Charles. 1998 [1872]. *The Expression of the Emotions in Man and Animals*. Oxford: Oxford University Press.

Eckel, Catherine C., and Philip Grossman. 1996. "Altruism in Anonymous Dictator Games." *Games and Economic Behavior* 16(2): 181–91.

———. 1998. "Are Women Less Selfish Than Men? Evidence from Dictator Games." *Economic Journal* 108(448): 726–35.

———. 1999. "Rebates Versus Matching: Does How We Subsidize Charitable Giving Matter?" Department of Economics working paper. Virginia Polytechnic Institute and State University, Blacksburg, Virginia.

———. 2001. "Chivalry and Solidarity in Ultimatum Games." *Economic Inquiry* 39(2): 171–88.

———. Forthcoming. "Differences in the Economic Decisions of Men and Women: Experimental Evidence." In *Handbook of Experimental Results*, edited by Charles Plott and Vernon Smith. New York: Elsevier.

Eckel, Catherine C., and Rick K. Wilson. 1999. "Reciprocal Fairness and Social Signaling: Experiments with Limited Reputations." Paper presented at the American Economic Association Meetings, New York (January 3–6).

Ekman, Paul. 1972. *Emotion in the Human Face: Guide-Lines for Research and an Integration of Findings*. Pergamon General Psychology Series, PGPS-11. New York: Pergamon Press.

———. 1982. *Emotion in the Human Face*. 2d ed. Studies in Emotion and Social Interaction. Cambridge: Cambridge University Press.

Ekman, Paul, and Wallace V. Friesen. 1982. "Felt, False, and Miserable Smiles." *Journal of Nonverbal Behavior* 6(4): 238–52.

Ekman, Paul, Wallace V. Friesen, and Maureen O'Sullivan. 1988. "Smiles When Lying." *Journal of Personality and Social Psychology* 54(3): 414–20.

Ekman, Paul, and Maureen O'Sullivan. 1991. "Who Can Catch a Liar?" *American Psychologist* 46(9): 913–20.

Fahr, René, and Bernd Irlenbusch. 2000. "Fairness As a Constraint on Trust in Reciprocity: Earned Property Rights in a Reciprocal Exchange Experiment." *Economics Letters* 66(3): 275–82.

Falk, Armin, and Urs Fischbacher 1998. "Kindness Is the Parent of Kindness: Modeling Reciprocity." Unpublished manuscript. Institute for Empirical Economic Research, Zurich, Switzerland.

Fehr, Ernst, Georg Kircksteiger, and Arno Reidl. 1993. "Does Fairness Prevent Market Clearing? An Experimental Investigation." *Quarterly Journal of Economics* 108(2): 437–59.

Fehr, Ernst, and Klaus M. Schmidt. 1999. "A Theory of Fairness, Competition, and Cooperation." *Quarterly Journal of Economics* 114(3): 817–68.

Fernández-Dols, José-Miguel, and Maria-Angeles Ruiz-Belda. 1995. "Are Smiles a Sign of Happiness? Gold Medal Winners at the Olympic Games." *Journal of Personality and Social Psychology* 69(6): 1113–19.

———. 1997. "Spontaneous Facial Behavior During Intense Emotional Episodes: Artistic Truth and Optical Truth." In *The Psychology of Facial Expression,* edited by James A. Russell and José-Miguel Fernández-Dols. Cambridge: Cambridge University Press.

Forsythe, Robert, Joel L. Horowitz, N. E. Savin, and Martin Sefton. 1994. "Fairness in Simple Bargaining Experiments." *Games and Economic Behavior* 6(3): 347–69.

Frank, Robert. 1988. *Passions Within Reason: The Strategic Role of the Emotions.* New York: W. W. Norton.

Frank, Robert, Thomas Gilovich, and Dennis Regan. 1993. "The Evolution of One-Shot Cooperation." *Ethology and Sociobiology* 14(4): 247–56.

Fridlund, Alan J., Paul Ekman, and Harriet Oster. 1987. "Facial Expressions of Emotion: Review of Literature, 1970–1983." In *Nonverbal Behavior and Communication,* 2d ed., edited by Aron W. Siegman and Stanley Feldstein. Hillsdale, N.J.: Lawrence Erlbaum.

Glaeser, Edward L., David I. Laibson, José A. Scheinkman, and Christine L. Soutter. 2000. "Measuring Trust." *Quarterly Journal of Economics* 115(3): 811–46.

Gopnik, Alison. 1993. *Mindblindness.* Unpublished essay, University of California, Berkeley.

Grandin, Temple. 1996. *Thinking in Pictures and Other Reports from My Life with Autism.* New York: Vintage Books.

Güth, Werner. 1995. "An Evolutionary Approach to Explaining Cooperative Behavior by Reciprocal Incentives." *International Journal of Game Theory* 24(4): 323–44.

Hoffman, Elizabeth, Kevin McCabe, Keith Shachat, and Vernon Smith. 1994. "Preference, Property Rights, and Anonymity in Bargaining Games." *Games and Economic Behavior* 7(3): 346–80.

Kimmel, Herbert D. 1957. "Three Criteria for the Use of One-Tailed Tests." *Psychological Bulletin* 54(4): 351–53.

Ledyard, John O. 1995. "Public Goods: A Survey of Experimental Research." In *Handbook of Experimental Economics,* edited by John H. Kagel and Alvin E. Roth. Princeton, N.J.: Princeton University Press.

McCabe, Kevin A., Stephen J. Rassenti, and Vernon L. Smith. 1998. "Reciprocity, Trust, and Payoff Privacy in Extensive-Form Bargaining." *Games and Economic Behavior* 24(1–2): 10–24.

O'Connell, Sanjida. 1998. *Mindreading: An Investigation into How We Learn to Love and Lie.* New York: Doubleday.

Ostrom, Elinor. 1998. "A Behavioral Approach to the Rational Choice Theory of Collective Action." *American Political Science Review* 92(1): 1–22.

Ridgeway, Cecilia L., Elizabeth H. Boyle, Kathy J. Kuipers, and Dawn T. Robinson. 1998. "How Do Status Beliefs Develop? The Role of Resources and Interactional Experience." *American Sociological Review* 63(3): 331–50.

Russell, James A. 1994. "Is There Universal Recognition of Emotion from Facial Expression?" *Psychological Bulletin* 115(1): 102–41.

Scharlemann, Jorn P. W., Catherine C. Eckel, Alex Kacelnik, and Rick K. Wilson. 2001. "The Value of a Smile: Game Theory with a Human Face." *Journal of Economic Psychology* 22(5): 617–40.

Smith, Vernon L. 1998. "The Two Faces of Adam Smith." *Southern Economic Journal* 65(1): 1–19.

Webster, Murray, Jr., and Stuart J. Hysom. 1998. "Creating Status Characteristics." *American Sociological Review* 63(3): 351–78.

Chapter 10

Strategic Analysis in Games: What Information Do Players Use?

KEVIN A. MCCABE AND VERNON L. SMITH

A LTHOUGH observations broadly consistent with the predictions of *noncooperative game theory* have been commonly observed in certain auction markets (Smith 1982), the theory has been markedly less successful in accounting for behavior in two-person interaction games between anonymous players. This condition is generally believed to favor the achievement of noncooperative outcomes by controlling for social influences and reputation formation—phenomena that have not yet been satisfactorily integrated into the structure of game theory (see, for example, Güth, Schmittberger, and Schwarze 1982; Roth et al. 1991; McCabe, Rassenti, and Smith 1996). Despite this "loading of the dice" in favor of noncooperation, we observe far too much cooperation in such games. Why?

In earlier work, we have hypothesized that people use principles of choice and information processing that differ from, but augment, the game-theoretic paradigm based on dominance and *backward induction* (McCabe, Rassenti, and Smith 1996; Hoffman, McCabe, and Smith 1998; Burnham, McCabe, and Smith 2000; McCabe, Smith, and LePore 2000). In the present work we summarize and report data from a research program motivated by concepts of reciprocity and intentionality detection that we propose as supplements to the standard game-theoretic principles. The question is not whether game-theoretic principles find application in the data—they do—but whether they suffice as the only principles that govern behavior.

One alternative research program is to postulate that the anomalous contradictions with theoretical predictions can be accommodated and rationalized by an appropriate learning model; that is, through experience in repeat interaction with different partners, players adapt through learning to play noncooperative equilibriums (Roth and Erev 1995; McKelvey and Palfrey 1995; Anderson, Goeree, and Holt 1998). Thus in voluntary-contribution-mechanism games, the initial tendencies toward cooperation fall victim to free riding in repeat play. In terms of the learning hypothesis, the problem is that cooperation increases when the group begins play again (Isaac and Walker 1988). Consequently, the "learning" does not stick, nor does it appear to carry over to other games; that is, people do not "learn" general principles from these experiences.

Rachel Croson (1998) has tested various hypotheses for explaining outcomes in voluntary-contribution-mechanism games and reports support for the reciprocity interpretation.[1] We provide data suggesting that fundamentally different principles of choice and information processing are needed and that learning models superimposed on the standard paradigm are not adequate to account for and understand the full range of the observations. Learning models describe rote directional responses to profitable experiences but do not themselves provide a framework for predicting or explaining the experience. Learning models are complementary to the principles of mental reciprocity accounting we propose, however, and remain important technical frameworks for describing changes in behavior over time based on these reciprocity principles. Furthermore, there is one condition on the environment in which statistical learning models do apply: private information. We present data showing that when each player knows only his or her own payoff, players gravitate over time toward the noncooperative outcome. In this case players cannot read one another's intentions, and rote statistical learning is expected, predicted, and observed.

A second alternative approach is to postulate that the failures of the noncooperative model are attributable to player types who are motivated by joint other-regarding and self-regarding preferences; that is, in a direct utilitarian sense, players care about the payoffs of their counterparts as well as their own (see Rabin 1993, for models, and Croson 1998, for tests of the "warm-glow" hypothesis in voluntary-contribution-mechanism games). We do not rule out a possible role for altruistic utility considerations; however, contrary to the assumptions of the traditional economic approach, preferences cannot be ultimate data. Utility is a proximate, not a fundamental, cause of what we observe—the phenotype, not the genotype. It is important to ask what evolutionary or cultural function is served by altruistic utility (Gintis and Romer 1998) and how it is able to survive invasion by selfish free riders, either in evolutionary time or even in the course of a repeat-interaction experiment with distinct partners in the laboratory.[2]

An important function of negative reciprocity is to punish those who defect (cheat) on cooperative exchanges across time (Cosmides 1989; Cosmides and Tooby 1992). Other-regarding utilitarian types neither cheat nor require punishment. Matthew Rabin's (1993) model of fairness accommodates both positive and negative equilibriums, but reciprocity in social exchange yields these outcomes as supporting the reputational self-interest, a special case of economic exchange, and need not require interpersonal utility.

Still a third alternative argument, often invoked over the years, is that the issue is moot in games in which the stakes are large. Concern that stakes can be important is probably the oldest issue in experimental economics, having emerged thirty-five to forty years ago among experimentalists, and has been extensively studied over that period (Siegel 1959; Siegel and Fouraker 1960; Smith 1965; for a review, see Smith and Walker 1993). This line of argument, however, does not resolve the anomalous failure of game theory to predict the high incidence of cooperation in two-person interactions: a hundred-thousand-fold increase in the stakes yields a hundred-thousand-fold increase in the benefits of cooperation. The high-stakes Federal Communications Commission auctions were not bereft of attempts to collude. Increasing the stakes sometimes affects outcomes substantially, sometimes not at all (Smith and Walker 1993; Camerer and Hogarth 1997). In any case, the level of the stakes is not a formal part of the apparatus of game theory but rather an ex post hoc argument appended to it. The theory is inadequate and incompletely specified so long as it cannot formally predict how the environment (including stakes), player information, player characteristics (including in-group versus out-group features), and whether the players use consultants impact cooperative versus noncooperative outcomes.

Hence the need for an in-depth empirical examination of how players view the games they play. As noted by Herbert Simon, "To predict how economic man will behave, we need to know not only that he is rational, but also how he perceives the world—what alternatives he sees and what consequences he attaches to them" (Simon 1956, 271). In this spirit we do not deny rationality in the work that follows. Rather, we explore hypotheses about how it is expressed through the social brain in the way people interpret one another's expectations in strategic interaction. This approach, however, does deny the traditional game-theoretic rational-actor assumption of common knowledge that each agent chooses dominant strategies within the analytical framework of backward induction. This view alone, however, is inadequate and fails to account for the play of sophisticated subjects (McCabe and Smith 2000).

Much of the data summarized here has been reported elsewhere in greater detail and with appropriate statistical tests provided (McCabe, Rassenti, and Smith 1996, 1997; McCabe, Smith, and LePore 2000). Our objective is to report some new experiments and to use the data as a whole to develop the principal themes that have permeated our research on two-person *extensive-form* (and *normal-form*) bargaining. That research program has been one in which each set of experiments raises new questions of interpretation relative to the game-theoretic and reciprocity paradigms, and it has not been possible in individual papers to articulate more fully how one set of results has motivated the design of new experiments. Specifically, we ask what can be inferred about players' modes of analysis, the information they use, and how the resulting behavior relates to game-theoretic versus reciprocity principles of strategic play.

There is clear evidence of reciprocal exchange in chimpanzees (de Waal 1996, 1997). Furthermore, there is strong evidence that reciprocity is a human universal (Gouldner 1960). Recent ethnological evidence in modern hunter-gatherer societies suggests large surplus production of calorie-rich goods by males aged eighteen and older (Hillary Kaplan, "Strong Reciprocity," conference organized at the University of Massachusetts, 1998). Such surplus production, together with the ability to engage in reciprocal exchange, would have permitted specialization, supporting greater reproductive success, long before trade between stateless societies emerged.

We find it particularly insightful to distinguish between personal and monetary forms of exchange, both of which have long been examined by experimental economists (Smith 1998). In personal exchange (see figure 10.1), I give you the good G at time t, (thus G_t), and in return you give me an implicit promise (that may, but need not, be specific) to repay me with something of value, H, in the future. Suppose, at some point in the future $(t + 1)$, you reciprocate by giving me the good $H_{(t+1)}$. What do I give you in return? Your promise? Not likely, given that it was not property to begin with (at least not in the absence of a highly developed legal system). Instead, my social brain credits you with "goodwill," making it more likely that I will trust you in future trading. In monetary exchange (figure 10.2), at time t you give me an amount of money, m, in return for the good, G, Money carries some promissory sense, as a medium of exchange in future transactions, but in exchanges of this sort, you do not generally make any promise to me, implicit or otherwise. At some later date $(t + 1)$, you may give me some other good, H, in return for which I

Figure 10.1   Schematic Diagram of Personal Exchange

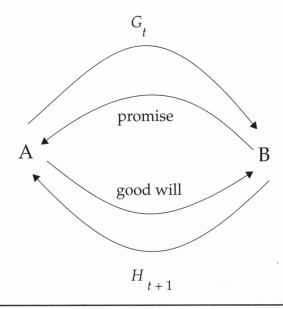

Source: Authors' configuration.

will give you an appropriate sum of money. This second exchange, however, is in no way implied by the first.

Goodwill, like money, allows individuals to overcome the double coincidence of wants found in a pure barter economy and to enjoy the long-run benefits of specialization. Barter solves the problem of long-distance trade with strangers, in which trust and goodwill cannot be relied upon as it can be in more closely knit in-group communities, and allows specialization to be extended beyond in-group boundaries.[3]

Note that, technically, a promise made by person B to person A could be described in terms of a "utility" marker; that is, A gets "utility" from—cares about—the value experienced by B; A's crediting B with goodwill could be similarly described. Such techniques, however, though they may be useful and productive, do not ask why, and on their own they will generate experiments different from those motivated by the reciprocity hypothesis.

In earlier work (McCabe and Smith 2000), we postulate a system of mental modules necessary for personal exchange. This system includes the existence of a "goodwill" accounting system, which tracks trading partners, together with a "mind-reading" system, which at-

Figure 10.2   Schematic Diagram of Monetary Exchange

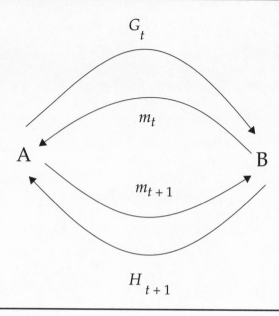

Source: Authors' configuration.

tributes mental states to partners to predict reciprocal behavior in achieving mutual gains (see ch. 6, this volume).

Once a person has formed some initial expectation about the likely value of a trading relationship with another person, he or she will continue to gather additional information to better understand the intentions of the other person in the specific trading instance. This requires the ability to make attributions on the mental states of others (examined in Leslie 1987, Frith 1989, and Baron-Cohen 1995). At this stage individuals are likely to use what Simon Baron-Cohen (1995) calls the shared-attention mechanism. Such a mechanism is used to convert a dyadic understanding of intentions, such as "He is hungry," to a triadic understanding, such as "He knows that I know that he is hungry." Triadic knowledge becomes the basis for reciprocity. For example, offering food as a way to "help" him meet his goal now implies a promise of reciprocity to keep the value of the relationship positive.

Baron-Cohen identifies mental modules, or mechanisms, that are hypothesized to exist; a variety of evidence supports this hypothesis. These four modules enable inferences to be made about mental phenomena in other agents based on their actions or words: an intentionality detector, an eye-direction detector, a shared-attention mechanism, and a theory-of-mind mechanism. The four are thought to be interconnected so that the intentionality and eye-direction detectors are inputs to the shared-attention mechanism, which is, in turn, an input to the theory-of-mind mechanism. The implications of this work for the analysis of strategic interaction differ substantially from the underlying postulates of game theory.

In bargaining-tree games played by anonymously matched pairs, such as those studied in economic laboratories, shared attention will operate on two kinds of information: *Focal points*, as discussed by Thomas Schelling (1960), are features of the strategic settings, such as symmetry and *Pareto dominance* of payoffs, which are likely to be observed by the other player and consequently promote triadic understanding. Move information promotes triadic understanding by communicating intentions through both forgone opportunities and what payoffs remain as admissible future opportunities.

The Games We Play: Three Extensive-Form Bargaining Environments

The comparisons that follow use the same extensive-form bargaining-tree structure and either vary the payoffs in a controlled manner or vary the matching protocol that assigns subjects to pairs, and to roles (player 1 or 2), in the bargaining tree. This discussion begins with three games, illustrated in figure 10.3: game 0, our elementary baseline, and games 1 and 2.

In figure 10.3, players 1 and 2 alternate moves, beginning with player 1, until a payoff bracket is reached. Player 1 receives the first payoff, player 2 the second. In games 0, 1, and 2, a move right at node x_6, in the right branch of the tree, results in the *subgame-perfect noncooperative equilibrium* (SP) outcome. In game 0 the SP payoff is (50,50), in games 1 and 2 it is (40,40). In games 0 and 1 a move left at node x_3 results in a symmetric cooperative (C) outcome in the left branch with a payoff outcome of (50,50). The C outcome requires reciprocal cooperative action by the players because it is not supported by the myopically self-interested game-theoretic principles of backward induction and the choice of dominant outcomes. If player 1 defects on player 2's attempt to achieve C, player 2 can punish such action by moving down at x_5, but this strategy is costly to player 2 and therefore not credible in extensive-form play. Game 2 is formed by interchanging the (50,50) and (60,30) payoffs in the left branch of game 1; consequently in game 2 a move left at x_3 enables player 1 to defect without any risk of punishment.

All three games provide ample scope for player 1s who are moti-

Figure 10.3   Two-Player Decision Tree for Games 0, 1, and 2

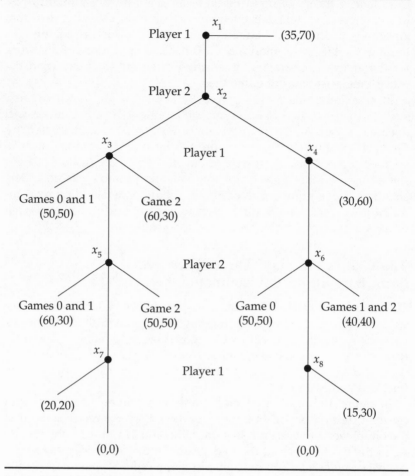

Source: Authors' configuration.

vated by a utility for the other's payoff. Thus if player 1 moves right at node x_1, player 2 receives 70 and player 1 receives 35. Relative to the SP "sure thing" in games 1 and 2, the opportunity cost for player 1 to provide a substantial payoff benefit to player 2 is only 5. If some player 1s care about the payoff to their counterpart player 2s, as implied in the analyses of Gary Bolton (1991), Matthew Rabin (1993), and Bradley Ruffle (1998), then we should observe no shortage of moves right at node x_1.

We originally began our study with game 1 motivated by game-theoretic reasoning. The resulting discrepancy with predictions soon led us to run experiments with game 0 to see whether the anomalous cooperative tendencies in game 1 were simply the "mistakes" of naïve and inexperienced traders or were a consequence of players' sensitivity to the opportunity cost of noncooperation in game 1. Moreover, we soon explored game 2 to determine how important the punishment option in game 1 was for the achievement of cooperation.

The experimental design is shown in table 10.1, which lists the treatment conditions and the number of pairs and trials for each experiment. For example, Random 1 uses game 1 with repeat trials and random pairing and assignment of roles (player 1 or 2) on each trial. Most sessions consisted of twelve subjects (six pairs); in Repeat Single 1, there were sixteen subjects (eight pairs), allowing fifteen trials in which each subject was matched with every other subject exactly once. In all repeat-play protocols (except Repeat Single 1), subjects did not know how many trials would be executed before the endgame. To make this credible, the subjects were recruited for two-hour sessions, and play was stopped after the twentieth trial, which consumed just over one hour of lab time.

In the repeated games 1 and 2 using the same pairs throughout all trials, we identify two equilibriums that are supported by trigger-threat strategies. The outcome (50,50) (on the left in figure 10.3) becomes an equilibrium if on trial t, contingent on defection by player 1 (down at x_3 in Same 1, left at x_3 in Same 2), player 2 moves right at node x_2 on trial $t + 1$, using SP to punish player 1's defection on trial t. Similarly, a move right at node x_1 with outcome (35,70) is a possible equilibrium if player 2 moves left at x_2 and down at x_6, yielding the outcome (15,30), an outcome that player 1 can avoid by moving right at x_1. Note that games 1 and 2 are equivalent with respect to these trigger-threat strategies.

From a game-theoretic perspective it might be thought that game 0 is trivial: SP on the right yields the same payoff vector as C on the left, but SP is an equilibrium whereas C is not. So why is game 0 an important baseline? There are two reasons: it establishes whether players, using their untutored natural instincts, can or cannot discern, and avoid, the strategic instability of C on the left; and it allows comparison with game 1, in which game theory also predicts the SP outcome, but it is payoff inferior to C. We control for distributional considerations by making the payoffs symmetric at both C and SP. Note that the instability in achieving outcome C on the left is based on the game-theoretic assumption of self-interested players and is not unstable if the players each have a utilitarian concern for payoff equity.

Table 10.1 Experimental Design and Treatments

Experiment Name	Game Type	Treatment Conditions Single or Repeat Play	Matching Protocol	Number of Pairs in Each Experiment	Number of Trials in Each Experiment
Random 0	0	Repeat	Random pairing and roles each trial	18	20
Random 1	1	Repeat	Random pairing and roles each trial	24	20
Single 1	1	Single	Random pairing and roles	30	1
Repeat Single 1 Alternating Roles	1	Repeat	Distinct pairing alternating roles each trial	24	15
Single 1 Experienced	1	Single, using experienced *Ss*	Random pairing and roles	17	1
Random 1 Same Roles	1	Repeat	Random pairing same roles each trial	24	20
Same 1	1	Repeat	Same pairing and roles each trial	22	20
Random Private 1	1 with private information	Repeat	Random pairing same roles each trial	24	20
Same Private 1	1 with private information	Repeat	Same pairing same roles each trial	24	20
Single 2	2	Single	Random pairing and roles	26	1
Same 2	2	Repeat	Same pairing and roles each trial	23	20

Source: Authors' compilation.

Player Types and Reciprocity

Suppose we analyze games 1 and 2 from the perspective of the players. Let player 2 have an assessment as to θ_d, the fraction of player 1s in the population sample who would defect if matched with a player 2 who chose to cooperate (move left at x_2) in a single play of game 1. Let player 1 have an assessment as to θ_p, the fraction of the population of player 2s who would cooperate and punish player 1s for defection. These types are relevant only for single play because in any repeat-play protocol any such baseline play propensity is subject to modification as a function of experience.

In game 1, a punishing-type player 2 will move to cooperate if the expected payoff exceeds the SP payoff in the right branch—that is,

$$\pi_p^2 = 50(1 - \theta_d) + 20\theta_d > 40,$$

if $\theta_d < 1/3$. Similarly, a nonpunishing-type player 2 will cooperate if the expected profit is

$$\pi_{\sim p}^2 = 50(1 - \theta_d) + 30\theta_d > 40,$$

or if $\theta_d < 1/2$. This last calculation also applies to game 2 because punishment is not possible.

Note that data from the Single 1 and Single 2 games in table 10.1 allow us to calculate, ex post, the expected payoff to player 2 conditional on choosing to cooperate. The more this payoff exceeds 40, the greater the prospect that cooperation will not deteriorate across repetition in the Repeat Single protocol. This is relevant to the results reported for both games 1 and 2.

In game 1, player 2 will defect if his or her expected profit is

$$\pi^1 = 60(1 - \theta_p) + 20\theta_p > 50,$$

or if $\theta_p < 1/4$. In game 2 the analysis is different because cooperation is possible only when trusting types are matched with trustworthy types. Let player 2 have an assessment as to θ_w, the fraction of player 1s in the population sample who are trustworthy—that is, who practice positive reciprocity in response to cooperators. A reasonable hypothesis is that $\theta_w = 1 - \theta_d$; that is, player 1s in game 1 who would refrain from defecting would be trustworthy in game 2.

Fundamental Principles in
Player Strategic Analysis

We report the data in a series of bar graphs, starting with game 0 and game 1, displaying the percentage of the outcomes by payoff box for all outcomes, as in figure 10.4, and for the individual principal outcomes, as in figures 10.5 to 10.9. More disaggregated versions of some of the repeat-play protocols are reported elsewhere (McCabe, Rassenti, and Smith 1996, 1997; McCabe, Smith, and LePore 2000). The research focused on ten questions related to players' strategic analysis.

Are naïve players capable of elementary strategic analysis? The answer is "yes," and the evidence is displayed in figure 10.4 in the dark shaded bars plotting outcomes for Random 0, by five trial blocks, adjacent to each payoff bracket. During the first five-trial block, more than 81 percent of the pairs end at SP (50,50), on the right (at x_6), and fewer than 9 percent at C, on the left (at x_3). In the remaining blocks about 95 percent of outcomes are at SP, and only 1 percent at C. Consequently, with SP and C equally attractive payoff alternatives, subjects have no difficulty quickly discerning the strategic instability of outcome C, on the left, and the stability of the same payoffs at SP, on the right. These results are contrary to the null alternative that players choose more or less randomly between right- and left-branch play and, by strategic learning through trial and error, gradually respond with moves discovered to be most profitable. The data also contradict the hypothesis that players are not strictly self-interested, for if that were the case, those who begin on the left would not encounter defection, and the frequency of the (50,50) payoff on the left would be maintained or even increase. These results alone, however, could mean merely that players in general are very fast SP game-theoretic learners, but this inference is denied by the results from Random 1.

Does player analysis identify only noncooperative incentives, as predicted by game theory? The answer to this question is "no." In Random 1, the payoff (at x_6) is reduced to (40,40) at SP on the right, while the (50,50) payoff at C on the left (at x_3) is retained. The higher payoffs at C can be achieved through reciprocity: player 2 must move left at x_2, giving up the "sure thing" SP outcome on the right, expressing the implicit intention of reaching C, provided that player 1 does not defect by moving down at x_3. The outcomes by five-trial blocks are indicated by the light shaded bars. Note that 39 percent of player 2s achieve outcome C in the first trial block; this proportion grows to 56 percent in the final trial block (figure 10.4). On the right we observe a corresponding decline in support for the SP outcome. Consequently, players in game 0, whose joint self-interest is served by the SP outcome, behave as if they initially, and correctly, analyze and respond over time to these incentives.

In game 1, however, in which there are gains from reciprocity exchange at C as shared attention increases, an increasing number of players correctly discern this prospect, extend goodwill, overcome the risk of defection, and achieve outcome C. They deliberately play the left branch, for which the reward is higher, and left-branch play stays high and increases. Punishments are less than half of defections in the first five trials, in which lower initial shared attention is forgiven as a mistake (see figure 10.3), but increase substantially in later trials. Thus player 2s are initially forgiving of defections, then increase the punishment rate, leading to increased cooperation, especially in the last five periods.

Do we observe any meaningful support for the hypothesis that subjects associate a positive utility for the payoff of their counterparts? No. Any player 1 is free to move right at node x_1, yielding the outcome (35,70) and a 75 percent increase to player 2 relative to SP at a cost of 12.5 percent to player 1. This move is extremely rare in all three games under all treatments except Same 1 and Same 2. Typical results are those shown in figure 10.4, in which 2.5 percent or less of the outcomes end at (35,70). As reported, and as discussed in earlier work (McCabe, Smith, and LePore 2000), when game 1 or game 2 is repeated with the same pairs, the occurrence of outcome (35,70) increases to 9.8 percent (Same 1) and 8.0 percent (Same 2). This is not attributable to other-regarding utility, however, and is the exception that proves the conclusion.

In these games we observe a corresponding increase in the frequency with which a player 2 moves right at x_2 and then down at x_6, in an obvious attempt to implement a trigger strategy designed to induce player 1 to move right at x_1 on the next trial. This strategy, however, works only with some player 1s, who respond to a move down at x_6 with a move down at x_8. Such an escalation, when employed, tends to neutralize the trigger strategy of player 2. These moves by sophisticated player 2s are interpreted as self-interested attempts to convert (35,70) into a *Nash equilibrium* outcome. The matching protocol for twelve players in Random 1 over twenty trials implies a positive probability for a subject to be rematched with the same person, which fact might conceivably account for the substantial tendency toward cooperation.

Does reciprocity require a positive probability of repeat interaction with the same person, as conjectured by our analysis of the trigger-threat strategy supporting C as an equilibrium? No. This is indicated by the data plotted in figure 10.5 for the three treatments, Single 1,

Figure 10.4 Are Subjects Aware of the Strategic Nature of Their Games?

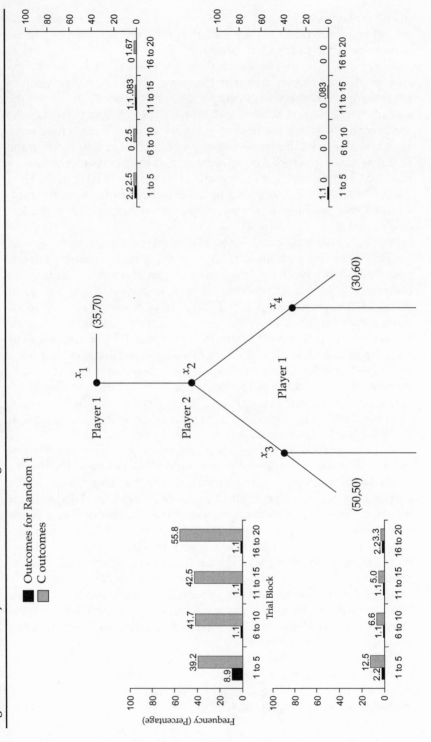

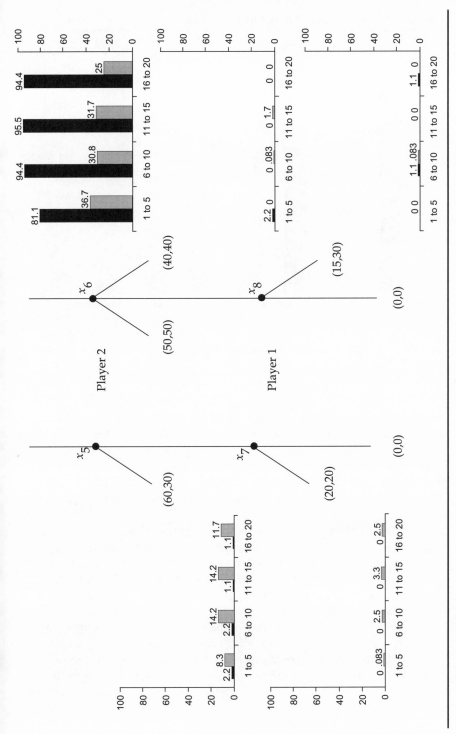

Source: Authors' configuration.

Figure 10.5   Does Experience Affect Reciprocity?

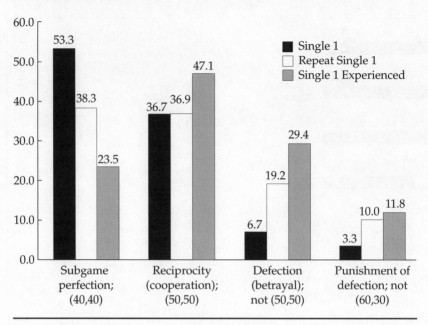

Source: Authors' configuration.

Repeat Single 1, and Single 1 Experienced. In Single 1, thirty pairs with no prior experience in any of these games played game 1 exactly once for twenty times the payoffs in cents shown along the x-axis in figure 10.5. In Repeat Single 1, twenty-four pairs with no prior experience played game 1 for fifteen trials, each trial with a distinct pairing. In Single 1 Experienced, seventeen of these last twenty-four pairs returned to play game 1 once for twenty times the payoffs shown in cents.

The Repeat Single 1 data have been aggregated across all fifteen trials. Note that the frequency of support for C does not deteriorate when we move from Single 1 (36.7 percent) to Repeat Single 1 (36.9 percent)[4] and increases when subjects return from the latter for Single 1 Experienced (47 percent). (Because seventeen of the twenty-four pairs in Repeat Single 1 returned for Single 1 Experienced, we cannot rule out some self-selection—that is, the pairs who do not return may have been more likely to play SP. Even if we assume that they all would have played SP, we still have 33.3 percent [8/24] ending at C.) Both defection and punishment increase with experience; game theory predicts defection but without costly punishment, whereas learning theory postulates that support for C should decline, and that for

Figure 10.6   Does Repeat Interaction Affect Reciprocity?

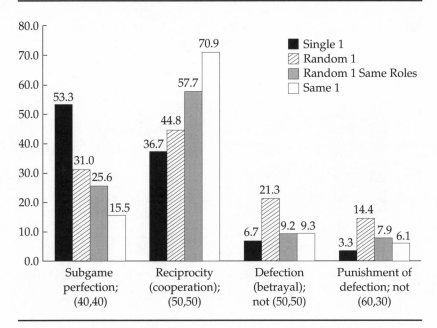

Source: Authors' configuration.

SP should rise, with experience. Theories based on other-regarding preferences predict support for C but fail to predict defection and punishments and their tendencies to increase with experience. Our cognitive theory predicts support for C but also the willingness of some subjects to incur the cost of punishment (negative reciprocity) when there is defection by nonreciprocators on offers to cooperate.

Does reciprocity increase with the probability of repeat interaction with the same person, as implied by our analysis of the repeated game? Yes, reputational effects as predicted by a goodwill-accounting module are alive and well. As we move across the four treatments, Single 1, Random 1, Random 1 Same Roles, and Same 1, the probability of any individual being rematched with the same person increases from zero for Single 1 to unity for Same 1. The bar graphs in figure 10.6 present the outcomes for all four treatments, and we note that the percentage of the observations supporting outcome C increases with the probability of the same pair being rematched: Single 1 (36.7 percent), Random 1 (44.8 percent), Random 1 Same Roles (57.7 percent), and Same 1 (70.9 percent). Concomitantly, there is a decline in support for SP that falls from 53.3 percent in Single 1 to 15.5 percent in Same 1.

Figure 10.7   Does Information Affect Reciprocity?

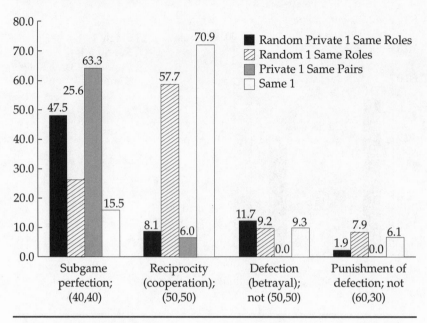

Source: Authors' configuration.

Do players use the payoffs of counterparts in their strategic analysis? Yes, but many players use the payoffs of their counterparts not only to identify SP but also to identify and try to achieve the outcome C through reciprocity, as has already been noted; it is when players know only their own payoffs (private information) that they predominantly converge to the SP outcome. This result extends to two-person extensive-form bargaining behavior—the tendency of markets to converge to competitive equilibriums under private information (Smith 1982). There is an important difference, however: in the market context, in the absence of external effects, noncooperative behavior yields *Pareto-efficient* outcomes, whereas the SP equilibriums in the games studied here are not efficient.

Our view is that in the bargaining environment, intentions cannot be assessed and reciprocity implemented unless the bargainers have complete information on one another's payoffs, a condition that is necessary but not sufficient to personalize the exchange relationship. Hence the prediction that private information will favor SP as compared with complete information. In Figure 10.7 we compare Random Private 1 with Random 1; in both cases players stay in the same roles but are randomly rematched with a counterpart on each trial. Figure

10.7 also presents a comparison between Private 1 Same Pairs and Same 1. In both sets of comparisons we find more SP outcomes under private information—nearly twice as frequent with random pairing, more than four times as frequent with the same pairing, and overwhelmingly more reciprocity with complete information where players can interpret moves in terms of intentions.

As in repetitive-market contexts, noncooperative theory gets easy supporting evidence under private information and little or mixed support under complete information in these two-person exchanges. It is the private-information condition that most naturally, and relevantly, leads to Nash statistical learning.[5] This supports the predictive power of the noncooperative equilibrium of evolutionary models in biology, in which the genotype is not presumed to be omniscient about the payoffs from alternative genetic combinatorial or mutational states.

Are player strategic analysis in game 1 and the frequency of left-game play explained by the availability of the punishment strategy at node x_5? No. Game theory postulates that, because the players are myopically self-interested, and because this is common knowledge (leading to the rationality of dominance and backward induction analysis), cooperative action depends crucially on trigger-threat punishment strategies. Although in game 1, as we have seen, player 2s do not always use the punishment option when responding to defection by player 1s, we cannot rule out the potential importance of the prospect of punishment. Does a player 1 read a left-branch move from player 2 as an implicit threat of punishment, even though in game-theoretic terms any such threat is not credible? None of the data rule out this psychological interpretation.

We confront this issue with game 2, which is derived simply by interchanging the payoffs (50,50) and (60,30) on the left branch of the tree for game 1 in figure 10.3. This makes the outcome (60,30) available to player 1 by moving left at x_3, though cooperation now requires player 1 to move down at x_3. The resulting game 2 is a pure trust game (in single play) because player 1 can defect on an offer to cooperate from player 2 by taking the (60,30) payoff and suffer no possibility of punishment. Hence achieving C depends only on positive reciprocity in the exchange between the two players.

Figure 10.8 presents a comparison of the key outcomes in Single 1 and Single 2. We observe no important change in left-branch play between Single 1 and Single 2 (the slight increase in Single 2 is no more than sampling variation). Reciprocity leading to C, however, declines, as expected, in going from Single 1 to Single 2 as the defection rate increases; that is, not every player 2 who moves left at x_2 is matched with a like-minded person.[6] What is remarkable, however, is

Figure 10.8   Does a Punishment Option Affect Reciprocity?

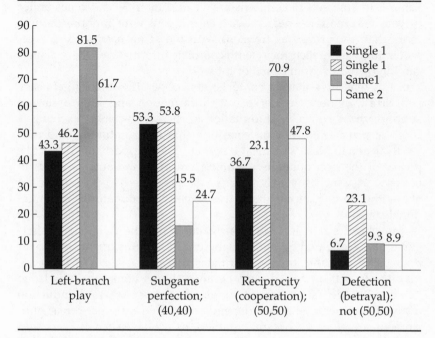

Source: Authors' configuration.

that player 2s largely rely on trust in attempting to achieve C, with no decline in left-branch play in the absence of a punishment option.

Do player 2s in both Same 1 and Same 2 use SP to punish defection on trial t by moving right on trial $t + 1$? No. Figure 10.8 also compares outcomes in Same 1 with those in Same 2. Contrary to the reasoning of repeated-game theory, when we compare the two games under the same partners' condition, left-branch play and the frequency of C outcomes decline considerably in supergame Same 2 relative to Same 1. This is because subjects in Same 1 under repetition do not punish defection on trial t with SP on trial $t + 1$, as implied by the trigger-threat mechanism. Instead, in Same 1 they use the direct and more costly option represented by moving down at x_5.

Table 10.2, which presents the next-period response conditional on the outcome occurring in period t, illustrates this pattern. Observe that in Same 1, 55 percent of the defections are followed by cooperation, whereas in Same 2 fewer than 3 percent of the defections are followed by the C outcome. In Same 2, however, 89 percent of the defections are followed by right-branch play, with a 38 percent transition frequency in Same 1. Thus, given a direct-punishment option,

Table 10.2   Conditional Responses for Same Pairs

Next-Period Move ($t+1$)

Same 1 \ Same 2	Cooperate	Defect	Right	Total
Cooperate	194 (.942) / 248 (.844)	6 (.029) / 26 (.088)	6 (.029) / 20 (.068)	206 / 294
Defect	1 (.029) / 22 (.55)	3 (.086) / 3 (.075)	31 (.886) / 15 (.375)	35 / 40
Right	15 (.107) / 32 (.432)	22 (.157) / 10 (.135)	103 (.736) / 32 (.432)	140 / 74
Total	31 / 302	210 / 39	140 / 67	381 / 408

(Row label: Base-Period Move (t). In each cell the upper-right value is the Same 2 count and the lower-left value is the Same 1 count.)

Source: Authors' compilation.
Note: Each entry lists the number of pairs choosing the row play on trial t followed by the column play on trial $t + 1$ for the Same 1 and Same 2 treatments. Fractions are given in parentheses.

players predominately use it, and this leads to a more rapid buildup of the frequency of cooperation over time. But is right play in Same 2 more likely to be followed by cooperation? No. Right play is four times more likely to be followed by C in Same 1 as in Same 2, in which right play is the overwhelming response to right play. In Same 2, players tend to get stuck on the right, although in the last five trials Same 1 and Same 2 achieve nearly identically high-branch conditional cooperation rates: 91.4 percent and 91.0 percent respectively (see Mc-Cabe, Rassenti, and Smith 1996, 13426–27).

Repeated-game analysis implies that the patterns of reputational achievement in Same 1 and Same 2 are identical because in both games the low-cost-defection punishment strategy is to respond with SP on the next trial. Behaviorally, however, the direct-punishment option in Same 1 is deployed, enabling the C outcome to be achieved more decisively than in Same 2. Consequently, although the "folk-theorem" prediction is satisfied—repetition favors cooperation—the dynamics of the process is contrary to the logic of repeated-game analysis.

In games 1 and 2, do player 2s who move right at x_2 for the SP outcome and player 1s who defect on attempts by player 2s to coop-

Table 10.3   Conditional Average Payoffs, by Treatment

Experimental Treatment	Expected Profit for Player 2s Who Move Left at x_2	Expected Profit for Player 1s Who Defect on Cooperation
Random 0	37.0	40.0
Random 1	40.7	30.8
Single 1	46.2	40.0
Repeat Single 1	41.5	39.1
Single 1 Experience	40.7	44.0
Random 1 Same Roles	45.8	23.6
Same 1	46.6	31.2
Random Private 1	37.1	53.2
Same Private 1	35.2	59.0
Single 2	40.0	—
Same 2	46.9	—

Source: Authors' compilation.

erate achieve higher expected payoffs than if they did not so move, as implied by game-theoretic analysis? No. As indicated in table 10.3, under all complete-payoff-information treatments with games 1 and 2, player 2s who move left at x_2 do not earn expected profits less than the 40 at SP, and player 1s who forgo the 50 at C by defecting uniformly earn less than the 50 they give up. On average, then, cooperation pays and defection does not under all complete-information treatments. Under private information, left-branch play is less profitable than the SP payoff of 40, and defection earns a return in excess of 50. The players cannot read intentions, they cannot do strategic analysis, and they do resort to effective statistical learning.

Do players use extensive-form move information in their strategic analysis? Specifically, do cooperative outcomes diverge when comparing the extensive and "equivalent" normal forms of a game? Yes. Move information is important because it provides information on the characteristics of a player's counterpart in two-person interactions. It allows greater scope for shared attention, cheater detection and goodwill accounting than the normal form. In traditional game-theoretic analysis, which hypothesizes common knowledge that agents are self-interested, there is nothing to be learned from move information that is not already known. However, this hypothesis, if entertained by a player 1, is seen by the player to be falsified the moment player 2 moves left at x_2. Such a move implies the selection of a dominated strategy and must mean that player 2 is attempting to achieve C. The normal form clouds the process of interpreting such move information.

Figure 10.9   Does Sequential Play Affect Reciprocity?

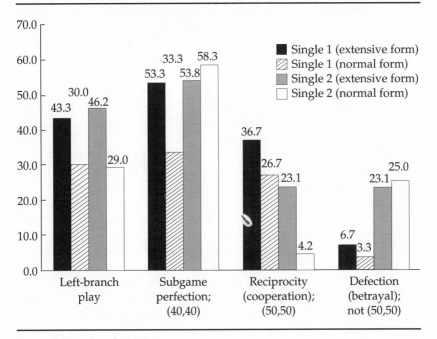

Source: Authors' configuration.
Note: Compares extensive and normal focus of games 1 and 2 under single-play proto-col.

Figure 10.9 presents a comparison of the extensive and correspond-ing normal forms of games 1 and 2 under the single-play protocol. We note first that left-branch play declines from 43.3 percent in extensive-form Single 1 to 30 percent in normal-form Single 1 and from 46.2 percent in extensive-form Single 2 to 29 percent in normal-form Sin-gle 2. Cooperation similarly declines from 36.7 percent to 26.7 percent in game 1 and from 23.1 percent to only 4.2 percent in game 2.[7]

Conclusions

Game theory accounts for strong observed support for the subgame-perfect noncooperative outcome under complete information condi-tional on play in the SP (right) branch of the tree, but it cannot ac-count for the conditional itself. As predicted by repeated-game theory, cooperation increases with the probability that subjects will be re-matched with the same counterpart; but it cannot account for the pat-tern of defection and punishment across the various treatments, nor can it account for differences in behavior between the trust and punishment versions of the game when repeated with the same pairs. Subgame-perfect theory receives its strongest support under private information, where Nash statistical learning most naturally applies.

Departures from game-theoretic behavior by subject players are rational in the sense that on average such moves earn players more money: cooperation pays and defection does not pay. A weakness of the game-theoretic model is that it postulates only one player type—the player who chooses only dominant strategies and uses only backward induction analysis—an assumption far too strong to account for the spectrum of subjects' behavior. An attempt to correct these weaknesses has been explored using a pretest—the Machiavellian test—to identify players likely to exhibit high, intermediate, or low propensities to defect on offers of positive reciprocity in trust games (Gunnthorsdottir, McCabe, and Smith 2002).

Our data fail to support the proposition that simple interpersonal utility models based on altruism or envy (or both) can be used to modify the standard game-theoretic model adequately, although we do not rule out the possibility that such models can be useful. Our own preference, however, is to build on the psychology of "mind reading"—intentionality defection, a shared-attention mechanism, and a theory-of-mind module—within the framework of reputation formation in the enlightened self-interest.

Support by a National Science Foundation grant, and its renewal under a special creativity competition, is gratefully acknowledged.

Notes

1. Similarly, Holly Ameden and her colleagues (1998) hypothesize that the decline in contributions over time in voluntary-contribution-mechanism games can be attributed to the preassignment of individuals to groups consisting of incompatible heterogeneity of types. They report that when subjects are sorted into groups (without informing subjects of the group selection criteria) with highest contributors forming the first group, next higher the second, and so on, they find significantly higher, often sustainable, contribution levels compared with a random-matching baseline. There is one exception: when the marginal per capital return (MPCR) is .75, random and sorted contributions are the same. When the MPCR is 0.75, however, free riding has a much weakened impact on the subjective sense of reciprocity felt by those trying to construct a cooperative solution. This case is the exception that proves the principle of reciprocity seeking.

2. For an evolutionary model of a population containing both self-interested and reciprocator utilitarian types, see Sethi and Somanathan (1998).

3. See James Coleman's (1990) descriptions of the many social arrangements designed to extend personal trade beyond that of barter.

4. Across the three five-trial blocks of Repeat Single 1, node-conditional cooperation rises gradually (63, 65, and 68 percent); punishment declines from the first to the second five-trial block (from 52 to 40 percent), then increases in the final five-trial block (to 62 percent). See McCabe, Rassenti, and Smith (1996, 13426, table 5).

5. In earlier work (McCabe, Rassenti, and Smith 1997), in which we examine a second, more demanding, private-information environment, the results are robust to at least one variation on the payoff conditions. It should be possible, we think, to find private payoff environments in which learning to play SP would be still more difficult and would perhaps fail.

6. See McCabe, Rassenti, and Smith (1996, 13427–28 and table 10), for specific data on this issue. The increased defection rate in Single 2 suggests that cooperation would decline when repeated with distinct pairing. This is confirmed in Burnham, McCabe, and Smith (2000).

7. For a more complete discussion, hypothesis tests, and a comparison of game forms in Same 1 and Same 2, see McCabe, Smith, and LePore (2000).

References

Ameden, Holly, Anna Gunnthorsdottir, Daniel Houser, and Kevin McCabe. 1998. "A Minimal Property Right System for the Sustainable Provision of Public Good." Unpublished paper. University of California, Berkeley.

Anderson, Simon, Jacob Goeree, and Charles Holt. 1998. "Rent Seeking with Bounded Rationality: An Analysis of the All-Pay Auction." *Journal of Political Economy* 106(4): 828–53.

Baron-Cohen, Simon. 1995. *Mindblindness: An Essay on Autism and Theory of the Mind.* Cambridge, Mass.: MIT Press.

Bolton, Gary E. 1991. "A Comparative Model of Bargaining: Theory and Evidence." *American Economic Review* 81(5): 1096–1136.

Burnham, Terence, Kevin McCabe, and Vernon Smith. 2000. "Friend-or-Foe Intentionality Priming in an Extensive-Form Trust Game." *Journal of Economic Behavior and Organizations* 43: 57–73.

Camerer, Colin, and Robin Hogarth. 1997. "The Effect of Financial Incentives on Performance in Experiments: A Review and Capital-Labor Theory." Working paper. Pasadena, Calif.: California Institute of Technology, Division of Humanities and Social Sciences.

Coleman, James. 1990. *Foundations of Social Theory.* Cambridge, Mass.: Harvard University Press.

Cosmides, Leda. 1989. "The Logic of Social Exchange: Has Natural Selection Shaped How Humans Reason? Studies with the Wason Selection Task." *Cognition* 31(3): 187–277.

Cosmides, Leda, and John Tooby. 1992. "Cognitive Adaptations for Social Exchange." In *The Adapted Mind*, edited by John Barkow, Leda Cosmides, and John Tooby. New York: Oxford University Press.

Croson, Rachel. 1998. "Theories of Altruism and Reciprocity: Evidence from Linear Public Good Games." Unpublished paper. University of Pennsylvania, Wharton School, Department of Operations and Information Management.

de Waal, Frans. 1996. *Good Natured*. Cambridge, Mass.: Harvard University Press.

———. 1997. "The Chimpanzee's Service Economy: Food for Grooming." *Evolution and Human Behavior* 18(6): 375–86.

Frith, Uta. 1989. *Autism: Explaining the Enigma*. Oxford: Blackwell.

Gintis, Herbert, and Paul Romer. 1998. "The Human Side of Economic Analysis: Economic Environments and the Evolution of Norms and Preferences." Working paper. University of Massachusetts, Department of Economics.

Gouldner, Alvin. 1960. "The Norm of Reciprocity: A Preliminary Statement." *American Sociological Review* 25: 161–78.

Gunnthorsdottir, Anna, Kevin McCabe, and Vernon Smith. 2002. "Using the Machiavellian Instrument to Predict Trustworthiness in a Bargaining Game." *Journal of Economic Psychology* 23: 49–66.

Güth, Werner, Rolf Schmittberger, and Bernd Schwarze. 1982. "An Experimental Analysis of Ultimatum Bargaining." *Journal of Economic Behavior and Organization* 3(4): 367–88.

Hoffman, Elizabeth, Kevin McCabe, and Vernon Smith. 1998. "Behavioral Foundations of Reciprocity: Experimental Economics and Evolutionary Psychology." *Economic Inquiry* 36(3): 335–52.

Isaac, R. Mark, and James Walker. 1988. "Communication and Free-Riding Behavior: The Voluntary Contributions Mechanism." *Economic Inquiry* 26(4): 585–608.

Leslie, Alan M. 1987. "Pretence and Representation: The Origins of 'Theory of Mind.'" *Psychological Review* 94(4): 412–26.

McCabe, Kevin, Stephen Rassenti, and Vernon Smith. 1996. "Game Theory and Reciprocity in Some Extensive-Form Bargaining." *Proceedings of the National Academy of Sciences* 93(23): 13421–28.

———. 1997. "Reciprocity, Trust, and Payoff Privacy in Extensive-Form Bargaining." *Games and Economic Behavior* 24(1–2): 10–24.

McCabe, Kevin, and Vernon Smith. 2000. "A Two-person Trust Game Played by Naïve and Sophisticated Subjects." *Proceedings of the National Academy of Sciences* 97(9): 3777–81.

McCabe, Kevin, Vernon Smith, and Michael LePore. 2000. "Intentionality Detection and Mindreading: Why Does Game Form Matter?" *Proceedings of the National Academy of Sciences* 97(8): 4404–09.

McKelvey, Richard, and Thomas Palfrey. 1995. "Quantal Response Equilibria for Normal-Form Games." *Games and Economic Behavior* 10(1): 6–38.

Rabin, Matthew. 1993. "Incorporating Fairness into Game Theory and Economics." *American Economics Review* 83(5): 1281–1302.

Roth, Alvin, and Ido Erev. 1995. "Learning in Extensive-Form Games: Experimental Data and Simple Dynamic Models in the Intermediate Term." *Games and Economic Behavior* 8(1): 164–212.

Roth, Alvin, Vesna Prasnikar, Masahiro Okuno-Fujiwana, and Shmuel Zamir. 1991. "Bargaining and Market Behavior in Jerusalem, Ljubljana, Pittsburgh, and Tokyo: An Experimental Study." *American Economic Review* 81(5): 1068–95.

Ruffle, Bradley J. 1998. "More Is Better, but Fair Is Fair: Tipping in Dictator and Ultimatum Games." *Games and Economic Behavior* 23(2): 247–65.

Schelling, Thomas. 1960. *The Strategy of Conflict.* Cambridge, Mass.: Harvard University Press.

Sethi, Rajiv, and E. Somanathan. 1998. "Preference Evolution and Reciprocity." Paper presented at the Conference on Modeling Strong Reciprocity. University of Massachusetts, Amherst (October 16–18, 1998).

Siegel, Sidney. 1959. "Theoretical Models of Choice and Strategy Behavior." *Psychometrika* 24(4): 305–16.

Siegel, Sidney, and Lawrence Fouraker. 1960. *Bargaining and Group Decision Making.* New York: McGraw-Hill.

Simon, Herbert. 1956. "A Comparison of Game Theory and Learning Theory." *Psychometrika* 21(September): 267–72.

Smith, Vernon. 1965. "Experimental Auction Markets and the Walrasian Hypothesis." *Journal of Political Economy* 73(4): 387–93.

———. 1982. "Microeconomics Systems As an Experimental Science." *American Economic Review* 72(8): 923–55.

———. 1998. "The Two Faces of Adam Smith." *Southern Economic Journal* 65(1): 1–19.

Smith, Vernon, and James Walker. 1993. "Monetary Rewards and Decision Costs in Experimental Economics." *Economic Inquiry* 31(2): 245–61.

Chapter 11

Trust in Children

WILLIAM T. HARBAUGH, KATE KRAUSE,
STEVEN G. LIDAY JR., AND LISE VESTERLUND

M ANY TRADE relationships are not covered by complete contracts. Although the involved parties may prefer a legally
binding agreement, it is often too costly to construct a contract that fully accounts for the possible contingencies of the relationship. Absent such contracts, otherwise advantageous trades may be
expected to fail as the parties each choose their payoff-maximizing
actions.

Many real-world examples demonstrate that this need not be the
case. In particular, there is substantial evidence that we instead rely
on a set of social contracts, whereby we trust that others will fulfill
their part of a nonbinding agreement and abide by such agreements
when they trust us to do so. Even when interacting with complete
strangers, we often work under the assumption that they can be
trusted. When traveling we encounter courteous cab drivers, waiters,
and porters who all believe, despite the *one-shot* interaction of our
relationship, that we will reward good service with a good tip. When
making one-time purchases, we trust that the conditions of delivery
will be acceptable. When selling fruit from an unattended road stand,
the farmer trusts that customers will pay for the produce.[1] By trusting
and rewarding trust we are able to sustain a society that is superior to
what we could expect absent substantial contractual agreements.

Despite their obvious advantages, trust and trustworthy behavior
are puzzling phenomena. In trusting others, self-interested people
purposefully put themselves in situations in which other self-interested
people can take advantage of them, and when rewarding trust we
choose costly actions that merely improve the well-being of others.

This raises the question of how we acquire these trusting behaviors. If their presence allows us to sustain a superior society, then it may be argued that these traits are an outcome of evolution. Perhaps we are genetically coded to be trusting and trustworthy. The substantial degree of heterogeneity in trust across both countries and individuals makes it questionable that genetic coding alone can explain these behaviors.[2]

Perhaps trust and the rewarding of trust are behaviors that develop over time. Children may learn from the innumerable lectures parents give about whom to trust, when to trust them, how far to trust, and how to respond when someone trusts them. Even if we take the skeptical view that these lectures are just talk, it is still possible that children learn from the many examples that parents set for their children in exhibiting trusting and trustworthy behavior. If these traits are developed over time, then how do they affect our behavior? Do we become more or less trusting as we get older? Do the conditions under which we trust become more refined with age? To answer these questions this chapter investigates trusting behavior among children.

We focus on trusting behaviors in children in the belief that this will provide insight into when and how certain aspects of trust behavior are formed. We report the results of an economic experiment that allows us to look at changes in these behaviors with the age of both the "truster" and the "trustee," and we also consider the effects of children's individual characteristics on trusting behavior. Because elements of trust are cognitively complex, involving reading and interpreting subtle nuances in the behavior of others as well as the ability to infer others' intentions and motivations, we might expect to find differences among young children, teenagers, and adults in their responses to trust dilemmas.

This research is part of a new effort to use economic methods and models to explore the behavior of children. In earlier work (Harbaugh, Krause, and Berry 2001) we show that by about age eleven, children's consumption choices are generally consistent with rational behavior. Elsewhere (Harbaugh, Krause, and Vesterlund 2001), we find that even seven-year-old children tend to value goods they own more than those they do not. We take this as evidence that children exhibit an endowment effect similar to that found in adults. In more complex economic interactions, we have found that bargaining ability among children is well developed at a surprisingly young age. By the age of seven, children appear to correctly consider the probability of rejection in bargaining games (Harbaugh, Krause, and Liday 2001). In situations involving choice under risk, we have found that children's choices are only slightly less consistent across choices than are undergraduates' choices; their behavior can be captured by variants of the same sorts of subjective expected probability models that are commonly used for adults (Harbaugh, Krause, and Vesterlund 2002).

On the other hand, our investigation into children's altruism has revealed some systematic differences between children's and adults' decisions. In one-shot *dictator games*, in which one player is asked to decide how much of a pie to give to an anonymous other player, the youngest children tend to make considerably smaller transfers than do older children and adults (Harbaugh, Krause, and Liday 2001). We find age differences in behavior across rounds in repeated linear *public-goods games*, in which individuals in a group must each decide whether to contribute to a *public good* and thereby sacrifice private payoffs for the benefit of the other group members (Harbaugh and Krause 2000). In multiple-round experiments, adults typically contribute less to the public good in the later rounds, possibly because they learn to free ride. On average, the six- to twelve-year-old children in our study actually contributed more to the public good in later rounds. However, the oldest among them behaved more like adults: participants who were eleven-and-a-half and older contributed less to the public good in the later rounds of the experiment. Although the public-good experiments were not designed to investigate trust, one plausible explanation for this result is that the younger children came to trust their (anonymous) group mates, whereas the older children realized either that their own trust could be violated or that they themselves could exploit others' trust in later rounds. This finding may be seen as evidence that trusting and trustworthy behaviors develop with age.

Economics and Trust: Competing Explanations

We use the trust game devised by David Kreps (1990) to examine trust in children. Chapter 1 of this volume describes the game and shows that if both participants of this game aim to maximize their monetary payoff then the standard *subgame-perfect-equilibrium* prediction is simply zero passed, zero returned. The initial experimental study of the trust game by Joyce Berg, John Dickhaut, and Kevin McCabe (1995) demonstrates the inadequacy of this prediction. Their study, as well as the many replications thereof, shows that most participants of the game display trust and trustworthiness. There is, however, substantial variance in the amounts that trusters allocate to trustees, and it is clear that they do not follow a single maximizing strategy. One possible explanation is that trusters are uncertain as to which strategy to use (Koford 2001). This is consistent with psychological research demonstrating that people behave with a degree of randomness when facing an uncertain or risky situation (for example, Herrnstein 1997).

Observing behavior inconsistent with the selfish equilibrium prediction is not unique to the trust game. Many experiments have revealed behaviors that suggest that participants are not only concerned for their own monetary payoff but also have a preference for the payoffs of others. To capture these behaviors, models of other-regarding preferences have been developed. These models have traditionally been classified as either outcome based or intention based. A common element of outcome-based models is that players are assumed to care about their own monetary payoff as well as their relative share of the total payoff.[3] Typically, the models assume that individuals have an inherent preference for an equal split of the overall payoff but that there is a trade-off between this preference and their own monetary payoff. Thus, holding relative payoffs constant, the individual prefers the largest possible monetary payoff, and, holding the monetary payoff constant, the individual prefers a more equal division.

Intention-based models argue, instead, that the preference for someone else's payoff depends on the intentions of this individual (see Rabin 1993, Dufwenberg and Kirchsteiger 1998, Falk and Fischbacher 1998, and Charness and Rabin 2001). Individuals may benefit from increasing the payoff of someone who is kind but may benefit from decreasing the payoff of someone who is unkind. Hence an intentionally kind act may be rewarded and an unkind act punished. Crucial for intention-based models is that they rely on individuals' attributing intentions to others. To determine whether behavior in the trust game is consistent with the outcome- or intention-based models, Kevin McCabe, Vernon Smith, and Michael LePore (2000) examine behaviors in the two simple two-person games illustrated in figure 11.1. They refer to these two games as the voluntary and involuntary trust games. In the voluntary trust game, player 1 can elect to stop the game, yielding payoffs of $20 for each player, or to pass control of the game to player 2. Player 2 can then either take $30, leaving $15 for player 1, or choose a payoff of $25 for each. Despite its one-shot nature this game can be seen as measuring trust and trustworthiness because player 1, in passing control to player 2, entrusts player 2 to determine his or her final endowment. The involuntary trust game is identical to the voluntary one except that player 1 does not have the option of stopping before player 2 chooses.

Player 2 faces exactly the same options (and absolute and relative payoffs) in the two variations of the trust game. Thus, if outcome-based models are accurate, there should be no difference in decisions by player 2 across treatments. However, if intention-based models are

Figure 11.1   A Test for Intention-Based Models

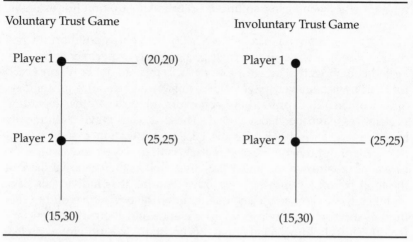

Source: Authors' configuration.

correct, we should find that player 2 is more likely to choose the co-operative outcome in the voluntary trust game than in the involun-tary one. The reason is that in the voluntary game player 1's decision to continue the game may be seen as an intentionally kind action. Consistent with the intention-based models but not the outcome-based ones, McCabe, Smith, and Michael LePore (2000) find that player 2s are much more likely to choose the cooperative outcome in the voluntary game.[4]

Harold D. Fishbein and Nancy K. Kaminski (1985) are among the few researchers to use salient payoffs in investigating the develop-ment of trust and reciprocity in children. Their study examines how the perceived motivations behind a kind act affect *reciprocal altruism* in children. In these experiments, six-, eight-, and eleven-year-olds were assigned partners in same-age, same-sex pairs. In some rounds player 1 was given the choice between a competitive move that would harm the other child and a cooperative move. In a subset of those rounds the experimenters openly instructed player 2 to move in a cooperative fashion, so that player 1 was aware that a cooperative move had been instructed. The authors compared the responses of non-confederate participants to this instructed move with responses when the confederate child appeared to cooperate voluntarily. The results did not "support the view that children's perceived motivation of the donor influenced . . . reciprocity" (Fishbein and Kaminski 1985, 397). This suggests that intention-based models may fail in predicting reciprocal behavior in children. Fishbein and Kaminski find no gender effects or age differences. This may be attributable to the limited age range that they examine or to the confounding factors involved when studying same-age and same-sex interactions.

Experiment Procedure and Participants

Although the experimental protocols were very different, a comparison of Berg, Dickhaut, and McCabe (2000) results with those of Fishbein and Kaminski suggests that children might approach trust tasks differently from adults. This suggests that trust or trustworthy behavior may develop over time, and thus models of evolution may fail in fully capturing these traits. To investigate the possibility that trust develops with age, we tested trust and reciprocity behavior in children using a modified version of Berg, Dickhaut, and McCabe's (1995) no-social-history, one-shot trust game.[5]

In our experiment, anonymous participants were matched in pairs. One person in the pair was assigned the role of truster, the other the role of trustee. For each decision each participant was given an endowment of four tokens. There were two stages to the task. At the first stage the truster decided how many, if any, of the four tokens to pass to the trustee in the pair. Every token passed to a trustee tripled in value. At the second stage the trustee was asked how many, if any, of his or her total tokens he or she would want to pass back to the truster. Each token sacrificed by the trustee increased the truster's payoff by one token.

We used the so-called strategy method to elicit the trustee's actual strategy. That is, rather than asking a trustee to respond to the amount actually passed by the truster, we did not reveal the amount passed and instead asked that the trustee decide how much he or she would pass if the initial transfer had been respectively $0, $1, $2, $3, and $4. We explained that we would match these responses with the actual transfer from the truster and that the payoff to each would then be tabulated.[6]

A total of 153 students in the Coquille, Oregon, public schools participated. Coquille is a rural logging town with an area population of approximately ten thousand people. Because school attendance by children is close to universal, conducting experiments in schools gives us a group of participants that is representative of the local population as a whole. On the other hand, the town is less diverse demographically than the country as a whole. The experiments were conducted in a total of eight public school classrooms, two each from the third, sixth, ninth, and twelfth grades. Children in these classes are typically aged eight, eleven, fourteen, and seventeen, respectively.

Within each grade, the students in one class were trusters, and those in the other class were the trustees.

One option in designing the experiment was to maintain the approach used in experiments in which individuals typically are paired with equals (generally, college students with college students). As we were interested in the general development of trust, we decided instead to ask each truster to make five separate transfer decisions—one to an anonymous trustee in each of the four grades including his or her own and one with an adult.[7] Similarly, the trustee was asked to make five separate transfer decisions with a truster from each of the five age groups. Participants were paid for the tokens earned in each of the five decisions. The benefit of this approach is that it allows us to make comparisons across grades.

In addition to controlling for the grade of the participants, we also included controls for a number of other individual characteristics. Experimental work by economists has generally been motivated by a desire to find results that are common to the experimental participants and to the general population. Relatively little effort has been made to explain the variation found in behaviors. The exceptions have looked at cross-cultural differences in bargaining (Roth et al. 1991), differences in altruism by gender (Andreoni and Vesterlund 2001), and the potential influence of training in economics on cooperative behaviors (Frank, Gilovich, and Regan 1996). To control more carefully for the development of economic behaviors, we have included a larger range of individual characteristics than is true in most economic experiments.[8]

Table 11.1 summarizes the individual characteristics of the trusters and trustees in this study. "Boy" is an indicator variable equal to 1 if the participant is a boy. Because birth order and height have been identified as statistically significant explanatory variables in previous studies of children's economic behavior, we included these measures in this study as well. Although there is no clear theoretical explanation for their relation to economic behavior, both are closely related to social development and status. "Height" is the participant's height in inches. "Birth order" denotes the participant's rank among his or her siblings, the oldest siblings in a family being given a value of 1. Values for this variable range from 1 to 5.

We also included a survey measure of trust. After completing the trust experiment but before payments were calculated, each participant responded to the following question: "Overall, can you trust most people?" Responses to this question were used to test consistency between experiment behavior and survey responses. "Survey trust" is an indicator for the participants' response to the question, and a response of "yes" equals 1.

Table 11.1   Survey Measures of Individual Characteristics

Category and Grade	Boy	Height	Birth Order	Survey Trust	Truster Risk
Trusters					
Third	0.42	51.7	1.8	0.65	2.27
Sixth	0.55	62.2	2.1	0.55	3.35
Ninth	0.35	65.8	2.6	0.30	3.45
Twelfth	0.44	67.3	1.5	0.38	3.06
Average	0.44	60.7	2.0	0.49	2.98
Trustees					
Third	0.29	55.3	2.3	0.67	
Sixth	0.48	59.3	2.2	0.71	
Ninth	0.87	67.7	2.0	0.47	
Twelfth	0.73	68.0	1.5	0.36	
Average	0.54	61.1	2.1	0.59	

Source: Authors' compilation.

Trusting another person entails the risk of defection. All else being equal we may expect more risk-averse individuals to be less likely to trust. To control for heterogeneity in risk attitudes we therefore asked trusters to complete a risk task after completing the trust game.[9] For this task, each truster was given five tokens and shown a spinner indicating a 60 percent chance of doubling the amount staked and a 40 percent chance of losing the amount staked. Trusters were asked to choose how many tokens they wished to stake on the spinner and how many they wished to keep. We use the number of tokens staked on the spinner as a measure of preference for risk.[10] The "truster risk" variable is the number of tokens that the truster staked in this risk experiment. This variable ranged from 0 to 5.

Although we use the terms "trustee," "truster," and "partners" in describing the experiment, our protocol used more neutral terminology: "first mover," and "second mover," and "person you are matched with." Both types of participants were asked how many tokens they wanted to "pass," and the word "trust" was never used in the protocol. The experiments were conducted over a three-day period: the truster session was conducted on the first day, the trustee session on the second day, and participants were paid on the last day. Third-graders used their accumulated tokens to purchase items from our experiment store. The experiment store stocks toys, school and art supplies, and games. Items are priced in tokens, using an exchange rate of about twenty-five cents per token. We have found that, to young children, cash is not as salient as the opportunity to immediately "purchase" items because children cannot independently go to a retail store to convert cash into goods of their own choosing. The experiment store makes the payoffs immediate and salient for these children. The children in sixth, ninth, and twelfth grade were paid a quarter for each token earned.

Our protocol differs in five ways from that used by Berg, Dickhaut, and McCabe. First, we use the strategy method, rather than showing each trustee the actual decision of the truster with whom they are matched. Second, each player is matched with multiple partners (one from each grade). Third, our experiment was blind, not double blind; that is, though the participants could not identify the person with whom they were matched, the experimenter could match the decisions to the individual making them. Fourth, the trustees could transfer any portion of their endowment and were not restricted to making transfers from the amount received from the trusters.[11] Finally, all the participants in this study had to wait a day or two for their payoffs, instead of receiving them immediately. These differences should be kept in mind when comparing our results with those of other experimenters.

Results

We begin by considering the decisions of the trusters and then turn to the trustees' responses. Table 11.2 summarizes the average passes from trusters, by grade of the truster and grade of the trustee. As has been found in the experiments on adults, the game-theoretic predictions for selfish preferences are not supported by our data. Average proposals from every grade and to every grade are always significantly different from zero. (Using one-sided t-tests, the highest p value is 0.002.) Of the 410 passing decisions that are made, only 112 (27 percent) were passes of zero tokens. Only five children out of eighty-two (6 percent) passed zero to every partner.

In contrast with the common perception, we do not find that young children are more trusting than older ones. In fact, the third-graders in our study passed the smallest number of tokens. On average, children make larger transfers to older trustees, and conditional on grade it appears that they are less trusting of members of their own cohort than those of older cohorts.

Surprisingly, the children and teenagers in this study appear to be less trusting than were the adults in the Berg, Dickhaut, and McCabe (1995) no-history treatment. In terms of percentage of endowment, the third-, sixth-, and twelfth-graders in our study all passed significantly fewer tokens (27, 30, and 28 percent of their endowments respectively) than did the no-history subjects in the Berg, Dickhaut, and

Table 11.2   Mean Passes from Truster to Trustee, by Grade of Truster and Grade of Trustee

Grade of Truster	Grade of Trustee					
	Third	Sixth	Ninth	Twelfth	Adults	Average
Third	0.73	1.19	1.23	1.31	1.04	1.10
	(1.15)	(1.13)	(1.21)	(1.41)	(1.25)	(1.23)
Sixth	1.25	1.10	1.25	1.15	1.35	1.22
	(0.91)	(0.85)	(0.91)	(0.88)	(0.93)	(0.88)
Ninth	1.85	1.85	1.65	1.95	2.05	1.87
	(1.39)	(1.14)	(1.18)	(1.32)	(1.19)	(1.23)
Twelfth	1.25	0.88	1.00	1.06	1.38	1.11
	(1.06)	(0.62)	(1.21)	(1.00)	(1.20)	(1.03)
Average	1.23	1.27	1.29	1.38	1.43	1.32
	(1.20)	(1.03)	(1.14)	(1.22)	(1.20)	(0.76)

Source: Authors' compilation.
Note: Maximum possible pass is four tokens. Standard deviations in parentheses.

McCabe study (52 percent). Only the ninth-graders passed almost the same percentage of tokens as did the adults (47 percent).[12] We do not find monotonic changes in passes across ages. Average passes increase with age between the third and ninth grades, but twelfth-graders, on average, pass approximately the same number of tokens as third-graders.

The differences between our results and those found by Berg, Dickhaut, and McCabe (1995) may be attributable to the differences in our protocol or to the fact that our subject pool is not selected on college attendance. The larger transfers to older trustees suggest that the difference arises from the much younger pool of trustees with whom our participants are matched. Future work will more carefully examine these possibilities. At the moment we note that, with the exception of ninth-graders, there is practically no difference in passes between ages eight and seventeen. This suggests that the degree to which we trust others is relatively unaffected by age. To examine more carefully the effect of age and to isolate the effects of individual variables on the pass amount, we estimated ordinary least squares panel regressions with random effects to account for the correlation of proposals across participants. Of course, these regressions assume that age and the other continuous variables have linear effects on behavior.

Table 11.3 provides the coefficients and t-statistics for seven variables and five (overlapping) sets of participants. We estimated separate models for each grade and found similar results for the sixth-, ninth-, and twelfth-graders. However, the results for the third-graders

Table 11.3   Regression Results for Passes by Trusters

Variable	All Participants	Third-Graders Only	Sixth-, Ninth-, and Twelfth-Graders	Boys Only	Girls Only
TrusteeGrade	0.018	0.029	0.013	0.01	0.024
	(1.46)	(1.27)	(0.88)	(0.51)	(1.57)
Boy	0.13	0.75**	−0.20	—	—
	(0.75)	(3.04)	(−0.89)	—	—
SurveyTrust	−0.29*	−0.319	−0.38**	−0.35	−0.306*
	(−1.81)	(−1.38)	(−1.98)	(−1.18)	(−1.79)
TrusterAge	0.01	−0.693**	−0.009	−0.037	0.07**
	(0.50)	(−2.62)	(−0.25)	(−0.78)	(2.60)
BirthOrder	0.16**	0.40**	0.10	0.03	0.22**
	(2.26)	(3.64)	(1.21)	(0.23)	(3.15)
TrusterRisk	0.06	−0.03	0.10	0.00	0.04
	(1.10)	(−0.58)	(1.37)	(0.00)	(0.80)
RelativeHeight	2.76*	9.38**	2.71	2.04	5.35**
	(1.91)	(4.24)	(1.41)	(0.81)	(3.04)
N	82	26	56	36	46

Source: Authors' compilation.
Note: * denotes significance at $p \leq 0.10$; **at $p \leq 0.05$. Adjusted t-statistics in parentheses.

were quite different. Therefore, we report pooled results for the sixth-through twelfth-graders but report results for the third-graders separately. "Truster age" is the truster's age in years. "Relative height" is the truster's height in inches, divided by the average height of the class. The variable "trustee grade" is the grade of the trustee.[13] This is the only trustee characteristic that we can plausibly include in the analysis of truster behavior, as all other characteristics were unknown to the truster.

Although the positive coefficient on trustee grade confirms that trusters are more trusting of older partners, we now see that the effect is not significantly different from zero. As expected, we also see that relatively risk-seeking individuals trust more, though the effect is not significant. Interestingly, male third-graders tend to be more trusting than female third-graders.[14] One possible explanation is that females tend to be more averse to risk. Although we have attempted to control for differences in risk attitudes, it may be that the risk involved in trusting others differs from the risk measure we use.

Estimated coefficients for birth order and for height suggest that these factors are positively correlated with trust behavior. The effects, both in terms of magnitude and statistical significance, are particularly pronounced among third-graders and girls. Russell Hardin (2001) provides a possible explanation for the significance of the two variables. He suggests that learning through experience is one path for the psychological development of the propensity or capacity to trust. The more positive reciprocity to their own cooperative trusting behavior people experience, the more likely they are to cooperate in the future. Our results are consistent with this explanation for the development of trust. It is likely that in face-to-face interactions taller children are more capable of enforcing reciprocity and therefore experience higher amounts of positive reciprocity. A similar explanation is plausible in the case of birth-order effects. Older brothers and sisters may be more likely to reciprocate than younger children, and thus younger siblings experience more instances of positive reciprocity than do older siblings. Obviously, the data cannot conclusively establish the existence of these mechanisms. However, they are possible explanations for systematic correlations and thus warrant further investigation.

The negative correlation between the dependent variable and the trust response from the survey bears mentioning. Individuals who answered that most people were trustworthy passed, on average, one-third of a token less than those who did not answer in the affirmative. This effect generally holds across the samples and is statistically significant among older trusters and girls. This result calls into question the validity of survey measures of trust and demonstrates that trust is a matter of context that cannot easily be summarized into a single question. This finding is not unique to children. E. L. Glaeser and colleagues (1999) have found that trustworthiness, but not the willingness to trust, corresponded to experiment participants' responses to survey questions. Individuals who were found to be more trusting in their experiments did not report that they were more trusting in the hypothetical survey questions (see also chapter 12, this volume).

Finally, the age of the truster has no general effect on the amount passed. Among third-graders, age is negatively correlated with pass amounts, and the effect is statistically significant. Among girls, age is positively correlated with pass amounts, but the magnitude of the effect is small. However, for the remaining subgroups of participants and for the sample as a whole, the estimated coefficients cannot be distinguished from zero. The data does not support the notion that the ability to trust develops between the third and twelfth grades.

Trustees

Next we turn to the trustee decisions. Table 11.4 presents the average amount returned by the trustees of each grade to the trusters of each

314   Trust and Reciprocity

Table 11.4   Mean Passes from Trustee to Truster, by Grade of Truster
and Trustee

Grade of Trustee	Grade of Truster				Adults	Average
	Third	Sixth	Ninth	Twelfth		
Third	7.13	9.13	10.21	9.63	10.92	9.40
	(5.78)	(8.04)	(10.03)	(8.44)	(11.02)	(7.93)
Sixth	10.90	11.43	11.24	12.19	11.38	11.43
	(9.74)	(9.23)	(12.45)	(12.37)	(11.88)	(10.91)
Ninth	9.40	8.73	8.20	8.60	9.60	8.91
	(8.40)	(5.68)	(7.64)	(7.05)	(8.09)	(6.54)
Twelfth	10.64	11.64	14.00	11.00	14.91	12.44
	(8.58)	(7.89)	(9.21)	(8.04)	(12.94)	(7.12)
Total	9.27	10.11	10.68	10.38	11.38	10.37
	(8.01)	(7.91)	(10.21)	(9.44)	(10.95)	(8.50)

Source: Authors' compilation.
Note: Standard deviations in parentheses.

grade. As was true of behavior for the trusters, trustees do not behave according to the predictions of *noncooperative game theory* with selfish preferences. We test the null hypothesis that average returns to each age group equal zero (adjusting for correlated errors across individuals) and that average returns to all ages equal zero (treating each individual as an observation). In both cases we can reject the null hypothesis at p values of 0.0000. Only three of the seventy-one children returned zero tokens for every decision with every partner.

Although the data presented in table 11.2 do not confirm the general perception that young children are more trusting than older ones, the data in this table lend slight support to the notion that younger children are less trustworthy. Ignoring the less generous ninth-graders it appears that trustworthiness increases with the age of the trustee. One might argue that this suggests that the trusters are acting rationally when they pass a slightly larger amount to the older and more trustworthy trustees.[15] Interestingly, it also appears that the amount returned increases with the age of the truster, though this pattern varies substantially across trustee grade. To determine the significance of these age effects we study them further in our econometric analysis.

Table 11.5 summarizes the average amounts returned by grade of the trustee and the amount passed by the truster. The children in our study did not display the same high levels of reciprocity, or sensitivity to the amount sent, as did participants in the studies by Berg, Dickhaut, and McCabe (1995) and Kenneth Koford (2001). In those studies,

Table 11.5   Average Number of Tokens Returned to Truster, by Grade of
Trustee and Number of Tokens Sent

	Tokens Sent by Truster				
Trustee Grade	0	1	2	3	4
Third	0.95	1.63	2.13	2.45	2.24
	(0.96)	(1.44)	(2.25)	(2.83)	(3.46)
Sixth	0.73	1.84	2.64	3.07	3.15
	(1.00)	(1.56)	(2.49)	(2.99)	(4.24)
Ninth	1.09	1.59	1.83	2.32	2.08
	(1.16)	(1.64)	(1.92)	(2.22)	(2.87)
Twelfth	1.04	1.95	2.58	3.44	3.44
	(1.05)	(1.52)	(2.02)	(2.76)	(3.32)
Average	0.93	1.73	2.29	2.76	2.66
	(1.04)	(1.53)	(2.24)	(2.77)	(3.60)

Source: Authors' compilation.
Note: Standard deviations in parentheses.

trusting behavior was generally rewarded, whereas in ours it is not. The average returns by tokens passed indicate relatively small differences in returns across differences in amount passed. For example, looking at the averages across all grades, at the bottom of table 11.5, we find that an increase in the amount passed from zero to one increases the amount returned by only 0.8 tokens, an increase from one to two by 0.6 tokens, and from two to three by 0.5 tokens; and the average returns are actually less for four tokens passed than for three. As a result, trusters who sent no tokens or one token did much better than those who were more trusting.

Neither the outcome-based nor intention-based models of fairness adequately explain the behavior of the trustees in this game. Both models would predict that the amount returned would increase consistently as the amount passed increased, either as a reaction to increased inequality or in response to a kinder action by the truster.

One possible reason for the discrepancy is our use of the strategy method to elicit trustees' responses. The experimental literature has yet to reach a consensus on whether using a strategy method results in responses that are different from what would be found had the players responded to the actual choice of their partners. For example, Jordi Brandts and Gary Charness (1998) investigate differences in responses among adults and find no difference between responses to observed action and responses elicited using the strategy method. Others, however, have found substantial differences (McCabe, Smith, and LePore 2000). Although the strategy method is not hypothetical,

Table 11.6   Comparisons of Average Returns, Monotonic and Nonmonotonic Trustees

Grade and Monotonicity	N	Percentage of Grade	Number Returned by Number Sent				
			0	1	2	3	4
Nonmonotonic							
Third	17	71	0.70	1.4	1.7	1.7	1.1
Sixth	13	62	0.52	1.4	1.9	1.7	0.9
Ninth	10	67	0.94	1.0	1.3	1.4	0.7
Twelfth	7	64	0.66	1.4	2.1	2.7	2.7
Monotonic							
Third	7	29	1.5	2.2	3.2	4.3	5.0
Sixth	8	38	1.1	2.6	3.9	5.2	6.7
Ninth	5	33	1.4	2.7	3.0	4.1	4.9
Twelfth	4	36	1.7	2.9	3.5	4.6	4.6

Source: Authors' compilation.

subjects may respond differently when they actually see the choice made by the truster. Indeed, it may be that this potential lack of salience is much more important for children than it is for adults.

Another explanation, which may be particularly relevant with children, is confusion. They may find it more difficult to understand how the strategy-method protocol will be implemented. Although our impression was that almost all trustees understood the meaning of the decision sheet on which they indicated responses, a majority of them behaved "nonmonotonically" at least once. We define monotonic trustees as those whose returns to trusters weakly increased with passes from trusters within a single grade. Nonmonotonic participants are those who, at least once, stated that they would return strictly fewer tokens in response to a higher pass from a truster within a single grade. Table 11.6 presents responses of monotonic and nonmonotonic trustees separately. This reveals that almost two-thirds of the trustees chose a nonmonotonic response at least once. Thus the intention- and outcome-based models can at best capture a minority of the trustees' choices. The obvious task for future research is to determine whether this nonmonotonic pattern is driven by the use of the less salient strategy method or should instead be seen as evidence that children perhaps exhibit a less refined degree of reciprocity than do adults.

Interestingly, though the average return is not sufficient to justify the truster's increasing the number of tokens passed, we see that the average returns to the subgroup of monotonic trustees make it worthwhile for them to increase the number of tokens passed. In our econo-

Table 11.7   Regression Results for Returns by Trustees

Variable	All	Nonmonotonic	Monotonic
TrusterGrade	0.03**	0.02	0.06**
	(3.01)	(1.43)	(3.26)
Boy	−4.74	−0.02	−1.28
	(−1.04)	(−0.07)	(−1.31)
SurveyTrust	0.68	0.14	1.15
	(1.55)	(0.40)	(1.23)
TrusteeAge	0.10	0.05	0.14
	(1.33)	(0.82)	(0.94)
Number of Siblings	−1.90	−0.04	−0.01
	(−1.27)	(−0.40)	(−0.02)
BirthOrder	0.05	0.11	0.76
	(0.18)	(0.61)	(1.27)
Tokens Passed	0.45**	0.15**	1.03**
	(15.15)	(4.78)	(19.25)
RelativeHeight	−2.25	−1.28	−0.66
	(−0.68)	(−0.48)	(−0.09)
N	71	47	24

Source: Authors' compilation.
Note: * denotes significance at $p \le 0.10$; **at $p \le 0.05$. Adjusted t-statistics in parentheses.

metric analysis we separately examine trustees with monotonic and nonmonotonic responses.

Table 11.7 reports the estimated coefficients, using random-effects ordinary least squares regressions to estimate trustee responses. As both the age and the gender of the trustee have little effect on their response, we report only the pooled results.

Neither relative height nor birth order is significant. This finding is not inconsistent with the learning model presented earlier. Individuals who experience high levels of positive reciprocity will not necessarily reciprocate themselves. We also note that the trustee's age has no significant effect on the amount passed. Combined with our earlier finding that trusters do not place significantly larger trust in older trustees, this suggests that they are correctly anticipating this response.

As expected, the amount sent is positively correlated with the amount returned. The coefficient is much larger among the monotonic than among the nonmonotonic subjects. Despite the nonmonotonic pattern, however, we find that, on average, an increase in the amount sent increases the amount returned. The truster's grade was also positively correlated with the trustee's return. This is possibly a reaction to an inferred higher status of older subjects. An analogous result has been found in adults. Glaeser and colleagues (1999) find that adult participants behave more trustworthily toward individuals of higher status. Alternatively, it may be that children believe that a different set of social standards applies for those who are older. Their parents and teachers do not lie to them or cheat them, which may not be the case with their peers. Their parents and teachers also actively reinforce social norms, including reciprocity. Therefore, participants may be hesitant to "cheat" adults.

Conclusions

Across the ages examined in this study we observe surprisingly little variation in trusting and trustworthy behavior. This suggests that if these traits develop with age then they are likely to do so when we are very young. This is consistent with what we have found in a series of other experiments, including those that involve altruistic preferences.

Surprisingly, the children in our experiment did not pass or return as many tokens as adults have in similar experiments. In addition, children did not vary their return amounts in response to the amount passed to the extent adults do. It may be that the trustees' behavior resulted from our use of the strategy method rather than age. Future work will have to investigate this possibility.

A number of factors are correlated with participants' trust behavior. Status appears to matter. Trusters tended to pass more tokens to older partners, and trustees returned more when paired with older partners. This effect, however, is significant only for trustees. Relative height and birth order are positively related to the truster's pass amount, possibly because taller children and younger siblings have experienced higher rates of positive reciprocity. These effects are largest among the youngest participants.

Self-reported trust is negatively correlated with the trusters' pass amount, with a small coefficient. It is positively (although insignificantly) correlated with trustees' return decisions, however, and these coefficients are generally large. The significance and robustness of this correlation suggests caution in the use of surveys to measure trust behavior in children.

Overall, we believe this experiment reinforces the argument that the sorts of experiments and models that economists are using to investigate and explain the behavior of adults can also be used with children, with suitable modifications to ensure salience and understanding. In particular, we find that even in this rather complicated experiment, children's trusting behavior is (broadly) qualitatively comparable to what has been found in adults and that individual characteristics matter, particularly among the youngest participants. However, we note that data from children is noisier (in both senses of the word) than that from adults; consequently, experiments need to be carefully designed and conducted with large samples to obtain reliable estimates of the effects of individual characteristics.

The research on which this chapter is based was funded by grant SES-0112157 from the National Science Foundation.

Notes

1. This example was first noted by Robyn Dawes and Richard Thaler (1988).

2. See, for example, the study by Stephen Knack and Philip Keever (1997) and chapter 13 in this volume. Note, however, that Nancy Buchan, Rachel Croson, and Eric Johnson (1999) find generally similar levels of trust across countries, when using experiments similar to those used by Berg, Dickhaut, and McCabe (1995).

3. Examples of outcome-based models are presented in Loewenstein, Thompson, and Bazerman (1989); Bolton (1991); Fehr and Schmidt (1999); and Bolton and Ockenfels (2000).

4. James Andreoni, Paul Brown, and Lise Vesterlund (2002) find a similar result in *public-good games*.

5. Instructions for obtaining the protocol used can be found online at *harbaugh.uoregon.edu/children/*.

6. The strategy method has previously been used in similar experiments on adults. See, for example, Falk, Fehr, and Fischbacher (forthcoming); Charness, Haruvy, and Sonsino (2001).

7. The adult was a hypothetical player. We matched each participant with the average play of adults in previous administrations of this game.

8. See Buchan and Croson (1999) for references on cross-country and gender differences in the trust game.

9. Catherine Eckel and Rick Wilson (2000) find that for adults, a truster's attitude toward risk affects his or her choice of more or less risky trust games.

10. This method is based on a procedure first suggested by Daniel Bernoulli in 1738.

11. James Andreoni, William Harbaugh, and Lisa Vesterlund (2002) find that adult trustees make transfers even when they have received nothing from the truster.

12. If we adopt the conservative approach of treating the average proposal from each person as a single observation, we can reject the hypothesis

that contributions equal the adult level of 52 percent of the endowment, at p values of 0.001 or below for students in all grades except the ninth. For ninth-graders, we cannot reject the null.

13. Grade is set to 14 for adults.

14. Eckel and Wilson (2000) find a similar gender result for adults.

15. This finding differs from that of René Fahr and Bernd Irlenbusch (2000). They examine trust games in which individuals' performance in a walnut-cracking task determines their initial endowments. They find that the trustee returns more when the truster has earned the higher endowment and that the truster sends more when the trustee has earned the higher endowment. Thus, the trusters tend to send more to trustees who subsequently reciprocate less. The individual differences in endowments, however, complicate a direct comparison between the two studies.

References

Andreoni, James, Paul Brown, and Lise Vesterlund. 2002. "What Makes an Allocation Fair? Some Experimental Evidence." *Games and Economic Behavior* 40(1): 1–24.

Andreoni, James, William Harbaugh, and Lise Vesterlund. 2002. "The Carrot or the Stick: Rewards, Punishments, and Cooperation." Working paper, Pittsburgh, Penn.

Andreoni, James, and Lise Vesterlund. 2001. "Which Is the Fair Sex? Gender Differences in Altruism." *Quarterly Journal of Economics* 116(1): 293–312.

Berg, Joyce, John Dickhaut, and Kevin McCabe. 1995. "Trust, Reciprocity, and Social History." *Games and Economic Behavior* 10(1): 122–142.

Bolton, Gary E. 1991. "A Comparative Model of Bargaining: Theory and Evidence." *American Economic Review* 81(5): 1096–1136.

Bolton, Gary E., and Axel Ockenfels. 2000. "ERC: A Theory of Equity, Reciprocity, and Competition." *American Economic Review* 90(1): 166–93.

Brandts, Jordi, and Gary Charness. 1998. "Hot Versus Cold: Sequential Responses and Preference Stability in Experimental Games." Working paper. Universitat Pompeu Fabra, Barecelona, Spain. Accessed August 7, 2002 at: *www.econ.upf.es/deehome/what/wpapers/postscripts/321.pdf*.

Buchan, Nancy, and Rachel Croson. 1999. "Gender and Culture: International Experimental Evidence from Trust Games." *American Economic Review, Papers and Proceedings* 89(2): 386–91.

Buchan, Nancy R., Rachel T. Croson, and Eric Johnson. 1999. "Getting to Know You: An International Experiment on the Influence of Culture, Communication, and Social Distance on Trust and Reciprocation." Working paper. Madison, Wisc.: University of Wisconsin, Department of Marketing.

Charness, Gary, Ernan Haruvy, and Doron Sonsino. 2001. "Social Distance and Reciprocity: An Internet Experiment." Unpublished manuscript, University of California, Santa Barbara.

Charness, Gary, and Matthew Rabin. 2001. "Social Preferences: Some Simple

Tests and a New Model." Unpublished manuscript, University of California, Santa Barbara.

Dawes, Robyn, and Richard Thaler. 1988. "Cooperation." *Journal of Economic Perspectives* 2(3):187–97.

Dufwenberg, Martin, and Georg Kirchsteiger. 1998. "A Theory of Sequential Reciprocity." Unpublished manuscript, University of Stockholm.

Eckel, Catherine, and Rick Wilson. 2000. "Whom to Trust? Choice of Partner in a Trust Game." Unpublished manuscript.

Fahr, René, and Bernd Irlenbusch. 2000. "Fairness As a Constraint on Trust in Reciprocity: Earned Property Rights in a Reciprocal Exchange Experiment." *Economics Letters* 66(3): 275–82.

Falk, Armin, Ernst Fehr, and Urs Fischbacher. Forthcoming. "On the Nature of Fair Behavior." *Economic Inquiry*.

Falk, Armin, and Urs Fischbacher. 1998. "A Theory of Reciprocity." Unpublished manuscript, Zurich, Switzerland.

Fehr, Ernst, and Klaus Schmidt. 1999. "A Theory of Fairness, Competition, and Cooperation." *Quarterly Journal of Economics* 114(3): 817–68.

Fishbein, H. D., and N. K. Kaminski. 1985. "Children's Reciprocal Altruism in a Competitive Game." *British Journal of Developmental Psychology* 3(4): 393–98.

Frank, Robert H., Thomas D. Gilovich, and Dennis T. Regan. 1996. "Do Economists Make Bad Citizens?" *Journal of Economic Perspectives* 10(1): 187–92.

Glaeser, E. L., David Laibson, J. A. Scheinkman, and C. L. Soutter. 1999. "Measuring Trust." *Quarterly Journal of Economics* 65(3): 811–46.

Harbaugh, William T., and Kate Krause. 2000. "Children's Altruism in Public Good and Dictator Experiments." *Economic Inquiry* 38(10): 95–109.

Harbaugh, William T., Kate Krause, and Timothy R. Berry. 2001. "GARP for Kids: On the Development of Rational Choice Behavior." *American Economic Review* 91(5): 1539–45.

Harbaugh, William T., Kate Krause, and Steven Liday. 2001. "Children's Bargaining Behavior." Working paper, Department of Economics, University of Oregon, Eugene.

Harbaugh, William T., Kate Krause, and Lise Vesterlund. 2001. "Are Adults Better Behaved Than Children? Age, Experience, and the Endowment Effect." *Economics Letters* 70(2): 175–81.

———. 2002. "Risk Attitudes of Children and Adults: Choices over Small and Large Probability Gains and Losses." *Experimental Economics* 5(1): 53–84.

Hardin, Russell. 2001. "Conceptions and Explanations of Trust." In *Trust in Society*, by Russell Hardin. New York: Russell Sage Foundation.

Herrnstein, R. J. 1997. *The Matching Law: Papers in Psychology and Economics.* Cambridge, Mass.: Harvard University Press.

Knack, Stephen, and Philip Keever. 1997. "Does Social Capital Have an Economic Payoff? A Cross-country Investigation." *Quarterly Journal of Economics* 112(4): 1252–88.

Koford, Kenneth. 2001. "Trust and Reciprocity in Bulgaria: A Replication of Berg, Dickhaut, and McCabe (1995)." Working paper 98-08, Department of Economics, University of Delaware, Newark, Delaware.

Kreps, David. 1990. "Corporate Culture and Economic Theory." In *Perspectives* on *Positive Political Economy,* edited by J. E. Alt and K. A. Shepsle. Political Economy of Institutions Decisions Series. Cambridge, New York, and Melbourne: Cambridge University Press.

Loewenstein, George, Leigh Thompson, and Max Bazerman. 1989. "Social Utility and Decision Making in Interpersonal Contexts." *Journal of Personality and Social Psychology* 57(3): 426–41.

McCabe, Kevin, Stephen J. Rassenti, and Vernon L. Smith. 1998. "Reciprocity, Trust, and Payoff Privacy in Extensive-Form Bargaining." *Games and Economic Behavior* 24(1–2): 10–24.

McCabe, Kevin, Vernon Smith, and Michael LePore. 2000. "Intentionality Detection and 'Mindreading:' Why Does Game Form Matter?" *Proceedings of the National Academy of Sciences* 97(8): 4404–9.

Rabin, Matthew. 1993. "Incorporating Fairness into Game Theory and Economics." *American Economic Review* 83(5): 1281–1302.

Roth, Alvin E., Vesna Prasnikar, Masahiro Okuno-Fujiwara, and Shmuel Zamir. 1991. "Bargaining and Market Behavior in Jerusalem, Ljubljana, Pittsburgh, and Tokyo." *American Economic Review* 81(5): 1068–95.

Chapter 12

Trust in Two-Person Games: Game Structures and Linkages

T. K. Ahn, Elinor Ostrom, David Schmidt, and James Walker

ONTRAST the following decision situation with the one described in the first chapter of this volume. Two individuals face the following choice. They are each endowed with $5. If individual 1 gives her $5 to individual 2, individual 2 receives $10. Similarly, if individual 2 gives his $5 to individual 1, individual 1 receives $10. Thus if both individuals give up their own $5, each receives a payoff of $10. If neither individual gives up $5, they both get to keep their own $5 and will receive nothing more. Of course, if one individual gives up $5 and the other does not, the individual giving up $5 receives a payoff of $0 and the other receives a payoff of $15.

Imagine that this decision game is to be played only once, that individuals cannot observe the decision of the other individual before making their own decisions, and that all decisions are completely anonymous. How might an individual go about making a decision in this situation? Clearly, if the individuals in this *one-shot* setting make choices based on maximizing their own pecuniary payoffs from the game, neither individual will give up $5, and each will walk away with a payoff of $5.

On the other hand, what if some individuals do, in fact, choose to give up their $5? Is there a rationale that might describe the motives of such an individual? Consider the following possibility. Imagine that person 1 prefers the outcome in which both individuals give up $5 to the outcome in which she keeps her $5 and person 2 gives up his $5. In this case, person 1 may or may not decide to give up her $5;

the decision depends upon what she expects person 2 to do. One might argue that in this scenario, the issue becomes one of whether person 1 trusts person 2, in the sense of having an expectation that he will give up his $5.

This situation is exactly the one faced by real subjects in a decision experiment we conducted in 1999 (Ahn, Ostrom, and Walker forthcoming). In this experiment, subjects played the game only once, they knew they would play the game only once, and they also knew that their decisions would be anonymous to the other players, as well as to the experimenters. Thirty-seven of the 104 subjects (36 percent) chose to give up their $5. Furthermore, before being informed of their earnings, the subjects completed a questionnaire, part of which focused on their preferences regarding possible outcomes of the game. Of these 104 subjects, 35 percent responded that they would prefer the outcome in which they both gave up their $5 to the outcome in which they kept their $5 and the person with whom they were anonymously matched gave up their $5, and 27 percent responded that they were indifferent between the two outcomes. In other words, only 38 percent of the subjects reported a preference ordering consistent with preferences based solely on maximizing their own pecuniary payoffs.

The subjects' preference orderings were found to be highly correlated to their actual behavior during the experiment. Among the thirty-six subjects who preferred the outcome in which both gave up $5, 61 percent gave up their $5. Among the twenty-eight subjects who were indifferent between the two outcomes, 39 percent gave up their $5. Among the forty subjects who revealed a preference ordering consistent with a *prisoner's dilemma game*, only 10 percent gave up their $5.

Ahn, Ostrom, and Walker also report results from an alternative sequential decision setting that more closely parallels the one-way trust game described in chapters 1 and 3 of this volume. In this setting, player 1 makes her decision first; her decision is reported to player 2, who then makes his decision. This is clearly a game of trust. If player 1 decides to give up her $5, can she trust player 2 to reciprocate that trust with a decision to give up his $5? Thirty-two subjects were in the role of player 1 making the first move. Eighteen (56 percent) of these subjects chose to give up their $5. What were the actions of the group of subjects in the role of player 2, when player 1 chose to give up their $5? Eleven of 18 (61 percent) chose to reciprocate the action of player 1 subjects and give up their $5.

A study recently conducted in Korea (Cho and Choi 2000) was designed to investigate this setting and to contrast results found in Korea with those observed in Japan and the United States. Among the 149 Korean subjects in the simultaneous-move condition, 68 (46 percent) chose to give up their 4,000 won (approximately $4). Eleven of

21 subjects (52 percent) making the first move in the sequential condition gave up their 4,000 won. When the individuals in the role of first mover chose to give up their 4,000 won, 8 of 11 individuals (73 percent) in the role of second mover reciprocated by giving up their own 4,000 won. On the other hand, none of the 13 American or the 10 Korean subjects in the second mover's role gave up their money when the first mover had not given up his or her own.

These results, for one-shot games, suggest two important themes related to experimental research on trust. First, evidence suggests that many subjects make decisions based on more than their own pecuniary payoffs. By choosing to cooperate and to reciprocate cooperative behavior, some subjects succeeded in reaching payoff outcomes, both individually and for their group, that were superior to those predicted by *noncooperative game theory* based strictly on their own pecuniary payoffs. Second, evidence suggests that the structure of the decision situation affects individuals' decisions, allowing them a degree of improvement in overall cooperation. On the other hand, the results also suggest that these types of decision settings truly represent a dilemma for many subjects with regard to whether to place trust in others. In a majority of the outcomes, groups end up at a deficient outcome from the perspective of overall potential pecuniary gains.

This chapter addresses these themes in the context of several studies designed to examine how elements of the decision situation affect individual choices in two-person games similar to the games described here. These games all have the monetary payoff structure of the well-known prisoner's dilemma game. As exemplified by the results reported in the preceding material, studies of *social dilemma games* typically find that the level of cooperation observed in such games is not consistent with noncooperative game-theoretic equilibrium predictions when all players are assumed to be purely self-interested—that is, when they are taken to care only about their own pecuniary rewards. The level of cooperative choices, however, varies substantially from very low to moderately high, depending on the experimental design.

Structures and Linkages of Decision Situations

To explain the substantial variation in cooperative choices, the theoretical literature focuses on factors within a game and in the environment surrounding a particular play of a game that are posited to affect individual motivation and behavior. For instance, considerable debate exists regarding the relative weight of pecuniary payoffs, subjects' orientations to fairness, trust, or reciprocity, and the way players in a game are linked to one another (Bolton and Ockenfels 2000; Camerer 1990; Kahneman, Knetsch, and Thaler 1986; Fehr and Schmidt 1999; Ochs and Roth 1989; Gunnthorsdottir et al. 2000). Strong evidence exists that all these factors affect, to some extent, the level of cooperation observed in social-dilemma situations. These studies suggest that the assumption that subjects who participate in experimental studies are narrowly self-interested is suspect. Thus equilibrium predictions based on this assumption are also suspect. If uncertainty about how subjects rank the possible outcomes exists, the experiment is best viewed as a Bayesian game.

In a particular experimental setting, in which the number of players and the sets of admissible actions are held constant, we see four basic elements related to the structure of the experimental setting that affect behavior. These are:

- pecuniary benefits;

- player types;

- information about player types; and

- linkages between players that occur in repeated-game situations.

These four elements can be utilized to explain observed behavior through their impact on player motivations and beliefs regarding the play of others. In the research reported here, we report evidence from a series of experimental studies related to behavior in two-person prisoner's dilemma games in which the pecuniary payoffs and the linkages among players are systematically varied while the type of information given to participants is controlled.[1]

Pecuniary Benefits

In noncooperative game theory, predicted game equilibriums depend on the utilities players receive from alternative outcomes. The traditional approach, when a game is operationalized in a laboratory, has been to assume that a player's pecuniary payoff is an appropriate proxy for the player's utility level. Much of the current debate within experimental social sciences is related to understanding when this approach yields predictions consistent with behavior. Once it is suggested that pecuniary benefits may not be a good proxy for utility, one must be careful about describing experimental environments using standard game-theoretic terminology. Throughout this chapter, when we describe an experimental setting as a prisoner's dilemma game, for instance, we mean that the game matrix obtained by using pecuniary payoffs as proxies for utilities has the structure of a prisoner's dilemma.

In the one-shot prisoner's dilemma game, both players have a dominant strategy known as defection (D). When both players choose their dominant strategy, the outcome is *Pareto inferior* to the outcome resulting when both players play their dominated strategy, known as cooperation (C). Experimental research across numerous designs based on games with the prisoner's dilemma structure in pecuniary benefits, however, does not support the prediction that all players will defect in such games. Even when double-blind test procedures are used in one-shot experiments, a significant number of individuals choose the dominated strategy of cooperation (see Hayashi et al. 1999 for relevant cites). Among the many possible explanations for this result, one that must be considered is that the pecuniary benefits do not fully account for the subjects' rankings of the outcomes.

Because we consider only symmetric games here, the pecuniary payoffs can be described by defining a payoff function, $\pi(\cdot,\cdot)$, in which the first argument is the player's own action and the second is the action of the other player. Prisoner's dilemma games are constructed so that $\pi(D,C) > \pi(C,C)$ and $\pi(D,D) > \pi(C,D)$. In comparing the relative payoffs of these outcomes, we adopt three terms used by Anatol Rapoport and Albert Chammah (1965) to describe the players' incentives in the game. First, if player 2 plays C, player 1's payoff is higher if he or she plays D rather than C. This gain, $\pi(D,C) - \pi(C,C)$, is referred to as "greed." Similarly, if player 2 plays D, player 1's payoff is again higher if he or she plays D instead of C, by an amount of $\pi(D,D) - \pi(C,D)$. This difference in payoffs is referred to as "fear." On the other hand, there is a group-level incentive to play C, because both players receive higher monetary payoffs by playing (C,C) than when they play (D,D). The magnitude of this incentive, $\pi(C,C) - \pi(D,D)$, is referred to as the "cooperators' gain."

In an experimental setting, if players' utilities are well represented by their monetary payoffs, subjects should defect in a one-shot prisoner's dilemma game, no matter the objective level of fear, greed, or cooperators' gain. Prior studies have shown, however, that increases in fear or greed lower the rate of cooperation in prisoner's dilemma games (Rapoport and Chammah 1965; Rapoport 1988a, 1988b; Saijo and Nakamura 1995) and that increases in the cooperators' gain increase the rate of cooperation (Komorita, Sweeny, and Kravitz 1980).[2]

Player Types

Scholars from diverse traditions have put forward the proposition that some subjects rank outcomes based on factors other than their own monetary payoffs (Sen 1974; Raub 1990). Psychologists have long argued that the social values held by individuals affect the way they transform a pecuniary payoff matrix into an effective matrix (Kelley and Thibaut 1978; Kramer, McClintock, and Messick 1986; Kuhlman, Camac, and Cunha 1986). Instead of assuming that all players maximize their pecuniary payoffs—ignoring the outcomes received by others or the morality of actions leading to outcomes—many scholars assume that players hold diverse orientations to games based on their own internal valuation systems and their linkages to others. Internal values, in turn, affect how pecuniary payoffs are transformed into utility. Matthew Rabin (1993), for example, recommends that one should derive "psychological games" from basic "material games" and include in the transformation the way players perceive the fairness of particular strategies taken by themselves and others (see also Binmore 1998).

Recent evidence suggests that at least some subjects facing a prisoner's dilemma game in terms of pecuniary benefits do not perceive the game as a prisoner's dilemma in terms of utilities.[3] For example, in an experimental investigation of a one-shot prisoner's dilemma game, based on questionnaire data, approximately 40 percent of a pool of 136 subjects revealed a preference ranking in which the outcome (D,C) was ranked below the outcome (C,C) and the outcome (C,D) was ranked below (D,D) (reported in Ahn, Ostrom, and Walker forthcoming).[4] If two players with these reported preferences were to play the game, and their preferences were common knowledge, the game would actually be an assurance game with two equilibriums in pure strategies: (C,C) and (D,D). We refer to a player with this type of preference as being an "assurance-type" player. On the other hand, most other players report preference orderings consistent with defection being a dominant strategy; we refer to these players as being "PD-type" players.

Evolving theories posit different internal mechanisms for transforming monetary payoffs into utilities that are consistent with these two types of preferences. In a model of inequity aversion developed by Ernst Fehr and Klaus Schmidt (1999), individuals' utility functions incorporate negative components based on relative payoffs in a game in addition to objective earnings. In the Fehr and Schmidt model, individuals are assumed to differ with respect to an aversion to payoff outcomes in which their own payoff outcome is less than or greater than the payoffs to other players in the game.[5] If a player's inequity aversion is of sufficient magnitude, defection may no longer be a dominant strategy, and players could have what we refer to as assurance-type preferences.

Work by Sue Crawford and Elinor Ostrom (1995) examines the role of norms represented by internal parameters of behavior added to or subtracted from objective payoffs. Werner Güth and Menahem Yaari (1992) propose an indirect evolutionary approach whereby selection operates on the objective payoffs obtained from interactions, but positive or negative internal weights are placed on objective outcomes as a result of the norms adopted by individuals. The distribution of particular norms in a population is thus indirectly affected by how well the carriers of these norms do in repeated interactions with others carrying different or similar norms (see also Güth and Kliemt 1998). This suggests a more dynamic model of the relation between outcomes and utilities than the static models discussed earlier.

Theories of reciprocity also provide an explanation for diverse internal transformations of pecuniary payoffs into expected utilities. Instead of presuming that individuals cooperate out of a concern for others alone, or only because they feel an action is the right thing to do, reciprocity as an explanation implies that players make choices contingent on their beliefs concerning the likely actions of others and what these actions reveal about the intentions of others (see Falk and Fischbacher 1998; Wagner 1998; Hoffman, McCabe, and Smith 1996; Ostrom 1998; Croson 1999).

In a study closely related to the work presented here, Anna Gunnthorsdottir and colleagues (2000) examine the consequences of sorting players by type in a multiround *public-goods game*. In their design, twelve subjects are sorted into groups of four in each decision round. Two treatment conditions are investigated. In the first, subjects are randomly sorted in each round into one of the three groups. In the second, subjects are sorted according to their contribution to the public good in the previous round. One group is composed of the four subjects making the highest contributions, one is composed of the four subjects making the next highest contributions, and the last is composed of the four subjects making the lowest contributions. In both designs, subjects know only that they will be regrouped for each round. They are not informed of the sorting procedure. Strong evidence is found supporting the notion of subject types. Based on first-period decisions, subjects are identified as free riders or cooperators. In both treatment conditions, cooperators tend to have made higher contributions than free riders across decision rounds. A significant sorting effect exists. Contributions are lower when subjects are sorted randomly rather than on the basis of contributions made in previous rounds. When free riders and cooperators interact more frequently, the rate of decay in contributions is greater than when subjects are sorted according to types.

Information About Player Types

Once it is granted that there may be more than one type of player, it is reasonable to assume that players make the same assumption. Consequently, subjects' decisions may be influenced by the kind of information they obtain about those with whom they are paired.

Michael Cain (1998) finds that expectations of play in a prisoner's dilemma game were affected by information regarding prior play in a *dictator game*. Stingy players—those who had retained at least 70 percent of their endowment in a prior dictator game—tended to predict that all players would defect. Nice players—those who gave away at least 30 percent of their endowment—tended to predict that nice players would cooperate and stingy players would defect (Cain 1998, 151). Information about prior actions also affected behavior—specifically, nice players chose cooperation 69 percent of the time when they were paired with other nice players and 39 percent of the time when they were paired with stingy players.

Expectations of others' play may be derived from repeated play in a setting or from experiences outside of the immediate setting. Evidence suggests that individuals may perceive the obligation to respond reciprocally at different levels depending on the person with whom they are paired and whether there are preexisting social linkages. Peter Kollock (1998) finds that the cooperation rates of fraternity brothers at the University of California at Los Angeles were strongly influenced by whether they thought they were paired with other members of their own fraternity, members of other fraternities, UCLA students at large, students at another university, or UCLA police officers.

Not only is information about the presence or absence of preexisting social connectedness or other player types an important source of different behavior, but knowing how much information about one's actions in a game will be conveyed to others is also a factor potentially affecting decisions. Knowing that your identity will be revealed to others after or during an experiment may increase the weight of internal norms triggered by external observation (Coleman 1988; Crawford and Ostrom 1995; Hoffman, McCabe, and Smith 1996; Bohnet and Frey 1999).

Linkages Among Players in Repeated Games

Within the literature on noncooperative game theory, cooperation in the prisoner's dilemma game is deemed possible if the game is repeated infinitely or, in a finitely repeated game, if there are certain types of asymmetric information. Prisoner's dilemma experiments typically last no more than a few hours, so the time horizon is clearly not infinite. The sequential equilibriums described by David Kreps and colleagues (1982) depend on the possibility of a player type who may respond to previous cooperative plays by playing cooperatively in the future. This result depends on players' abilities to form reputations, which is something that varies over different experimental designs.

If subjects in prisoner's dilemma experiments have beliefs that some other subjects have assurance-type preferences, PD-type players may mimic assurance-type players in the early rounds of a sequential equilibrium. Because most players would be acting as if the game were an assurance game, in which (C,C) is presumably the payoff dominant equilibrium, they would face an equilibrium selection problem between (C,C) and (D,D). Experimental research on assurance games has shown that information about prior play, and matching protocols affect players' abilities to resolve the equilibrium selection problem (Schmidt et al. 2002).

Furthermore, the exact form of the linkages between players' actions and resulting outcomes may affect the level of cooperation; one example is whether the game is sequential or simultaneous (Clark and Sefton 2001; Yamagishi and Cook 1993). Finally, if players believe that the persons with whom they will be matched in future decisions will be influenced by current decisions, such linkages could affect behavior.[6]

Decisions in a One-Shot Prisoner's Dilemma Setting

Subjects in our study were volunteers from introductory undergraduate courses in economics at Indiana University.[7] Before volunteering, subjects were informed that they would participate in a decision-making exercise and would be paid in cash an amount dependent upon their decisions and the decisions of others in the experiment. Upon arriving for the experiment, subjects privately read through a set of instructions that explained the game situation. After reviewing the instructions for the game, the experimenter presented publicly, on an overhead projector, further instructions that explained the decision environment. Following this review, subjects completed a questionnaire designed to check their understanding of the decision task.

The games played were described as board games with a row and a column player. Each subject would make a choice between cooperation and defection (which were actually labeled "A" and "B" in the experiments). Subjects were given complete information about the payoff structure. All subjects always saw themselves as row players. Subjects were informed that at the end of the experimental session they would receive their earnings privately, in cash, plus $5 for having kept their experiment appointment.

In private, the subjects completed a game sheet that contained the four prisoner's dilemma games shown in figure 12.1. The levels of

Figure 12.1   Game Parameters for One-Shot Games

	Player 2 D	Player 2 C
Player 1 D	60,60	110,50
Player 1 C	50,110	100,100

Game 1
(Fear = 10, greed = 10,
cooperators' gain = 40)

	Player 2 D	Player 2 C
Player 1 D	60,60	110,20
Player 1 C	20,110	100,100

Game 2
(Fear = 40, greed = 10,
cooperators' gain = 40)

	Player 2 D	Player 2 C
Player 1 D	60,60	140,50
Player 1 C	50,140	100,100

Game 3
(Fear = 10, greed = 40,
cooperators' gain = 40)

	Player 2 D	Player 2 C
Player 1 D	60,60	140,20
Player 1 C	20,140	100,100

Game 4
(Fear = 40, greed = 40,
cooperators' gain = 40)

Source: Authors' configuration.

fear, greed, and cooperators' gain for each game are also reported in this figure. Cooperators' gain was held constant, allowing us to systematically vary fear and greed. All games were completed without feedback. Subjects were matched with a different participant for each individual game. Subjects were informed that their payoff in each individual game would depend on their decision in that game and the decision of another participant in the room, randomly chosen without replacement. Game sheets were collected after all subjects had completed the task. Earnings were computed, and each subject was privately paid his or her earnings for the experiment.

Thirty-three of the forty subjects who participated in this experiment had completed an in-class questionnaire on the first day of the semester in which they were asked to play a prisoner's dilemma game (not for actual payoffs) and asked several survey questions about the game—five questions related to their preferences over game outcomes and three questions regarding their views of trust in others.[8] (The complete questionnaire and the three additional ques-

Table 12.1   Cooperation Rates in One-Shot Prisoner's Dilemma Games

Experiment Group	Game 1	Game 2	Game 3	Game 4
All subjects ($N = 40$)	27.5	30.0	30.0	22.5
Subjects who completed question-				
naire ($N = 33$)	24.2	27.3	30.3	18.4

Source: Authors' compilation.

tions are given in the appendix to this chapter.) From this survey data we compute measures of subject "type" and subject "trust." As noted, a subject is classified as being an assurance-type player if from the questionnaire he or she ranked the outcome (C,C) over (D,C). A subject is classified as being a PD-type player if he or she ranked the outcome (D,C) over (C,C). A subject is classified as being indifferent if he or she ranked the outcome (C,C) equal to (D,C). The measure for trust was calculated based on the subjects' answers to the three trust questions, which have been used extensively in empirical studies of trust based on survey research. A positive answer was scored as 1, a negative answer as 0, and a "Don't know" response as 0.5. The trust level for a subject is the sum of the three measures.

We organize our reporting of the data around summary observations. The first row of table 12.1 reports overall cooperation rates from the decisions made by forty subjects recruited to participate in this

Table 12.2   Distribution of Cooperative Choices in One-Shot Prisoner's Dilemma Games, by Sex, Preference Type, and Trust Level

| Characteristic | N | Cooperative Choices Made[a] | | | | |
		0	1	2	3	4
Sex						
Male	20	60.0	10.0	0.0	20.0	10.0
Female	13	69.2	7.7	7.7	0.0	15.4
Preference type						
Assurance	8	50.0	12.5	12.5	12.5	12.5
Indifferent	6	50.0	0.0	0	33.3	16.7
Prisoner's dilemma	19	73.7	10.5	0	5.3	10.5
Average trust level	1.15[b]	1.21	1.67	0.0	0.25	1.63
All	33	63.6	9.1	3.0	12.1	12.1

Source: Authors' compilation.
[a]As percentage of all decisions made.
[b]Mean trust level.

experimental setting; the bottom row focuses on the behavior of the thirty-three individuals who completed the first-day questionnaire. Table 12.2 organizes the data on cooperation rates based on the number of times an individual chose to cooperate in the four decision games. These individuals are classified according to sex, preference type, and trust.

We draw three summary observations from the data. First, cooperation rates are low and vary little across the different game settings. Clearly, this "one-shot" setting has created a situation in which subjects do not trust one another and are reluctant to play the cooperative strategy. Furthermore, the game parameters, at least for this setting, appear to have little impact on cooperation rates—ranging from a low of 23 percent in game 4 to a high of 30 percent in games 2 and 3.

Second, there is considerable variation across subjects concerning play in the four games. Of the thirty-three subjects who completed the questionnaire, 64 percent chose never to cooperate, and only 12 percent cooperated in every game.

Third, responses from the preexperiment questionnaire are of little help in organizing the data. No general pattern emerges that separates one player type from another (table 12.2). PD-type players appear to be marginally more likely never to have cooperated, but the differences between the player types are not pronounced. Similarly, no obvious pattern is observed with respect to average trust score by preference type.

The lack of a strong correlation between game parameters, player type, and trust level is supported by a more formal statistical analysis of the data. Using a logit model, and regressing the decision to cooperate on dummy variables for game and player type, as well as the trust measure, yields no systematic significant coefficients for any of these classes of variables. Thus survey responses (gathered weeks earlier) do not offer strong evidence regarding the prediction of player behavior. Note that this result is somewhat at odds with the evidence from the prisoner's dilemma experiment presented in chapter 1, in which the survey instrument was completed by subjects immediately following their participation in the experiment but before being informed of their payoffs.

The Repeated Prisoner's Dilemma Setting

The one-shot decision setting is a minimal, and quite harsh, environment for investigating the propensity of subjects to cooperate in dilemma games. The subjects have no opportunity for the learning or reputation building that may come from repeated play. David Schmidt

Figure 12.2   Game Parameters for Repeated Games

Player 2

	D	C
D	40,40	110,10
C	10,110	80,80

Player 1

Game 1
(Fear = 30, greed = 30,
cooperators' gain = 40)

Player 2

	D	C
D	50,50	110,10
C	10,110	70,70

Player 1

Game 2
(Fear = 40, greed = 40,
cooperators' gain = 20)

Player 2

	D	C
D	50,50	110,10
C	10,110	90,90

Player 1

Game 3
(Fear = 40, greed = 20,
cooperators' gain = 40)

Player 2

	D	C
D	60,60	110,10
C	10,110	80,80

Player 1

Game 4
(Fear = 50, greed = 30,
cooperators' gain = 20)

Player 2

	D	C
D	30,30	110,10
C	10,110	70,70

Player 1

Game 5
(Fear = 20, greed = 40,
cooperators' gain = 40)

Player 2

	D	C
D	40,40	110,10
C	10,110	60,60

Player 1

Game 6
(Fear = 30, greed = 50,
cooperators' gain = 20)

Source: Authors' configuration.

and colleagues (2001) conducted a set of experiments in which subjects made a series of decisions in a repeated-game context. Two designs were used to explore how information about player behavior and linkages among players affect cooperation. In addition, each experiment consisted of two phases designed to investigate further the ways in which information regarding player type may affect behavior. The six prisoner's dilemma games are shown in figure 12.2.

In the first design, referred to as random matching, eight subjects first play twelve rounds (two rounds of each of six payoff matrixes) of a prisoner's dilemma game in phase 1. For each round, subjects are randomly and anonymously matched in four pairs. The subjects play each of the six games and then repeat play of the games in the same order. In phase 2, they are assigned into two groups of four players and provided with a history of the choices made by the members of both groups, based on a subject identification number (without personally identifying individuals). One group is composed of those subjects with the highest cooperation rates in the first twelve rounds. The other is composed of those with the lowest cooperation rates. This provides subjects in phase 2 with information about the distribution of past actions of the population of players involved in the experiment and in their group.

The second design, referred to as fixed matching, was created to parallel the first design but with a fixed-match protocol. Subjects were anonymously matched with the same person for all twelve rounds of phase 1 of the experiment. They were then randomly rematched with one person for phase 2. This design strengthens the linkages between players, thus allowing for greater levels of coordination and reciprocity. In all experimental sessions, subjects were informed of the structure and information conditions of both phases before the game was begun. In each phase, each of the six games was played twice. The order of play was based on game number and proceeded from the first through the sixth game two times.

Subjects were recruited to the experimental laboratory in cohorts of eight players. Upon arriving at the laboratory, they were randomly seated at computer monitors. Subjects privately read through a set of computerized instructions that explained the game situation for phases 1 and 2. After reviewing the instructions for the game, the experimenter presented publicly, on an overhead projector, further instructions that explained the decision environment. The subjects did not know at any time with whom they were paired in any of the decision trials and were told that their decisions would remain anonymous throughout and after the experiment.

Payoff Parameters

Our prior research (Ahn et al. 2001) suggests that, in place of absolute measures of fear, greed, and cooperators' gain, normalized measures of these factors are better predictors of cooperation rates. Normalized measures are created by dividing the absolute values of each of these measures by the difference between the maximum and minimum possible payoffs, $\pi(D,C)$ and $\pi(C,D)$, respectively. That is, normalized fear $(Fn) = [\pi(D,D) - \pi(C,D)] / [\pi(D,C) - \pi(C,D)]$,

normalized greed $(Gn) = [\pi(D,C) - \pi(C,C)] / [\pi(D,C) - \pi(C,D)]$,

and

$$\text{normalized cooperators' gain} \\ (CGn) = [\pi(C,C) - \pi(D,D)] / [\pi(D,C) - \pi(C,D)].$$

This normalization has the attractive feature that

normalized fear (Fn) + normalized greed (Gn) + normalized cooperators' gain $(CGn) = 1$.

Thus the measure allows for a useful way to understand how changing one dimension of the game affects other dimensions. We propose the following three behavioral conjectures:

1. The rate of cooperation is negatively related to the level of normalized fear.

2. The rate of cooperation is negatively related to the level of normalized greed.

3. The rate of cooperation is positively related to the level of normalized cooperators' gain.

The six games shown in figure 12.2 systematically vary CGn, Fn, and Gn, as shown in table 12.3. With these conjectures in mind, the variations in CGn, Fn, and Gn, presented in the top panel of table 12.3, allow us to examine the seven hypotheses listed at the bottom of the table. For example, hypothesis 1 predicts that the rate of cooperation will be higher in game 1 than in game 2. This follows from the three conjectures because the value for CGn is higher and those for Fn and Gn are lower in game 1 than in game 2.

Results

Our summary analysis of the data is organized around two forms of presentation. First, we report data on overall rates of cooperation across the various games and design conditions. This gives us a broad view of how decisions vary with game conditions. We follow this analysis with a multivariate analysis of a logit model designed to allow us to examine various components of the decision environment statistically, as well as characteristics of players ascertained from a postexperiment survey. The survey contained the eight questions

**Table 12.3   Experimental Design: Game Parameters and
Game Hypotheses**

Normalized Value	High CGn	Low CGn
$Fn = Gn$	CGn = .4 (Game 1)	CGn = .2 (Game 2)
	Fn = .3	Fn = .4
	Gn = .3	Gn = .4
$Fn > Gn$	CGn = .4 (Game 3)	CGn = .2 (Game 4)
	Fn = .4	Fn = .5
	Gn = .2	Gn = .3
$FN < Gn$	CGn = .4 (Game 5)	CGn = .2 (Game 6)
	Fn = .2	Fn = .3
	Gn = .4	Gn = .5

Hypothesis	Basis for Hypothesis
1. Cooperation in game 1 > cooperation in game 2	Fn, Gn, CGn
2. Cooperation in game 3 > cooperation in game 4	Fn, Gn, CGn
3. Cooperation in game 5 > cooperation in game 6	Fn, Gn, CGn
4. Cooperation in game 1 > cooperation in game 4	Fn, CGn
5. Cooperation in game 5 > cooperation in game 2	Fn, CGn
6. Cooperation in game 1 > cooperation in game 6	Gn, CGn
7. Cooperation in game 3 > cooperation in game 2	Gn, CGn

Source: Authors' compilation.

listed in the appendix to this chapter as well as other questions related to subject characteristics.

Cooperation Rates   Table 12.4 reports the cooperation rates observed across the six games for the games in the random-matching and fixed-matching designs. Our fourth observation is based on the data in this table: Rates of cooperation are much higher in the fixed-matching design than in the random-matching design. Focusing on the last row of table 12.4, where cooperation rates are pooled across the games uniformly, higher cooperation rates can be seen in the fixed-matching design, averaging 32 percent, whereas the average rate in the random-matching design is only 10 percent. Allowing subjects the opportunity to build reciprocal relationships helps to build trust between some pairs of decision makers, leading to higher levels of cooperation.

Table 12.4 also brings us to our fifth observation: Rates of cooperation are generally lower in phase 2 than in phase 1. Across both protocol settings there is clearly a tendency for cooperation to decline with repetition of the game. This is an empirical result that is consis-

Table 12.4   Cooperation Rates Across Game Structures in Random-Matching and Fixed-Matching Designs (Percentage)

	Random Matching		Fixed Matching	
Game Parameters	Phase 1	Phase 2	Phase 1	Phase 2
High (CGn = .4)				
Game 1 (Fn = .3, Gn = .3)	31.3	22.9	35.4	43.8
Game 3 (Fn = .4, Gn = .2)	18.8	27.1	37.5	33.3
Game 5 (Fn = .2, Gn = .4)	27.1	20.8	43.8	29.2
Average	25.7	23.6	38.9	35.4
Low (CGn = .2)				
Game 2 (Fn = .4, Gn = .4)	14.6	12.5	31.3	33.3
Game 4 (Fn = .5, Gn = .3)	8.3	6.3	25.0	27.1
Game 6 (Fn = .3, Gn = .5)	6.3	4.2	29.2	20.8
Average	9.7	7.6	28.5	27.1

Source: Authors' compilation.
Note: Total observations per game = 96.

tent with other studies focusing on repeated prisoner's dilemma and *public-goods games* (see chapter 2, this volume, for citations). In the current setting, the introduction of information regarding the cooperative behavior of others with whom a subject will be playing does not affect this repeatedly found decline in cooperation.

Our sixth observation is that, based on the three conjectures presented earlier, variations in fear, greed, and cooperators' gain have the expected impact on play. In the random-matching design, cooperation rates are almost three times higher in games with high CGn than in games with low CGn. The direction of this effect also holds in the fixed-matching design, though the impact is smaller. One can examine the paired-game hypotheses listed in table 12.3 by matching games within the four design conditions (two matching protocols and two phases). This allows for twenty-eight (seven times four) paired comparisons. The direction of the hypothesis is supported in twenty-six of the twenty-eight possible comparisons.

Multivariate Analysis   It is clear from the foregoing discussion that subjects' experiences and their expectations about the experiences of others influence their decisions in future games. To analyze this more dynamic story, and to investigate more fully the impact of variables related to game parameters and subject characteristics ascertained from the postexperiment survey, we turn to a logit regression analysis of the data.

Tables 12.5 and 12.6 present results from a logistic model designed for predicting cooperative play in phase 1 and phase 2, respectively.

Table 12.5   Logit Analysis of Game Parameters, History, and Survey Results: Phase 1

Variable	Random Matching Coefficient	Random Matching p-value	Fixed Matching Coefficient	Fixed Matching p-value
Constant	0.09	0.99	−4.45	0.23
CGn	9.31	0.00	6.94	0.00
Gn	2.48	0.28	2.80	0.21
Round	−0.11	0.10	−0.09	0.15
PrevRnd-DC	0.79	0.17	0.84	0.13
PrevRnd-CD	−0.34	0.62	0.81	0.13
PrevRnd-CC	2.69	0.00	4.64	0.00
TypeIndifferent	0.57	0.55	0.29	0.59
TypeAssurance	0.12	0.84	0.64	0.15
Trust-level	−0.08	0.71	0.37	0.18
Gender	0.44	0.36	−0.01	0.97
Age	−0.28	0.50	−0.02	0.90
Number of observations	264		264	
LR $\chi^2(11)$	34.00		135.89	
Prob $> \chi^2$	0.00		0.00	
Pseudo R^2	0.15		0.41	
LnL	−97.00		−99.40	

Source: Authors' compilation.

Results are reported separately for each matching protocol. Coefficient values and corresponding p values are reported for each variable. The dependent variable—1 if the decision is C, 0 if the decision is D—is regressed on the following set of variables defined for player i, created to capture key elements of the game parameters and history of play within a decision environment. Based on game parameters,

- CGn is the value of normalized cooperators' gain in the specific game being played;
- Gn is the value of normalized greed in the specific game being played.

Based on decision experience in the previous round,

- PrevRnd-DC is 1 if subject i defected in the previous round but the other player cooperated;
- PrevRnd-CD is 1 if subject i cooperated in the previous round but the other player defected;

Table 12.6   Logit Analysis of Game Parameters, History, and Survey Results: Phase 2

Choice	Random Matching Coefficient	p-value	Fixed Matching Coefficient	p-value
Constant	25.18	0.07	4.02	0.50
Gain	13.95	0.00	3.60	0.17
Greed	0.99	0.74	−0.66	0.80
Round	−0.37	0.00	−0.07	0.34
Phase1-C-Self	0.78	0.02	0.05	0.46
Phase1-C-Others	0.12	0.29	−0.03	0.44
PrevRnd-DC	−0.68	0.50	1.67	0.01
PrevRnd-CD	1.23	0.15	1.35	0.03
PrevRnd-CC	1.13	0.28	4.73	0.00
TypeIndifferent	3.97	0.02	1.21	0.04
TypeAssurance	1.92	0.03	0.42	0.41
Trust-level	0.26	0.47	0.55	0.15
Gender	−2.62	0.01	−0.22	0.68
Age	−1.68	0.02	−0.38	0.18
Number of observations	264		264	
LR $\chi^2(11)$	98.40		156.83	
Prob > χ^2	0.00		0.00	
Pseudo R^2	0.46		0.49	
LnL	−57.70		−81.80	

Source: Authors' compilation.

- PrevRnd-CC is 1 if subject i and the other player cooperated in the previous round.

Based on the type of player as measured by responses to the questionnaire,

- TypeIndifferent is indifferent to outcomes (C,C) and (D,C) (1 if indifferent, 0 otherwise);
- TypeAssurance prefers outcome (C,C) to (D,C) (1 if subject prefers [C,C], 0 otherwise);
- Trust-level is the trust score derived from the three survey questions on trust.

Based on personal characteristics,

- Gender is the gender of the subject (1 if female, 0 if male);[9]
- Age is the age of the subject.

Note that the analysis does not contain a variable for Fn. By definition, the sum of Fn, Gn, and CGn is 1. Any change in one of the measures must be offset by a change in one or both of the other variables. This implies that there is perfect multicollinearity between the sum of these variables and the constant term. Thus, in our analysis, the estimated coefficients for Gn and CGn are interpreted as the behavioral effect of these variables when there is a numerically offsetting change in Fn. Similarly, the measured effects of TypeIndifferent and TypeAssurance are relative to a base condition of TypePD; PrevRnd-DC, PrevRnd-CD, and PrevRnd-CC are relative to a base condition of PrevRnd-DD; and Gender measures the effect on cooperation rates of females relative to males.[10]

The summary observations reported here focus on three classes of variables: game parameters, history of play, and subject characteristics based on the postexperiment questionnaire. We begin with a summary related to phase 1, displayed in table 12.5.

In phase 1, CGn is statistically significant in both the random- and fixed-matching designs, but Gn is not. Thus there is consistent evidence that an increase in the normalized value of cooperator's gain, when offset by a decrease in the normalized value of fear, increases cooperation rates. Furthermore, the coefficient on normalized greed is not significantly different from zero, implying that the impact on cooperation rates of a change in Gn, offset by an opposing change in Fn, has no impact on cooperation rates.

There is strong evidence that cooperation rates in phase 1 decrease with repetition of the game and that cooperation by both players in the previous round is a strong predictor of continued cooperation. The variables Round and PrevRnd-CC are statistically significant in phase 1 of both the random- and fixed-matching designs. The importance of PrevRnd-CC is clear for the fixed-matching design. That both subjects cooperated in a previous round suggests the building of a reciprocal relationship and trust in that relationship. Interestingly, however, the fact that this variable is significant in the random-matching design suggests that this type of behavioral effect is maintained even when the subjects know that the person with whom they will be matched in the next round is chosen at random. Note that the variables PrevRnd-DC and PrevRnd-CD are not statistically significant. This implies that if a subject did not cooperate in the last round but the person with whom he or she was matched did cooperate, or if a subject cooperated in the last round but the person with whom he or she was matched did not, the impact on cooperation (positive or negative) is not significantly different than if neither player cooperated.

In phase 1, there is no general support for the hypothesis that cooperation rates are correlated with type of player, as measured by survey questions. Consistent with the results presented in the discussion on decision making in one-shot prisoner's dilemmas, in neither the random- nor the fixed-matching designs do we observe any statistically significant coefficients for either the type variables or the trust scale. Furthermore, no support is found for gender or age as significantly affecting behavior.[11]

Table 12.6 focuses on the analysis of phase 2 data. In phase 2, the subjects are grouped according to the decisions they made in phase 1. Those who played C the most often are grouped together, and those who played D the most often are grouped together. The multivariate analysis contains two new variables related to this design difference:

- Phase1-C-Self is the overall rate of cooperation by subject i in phase 1;

- Phase1-C-Others is the overall rate of cooperation in phase 1 by others in subject i's phase 2 subgroup.

The logit model results from phase 2 are similar to those from phase 1, with a few notable exceptions. In the random-matching design, the newly included variable Phase1-C-Self is significant, as expected, with a positive coefficient. Interestingly, the variable Phase1-C-Others is not statistically significant. In addition, there does appear to be an effect of gender and age in this design condition. The coefficients for gender and age are negative, suggesting a decrease in cooperation rates by females and older subjects in phase 2 of the random-matching design.

In the fixed-matching design, the most notable change is the lack of significance of CGn and the significance of PrevRnd-DC, PrevRnd-CD, and PrevRnd-CC. These results suggest the clear importance of the level of trust in the reciprocal relationship that is or is not built in a design with repeated encounters between the same two subjects. The magnitude of the variable PrevRnd-CC is much larger than the other two, implying the importance of a situation in which both subjects are cooperating. Interestingly, however, both PrevRnd-DC and PrevRnd-CD have positive coefficients. This suggests that the rate of cooperation in the next round is increased by either player's having cooperated in the previous round, relative to the situation in which both defected.

Concluding Comments

If subjects make decisions based purely on pecuniary returns, noncooperative game theory makes a single, unambiguous prediction of the behavior likely to occur in one-shot or finitely repeated prisoner's dilemma games. All subjects are expected to play the dominant strategy of defection. Behavior in prisoner's dilemma experiments, however, tends to vary from very low levels to somewhat moderate levels of cooperation. As this chapter has demonstrated, several factors may affect the likelihood of individuals' trusting one another sufficiently to play the dominated strategy in a prisoner's dilemma game (as measured by pecuniary payoffs): the specific relations among the pecuniary payoffs, the types of players involved, the information made available to players about player types, and the linkages among players in repeated games.

The results from the one-shot game settings lead to several puzzles. In our initial study (Ahn, Ostrom, and Walker forthcoming), we found that approximately one-third of the population of subjects chose the cooperative outcome over the defection outcome in a simultaneous-play prisoner's dilemma game. Furthermore, when subjects were allowed to play in a sequential version of the game, more than half of the subjects chose to cooperate and trusted their counterparts to do the same. Based on responses to a questionnaire administered at the time of the experiment, there is a strong correlation between subjects' choices and their responses regarding preferences for cooperative outcomes.

In the second study reported here, subjects played multiple prisoner's dilemma games in a one-shot setting. In this setting, the level of cooperation and trust was lower. For some game parameters, the choice of the cooperative outcome was as low as 23 percent. Specific payoff parameters had only a marginal impact on subjects' behavior in this setting. Moreover, the measures of player type and level of general trust obtained from a questionnaire administered several weeks before the experiment was conducted had little correlation with behavior.

The repeated-game setting, on the other hand, generated support for several of the conjectures regarding factors that might influence play. Increasing the joint benefit that subjects could achieve—cooperators' gain—is associated with higher levels of cooperation in the first phase of both designs and, in phase 2, when the players are randomly matched. Although noncooperative game theory treats all payoff configurations that fit a prisoner's dilemma structure as if they were the same, subjects in a repeated-game setting do not. Payoff configurations make a difference.

Subjects in a repeated game are most responsive in those settings in which they receive direct information about the type of player with whom they are playing as a result of being matched with one player for a series of plays. In the fixed-matching design, the strongest impact on a subject's cooperation was having just experienced a round of play in which both players cooperated. Furthermore, cooperative play by just one player in the previous round also increased cooperation relative to joint defection in the previous round.

On the other hand, questionnaire measures for the type of player and for the trust that a player brings to a game setting did not have an impact on behavior, as was also the case in the second one-shot study. In this case, the questionnaire was administered at the time of the experiment. This lack of a close correlation between behavior and questionnaire responses should be of concern to researchers focusing on similar issues. It is quite striking that the three questions most often used in survey research to measure general trust were not predictive of the likelihood that subjects will trust each other even in a repeated setting. Subjects may well be responding in a glib manner to this survey instrument, as Russell Hardin worries in chapter 3 of this volume.

At the time we designed our study and presented the paper on which this chapter is based, we did not know of any other research study that had examined whether responses to the basic questions used on many surveys to measure trust were predictive of trusting or trustworthy behavior in a dilemma setting. Independently, Edward Glaeser and colleagues (2000) have conducted an interesting study using a survey instrument containing the same questions as we asked on our questionnaire (plus others). They then conducted several versions of the trust game described in chapter 1 of this book (see also Berg, Dickhaut, and McCabe 1995). Their findings are similar to ours. None of the standard General Social Survey questions predicted trusting behavior in any of their experimental designs. They did find, however, that specific questions about past experiences of being trusted or extending trust in the past were positively associated with trusting behavior. Moreover, the General Social Survey questions were positively related to trustworthy, if not trusting, behavior. Thus, from our own study and studies by others reported elsewhere, we recognize that much more work is needed to examine the relation between trust as measured in survey research and trust as embodied in behavior in one-shot or repeated social dilemmas.

This chapter does not represent the views of the Federal Trade Commission or any individual commissioner. The authors would like to thank the American Academy of Arts and Sciences and the National Science Foundation (Grant #SBR 93 19835) for funding support for the experiments reported in this research. We would like to thank the Russell Sage Foundation for its support for two conferences at which the findings were presented. We thank the participants in both conferences for their thoughtful suggestions, Ron Baker for his useful comments, and Patty Zielinski for her outstanding editing.

Appendix

Questions Related to Preferences over Outcomes

1. How satisfactory would it be to you if both you and the other player chose B [the defection option]?

1 2 3 4 5 6 7

Very Unsatisfactory   Very Satisfactory

2. How satisfactory would it be to you if both you and the other player chose A [the cooperation option]?

1 2 3 4 5 6 7

Very Unsatisfactory   Very Satisfactory

3. How satisfactory would it be to you if you chose B and the other player chose A?

1 2 3 4 5 6 7

Very Unsatisfactory   Very Satisfactory

4. How satisfactory would it be to you if you chose A and the other player chose B?

1 2 3 4 5 6 7

Very Unsatisfactory   Very Satisfactory

5. To what extent do you think that most other students in this class would select B when answering this class survey?

1 2 3 4 5 6 7

Not Very Much   Very Much

Questions Related to Trust

6. Generally speaking, would you say that most people can be trusted or that you can't be too careful dealing with people?

    Most people can be trusted _____ Can't be too careful _____ Don't know _____

7. Would you say that most of the time people try to be helpful or that they are mostly just looking out for themselves?

    Try to be helpful _____ Just look out for themselves _____ Don't know _____

8. Do you think that most people would take advantage of you if they got a chance or would they try to be fair?

    Most people would take advantage _____ They would try to be fair _____ Don't know _____

Notes

1. This discussion as well as many of the empirical results provided in this chapter draw significantly from Schmidt et al. (2001).

2. In a related study, Ken Clark and Martin Sefton (2001) find that increasing greed significantly lowered levels of cooperation in one-shot prisoner's dilemma games in which one subject moves first and the second mover has knowledge of the choice of the first subject.

3. See Hayashi et al. (1999) for a discussion of the literature related to this view.

4. The questionnaire was administered, double blind, after subjects had made their own game decisions but before they had learned of the decisions of the persons with whom they were matched in the prisoner's dilemma game (see also Watabe et al. 1996, for similar findings from Japan, and Hayashi et al. 1999, for a comparison of responses from Japan and the United States).

5. An alternative explanation might be found in the work of Thomas Palfrey and Jeffrey Prisbrey (1997). They specify a utility function, in the context of voluntary-contribution experiments, that includes the warm-glow term and other subjects' payoffs as well as a player's own monetary payoff. Also see Bolton and Ockenfels (2000).

6. In related research, James Andreoni and John Miller (1993) investigate random matching and fixed matching in two-person prisoner's dilemma

games. Subjects are paired with human subjects or computerized decision makers. Thomas Palfrey and Howard Rosenthal (1994) investigate the impact of random and fixed matching in a repeated step-level public-goods game with groups of three and four subjects. Both studies find more cooperation in fixed-match settings than in settings in which subjects are randomly matched.

7. Fewer than 2 percent of the students in these classes are economics majors, although many are business majors.

8. These questions have been used repeatedly on the General Social Survey conducted by the National Opinion Research Center. See Putnam (1995) and Rahn and Transue (1998) as examples of studies relying on these questions to measure trust.

9. We are simply introducing two attributes of individuals—age and gender—as control variables. Both are frequently thought to affect trust and cooperative behavior. On the impact of gender, see Eckel and Grossman (1998).

10. Note that comparisons are relative to the base condition in which neither subject cooperated in the previous round.

11. We have also checked to see if there is any significant correlation between behavior and either the type variables or the trust scale using only the data from the first round of each design. The results were identical to those using data from all rounds; there was no significant correlation between behavior and type or trust level as revealed by the responses to the survey questionnaire.

References

Ahn, T. K., Elinor Ostrom, David Schmidt, Robert Shupp, and James M. Walker. 2001. "Cooperation in PD Games: Fear, Greed, and History of Play." *Public Choice* 106(1–2): 137–55.

Ahn, T. K., Elinor Ostrom, and James M. Walker. Forthcoming. "Incorporating Motivational Heterogeneity into Game Theoretic Models of Collective Action." *Public Choice.*

Andreoni, James, and John H. Miller. 1993. "Rational Cooperation in the Finitely Repeated Prisoner's Dilemma: Experimental Evidence." *Economic Journal* 103(418): 570–85.

Berg, Joyce, John Dickhaut, and Kevin McCabe. 1995. "Trust, Reciprocity, and Social History." *Games and Economic Behavior* 10(1): 122–42.

Binmore, Ken G. 1998. "The Evolution of Fairness Norms." *Rationality and Society* 10(3): 275–302.

Bohnet, Iris, and Bruno S. Frey. 1999. "The Sound of Silence in Prisoner's Dilemma and Dictator Games." *Journal of Economic Behavior and Organization* 38(1): 43–57.

Bolton, Gary, and Axel Ockenfels. 2000. "ERC: A Theory of Equity, Reciprocity, and Competition." *American Economic Review* 90(1): 166–93.

Cain, Michael. 1998. "An Experimental Investigation of Motives and Information in the Prisoner's Dilemma Game." *Advances in Group Processes* 15:133–60.

Camerer, Colin. 1990. "Behavior Game Theory." In *Insights in Decision Making: A Tribute to Hillel J. Einhord*, edited by Robin Hogarth. Chicago: University of Chicago Press.

Cho, Kisuk, and Byung-il Choi. 2000. "A Cross-Society Study of Trust and Reciprocity: Korea, Japan, and the U.S." *International Studies Review* 3(2): 31–43.

Clark, Ken, and Martin Sefton. 2001. "The Sequential Prisoner's Dilemma: Evidence on Reciprocation." *Economic Journal* 111: 51–68.

Coleman, James. 1988. "Free Riders and Zealots: The Role of Social Networks." *Sociological Theory* 6(1): 52–57.

Crawford, Sue E. S., and Elinor Ostrom. 1995. "A Grammar of Institutions." *American Political Science Review* 89(3): 582–600.

Croson, Rachel. 1999. "Theories of Altruism and Reciprocity. Evidence from Linear Public Goods Games." Working paper. University of Pennsylvania, Wharton School.

Eckel, Catherine C., and Philip J. Grossman. 1998. "Are Women Less Selfish Than Men? Evidence from Dictator Experiments." *Economic Journal* 108(448): 726–35.

Falk, Armin, and Urs Fischbacher. 1998. "A Theory of Reciprocity." Working paper. Zurich, Switzerland: University of Zurich, Institute for Empirical Research.

Fehr, Ernst, and Klaus M. Schmidt. 1999. "A Theory of Fairness, Competition, and Cooperation." *Quarterly Journal of Economics* 114(3): 817–68.

Glaeser, Edward L., David I. Laibson, José A. Scheinkman, and Christine L. Soutter. 2000. "Measuring Trust." *Quarterly Journal of Economics* 115(3): 811–46.

Gunnthorsdottir, Anna, Daniel Houser, Kevin McCabe, and Holly Ameden. 2000. "Excluding Free-Riders Improves Reciprocity and Promotes the Private Provision of Public Goods." Working paper. Tucson: University of Arizona, Department of Economics.

Güth, Werner, and Hartmut Kliemt. 1998. "The Indirect Evolutionary Approach: Bridging the Gap Between Rationality and Adaptation." *Rationality and Society* 10(3): 377–99.

Güth, Werner, and Menahem Yaari. 1992. "An Evolutionary Approach to Explaining Reciprocal Behaviour in a Simple Strategic Game." In *Explaining Process and Change*, edited by Hartmut Kliemt. Ann Arbor: University of Michigan Press.

Hayashi, Nahoko, Elinor Ostrom, James M. Walker, and Toshio Yamagishi. 1999. "Reciprocity, Trust, and the Sense of Control: A Cross-societal Study." *Rationality and Society* 11(1): 27–46.

Hoffman, Elizabeth, Kevin McCabe, and Vernon Smith. 1996. "Social Distance and Other-Regarding Behavior in Dictator Games." *American Economic Review* 86(3): 653–60.

Kahneman, Daniel, Jack L. Knetsch, and Richard H. Thaler. 1986. "Fairness and the Assumptions of Economics." *Journal of Business* 59(4): S285–S300.

Kelley, Harold H., and John W. Thibaut. 1978. *Interpersonal Relations*. New York: Wiley.

Kollock, Peter. 1998. "Transforming Social Dilemmas: Group Identity and Cooperation." In *Modeling Rationality, Morality, and Evolution*, edited by Peter Danielson. Oxford: Oxford University Press.

Komorita, Samuel S., James Sweeny, and David A. Kravitz. 1980. "Cooperative Choice in the N-Person Dilemma Situation." *Journal of Personality and Social Psychology* 38(3): 504–16.

Kramer, Roderick M., Charles G. McClintock, and David M. Messick. 1986. "Social Values and Cooperative Response to a Simulated Resource Conservation Crisis." *Journal of Personality* 54(3): 576–92.

Kreps, David M., Paul Milgrom, John Roberts, and Robert Wilson. 1982. "Rational Cooperation in the Finitely Repeated Prisoner's Dilemma." *Journal of Economic Theory* 27(2): 245–52.

Kuhlman, D. Michael, Curt R. Camac, and Denise A. Cunha. 1986. "Individual Differences in Social Orientation." In *Experimental Social Dilemmas*, edited by Henk A. M. Wilke, David M. Messick, and Christel G. Rutte. Frankfurt, Germany: Peter Lang.

Ochs, Jack, and Alvin E. Roth. 1989. "An Experimental Study of Sequential Bargaining." *American Economic Review* 79(3): 355–84.

Ostrom, Elinor. 1998. "A Behavioral Approach to the Rational Choice Theory of Collective Action." *American Political Science Review* 92(1): 1–22.

Palfrey, Thomas R., and Jeffrey E. Prisbrey. 1997. "Anomalous Behavior in Public Goods Experiments: How Much and Why?" *American Economic Review* 87(5): 829–46.

Palfrey, Thomas R., and Howard Rosenthal. 1994. "Repeated Play, Cooperation, and Coordination: An Experimental Study." *Review of Economic Studies* 61(3): 545–65.

Putnam, Robert D. 1995. "Tuning In, Tuning Out: The Strange Disappearance of Social Capital in America." *PS: Political Science and Politics* 28(4): 664–83.

Rabin, Matthew. 1993. "Incorporating Fairness in Game Theory and Economics." *American Economic Review* 83(5): 1281–1302.

Rahn, Wendy M., and John E. Transue. 1998. "Social Trust and Value Change: The Decline of Social Capital in American Youth, 1976–1995." *Political Psychology* 19(3): 545–66.

Rapoport, Anatol. 1988a. "Experiments with N-Person Social Traps I: Prisoner's Dilemma, Weak Prisoner's Dilemma, Volunteer's Dilemma, and Largest Number." *Journal of Conflict Resolution* 32(3): 457–72.

———. 1988b. "Experiments with N-Person Social Traps II: Tragedy of the Commons." *Journal of Conflict Resolution* 32(3): 473–88.

Rapoport, Anatol, and Albert M. Chammah. 1965. *Prisoner's Dilemma: A Study in Conflict and Cooperation*. Ann Arbor: University of Michigan Press.

Raub, Werner. 1990. "A General Game-Theoretic Model of Preference Adaptations in Problematic Social Situations." *Rationality and Society* 2(1): 67–93.

Saijo, Tatsuyoshi, and Hideki Nakamura. 1995. "The 'Spite' Dilemma in Voluntary-Contributions-Mechanism Experiments." *Journal of Conflict Resolution* 39(3): 535–60.

Schmidt, David, Robert Shupp, James Walker, T. K. Ahn, and Elinor Ostrom.

2001. "Dilemma Games: Game Parameters and Matching Protocols." *Journal of Economic Behavior and Organization* 46(4): 357–77.

Schmidt, David, Robert Shupp, James M. Walker, and Elinor Ostrom. 2002. "Playing Safe in Coordination Games: The Role of Risk Dominance, Payoff Dominance, and History of Play." Working paper. Bloomington: Indiana University, Workshop in Political Theory and Policy Analysis.

Sen, Amatrya. 1974. "Choice, Orderings, and Morality." In *Practical Reason: Papers and Discussions*, edited by Stephan Körner. Oxford: Blackwell.

Wagner, Thomas. 1998. "Reciprocity and Efficiency." *Rationality and Society* 10(3): 347–76.

Watabe, Motoki, Shigeru Terai, Nahoko Hayashi, and Toshio Yamagishi. 1996. "Cooperation in the One-Shot Prisoner's Dilemmas Based on Expectations of Reciprocity." *Japanese Journal of Experimental Social Psychology* 36(2): 183–96. (In Japanese, with an English summary.)

Yamagishi, Toshio, and Karen S. Cook. 1993. "Generalized Exchange and Social Dilemmas." *Social Psychology Quarterly* 56(4): 235–48.

Chapter 13

Cross-Societal Experimentation on Trust: A Comparison of the United States and Japan

I T IS generally believed that Japanese society and, in particular, business relations in Japan are characterized by a high level of trust. Collectivist preferences for in-group harmony and mutually cooperative practices in Japan are believed to underlie the high level of general trust, particularly in contrast with the individualistic and competitive pursuit of private as against collective goals in American society. At the same time, insightful social observers such as Alexis de Tocqueville (1945 [1835–40]) and Francis Fukuyama (1995) have characterized American society as having a high level of general trust. Fukuyama argues that strong family ties in societies such as China, France, and southern Italy prevent trust from developing beyond the confines of the family; whereas the absence of strong familism in such countries as the United States, Japan, and Germany breeds general trust that extends beyond the narrow confines of the family.

Neither characterization—of Americans as nontrusting and Japanese as trusting or of both as trusting societies—is consistent with empirical findings, however. Past research comparing the United States and Japan has repeatedly demonstrated that the level of general trust is much higher in American society than in Japanese society. A cross-societal questionnaire survey has demonstrated that the average level of general trust is higher among Americans than among Japanese (Yamagishi and Yamagishi 1994). Although this survey did not use nationally representative samples, another more representative study conducted by the Japanese Institute of Statistical Mathematics (Hayashi et al. 1982), using representative national samples, reports a similar cross-national difference. According to this study, 47 percent of the American sample (n = 1,571), when asked, "Do you think you can put your trust in most people, or do you think it's always best to be on your guard?" answered that "people can be trusted." In contrast, only 26 percent of the Japanese sample (n = 2,032) gave the same response. Similarly, in response to the question, "Would you say that most of the time people try to be helpful, or that they are mostly just looking out for themselves?" 47 percent of the American sample, compared with 19 percent of the Japanese sample, replied that people try to be helpful.

The apparent inconsistency between the widely shared view of American and Japanese societies and the results of the cross-societal questionnaire studies can be resolved by understanding the distinction between trust and "assurance" (Yamagishi and Yamagishi 1994). Japanese society is characterized by a prevalence of commitment networks, such as keiretsu networks among business firms, and an "assurance" of mutual cooperation in such commitment relations. In an environment in which all transactions are conducted within commitment relations, "trustworthy" behavior from interaction partners is assured by the nature of the incentives. This assurance of mutual cooperation in Japan, however, does not imply that the Japanese are generally trusting. Whether or not one has a high level of default expectation of other people's trustworthiness—the definition of "general trust" used in the construction of interpersonal trust scales (Rotter 1967; Yamagishi and Yamagishi 1994)—is logically independent from the social security of the situation in which an individual lives.[1] Even a person who believes strongly in the trustworthiness of people in general would not feel comfortable walking alone down an alley in downtown New York after midnight. Japanese society provides various assurance mechanisms in business, employment, and other areas that include mutual monitoring and sanctioning systems (Hechter and Kanazawa 1993) which induce people to act in a "trustworthy" manner. This does not mean, however, that the Japanese believe in the trustworthiness of people in general (especially when dealing with "outsiders").

The distinction between sociorelationally based "assurance," on the one hand, and trust as a belief in general human trustworthiness, on the other, may be easier to understand in the following imaginary experimental situation. Participants in this experiment play a game of trust in which the first player decides whether to accept $10 directly from the experimenter or instead to entrust $30 to a partner (the second player). The second player receives $10 if the first player accepts the $10 directly from the experimenter. If the first player decides to entrust $30, the second player is given $30 from the experimenter, leaves whatever amount he or she wants to allocate to the first player in an envelope, pockets the remainder, and leaves the laboratory. The first player receives whatever amount has been put in the envelope. Anonymity of players' choices, both to each other and to the experimenter, is completely assured.

The first player's choice in this imaginary experiment should depend on the expectation of how much the second player will leave in the envelope. How much the second player will leave in the envelope should depend on two factors: the utility he or she derives from leaving a "fair" amount in the envelope relative to the utility derived from the extra income from leaving nothing in the envelope, and the expected future consequences of leaving an "unfair" amount in the envelope. The second factor is negligible in the setting of this example because there is no further interaction between the two players. Thus the first player's choice should depend on the level of general trust (that is, the default expectation of how much utility the partner derives from leaving a "fair" amount in the envelope). In other words, the first player's choice should depend on what kind of a model of a human being he or she applies to the second player, about whom the first player knows nothing.

Adding an option for the first player to "punish" the second may dramatically affect the amount the second player leaves in the envelope. Suppose that the first player is given a choice, after learning how much the second has left in the envelope, to give a bonus of $100 to the second player. The first player's choice—whether or not to give the bonus (experimenter's money) to the second player—does not affect the first player's own income. The first player's control of the bonus for the second player provides an award for the second player's "fair" behavior. Thus the opportunity to earn the bonus helps to assure trustworthy behavior. Under these circumstances, very few second players would dare leave less than $10 in the envelope. The first player's choice in this experiment depends on his or her assessment of two factors: the level of assurance of the second player's "fair" behavior that the incentives to the second player provide, and how much he or she trusts the second player in the absence of such assurance.

What I call assurance is what Russell Hardin, in chapter 3 of this volume, calls incentive-based trust, and I reserve the term trust to refer to what Hardin calls normatively based trust. When my reason to expect a benign and cooperative behavior from you is based on rational calculation of your interest, I call the expectation assurance. When it is based on my belief that my interest means something to you, I call the expectation trust. With this distinction between trust and assurance in mind, I argue that Japanese society might be better characterized as a high-assurance society than a high-trust society. High expectations among Japanese of cooperative behavior from others are based on the nature of social relations and incentives that derive from them rather than on the belief that others generally take my interest into account in their decisions. A series of cross-societal experiments that supports this view follows.

I use the term "cross-societal," rather than the more widely used "cross-cultural," in referring to experiments that compare American and Japanese participants' behaviors. The goal of cross-cultural experiments in psychology is to discern the universal from the culturally specific in the working of the human mind through comparisons of responses of people from various cultures. The goal of what I call "cross-societal" experimentation (Yamagishi 1998; Yamagishi, Cook, and Watabe 1998) is quite different: to extract the effect of sociorelational factors from the so-called cultural differences. This is done by systematically controlling the theoretically specified sociorelational factors and observing whether the cross-cultural differences in participants' responses disappear. If we still find a "cultural difference," even after experimentally controlling the theoretically relevant variables, then we are further encouraged to look more deeply into the aspects of culture that are responsible for the residual differences. If we succeed in finding relevant factors that are responsible for the residual differences, then we do not need to revert to culture to explain the existing cultural differences. In brief, the goal of cross-societal experimentation is to demonstrate that cultural differences can be investigated more fully by experimentally controlling or manipulating the theoretically relevant variables.

Cultural Collectivism and Cooperation Among Group Members

In 1988 I conducted an experiment on free riding and exit from the group using the cross-societal experimentation methodology to separate the sociorelational factors from cultural factors (Yamagishi 1988a). In this *public-good experiment* I compare the tendencies of American and Japanese participants to leave a group that contains free riders. The common view of the cultures in American and Japanese societies—the former characterized by individualism and the latter by collectivism—would imply that Japanese participants, compared with American participants, have a stronger preference for staying in the group, despite the occurrence of free riding on the part of other group members. The results of this experiment contradict this simplistic view of American and Japanese cultures: Americans exhibited a much stronger tendency to remain in the group than Japanese. American participants exited the group, on average, in only slightly more than one in twenty trials when the cost of exit was high (that is, when they incurred monetary costs for leaving), whereas Japanese participants exited the group much more frequently in approximately eight in twenty trials, though they earned much less money by doing so.

There was no such difference in exit rates, however, when the exit costs were low. These results indicate that although both American and Japanese participants disliked staying in a group with free riders (as evidenced by the high level of exit responses among both national groups in the low-cost condition), American participants stayed in the group when the exit response was sufficiently costly, whereas Japanese participants were willing to pay the extra cost for the exit option. These results would be difficult to explain under the traditional view of culture. If the Japanese are collectivist in the sense that they prefer to be part of the group rather than independent from the group, and if Americans are individualistic in the sense that they value independence from the group, then American participants should have exited more often than the Japanese participants.

This seemingly counterintuitive pattern of findings was predicted based on an institutional view of culture. According to this view, the Japanese often "prefer" to belong to groups and place group interests above their own individual interests not because of an intrinsic tendency but because it is in their own long-term interest to do so (see Hamaguchi 1982 for a similar view). In the context of a collective work group, Japanese society has developed systems of mutual monitoring and sanctioning to curtail free riding (Hechter and Kanazawa 1993), and these systems work for the group insofar as such a "collective solution" to the free rider problem is in place. However, in groups artificially created in the laboratory in which individuals lack opportunities for interacting with one another in person—the condition of this experiment—such collective solutions as informal mutual monitoring and sanctioning do not exist. In these situations, Japanese tend to choose to leave the group, at least more strongly so than American participants, as indicated by the experimental results.

Another 1988 experiment of mine provides an even clearer contrast between the traditional view of culture and the institutional view of culture. In a cross-societal experiment comparing cooperative tendencies in *social dilemmas* in the United States and Japan (Yamagishi 1988b), participants in four-person groups were each given $.50 in the United States or 100 yen in Japan (roughly equivalent amounts at the time of the experiment) and were asked how much of the money they wanted to provide for the welfare of the other group members. They could contribute any amount, from zero to the total. Amounts given to the group by participants were doubled in value, and the total was divided equally among the other three members at the end of each trial. Thus if all four contributed the full amount, each earned $1.00 or 200 yen. However, a single participant could have earned more ($1.50 or 300 yen) if he or she had not contributed anything and the other three had fully contributed.

The decision was repeated twelve times in Japan and sixteen times in the United States; thus the pure free rider could potentially earn $1.50 times sixteen (or $24.00) or 300 yen times twelve (or 3,600 yen) if all other members of the groups always contributed. This amount is larger than the amount they would have obtained if all four had contributed in full ($16.00 or 2,400 yen). Thus the dominant or "rational" choice was not to contribute. However, if everyone had chosen this dominant response, each would have earned only $.50 cents or 100 yen per trial and $8.00 or 1,200 yen in total. This situation represents a social dilemma in which each member has a choice between C (cooperation, contributing the full amount) and D (defection, contributing nothing); the choice of D produces a better outcome for a member than the choice of C, regardless of the choices of the other members; and yet the individual outcome when all members choose D is worse than the individual outcome when all choose C (see Dawes 1980; Kollock 1998; Messick and Brewer 1983; and Yamagishi 1995 for reviews of the social dilemma literature).

According to the individualistic view of culture—the view that Japanese individuals value group interests over individual interests more than Americans do—it is presumed that Japanese participants will cooperate more in this experiment than will American participants. According to the institutional view of culture—the view that Japanese individuals cooperate with the group because there exists a system of formal and informal mutual monitoring and sanctioning—Japanese participants should cooperate less than American participants in such an experimental social dilemma. This is because the Japanese are so accustomed to the sociorelationally based assurance system in which collective systems of mutual sanctioning guarantee mutual cooperation in the group that they would feel insecure in a social environment lacking such a system.

Based on this reasoning, I predicted that Japanese participants would have a lower level of trust in strangers and would cooperate less in social dilemmas involving strangers than American participants. This prediction received clear empirical support. American participants in this experiment cooperated more (contributing, on average, 56.2 percent of $.50 cents per trial) than Japanese participants (who contributed, on average, 44.4 percent of 100 yen per trial). Furthermore, the participants' responses to a questionnaire they had filled out a few weeks before participating in this experiment indicates that the American participants had higher levels of general trust than the Japanese. That is, in a group consisting of strangers, and lacking a sociorelational system that assured mutual cooperation, American participants voluntarily cooperated more—contributing more to the welfare of the group—than did the Japanese participants.

On the other hand, when participants were given opportunities to sanction one another, Japanese participants became much more cooperative. With the addition of opportunities for mutual sanctioning, Japanese participants' average cooperation level increased from 44.4 percent to 74.6 percent, an improvement of 30 percentage points. In contrast, the sanctioning opportunities did not have as strong an effect on the Americans. The sanctioning opportunities improved the average cooperation level of the American participants' from 56.2 percent to 75.5 percent, an improvement of 19 percentage points. This finding suggests that the "collectivist" behavior—cooperation for the welfare of the group as a whole—among the Japanese participants was maintained to a large extent by the system of mutual monitoring and sanctioning that assures mutual cooperation rather than by their presumed "value system" according to which each individual places the group's welfare above his or her own self-interest.

Uncertainty, Trust, and Commitment Formation

In a later study, Karen Cook, Motoki Watabe, and I compared American and Japanese participants' inclination toward forming commitment relations when presented with a socially uncertain situation (Yamagishi, Cook, and Watabe 1998). In this experiment, we pursued the implications of earlier experiments and showed that the cross-cultural difference in the collectivist behavioral pattern of forming commitment relations with particular partners and maintaining such secure relations disappear when the underlying factors responsible for such a behavioral pattern are experimentally controlled.

Trust and commitment formation are alternative solutions to the problem of social uncertainty (Yamagishi and Yamagishi 1994). We engage in social interactions with others to improve our own welfare, material or psychological. However, in interacting with others we make ourselves vulnerable. I use the term "social uncertainty" to refer to the risk of being exploited in social interactions. When we face social uncertainty in this sense, commitment formation is one of the most commonly used behavioral responses. Peter Kollock (1994) compares rice and rubber markets in Southeast Asia as an example of how social uncertainty promotes commitment formation. The quality of rice is immediately apparent upon simple inspection. The buyer has little risk of being cheated on the quality of rice and thus faces a low level of social uncertainty. In contrast, the quality of raw rubber is hard to judge; its quality can be known only after it has been processed. Cheating on quality is easier, and the consequence of being cheated in this situation is extremely serious. Thus the buyer of raw rubber faces a high level of social uncertainty.

This difference in social uncertainty concerning the quality of the products, Kollock argues, explains the observed difference in the dominant form of trade. Rice is usually traded in open markets between strangers, whereas rubber is often traded between a particular producer and broker who have formed a long-term relationship, often extending over several generations. A high level of social uncertainty concerning the quality of rubber is the determining factor in the development of such commitment relations between rubber producers and brokers.

Commitment formation as a solution to the problem of social uncertainty, however, has a weakness. Although it reduces the risk of being duped in interactions with unfamiliar people, it constrains opportunities that might exist outside the current relationship. Using terminology borrowed from economics, commitment formation reduces transaction costs, on the one hand, but imposes opportunity costs, on the other. In forming a commitment relationship with a particular partner, one obtains security (a reduction in social uncertainty) in exchange for reduced opportunities. Thus commitment formation is an efficient means for reducing uncertainty when outside opportunities are limited. On the other hand, such commitments become a liability rather than an asset as traders face more and better opportunities outside their current, mutually committed relationships. The levels of social uncertainty and opportunity costs for staying in commitment relations are the two fundamental factors that determine the level of the collectivist behavioral pattern of commitment formation. The third factor that affects the strength of the collectivist behavioral pattern is the level of general trust. General trust provides a springboard for people who have been "confined" to committed relationships to move out into the larger world of opportunities. In this way general trust emancipates people from the confines and security of stable commitment relations.

The stability of interorganizational, as well as interpersonal, relations makes exploitative, short-term profit-maximizing behavior less successful in Japan than in American society. The one who leaves a relationship for quick profit will have a harder time in a society in which other relationships are mainly closed to outsiders. The stable nature of social and organizational relations reduces social uncertainty and provides security inside of such relationships. This sense of security is what is often considered "trust" when characterizing the Japanese. However, in the absence of such sociorelational bases of security, the Japanese may feel more insecure than Americans. They may be more distrustful of strangers in general. This explains why Japanese respondents in the first two experiments trusted fewer of their fellow participants, cooperated less in a social dilemma setting, and more often left groups that included free riders. In the experiments presented in the remainder of this chapter, these three theoretically relevant factors—social uncertainty, opportunity cost, and general trust—were experimentally controlled in the comparisons of American and Japanese participants' collectivist behavioral pattern.

Experiments on Markets

Kollock (1994) conducted an experiment in which he simulated transactions between buyers and sellers in rice and rubber markets. In one condition, the true quality of the goods sold by sellers was known only to the seller. The seller made claims about the quality of the goods to potential buyers, but buyers had no information on which to judge the seller's claims and could be deceived concerning the quality of the goods they were buying. This condition represented the market for rubber. In the other condition, the quality of all goods offered for sale was transparent to both the sellers and the buyers. This condition represented the market for rice. Pairs of sellers and buyers emerged more frequently in the high uncertainty condition (the rubber market) than in the low certainty condition (the rice market) in which they exclusively traded with each other. With the use of this design, Kollock successfully demonstrated that social uncertainty promotes commitment formation between particular sellers and buyers.

My colleagues and I also simulated trading practices between buyers and sellers in an experiment that compared American and Japanese participants' responses to the two levels of social uncertainty (Yamagishi, Cook, and Watabe 1998). We predicted that the level of commitment formation would be the same among Americans and Japanese when they faced the same level of social uncertainty and when they were matched on their levels of general trust. In each country, the experiment took place in a comparably designed social psychology laboratory complex consisting of a control room and several compartments for the participants. Participants were provided with relevant information displayed on a computer located in front of them in each compartment, and their responses were entered into the computer through the keyboard.

Subjects were drawn from a participant pool that had been recruited several weeks before the experiment. Potential participants were divided into a high-trust group and a low-trust group, using a median split on a trust scale I had developed some years earlier (Yamagishi 1986, 1988b, 1988c, 1992). The questionnaire was administered upon recruitment into the participant pool. Equal numbers of high-trusters and low-trusters (fifty of each) were selected from the participant pool in each country, five or six of whom were scheduled for each experimental session. Participants were led to a private compartment as soon as they arrived at the laboratory and did not have a chance to meet other participants. However, the compartments were not well insulated, and they could hear the experimenter talking to other participants. The physical setup of the laboratory thus helped reduce the participants' suspicion that they might be interacting only with a computer, not with other participants, while also maintaining anonymity.

Although participants were told that they would be randomly assigned the role of either buyer or seller and would repeatedly conduct transactions, all were actually assigned the role of buyer. Buyers were provided with an initial endowment of $5.00 to use in the trading sessions, and at the end of the experiment they were paid that amount plus profits and minus losses. In each trading session, each buyer was matched with two sellers (actually computer responses) and was required to buy a commodity from one of them. Each transaction period began with sellers announcing the price of the commodity they were selling. Buyers did not know the actual quality of the commodity. If the quality of the commodity was standard, the experimenter would buy the commodity for $1.40 (or 140 yen). Thus, if the quality of the commodity was standard and the purchasing price was less than $1.40, the seller made a profit. If the quality was below standard, the resale price to the experimenter was less than $1.40. If the quality was above standard, the resale price was more than $1.40. The buyer knew neither the quality of the commodity nor the resale price reflecting the true quality until he or she resold it to the experimenter. Sellers could not control the quality of the commodities they sold; they could decide only on the price. Furthermore, sellers had only limited information about the quality of their commodities, and so buyers could not judge whether overpricing was intentional or not. Actually, the computer program randomly determined the offer price such that the maximum profit for the buyer was $0.50 and the maximum loss was $0.10 in each transaction from all sellers. During the first twenty trading sessions, each participant traded with two sellers

(sellers A and C). There was no programmed difference between the two sellers with regard to offers. However, there was a substantial difference between them with respect to their tendency to take advantage of an "extortion chance" after a transaction. "Extortion chances" were introduced to make the amount of social uncertainty clearly visible to participants. After each transaction, the computer gave the seller an "extortion chance" with a small probability. This information was public to the buyer. When the seller was given this opportunity, A and C were differently programmed regarding whether to use the opportunity. If the seller took advantage of an "extortion chance," a certain amount of money was taken from the buyer to whom the seller had sold the commodity. The amount of money that the seller could "extort" from the buyer increased as the trading continued: the seller could extort $1.20 (or 120 yen) from a buyer during the first seven transaction periods, $1.90 during the eighth to fourteenth periods, and $2.50 during the final six periods.

The computer was programmed such that each of the two sellers would have the extortion chance twice during the first twenty transactions. Seller A was programmed to take advantage of both opportunities; seller C was programmed never to use the extortion chance. In other words, A was programmed to act like an egoist who took advantage of any opportunity for self-aggrandizement, whereas C was programmed to behave like an honest person who did not exploit others even when given the opportunity to do so.

After the twentieth transaction period, partners were replaced, and seller F replaced seller A (the egoist). The transactions up to this point were preparation for the experimental manipulation. The actual experiment started with the twenty-first transaction period. Buyers now traded with a new set of sellers: seller C (who, from the experience of the previous twenty trading sessions, was known to be an honest person) and seller F (a stranger with whom the buyer had no previous experience). The buyer had to decide with whom to complete a transaction. Transactions with C were safe with regard to extortion opportunities, but F was programmed to offer a price lower than C's.

The independent variable, the level of social uncertainty, was manipulated by keeping or removing the "extortion chances" for the twenty-first to thirtieth transaction periods, the ten periods during which the buyer dealt with sellers C and F. In the low-uncertainty condition, buyers were told at the beginning of the twenty-first round that the extortion opportunities would no longer be available. In the high-uncertainty condition, not only did the "extortion chances" remain, but the amount of money extorted also increased to $4.00 (or 400 yen). However, the roulette wheel (the probability factor) never struck during the final ten sessions, and neither C nor F was actually given the chance to extort from the participant. Thus the two conditions were equivalent with respect to the actual behavior of C and F. The main dependent variable, the level of commitment formation, was the number of trades the participant made during the last ten trading sessions with the "honest" seller, C, rejecting the better offer from unknown seller F.

The result of this experiment clearly shows the effect of social uncertainty on commitment formation. The new seller, F, was programmed to offer lower selling prices. If the likelihood that F would behave selfishly was small, the buyer would be better off trading with F than with C. In the low-uncertainty condition, in which there was no "extortion chance," participants traded with F in about half of the last ten transaction periods. In the high-uncertainty condition, in which the buyer could suffer a big loss from the seller, the buyer concluded about twice as many transactions with C, who was safe but offered higher prices, as with F, whose degree of honesty the buyer did not know. This difference between conditions was statistically significant. Furthermore, responses to one of the postexperimental questionnaire items—"How important was it to keep the same seller as a trade partner in order to develop a trusting relationship with him or her?"—indicate that building a trusting relationship with trade partners was more important to participants in the high-uncertainty condition than in the low-uncertainty condition. These results indicate that the greater the level of social uncertainty, the stronger the tendency for people to form commitment relationships.

Our findings also suggest that there is little difference in the degree of commitment formation (in this case, the frequency of keeping seller C as transaction partner) between Japanese participants and American participants. It was thus demonstrated that the seeming difference in the collectivist behavioral pattern among Americans and Japanese—that is, their differential inclination to form commitment relations—can be explained by controlling for the theoretically relevant factors.

The finding support the proposition that social uncertainty facilitates commitment formation between particular exchange partners. It further demonstrates that social uncertainty has comparable effects on the collectivist behavioral pattern of commitment formation among American participants and Japanese participants when the two national samples are matched on their levels of general trust, social uncertainty, and opportunity cost (the difference in the offering prices of C and F). Another follow-up study (Yamagishi, Cook, and Watabe 1998) replicated these findings. The follow-up experiment also demonstrated that low-trusters are more strongly inclined to form commitment relation with particular partners than are high trusters.

The finding that nationality of the participants did not play a major role in determining the level of commitment formation requires special attention. This finding suggests that cross-societal experimentation can be a powerful tool for exploring what has been relegated to the category of general "cultural differences." In this study, we started with a theoretical prediction that the level of commitment formation between particular partners will be determined by the levels of social uncertainty and opportunity costs in the environment and the level of general trust of the partners. The "cultural difference" that the Japanese tend to form stable, long-term relationships between particular partners or within particular groups should thus disappear once these three factors are experimentally controlled. This is exactly what happened in the experiments reported in this chapter.

Trust and Reciprocity

The last piece of cross-societal experimentation to be discussed in this chapter is one conducted by Nahoko Hayashi, Elinor Ostrom, James Walker, and me (Hayashi et al. 1999). We started with the standard finding in the social-dilemma research that players of the *prisoner's dilemma* experiment are more likely to cooperate when they expect their partners to cooperate than when they anticipate defection (Dawes, McTavish, and Shaklee 1977; Marwell and Ames 1979; Messick et al. 1983; Sato and Yamagishi 1984; Tyszka and Grzelak 1976; Yamagishi 1986, 1988a, 1992; Yamagishi and Cook 1993; Yamagishi and Sato 1986). This finding has been obtained with both American participants and Japanese participants. On the other hand, Hayashi and colleagues thought that the source of the expectation might be different in the two groups. Compared with the Japanese, Americans have a higher level of general trust, and thus their expectation that the partner would cooperate is more strongly based on a general belief that most people would cooperate in such a situation.

In contrast, the Japanese would expect cooperation from the partner only within relationships in which mutual monitoring and control are possible. Such a possibility of monitoring and sanctioning the partner, of course, does not exist in the *one-shot* prisoner's dilemma played between anonymous partners. However, it is conjectured (and supported by experimental evidence) that prisoner's dilemma players often entertain the illusion of control of the partner's behavior (Karp et al. 1993; Morris, Sim, and Girotto 1998; Watabe et al. 1996; Yamagishi and Kiyonari 2000). In the ordinary, one-shot prisoner's dilemma, these two sources of expectation—general trust that people would generally cooperate in such a situation and the illusion of control—are both likely to exist. Hayashi and colleagues separated the two usually confounded sources of the partner's expectation by using a sequential form of the one-shot prisoner's dilemma. To keep the story simple, I am presenting here only two of the six conditions used in this cross-societal experiment. The first condition was the ordinary one-shot prisoner's dilemma in which the players simultaneously make the choice between cooperation and defection without knowing their partner's choice. The second was the sequential one-shot prisoner's dilemma in which the one player makes a decision only after the other has already made his or her move. In this condition (partner-first and no-knowledge), the second player knows that the first player has already made his or her decision but is not informed of that choice (cooperation or defection) until his or her own decision has been made. Logically speaking, those two conditions—simultaneous decision making and the partner-first and no-knowledge condition—are identical: in both cases, the player makes a decision whether to cooperate or defect without the knowledge of the partner's choice.

On the other hand, Hayashi and colleagues argue, an illusion of control could play different roles in the two conditions. As mentioned earlier, illusion of control is mixed with general trust in the player's expectation of the partner's cooperation in the simultaneous condition. However, the knowledge that the partner has already made his or her decision makes it difficult for such an illusion to operate in the partner-first and no-knowledge condition. The difference between cooperation rates in the two conditions is thus considered to represent the portion of the expectation for the partner's cooperation that is attributable to the illusion of control (see Morris, Sim, and Girotto 1998 for a similar reasoning). The cooperation rate in the partner-first and no-knowledge condition is considered to represent the portion attributable to generalized trust.

The results of this experiment are consistent with the central argument presented earlier. First, illusion of control played a much greater role among Japanese participants (whose cooperation rate drastically increased from 12 percent in the partner-first and no-knowledge condition to 56 percent in the simultaneous-decision condition) than among American participants, for whom the cooperation rate was not affected (38 percent in the partner-first and no-knowledge condition and 36 percent in the simultaneous-decision condition). The wide gap between the two samples in the partner-first and no-knowledge condition (12 percent among Japanese, 38 percent among Americans) indicates a stronger presence of general trust among American than Japanese participants in promoting cooperation in the prisoner's dilemma. The gap in the simultaneous-decision condition (56 percent among Japanese, 36 percent among Americans), together with the

two comparisons already noted, indicates the collectivist nature of cooperation among Japanese participants—that is, their tendency to cooperate in the situation in which mutual monitoring and sanctioning
is considered to operate, even if in an illusory form.

Hayashi and colleagues' study represents another use of the cross-
societal experiment. I have already presented the argument that the
goal of cross-societal experimentation is eliminate the effects of cross-
cultural differences by controlling the theoretically relevant variables.
Hayashi and colleagues went one step further along these lines: they
use cross-societal experimentation to test hypotheses concerning "cultural differences" derived from the underlying mechanisms of the
cultural bundle clarified by earlier cross-societal experiments. Carefully planned cross-societal experiments are powerful tools for resolving the puzzle of cultural differences.

Conclusion

I have tried to demonstrate in this chapter that cross-societal experimentation can be used to identify sociorelational foundations that
lead to so-called cultural differences. It is commonly believed that the
Japanese are more collectivist than Americans; and this difference is
commonly considered to imply that Japanese individuals have collectivist preferences for group life and for group as against individual
interest. However, Japanese participants who were placed in artificially created groups in which no formal or informal system of mutual monitoring and sanctioning existed exhibited no more collectivist
behavioral patterns—willingness to stay in the group or to contribute
to the welfare of the group—than did American participants.

The first two experiments presented in this chapter provide strong
evidence against the commonly held, naïve view of culture as the
internal source of a particular behavioral pattern. The counterintuitive
finding that Americans are more collectivist than Japanese—the former staying with the group more often and contributing more to the
welfare of the group—has been attributed to the difference between
the two societies in the prevalence of commitment relations. The last
two experiments reveal the mechanisms responsible for another aspect of the collectivist behavioral pattern—preference for stable and
committed relations. It has been demonstrated, first, that participants'
inclination to form committed relations with particular partners is a
function of the level of social uncertainty and general trust; and second, that when those two factors are controlled, no such difference
exists between Japanese and American participants. Taken together,
those cross-societal experiments demonstrate that the commonly held
notion of cross-cultural differences between the Japanese and Ameri-

cans—the former being collectivists and the latter individualists—cease to exist once all the theoretically relevant factors are experimentally controlled. At the same time, the theoretically relevant factors have been shown to operate in a similar manner among both Japanese and American participants.

The last point I would like to make here is that trust played a pivotal role in those cross-societal experiments. The results of the first experiment suggest that cooperation among American participants was based on trust of others, whereas cooperation among Japanese participants was based on the system of mutual monitoring and sanctioning, in relative terms, of course. The results of my second experiment (Yamagishi, Cook, and Watabe 1998) demonstrate that people form commitment relations in response to a lack of trust. Given the survey results (Hayashi et al. 1982; Yamagishi and Yamagishi 1994) that Japanese are less trustful of others than Americans, it is suggested that the Japanese have a stronger tendency to form commitment relations than Americans because they are less trustful of others in general. The overall picture emerging from this discussion is that the lack of general trust among Japanese people constitutes a piece in the cultural complex of collectivism. The core of the collectivist behavioral pattern is commitment formation that produces assurance for mutual cooperation and high cost of exit. Once this pattern emerges, trust is seen as confined within the closed circle of commitment relations, and development of general trust that extends beyond the closed circle is hampered.[2] The resulting lack of general trust further motivates people to avoid interacting with "outsiders" and thus to strengthen the existing commitment relations.

Notes

1. As shown in Julian Rotter's (1980) review article, empirical studies predominantly indicate that general trust—"default" expectation of other people's trustworthiness—is independent of gullibility or credulousness. Furthermore, my colleagues and I have found that high-trusters are more sensitive than low-trusters to information suggesting the lack of trustworthiness in others and more accurate in predicting other people's choices in prisoner's dilemma games played between anonymous players (Kikuchi, Watanabe, and Yamagishi 1997; Kosugi and Yamagishi 1998; Yamagishi 2001; Yamagishi, Kikuchi, and Kosugi 1999; Yamagishi and Kosugi 1999).

2. See Fukuyama (1995) for a similar logic applied to trust that is confined within family ties in familist countries.

368   Trust and Reciprocity

References

Dawes, Robyn M. 1980. "Social Dilemmas." *Annual Review of Psychology* 31: 169–93.

Dawes, Robyn M., Jeanne McTavish, and Harriett Shaklee. 1977. "Behavior, Communication, and Assumptions About Other People's Behavior in a Commons Dilemma Situation." *Journal of Personality and Social Psychology* 35(1): 1–11.

Fukuyama, Francis. 1995. *Trust: The Social Virtues and the Creation of Prosperity.* New York: Free Press.

Hamaguchi, Eshun. 1982. "What Is Japanese Collectivism?" In *Japanese Collectivism* (in Japanese), edited by Eshun Hamaguchi and Shunpei Kumon. Tokyo, Japan: Yuhikaku.

Hayashi, Chikio, Masakatsu Murakami, Giichiro Suzuki, and Tatsuzo Suzuki. 1982. *A Study of Japanese National Character,* vol. 4 (in Japanese, with an English summary). Tokyo, Japan: Idemitsushoten.

Hayashi, Nahoko, Elinor Ostrom, James Walker, and Toshio Yamagishi. 1999. "Reciprocity, Trust, and the Sense of Control: A Cross-societal Study." *Rationality and Society* 11(4): 27–46.

Hechter, Michael, and Satoshi Kanazawa. 1993. "Group Solidarity and Social Order in Japan." *Journal of Theoretical Politics* 5(4): 455–93.

Karp, David, Nobuhito Jin, Toshio Yamagishi, and Hiromi Shinotsuka. 1993. "Raising the Minimum in the Minimal Group Paradigm." *Japanese Journal of Experimental Social Psychology* 32(3): 231–40.

Kikuchi, Masako, Yoriko Watanabe, and Toshio Yamagishi. 1997. "Judgment Accuracy of Other's Trustworthiness and General Trust: An Experimental Study" (in Japanese, with an English summary). *Japanese Journal of Experimental Social Psychology* 37(1): 23–36.

Kollock, Peter. 1994. "The Emergence of Exchange Structures: An Experimental Study of Uncertainty, Commitment, and Trust." *American Journal of Sociology* 100(2): 313–45.

———. 1998. "Social Dilemmas: The Anatomy of Cooperation." *Annual Review of Sociology* 24: 183–214.

Kosugi, Motoko, and Toshio Yamagishi. 1998. "General Trust and Judgments of Trustworthiness" (in Japanese, with an English summary). *Japanese Journal of Psychology* 69(5): 349–57.

Marwell, Gerald, and Ruth E. Ames. 1979. "Experiments on the Provision of Public Goods," part 1, "Resources, Interest, Group Size, and the Free-Rider Problem." *American Journal of Sociology* 84(6): 1335–60.

Messick, David M., and Marilyn B. Brewer. 1983. "Solving Social Dilemmas: A Review." In *Review of Personality and Social Psychology,* vol. 4, edited by Ladd Wheeler and Phillip Shaver. Beverly Hills, Calif.: Sage.

Messick, David M., Henk Wilke, Marilyn B Brewer, Roderick M. Kramer, Patricia E. Zemke, and Layton Lui. 1983. "Individual Adaptations and Structural Change As Solutions to Social Dilemmas." *Journal of Personality and Social Psychology* 4(2): 293–309.

Morris, Michael W., Damien L. H. Sim, and Vittorio Girotto. 1998. "Distinguishing Sources of Cooperation in the One-Round Prisoner's Dilemma: Evidence for Cooperative Decisions Based on the Illusion of Control." *Journal of Experimental Social Psychology* 34(5): 494–512.

Rotter, Julian B. 1967. "A New Scale for the Measurement of Interpersonal Trust." *Journal of Personality* 35(4): 651–65.

———. 1980. "Interpersonal Trust, Trustworthiness, and Gullibility." *American Psychologist* 35(1): 1–7.

Sato, Kaori, and Toshio Yamagishi. 1984. "Two Psychological Factors in the Problem of Public Goods" (in Japanese, with an English summary). *Japanese Journal of Experimental Social Psychology* 26(1): 89–95.

Tocqueville, Alexis de. 1945 [1835–40]. *Democracy in America.* 2 vols. New York: Vintage Books.

Tyszka, Tadeusz, and Janusz N. Grzelak. 1976. "Criteria of Choice in Non-Constant Zero-Sum Games." *Journal of Conflict Resolution* 20(2): 357–76.

Watabe, Motoki, Shigeru Terai, Nahoko Hayashi, and Toshio Yamagishi. 1996. "Cooperation in the One-Shot Prisoner's Dilemma Based on Expectations of Reciprocity" (in Japanese, with an English summary). *Japanese Journal of Experimental Social Psychology* 36(2): 183–96.

Yamagishi, Toshio. 1986. "The Provision of a Sanctioning System As a Public Good." *Journal of Personality and Social Psychology* 51(1): 110–16.

———. 1988a. "Exit from the Group As an Individualistic Solution to the Public Good Problem in the United States and Japan." *Journal of Experimental Social Psychology* 24(6): 530–42.

———. 1988b. "The Provision of a Sanctioning System in the United States and Japan." *Social Psychology Quarterly* 51(3): 265–71.

———. 1988c. "Seriousness of Social Dilemmas and the Provision of a Sanctioning System." *Social Psychology Quarterly* 51(1): 32–42.

———. 1992. "Group Size and the Provision of a Sanctioning System in a Social Dilemma." In *A Social Psychological Approach to Social Dilemmas,* edited by W. B. G. Liebrand, David M. Messick, and Henk A. M. Wilke. New York: Pergamon Press.

———. 1995. "Social Dilemmas." In *Sociological Perspectives on Social Psychology,* edited by Karen S. Cook, Gary Fine, and James House. Boston, Mass.: Allyn and Bacon.

———. 1998. *The Structure of Trust: The Evolutionary Game of Mind and Society* (in Japanese). Tokyo, Japan: University of Tokyo Press.

———. 2001. "Trust As a Form of Social Intelligence." In *Trust in Society,* edited by Karen S. Cook. New York: Russell Sage Foundation.

Yamagishi, Toshio, and Karen S. Cook. 1993. "Generalized Exchange and Social Dilemmas." *Social Psychology Quarterly* 56(4): 235–48.

Yamagishi, Toshio, Karen S. Cook, and Motoki Watabe. 1998. "Uncertainty, Trust, and Commitment Formation in the United States and Japan." *American Journal of Sociology* 104(1): 165–94.

Yamagishi, Toshio, Masako Kikuchi, and Motoko Kosugi. 1999. "Trust, Gullibility, and Social Intelligence." *Asian Journal of Social Psychology* 2(1): 145–61.

Yamagishi, Toshio, and Toko Kiyonari. 2000. "The Group As the Container of Generalized Reciprocity." *Social Psychology Quarterly* 63(2): 116–32.

Yamagishi, Toshio, and Motoko Kosugi. 1999. "Character Detection in Social Exchange" (in Japanese, with an English summary). *Cognitive Studies* 6(2): 179–90.

Yamagishi, Toshio, and Kaori Sato. 1986. "Motivational Bases of the Public Goods Problem." *Journal of Personality and Social Psychology* 50(1): 67–73.

Yamagishi, Toshio, and Midori Yamagishi. 1994. "Trust and Commitment in the United States and Japan." *Motivation and Emotion* 18(2): 129–66.

PART V

CONCLUSIONS

Chapter 14

The Transformation of a Skeptic: What Nonexperimentalists Can Learn from Experimentalists

MARGARET LEVI

READING through this collection of papers for the purpose of writing a concluding note on "what social scientists can learn" has proved a daunting task. My own work is in historical and comparative political economy. My role in the scholarly division of labor is to reveal the micro foundations of macro events and outcomes that are often unique and then to provide the link between the micro and the macro. Even in the finest comparative research, the capacity to control for the diversity of independent variables and multiple motivations is at best limited and, more often, hopeless; it is certainly just about impossible to proceed as systematically and rigorously as the experimentalists do. At first glance, then, nothing could be further from what I do than the very micro, carefully controlled experiments documented in this book.

Moreover, mine is the view of someone who is skeptical as well as ignorant about experiments. I am in awe of the rigor of experimentalists, and I am persuaded by many of their findings. At the same time, like other social scientists who deal with data derived from the events and behaviors associated with real polities and economies, I often have had difficulty understanding how to translate the insights of experimental research into the ways the people I observe regularly interact with one another and the conditions under which they interact. Second, much of the experimental research of the past conflates trust and cooperation or trust and reciprocity. I am concerned about the extent to which experiments can actually get at the question of trust as opposed to the behavior and choices that trust elicits. Third, despite the popularity of evolutionary theory among some of the social scientists I most respect and admire, I remain dubious of the usefulness of expending so much intellectual effort in forging links with this research program.

My ignorance is also multifaceted. I am not conversant with the nuances of experimental research, of how experimenters ensure that they actually get at what they want and in an uncontaminated way. Only by attending the workshop that produced these papers did I finally begin to grasp the distinctions among the disciplinary approaches to experimental research. I am just beginning to get a good feel for the complexity of the relation between game theory and experimental design.

Reading these papers has eliminated some of my most egregious forms of ignorance and thus alleviated at least part of my skepticism. Moreover, I am now far more aware than before of how experimental research can inform other kinds of social science scholarship. In particular, I believe experimentalists have something to teach the rest of us about the methodological issues in studying the relations among trust, cooperation, and reciprocity; the limits of game theory and of the standard model of rationality; the value added of other theoretical approaches, most especially those derived from cognitive science and evolutionary biology; and, of course, the substantive issues of the inquiry: trust, trustworthiness, cooperation, and reciprocity.

Methodological Issues

In chapter 3 of this volume, Russell Hardin, a political philosopher, emphasizes conceptual distinctions, and his kind of work is sometimes faulted for overconcern with the fine points of linguistic differentiation. However, useful experiments demonstrate why such distinctions matter. Precision regarding the rules, the decision to participate, the order and direction of moves, and the scenario facilitate distinction among various motivations and behaviors. It is not that all agree on the terms. For example, when referring to the belief that emerges from thick, ongoing relationships, Hardin uses the term "trust" for what Toshio Yamagishi, in chapter 13 of this volume, labels "assurance." Karen Cook and Robin Cooper (chapter 8, this volume) think Hardin may be right that risk is what is at issue to the first mover in the trust-honor game, but Kevin McCabe, Vernon Smith, Catherine Eckel, and Rick Wilson (in chapters 6, 9, and 10 of this volume) consider trust to be in play. The usage of the terms may differ, but what is important here is that the analysts are clear in what they mean and can justify their inference that the experimental design tells us something about what they claim to be investigating.

This pluralism about terms does not obviate the fact that experimentalists often conflate trust and cooperation, but they are increasingly attempting to measure trust as distinct from cooperation and reciprocity. Cook and Cooper confirm my perception that this has been a problem in the literature; many early researchers have tended to treat cooperative behavior as an indicator of trust among the partners. However, there has been real progress recently in differentiating these concepts. Cook and Cooper cite experiments that permit players the choice not to play the game; if they choose to play at all, players are exhibiting trust, which is then followed by a decision to cooperate or not. The major innovation has been the trust-honor game, a sequential *prisoner's dilemma game* in which the first player must decide whether to make a risky investment that may or may not be honored. The taking of the risk is the indicator of trust. Variations of this game permit greater refinements of the relations among trust, risk, and reciprocity. Yamagishi, McCabe, and Smith all make use of more nuanced experiments—protocols the authors helped develop initially. James Hanley, John Orbell, and Tomonori Morikawa (chapter 7) use computer simulations to sharpen further such distinctions.

The other way to distinguish trust from cooperation is by means of a survey, taken before and, sometimes, following the experiment. Combining attitudinal and behavioral measures has been popular since Julian Rotter's (1967) pioneering work. This procedure is used by T. K. Ahn, Elinor Ostrom, David Schmidt, and James Walker and by Catherine Eckel and Rick Wilson (chapters 12 and 9). There are problems with this approach, however, as the findings in this volume indicate. The most important, noted by Cook and Cooper, is that "survey work can get at only self-reported intentions to behave in specific ways or self-reported estimates of the frequency of a behavior such as volunteering" (chapter 8, this volume). Thus it is not surprising that Ahn and colleagues and Eckel and Wilson find such a weak relationship between the attitude and the behavior, or that William Harbaugh, Kate Krause, Steven G. Liday Jr., and Lise Vesterlund (chapter 11) find a negative relationship.

There is an additional problem, having to do with the survey questions themselves. Controversy persists, even among the most sophisticated survey researchers, about how to capture trust through surveys and what exactly the questions are measuring (Levi and Stoker 2000). In particular disrepute are the General Social Survey questions, meant to measure generalized text. Although widely used, including in chapter 12 of this volume, they are, as Yamagishi notes, more likely to be capturing social security or insecurity than trust (chapter 13, this volume; Yamagishi and Yamagishi 1994). Nonetheless, survey material can sometimes be quite illuminating in combination with experimental evidence about behavior. For example, Yamagishi (2000) uses questionnaires to determine which members of his participant pool are high-trusters and which are low-trusters, an attribute that has testable implications for how subjects play the game.

The most important development in experimental research—from my limited perspective—is the emphasis on social context. This is apparent in several of the experiments reported in this volume. It is at the heart of what Yamagishi is doing when he offers a means by which to make cross-societal comparisons. Illuminating the role of social context is what Ostrom (chapter 2) and Cook and Cooper advocate as well. By social context, they mean "factors that are external to the game, such as the social identities of the actors, the size of the group to which the individual belongs, the degree of *communication*, the existence of time pressure, and third-party effects, among others" (chapter 8, this volume). There is considerable work now that investigates and varies each of these factors, and the findings of this research are reported in this volume. It is nice, for example, to see Harbaugh and colleagues (chapter 11) consider why children exhibit less trust behavior than adults. They focus on a range of variables. The suggestive finding that norms of reciprocity and fairness are less developed in children is one—among many—that deserves further exploration.

Of most interest to me as a comparative political economist are the ways experimentalists are able to get at institutional and national variations. In some instances, the institutional variation is investigated through manipulation of the rules of the game. Although this research certainly provides some real insight, it often suffers from problems of external validity, making it difficult to translate into the settings in which real people (as opposed to experimental subjects) make real decisions in real contexts. Ostrom and others are beginning to point to ways out of this predicament by using experimental findings and then testing them with fieldwork and other nonexperimental empirical research. One of the implications of this volume is that triangulation, the current shibboleth of methodologists, should include experiments.

Work on cross-societal variation seems to suffer less from problems of external validity. Exemplary is the research program of Yamagishi and his colleagues (Yamagishi, Cook, and Watabe 1998; Yamagishi and Yamagishi 1994) as well as that of anthropologist Jean Ensminger (1999) and others involved in the MacArthur Foundation cross-cultural experiment project. There is also very interesting research on variation in social and economic exchange settings. I have always been fascinated by Peter Kollock's (1994) study of the different kinds of commitment relationships that emerge among exchange partners with variation in the nature of the market—and the uncertainties inherent in that market structure. Such research both draws on and has important implications for other kinds of scholarship on exchange and on principal-agent relationships.

Rational Choice and Game Theory

As these papers reveal, game theory forms the basis of most of the experiments on trust. Game theory is one means by which to discipline the complex narratives that we comparativists confront and construct (Bates et al. 1998), and experimentalists use it in that way, too. At the same time, experimentalists also use game theory to transform our understanding of rationality. In fact, the reliance on game theory has been crucial to one of the major contributions of experimental research: the revelation of the limits of classical *rational choice theory*. Reinhard Selten, awarded a Nobel Prize for the development of *subgame perfection*, is also a leading experimental economist who argues that game theory offers a normative account of rationality that must be evaluated against empirical evidence (Selten 1999). Like McCabe, Ostrom, and Smith, he has demonstrated that the capacity to engage in *backward deduction* and other high-level calculations, which game theory presumes, is not always how people think. Most important, game theory—and rational choice theory more generally—significantly underpredicts reciprocity and, therefore, cooperation.

Game theory provides a null hypothesis. Experimentalists have demonstrated the specific conditions under which its predictions hold and have begun to specify where the "theory is inadequate and incompletely specified" (chapter 10, this volume). Heuristics, "goodwill accounting," emotions, and other influences on cognition become part of the account.

Value Added of Cognitive and Evolutionary Models

Robert Kurzban (chapter 4) provides a useful review of evolutionary theory, clarifying how it can account for what appears to be "nonrational" or what Leda Cosmides and John Tooby (1994) label "better than rational" behavior. Evolutionary theory seems to hold the key to the characteristics of individuals that make it possible for them to trust others. The link here is with the expectation of reciprocity. Without good reason to presume the other will "honor" one's trust, there will be no trust, either in the form of risk taking or as a cognitive belief about another. What makes trust possible, then, is the capacity to evaluate others' trustworthiness and to recognize others so as to be able to punish or reward their trustworthiness in future interactions.

Frans de Waal (chapter 5) reports on evidence of *reciprocal altruism* among chimpanzees. The importance of his work is that it finds that chimpanzees and, by extension, humans possess evolved capacities for recognizing others who are likely to reciprocate one's trust.

Hanley, Orbell, and Morikawa emphasize both the human capacity to penetrate lies and assess information and the unequal endowments of such capacities. Using computer simulation, they model an environment in which there are multiple possible games. Their focus is on the evolution of the "mean population values for agents' cognitive attributes and for their cooperativeness" when individuals can play only the prisoner's dilemma and when there is the possibility of either the prisoner's dilemma or the hawk-dove game. Interestingly, they find that where there is only the PD, there is a tendency toward defection as an effect of selection for perceptiveness and that the added option to fight supports cooperation. Trust, for the authors, is the expectation of cooperation. It is a cognitive evaluation of what others are likely to do and drives the decision about which game to play. The authors' simulations lead them to conclude that trust relies heavily on information-processing capabilities, which are the effect of separate yet interdependent evolutionary processes.

While Hanley, Orbell, and Morikawa indicate where and how cognition plays a role in trust and cooperation, McCabe and Smith want to delve into the mind in order to uncover the influences on cognition. McCabe and Smith cite research (Baron-Cohen 1995) that describes hypothesized mechanisms or mental modules that are likely to facilitate reciprocity: an intentionality detector, an eye-direction detector, a shared-attention mechanism, and a theory-of-mind mechanism. These mechanisms are thought to be interconnected in such a way that the intentionality and eye-direction detectors are inputs to the shared-attention mechanism, which is, in turn, an input to the theory-of-mind mechanism. These modules enable inferences to be made about mental phenomena in other agents based on their actions or words. The implications of this work for the analysis of strategic interaction differ substantially from the underlying postulates of game theory.

McCabe and Smith explore these mechanisms in their own experiments reported in this volume. So, too, do Eckel and Wilson, whose experimentation with facial expressions is designed to get at the extent to which individuals can "read" one another's minds—as well as how emotions affect cognitive capacities.

The research inspired by advances in cognitive science and evolutionary theory claims that reciprocity rests on the capacity for information processing sophisticated and flexible enough that future play can be contingent upon past interactions. This is a necessary but not sufficient condition, however. When trust is at issue, there must also exist an ability to detect cheaters. This can be a result of evolution, as Cosmides and Tooby (1992) have it, of socialization and experience, as Yamagishi (2000) seems to suggest, or of the combination of the two, as Ostrom implies. There must also exist the ability to delay gratification to ensure an ongoing and sequential reciprocity. Deferred gratification rests, in turn, on what McCabe and Smith label "goodwill accounting." By that they mean a running record of who reciprocates and who does not, whom one owes and whom one should punish.

The identification of these cognitive requirements is generating a whole new program of experimental research. The experiments with facial expressions are one kind of direction this work is taking. Yet another involves the effort to understand what is actually going on in the mind as choices are made. McCabe, for example, discusses his research using magnetic resonance imaging to identify when the "hot" and "cool" systems of the brain come into play; it is his argument that delayed gratification rests on a "cool narrative" that involves cognition and strategy rather than emotional reaction.

What Have We Learned About
Trust and Trustworthiness?

Although the language of most of these papers concerns trust and reciprocity, I must concur with Hardin that most of the experimental research is about trustworthiness. What I take away from this largely has to do with the incentives, norms, and, more dynamically, mechanisms that make people likely to reciprocate the trust placed in them—that is, the factors that make them trustworthy. It also tells me something about the signals people must give to let others know they are trustworthy. We already know, of course, that constraints and institutions can make commitments credible and those making the commitments trustworthy. The research in this volume demonstrates empirically how trustworthiness can emerge from repeat interactions and exchange networks, commitment formation (discussed in chapters 8 and 13), or goodwill accounting. It is this kind of trustworthiness that the experimentalists document. Moreover, it is this kind of trustworthiness that seems to evoke what they mean by behavioral trust—that is, the willingness to play the game, invest, and so on.

The experiments reported here identify an important role for trust, defined as a cognitive belief that others will positively reciprocate one's willingness to take a risk—for example, McCabe's work identifying different reactions in the brain that are more or less likely to stimulate trusting beliefs, and Yamagishi's work identifying high- and low-trusters. This only leads us to further questions having to do with the sources of these variations. McCabe's instinct is to investigate the brain itself. Mine is closer to Cook and Cooper's: "to provide insights into the role of trust in the larger society, experimental work will need to include a more complete treatment of the effects of social context factors." There is a large and fruitful research program here and one that I—as a redeemed skeptic—most enthusiastically endorse.

References

Baron-Cohen, Simon. 1995. *Mindblindness: An Essay on Autism and Theory of the Mind.* Cambridge, Mass.: MIT Press.

Bates, Robert H., Avner Greif, Margaret Levi, Jean-Laurent Rosenthal, and Barry R. Weingast. 1998. *Analytic Narratives.* Princeton, N.J.: Princeton University Press.

Cosmides, Leda, and John Tooby. 1992. "Cognitive Adaptations for Social Exchange." In *The Adapted Mind*, edited by Jerome H. Barkow, Leda Cosmides, and John Tooby. New York: Oxford University Press.

———. 1994. "Better than Rational: Evolutionary Psychology and the Invisible Hand." *American Economic Review* 84(2): 327–32.

Ensminger, Jean. 1999. "Examining Trust, Cooperation, and Fairness: A Cross-cultural Study Using Experimental Economics." Unpublished paper, Pasadena, Calif.: California Institute of Technology.

Kollock, Peter. 1994. "The Emergence of Exchange Structures: An Experimental Study of Uncertainty, Commitment, and Trust." *American Journal of Sociology* 100(2): 313–45.

Levi, Margaret, and Laura Stoker. 2000. "Political Trust and Trustworthiness." *Annual Review of Political Science* 3: 475–507.

Rotter, Julian B. 1967. "A New Scale for the Measurement of Interpersonal Trust." *Journal of Personality* 35(4): 1–7.

Selten, Reinhard. 1999. "Response to Shepsle and Laitin." In *Competition and Cooperation*, edited by James Alt, Margaret Levi, and Elinor Ostrom. New York: Russell Sage Foundation.

Yamagishi, Toshio. 2000. "Trust As a Form of Social Intelligence." In *Trust in Society*, edited by Karen S. Cook. New York: Russell Sage Foundation.

Yamagishi, Toshio, Karen S. Cook, and Motoki Watabe. 1998. "Uncertainty, Trust, and Commitment Formation in the United States and Japan." *American Journal of Sociology* 104(1): 165–94.

Yamagishi, Toshio, and Midori Yamagishi. 1994. "Trust and Commitment in the United States and Japan." *Motivation and Emotion* 18(2): 129–66.

Chapter 15

Conclusion

JAMES WALKER AND ELINOR OSTROM

A CENTRAL question lies at the core of the social sciences: How do individuals form and sustain agreements or relationships with others to counteract individual temptations to select actions based only on short-sighted, individual incentives? In other words, how do individuals trust one another and behave in a trustworthy manner? Thomas Hobbes's answer was that communities have to rely on an external authority to impose and enforce their own agreements with one another. Furthermore, to overcome incentives to free ride, there must be a central authority that directs "involuntary contributions" so as to finance the provision of the large number of goods and services that citizens desired.

The modern approach to the Hobbesian question is the puzzle of how individuals cope with *social dilemmas*. The answer that has often been given, using *noncooperative game theory* as the source of the argument, is effectively the same as that of Hobbes: to be followed, agreements must be enforced by external authorities. These grim predictions, however, evoke considerable empirical challenges from a wide assortment of studies based on field and experimental testing. Scholars do not always observe ubiquitous free-riding behavior, nor do they observe a total lack of trustworthy and trusting behavior in settings in which external authority is absent. Some individuals learn to cooperate with one another to solve many, though not all, social dilemmas themselves.

The conflict between theory and behavior implies an important problem for the social sciences: the development of a class of theories that can be used to explain the emergence of cooperation in settings in which myopic self-interest would suggest a lack of cooperation.

The development of such theories is important not only for our scientific understanding but also for the design of institutions to facilitate individuals achieving higher levels of productive outcomes in social-dilemma situations.

At the core of understanding cooperation is an understanding of the foundations of trust and reciprocity. Definitions of the concept of trust still slightly differ from one scholar to another. A core meaning, however, underlies all of the more specific definitions. The scholars in this volume share a broad definition of trust as the willingness to take some risk in relation to other individuals on the expectation that the others will reciprocate.

The differences in definitions of trust relate to whether trust is based only on narrow self-interest, on normative foundations, or on both. These important differences underlie essential theoretical questions in the social sciences today. As experimental studies of trust demonstrate, models of individual choice that begin with an assumption that all individuals make decisions based only on their own material payoffs do not fully account for observed behavior. Complementing field studies, controlled experiments reveal that many individuals act in a trusting or trustworthy manner, and the proportion varies systematically with variation in experimental conditions (Fehr and Gächter 2000). Consequently, these and related experiments provide important insights for the study of trust and also as a foundation for understanding social interactions more generally.

As a result of theoretical reformulations based on experimental evidence—in, for example, the chapters in part III of this volume and the citations referenced in these chapters—we expect that a growing number of studies will analyze behavior more explicitly by assuming the existence of multiple types of players, in contrast with the previous view that all players use the same rationality in approaching all situations (see, for example, Ahn, Ostrom, and Walker forthcoming). Types of players differ in the degree to which they exclusively focus on their own material well-being, on norms of reciprocity, on trustworthiness, and on willingness to trust.

In a world populated strictly by narrow egoists who focus entirely on their own material payoffs, the context within which individuals interact in dilemma situations makes little difference. Without external monitoring and sanctioning capabilities, the expected gains from association are minimal. In a world populated by different types of individuals who vary with respect to their normative commitments and regard for others, considerably more aspects of the decision context become relevant for predicting and understanding when trust is likely to be extended and reciprocated. Although many social scientists will not be surprised by such a conclusion, those who are committed to using *rational-choice theory* as the foundation for understanding social life will find it necessary to delve deeper into models and frames for empirical testing that account for multiple types of players.

One thing is clear from recent experimental research; the degree of trust and trustworthiness varies substantially across cultures and across groups within cultures.[1] Evidence from field and experimental data suggest a variety of contextual factors associated with the structure of a decision-making setting that help to explain the variance: the type of economic activities engaged in and the degree to which mutual trust is necessary to support such activities, normative preferences based on positive or negative reciprocity, prior experience with the decision setting, the capacity to learn more about the personal characteristics of each other, and the capacity to gain a reputation all appear to affect decisions to trust or to act in a trustworthy manner. The puzzle is this: how does one begin to understand and build the foundations and regularities of relationships based on trust into one's theories in a systematic way?

As seen in the early chapters of this book, evolutionary theory serves as a natural point of origin for developing a framework to serve as a guide for building a more comprehensive theory of trust, reciprocity, and cooperation. In chapter 4, Robert Kurzban provides the reader with the rudiments for understanding how an evolutionary approach can serve as the basis for such a framework. Trust, cooperation, and reciprocity appear to be in conflict with the principles of natural selection, the cornerstone of modern evolutionary theory. Understanding how these behavioral attributes may have evolved hinges on understanding how benefits from association are delivered as contingent or reciprocal claims and understanding the characteristics of environments that will be conducive to such claims. As Kurzban explains, however, this evolutionary argument does not suggest that humans will necessarily act as rational *reciprocal altruists,* in the sense of calculating probabilistic costs and benefits of possible actions. Instead, the approach suggests that the structure of environments that lead to trust and reciprocity have impacted human cognitive adaptations. The cognitive systems built by the processes of natural selection impact modern human behavior.

This conceptual framework for understanding modern human behavior lies at the core of the work presented by Kevin McCabe in chapter 6. As McCabe notes,

Trust and conciliation are relatively easy to explain once reciprocity is established, but how does one explain reciprocity? A game-theoretic analysis of reciprocity assumes that subjects will take actions that maximize their self-interest at every stage of the decision process—that they will always act from myopic self-interest. This means that when it comes time to reciprocate, subjects should instead defect in their myopic self-interest. If the subjects moving first know this, then they should not "trust" or engage in "conciliatory" actions. Therefore, reciprocity can be viewed as a form of commitment to a certain course of voluntary action.

An approach to understanding reciprocity as the basis for trust and subsequent cooperation is built upon several integrated themes discussed by McCabe. This approach is constructed on four premises. The first premise draws on the evidence related to the adaptation of the human mind over time, thus allowing for increasingly more complex commitments to reciprocal actions. The argument is made that humans long ago developed mental mechanisms such as "cheater-detection" and "theory-of-mind" modules. These allowed humans to develop reciprocal behavior that initially emerged from food sharing and later expanded to many other activities. The second premise is the existence of a psychological mechanism for commitment based on the notion that delay of gratification involves the intervention of cognitively cool neural mechanisms to overcome hot mechanisms' demand for immediate gratification. The third premise draws on a system of "goodwill accounting" that allows relationships to be built on a history of association. The final premise relies on a theory-of-mind system, a necessary component for the implementation of a goodwill accounting system to allow individuals to "read" the level of goodwill.

This evolutionary focus in analyzing issues of reciprocity and trust can be seen as a cornerstone for theoretical and empirical analyses designed to model and understand behavior in complex systems that require reciprocal commitments. The cognitive approach can be thought of as supplementary to standard game-theoretic principles. Game theory can explain some aspects of all of the data presented in this volume. The problem is, however, that noncooperative game theory is not sufficient as a full explanation for the data presented here. We all rely on the insights of Herbert Simon in his argument that "to predict how economic man will behave, we need to know not only that he is rational, but also how he perceives the world—what alternatives he sees and what consequences he attaches to them" (Simon 1956, 271). The contributors to this volume do not deny human rationality. In the words of McCabe and Smith,

> Rather, we explore hypotheses about how it is expressed through the social brain in the way people interpret one another's expectations in strategic interaction. This approach, however, does deny the traditional game-theoretic rational-actor assumption of common knowledge that

each agent chooses dominant strategies within the analytical framework of *backward induction*. This view alone, however, is inadequate and fails to account for the play of sophisticated subjects. (See also McCabe and Smith 1999.)

Summary Observations

The foregoing overview outlines the conceptual and methodological foundations for the research presented in this volume. At the core is the fundamental belief that empirical and theoretical inquires must go hand in hand in building a conceptual framework that is validated by sound empirical evidence. In this light, we draw the reader's attention to several broad empirical conclusions that can be drawn from the studies presented here:

- In support of an evolutionary origin of the capacity to learn trust and reciprocity, rigorous empirical methodology, using chimpanzees as subjects, demonstrates that reciprocity rests on an exchange mechanism in which social services are provided contingent on previous receipt of services from the same partner (chapter 5).

- Trust is conditional. Individuals use clues outside of game parameters to assess the trustworthiness of others (chapter 9). Past moves matter, especially in environments in which reputations can be formed (chapters 6 and 12).

- Understanding the evolution of cooperation may depend crucially on outside options (chapter 7).

- *Social distance* serves as an important variable in explaining deviations based on purely self-interested payoff maximization (chapter 8).

- Critical to understanding the foundations of trust across diverse settings is the distinction between associations based on general trust and those based on assurance—what might be called within-group trust (chapter 13).

Finally, we must point out the obvious. The empirical evidence presented in this volume presents only a sampling of the type of research that is currently being conducted in the social sciences on issues of trust, reciprocity, and cooperation. Extensive work is currently being undertaken by scholars in all disciplines to discover how to develop rigorous models of bounded rationality that help to explain empirical findings. A recent set of studies on tax compliance raises important questions about the trust heuristics used by citizens and their reactions to governmental efforts to monitor compliance (see Scholz 1998).

Too much monitoring may have the counterintuitive result that individuals feel they are not trusted and thus become less trustworthy (Frey 1993). Bruno Frey (1997) questions whether some formal institutional arrangements, such as social insurance and paying people to contribute effort, reduce the likelihood that individuals will continue to place a positive intrinsic value on actions taken mainly because of internal norms. Rather, they may assume that formal organizations are charged with the responsibility of taking care of joint needs and that reciprocity is no longer needed (see also Taylor 1987).

Scholars from the fields of animal biology, anthropology, artificial intelligence, economics, philosophy, and psychology have recently developed a framework of bounded rationality to aid in understanding how individuals use an "adaptive toolbox" of simple heuristics and how these are related to social norms, institutions, and other cultural tools (see Gigerenzer and Selten 2001). The Russell Sage Foundation has itself sponsored an extensive series of conferences and workshops on trust and has already published five books that summarize the findings from these efforts (see p. vi, this volume). We hope that this book, as the sixth volume in this series, adds significantly to our common understanding of trust and cooperation in social-dilemma settings.

It may be surprising to some that we have relied so extensively on experimental research in this volume. We do so for several reasons. As theory becomes an ever more important core of social science, experimental studies will join the ranks of basic empirical research methods for social scientists. Large-scale field studies will continue to be an important source of empirical data, but such studies are frequently an expensive and inefficient method for addressing how institutional incentives combine to affect individual behavior and outcomes. Advancement is likely to come much sooner if social scientists examine hypotheses that include some contested elements among diverse models or theories of a coherent framework. Careful experimental research designs frequently help sort out competing hypotheses more effectively than attempts to find the precise combination of variables in the field. By adding experimental methods to the battery of field methods already used extensively, the social sciences of the twenty-first century will move more rapidly in acquiring well-grounded theories of human behavior and of the effect of diverse institutional arrangements on behavior. It is hoped that this volume convinces more than one skeptic of the importance of studying trust through a theoretical and experimental lens.

Note

1. See Henrich et al. 2001 for a brief overview of an outstanding study of a set of parallel experiments conducted in fifteen small societies.

References

Ahn, T. K., Elinor Ostrom, and James M. Walker. Forthcoming. "Incorporating Motivational Heterogeneity into Game-Theoretic Models of Collective Action." *Public Choice.*
Braithwaite, Valerie, and Margaret Levi, eds. 1998. *Trust and Governance.* New York: Russell Sage Foundation.
Cook, Karen S., ed. 2001. *Trust in Society.* New York: Russell Sage Foundation.
Fehr, Ernst, and Simon Gächter. 2000. "Fairness and Retaliation: The Economics of Reciprocity." *Journal of Economic Perspectives* 14(3): 159–81.
Frey, Bruno S. 1993. "Does Monitoring Increase Work Effort? The Rivalry with Trust and Loyalty." *Economic Inquiry* 31(4): 663–70.
———. 1997. *Not Just for the Money: An Economic Theory of Personal Motivation.* Cheltenham, England: Edward Elgar.
Gigerenzer, Gerd, and Reinhard Selten. 2001. *Bounded Rationality: The Adaptive Toolbox.* Cambridge, Mass: MIT Press.
Henrich, Joseph, Robert Boyd, Samuel Bowles, Colin Camerer, Ernst Fehr, Herbert Gintis, and Richard McElreath. 2001. "In Search of Homo Economicus: Behavioral Experiments in Fifteen Small-Scale Societies." *American Economic Review* 91(2): 73–78.
McCabe, Kevin, and Vernon Smith. 1999. "A Comparison of Naïve and Sophisticated Subject Behavior with Game Theoretic Predictions." Working paper. Tucson, Ariz.: University of Arizona, Economic Science Laboratory.
Scholz, John T. 1998. "Trust, Taxes, and Compliance." In *Trust and Governance,* edited by Valerie Braithwaite and Margaret Levi. New York: Russell Sage Foundation.
Simon, Herbert A. 1956. "A Comparison of Game Theory and Learning Theory." *Psychometrika* 21(September): 267–72.
Taylor, Michael. 1987. *The Possibility of Cooperation.* New York: Cambridge University Press.

Glossary

Backward Induction: A strategic choice criterion often used in games that consists of a finite sequence of decisions that are made with perfect knowledge of the decisions made in prior decision stages of the game. Decision makers initially consider the game from the perspective of play in the final decision nodes of the game, determining which decisions are optimal at each of these nodes. These optimal decisions are then taken as given, so that reaching each final node is seen as being equivalent to achieving the outcome associated with the optimal decision at that node. Consequently, decisions in the next-to-last decision round are seen as leading directly to outcomes; in other words, they are now thought of as being like final decision nodes. The optimal decisions for each of these nodes can then be determined, and those decisions can be taken into account in the decisions that immediately precede these nodes. This process can be repeated all the way back to the initial decision node. This analytical approach is used sequentially to determine play in all rounds of the game. This mode of reasoning helps players to eliminate noncredible threats or commitments in later decision nodes in finding rational play for earlier decision nodes.

Chicken Game: A two-person bimatrix game often used to model situations with conflict of interests. Each player has two strategies, which can be characterized as "assertive" and "reserved." Each player has an incentive to be assertive as long as the other plays the reserved strategy. When both players play the assertive strategy, however, the social outcome is Pareto inferior to both players' playing the reserved strategy. Unlike the prisoner's dilemma game, players in the chicken game do not have a dominant strategy, and the equilibriums consist of outcomes in which either one plays the assertive and the other plays the reserved strategy or the players randomize between the two strategies.

Collective Action: A term used broadly to define actions that are taken at a group (or subgroup) level with coordination among group members.

COMMON-POOL RESOURCE: A natural or man-made resource or good that provides a flow of harvestable output that is rival in consumption—that is, one person's consumption of the output precludes others' consumption of the same output. The resource is accessible to members of a group without property rights having been assigned to group members.

COMMUNICATION: Some experimental settings are designed to allow decision makers to communicate before choosing a strategy. Forms of communication vary. For example, in some instances the communication is face-to-face, in other cases it may be achieved through computer terminals. Generally, communication is nonbinding in that subjects are not required to adhere to promises made during communication.

DICTATOR GAME: A two-person game in which the first person chooses how to divide a given resource with the other person. The second person receives only what is allocated to him or her, having no choice in regard to the split.

EXTENSIVE-FORM GAMES: Games presented in the form of a game tree, with branches reflecting alternative strategies.

FOCAL POINT: An equilibrium is a focal point if its characteristics distinguish it from other equilibriums and appeal to players. Use of focal points as a way of choosing among multiple equilibriums was first proposed by Thomas Schelling. A famous example is the meeting at Grand Central Terminal: multiple individuals need to meet in New York City but have no chance to coordinate among themselves where to meet. Other characteristics of an equilibrium, such as its Pareto superiority or symmetry or its simply being located in the upper-right cell of a game matrix, may also render the equilibrium more conspicuous to players and, thus, make it a focal point.

GIFT-EXCHANGE GAME: A particular framing of the prisoner's dilemma situation in experiments to facilitate the study of reciprocal behavior. Typically, there are two players, each of whom decides whether or not to give a gift to the other. When each player gives a gift to the other, both are better off. Each player is better off, however, when he or she does not give the gift to the other player, regardless of the latter's decision.

HAWK-DOVE GAME: Two players encounter a resource v that can be consumed by either. A hawk choice indicates a willingness to fight, whereas a dove choice is to back off, leaving the resource in the undisputed control of the other. If both players play hawk, a fight ensues, with a winner capturing v and a loser being obliged to pay the cost c. In most formulations, both players playing dove results in each player having a .5 probability of capturing v.

MORAL HAZARD: A concept that applies to problems of exchange in which there is uncertainty over outcomes, and parties in the exchange have asymmetric information regarding probability distributions over outcomes. In such cases, one party may have incentives to take actions that are not in the best interest of the other party, but the second party cannot observe the source of the actions. An example includes insurance: the insured may take actions that increase the chances of the occurrence of an insured outcome (thereby increasing the liability to the insurer), but the insurer cannot distinguish the source of the increased liability.

NASH EQUILIBRIUM: A set of strategies for the players in a game with the property that no player can benefit by deviating from his or her strategy, and thereby improve his or her payoffs while the strategies of other players are unchanged.

NON-COOPERATIVE GAME THEORY: An analytical framework for studying decision making by groups of individuals whereby each decision maker unilaterally chooses over alternative strategies, but each individual's payoffs can be influenced by others' choices in addition to his or her own.

NORMAL-FORM GAME: A game presented in a matrix formulation in which outcomes of alternative combinations of choices are presented as cells of the matrix.

ONE-SHOT GAME: A conceptualization of a game situation in which decision makers view the game as a single choice, with no ramifications for future interactions.

PARETO EFFICIENT, PARETO OPTIMAL: An outcome is Pareto efficient if there is no alternative outcome that makes some individuals better off and leaves all other individuals at least as well off.

PARETO SUPERIOR, PARETO DOMINANT: An allocation is Pareto superior to another allocation if it makes at least one person better off and all others at least as well off relative to the initial allocation.

PRISONER'S DILEMMA GAME: A binary choice game based on the following scenario: Two partners in a crime have been apprehended.

The prosecutor separately offers a reduced punishment to each prisoner if he or she will discuss the involvement of the other. If only one prisoner defects—that is, gives the prosecutor the information he is seeking—he or she stands to gain; if both prisoners defect, both stand to lose. If neither defects, however—that is, if they cooperate with each other—both prisoners will avoid penalty. Prisoner's dilemma games are generally conceptualized from the perspective of a choice between C (to cooperate) and D (to defect). In a two-person version of this game, mutual cooperation maximizes group earnings, whereas mutual defection minimizes group earnings. Play of D by one person and C by the other leads to an outcome that maximizes earnings to the person choosing D and minimizes the earnings to the person choosing C.

PROVISION-POINT PUBLIC GOOD: A public good in which a minimal (nonzero) allocation of resources is necessary for provision.

PUBLIC GOOD: A natural or man-made resource or good that provides a flow of benefits that is nonrival in consumption—that is, one person's benefit from the good does not preclude others from benefiting from the good. The benefit of a public good is received regardless of an individual's contribution to the provision of the good.

PUBLIC-GOODS GAME: A multiperson game in which players choose an allocation of their resources to a group good. Benefits from the group good are received by all players, regardless of the size of their allocation to the group good. Strategically, players have an incentive to withhold resources from the group good, relying on others to provide the group good. The outcome of this strategy yields a payoff to the group that is less than the payoff possible if group members were to cooperate in their allocations to the group good.

RATIONAL-CHOICE THEORY: The conceptualization of a theory of choice in which decision makers choose strategically by "rationally" comparing and choosing from among alternative strategies based on the outcomes of possible combinations of strategies. Decision makers are seen as calculating agents with the ability to compare among strategies and outcomes presented in the decision problem.

RECIPROCAL ALTRUISM: A theory to explain why animals, including humans, incur costs to help others to whom they are unrelated. Costly behavior that benefits others is defined as "altruism," the evolution of which requires that recipients repay the actor with either the same or other benefits. Reciprocal altruism requires a time delay between giving and receiving: if such delay is absent (that is, if benefits are exchanged simultaneously or in quick succession), biologists speak of "mutualism."

Second-Order Social Dilemma: A situation in which dilemma problems are "nested," one within another. For example, the provision of a sanctioning mechanism for limiting harvesting from a common-pool resource could be viewed as a public-goods problem nested in a common-pool-resource problem.

Social Distance: The conceptual notion that decision makers vary in decision-making contexts in regard to the "social closeness" with other decision makers. For example, even when there is no communication between decision makers, one would regard friends as being closer, in terms of social distance than complete strangers.

Social Dilemma: The class of games in which the outcome that is achieved when subjects follow a strategy based on pure self-interest is inferior to an outcome that would be achieved if subjects chose strategies based on the interests of all group members. Types of social dilemma games include the prisoner's dilemma game, public-goods games, and common-pool-resource games.

Subgame-Perfect Nash Equilibrium: A game's equilibrium strategy implies a plan of play for each subgame of the original game. An equilibrium strategy is subgame perfect if that equilibrium implies the play of an equilibrium for every subgame.

Tit-For-Tat: A strategy to cooperate on the first move of a repeated social-dilemma game and then on subsequent trials do whatever the other player did on the previous move. In this way, tit-for-tat conditionally rewards the other player for cooperative moves by cooperating on the next trial.

Tragedy of the Commons: Garrett Hardin (1968; see chapter 2 references) used this term to define the outcome of a social-dilemma game played in the context of a common-pool resource without property rights defining the use of the resource. Sometimes erroneously applied to contexts in which common-property regimes are well defined but individuals do not have separable rights.

Ultimatum Game: A two-person game in which the first person proposes a "split" of a given resource to the other player. The second player can accept or decline the split. If the second player accepts, the resource is shared as defined by the first player's proposal. If the second player declines the split, both players receive nothing.

Index

Numbers in **boldface** refer to figures and tables.

common-pool resource dilemmas, 20, 52, 65n5, 390. *See also* public-goods dilemmas

communication: backward induction violation, 36; cheap talk, 65n8; cheating-defecting control, 53–54; and cooperation, 22, 52–53, 212; definition, 390; and intention detection, 198n10; non-verbal, 245–54; and sanction effects on outcomes, 37; social dilemma role, 29, 31–34; and trust development, 4, 226, 228–29. *See also* face-to-face communication; information; intentionality detection

competition-competitive players, 54, 171–72, 211–12, 218–19. *See also* conflict games

complete vs. bounded rationality models, 39–49, 54–61, 62–64, 64n3

complete vs. private information environments, 292–93, 295–96, 298

computers vs. humans as partners in games, 166–67

conditional cooperators, humans as, 245, 267, **295**, 305, 310

confidence vs. trust, 94, 213

conflict games: influence on cooperation, 11–12, 170–71, 185–86, **187–90**, 191–97; value of, 201n31–33

context, social: effect on social dilemmas, 38–49; evolutionary basis for cooperation, 110, 115–17, 147, 148–49, 156–58; in experimental approach, 227–31, 376; game theory limitations, 98, 170–71; modern vs. ancestral, 119; multiple player types, 382–83; norm usage, 41; and rational-choice theory, 26; and smiling signal, 253–54; social intelligence hypothesis, 171–74; thick relationships, 92–95; in trust development, 5, 14–15, 92, 99–100, 313

contingent agreements: chimpanzee study, 130, 140; contingent benefits strategy, 120–21; neurological handling of, 149–50; punishment, 52–

53; and reciprocity, 9, 51–52, 110, 111

control, sense of, 230, 364–66

Cook, Karen, 221, 233–34

cooperation: Anticipatory Interactive Planning Simulation methodology, 174–79; and assurance vs. trust, 355; behavioral theory for, 24-25; and communication, 22, 24, 29, 34, 49, 52–54, 67n31, 212; complexity of, 39; conflict games as influencing, 11–12, 170–71, 185–86, **187–90**, 191–97; cooperation-only world simulation, 179–80, **181–82**, 183, **184**, 185, 199n19; evidence for high levels, 22, 23, 27–29, **30**, 31–34, 36; as exchange, 231; vs. game theoretical predictions, 246, 382; in high-stakes games, 277, 356; initial tendency toward, 88, 96, 97, 98, 99, 154; in large vs. small groups, 54–56, **57**, 58, **59**, 60–61; as learned response, 44, 159; motivations for, 97, 211–12, 323–24; neural patterns for, 166–67; and past experience, 250, 339–40; as personal rule, 45–47; and player types, 211–12, 219, 235–36n2, 342–43; punishment incentives for, 14, 36–37, 43, 154, 293–95; relationship to trust, 12, 80, 209–10, 212–13, 216–18, 221, 234–35, 323–24, 375; and social commitment, 40–41; and social context, 110, 115–17, 147, 148–49, 156–58; and social intelligence theory, 171–74. *See also* evolutionary considerations; prisoner's dilemma; reciprocity

coordination games, 65n8–9

corruption and tight circles of trust, 45

Cosmides, Leda, 106, 117, 120, 121, 148, 158, 377

Crawford, Sue, 40, 328–29

credibility and promise-keeping, 87. *See also* reputation

credible-commitment dilemma. *See* social dilemmas

mimesis, 157–58
mind, origins of human, 156–57
mind reading. *See* theory of mind
Mischel, Walter, 149, 158
modular vs. general-purpose information processing, 172–73
Moir, Rob, 33
Molm, Linda, 232, 233, 234
monetary vs. personal exchange, 278–79. *See also* pecuniary benefits as game incentive
monotonic vs. nonmonotonic trustees in children study, 316–18
moral hazard: definition, 391. *See also* norms; social dilemmas
Mori, Kumiko, 228
motivations: beyond pecuniary payoff, 325; for cooperation, 97, 211–12, 323–24; experimental approach, 218–23; vs. incentives, 236n9; measurement limitations of prisoner's dilemma, 86–87; and norm usage, 54–55
Mueller, Dennis, 44
music and trust, 229
Mutual Aid (Kropotkin), 128
mutual benefits and evolution of cooperation, 110
mutual-cooperation payoff, 192, 193, 202n36
mutualism and simultaneous reciprocity, 130
mutual trust: as byproduct of commitment, 234; definition, 8; and game theory, 85–87; and group identity, 227; in hostage posting strategy, 225–26; motivations to cooperate, 211–12; vs. negotiated exchange, 232

Nash equilibrium: and cooperation games, 28, 65n9; definition, 391; and payoff matrix changes, 66n14; predictive capacity of, 34–35; research focus on, 65n9; and social dilemma model, 22–23
National Election Studies, 215
nationality. *See* culture

National Opinion Research Center (NORC), 90
natural selection, 9–10, 105–23, 178–79
neediness and treatment in dictator games, 251
negative reciprocity. *See* punishment
negotiated vs. reciprocal exchange, 232–34, 239n23
neighborhood size and trust, 228, 238–39n19
net-generalized exchange, 233
neural correlates for reciprocity, 147–50, 156–57, 165–67
Noë, Ronald, 131
noncooperative game theory: communication in, 29; definition, 391; and external authority, 19; predictive limitations, 38, 275–81, 384; in public-goods games, 27–29, **30**, 31–38; punishment of noncooperators, 24; self-interest as basis for, 218; vs. trust relationships, 14. *See also* backward induction; defecting strategy-defectors
nonexperimental vs. experimental approaches, 14–16, 373–80. *See also* field studies; survey methods
nonsimultaneous vs. simultaneous exchange, 117–18, 161, 217, 331, 365–66
nonverbal action modeling, 157–58
NORC (National Opinion Research Center), 90
normal-form vs. extensive-form games, 161, 296–97, 391
norms: in bounded rationality, 40–47; equity and equality, 154–55; and general trust of others, 354; in human behavior motivation, 25, 54–55; and initial cooperation, 96; and one-shot game limitations, 98; and player types in game analysis, 327–28; vs. rational incentives for trust, 83–85; vs. reciprocal altruism, 119; reciprocity as, 224; tit-for-tat, 67n30; and trustworthiness, 8; variations in payoff response, 328–29. *See also* reciprocity

Van Vugt, Mark, 227
vervet monkeys, 116
Vesterland, Lise, 251
voluntary and involuntary trust
  games, 305–7
voluntary-contribution-mechanism
  games, 276, 298n1

Walker, James, 28–29, 31, 32, 33, 35,
  37, 52, 53, 324, 364
Warglien, Massimo, 34
Wason selection task, 158
Watabe, Motoki, 221, 233
Watanabe, Yoriko, 51
Wieland, Carole, 229

Williams, Arlington, 28–29, 33
Williams, Bernard, 93–94, 95
Williams, George, 105
Wilson, David, 112
Wilson, Rick, 34
win-stay, lose-shift game, 197n2
Wright, Robert, 178
Wright, Thomas, 222

Yaari, Menahem, 328–29
Yamagishi, Midori, 215
Yamagishi, Toshio, 36, 51, 85, 215,
  217–18, 219–21, 222–23, 224, 229–
  30, 233, 364
Yoon, Jeongkoo, 232